TWO TESTAMENTS, ONE BIBLE

TWO TESTAMENTS, ONE BIBLE

A study of some modern solutions to the theological problem of the relationship between the Old and New Testaments

by D.L. Baker

Inter-Varsity Press

Inter-Varsity Press
Universities and Colleges Christian Fellowship
38 De Montfort Street, Leicester LE1 7GP

First published 1976

ISBN 0 85111 500 4

Printed in Great Britain by offset lithography by
Billing & Sons Ltd, Guildford, London and Worcester

Two Testaments, One Bible: A study of some modern solutions to the theological problem of the relationship between the Old and New Testaments

by D.L. Baker

SUMMARY

The relationship between the two Testaments of the Christian Bible is a fundamental problem in biblical studies. As well as many exegetical studies of particular aspects, there are numerous more general works which present solutions to the problem as a whole. It is the concern of this thesis to undertake a much-needed analytical and critical study of these modern solutions.

Preliminary research led to the isolation of eight distinct, though not all mutually exclusive, major solutions. A basic requirement for understanding these is to consider their biblical and historical background, and this is outlined in Part One. The solutions are then subjected to detailed analysis, criticism and comparison. In Part Two the 'Old Testament' solutions of van Ruler and Miskotte are considered, appreciated and rejected because the undue priority they give to the Old Testament, though creating a certain incisiveness, leads to an inadequate appreciation of the New Testament's contribution to the relationship. In Part Three the 'New Testament' solutions of Bultmann and Baumgärtel are likewise reluctantly rejected.

It is argued that a satisfactory solution will take the evidence as it stands - two Testaments in one Bible - and refuse to presuppose that either Testament is more important than the other. Four such 'biblical' solutions are considered in Part Four, which thus constitutes the most important part of the work: Vischer's frequently misunderstood Christological solution is rehabilitated; a new approach to typology is developed and used to illuminate the relationship between the Testaments; the popular 'salvation history' solution, especially as presented by von Rad and his associates, is surveyed and accepted, with some reservations; and the study is completed by a discussion of the important though less often mentioned idea of tension between continuity and discontinuity.

CONTENTS

PART THREE: 'NEW TESTAMENT' SOLUTIONS

3. The New Testament is the essential Bible, the Old Testament its non-Christian presupposition

4. The New Testament shows the Old Testament to be a witness to the promise in Christ

PART FOUR: THE SEARCH FOR A 'BIBLICAL' SOLUTION

5. The Old and New Testaments are equally Christian Scripture

6. The Old and New Testaments correspond to each other

8. The Old and New Testaments are continuous and discontinuous

CONCLUSION

APPENDICES

ABBREVIATIONS AND BIBLIOGRAPHY

INDEXES

PREFACE

This study is essentially a Ph.D. thesis, originally entitled 'The Theological Problem of the Relationship Between the Old Testament and the New Testament: A Study of Some Modern Solutions', which was accepted by the University of Sheffield in 1975. Indexes and a supplementary bibliography have been added, and a few corrections and minor alterations have been made in the text.

The research for the thesis was carried out under the supervision of Mr D.J.A.Clines, Senior Lecturer in the University of Sheffield, in the Department of Biblical Studies of that University (1971-3) and at Tyndale House Cambridge (1973-5). I am grateful for the guidance of my supervisor and other academic staff in Sheffield and Cambridge, the use of the research facilities offered by these two institutions, and permission to read in several other libraries. I acknowledge my debt to friends and colleagues who have contributed directly or indirectly to the completion of this work. Financial support was provided by a major State Studentship, a grant from the Tyndale Fellowship for Biblical Research, and the hard work of my wife, and without these I could never have undertaken the project.

The method of documentation used here follows essentially that of the new journal Semeia, which is also that generally used in modern scientific scholarship. Full bibliographical details of all works consulted are given in the bibliography. Within the text parentheses rather than footnotes are used for documentation, and the information given is generally limited to surname of author, date of first publication, and relevant page or section number: e.g.
Scott (1972: 234) argues that...;
it is sometimes suggested (e.g. Brown 1958) that...;
Smith (1974) has shown this (p.3) and that (p.18).
Some of this information may be omitted if it is obvious (e.g. in a section specifically on Bultmann, works by him are cited by date and page number only) or unnecessary (e.g. page numbers are omitted if most or all of a book or article is relevant to a particular point or if the article is very short). Occasionally extra information is given if necessary (e.g. if two or more works by the same author in the same year are cited, they are distinguished by suffixes - a, b, etc. - after the date). Pagination in two

different editions or printings is indicated thus: Vriezen 1954/66: 77/89; van Ruler 1955: 33/35 (details of the relevant editions are given in the bibliography - the earlier one is always given first). In the course of an argument it is usually sufficient to know which scholar provided a particular piece of evidence and when he did so. The method employed here means that this essential information is more accessible, being in parentheses rather than at the foot of the page or - as is becoming increasingly common - at the end of the work, and further details for following up references are readily available in the bibliography. In the present work this method of documentation is supplemented in two ways. First, titles of exceptionally important works that are discussed in detail are given in the text, along with other information as appropriate. Secondly, interim bibliographies of particular topics and authors are frequently provided in single-space type at the end of the relevant section of the text. In these are given the titles or abbreviated titles of works (plus, in the case of an article, the title of the journal or editor of the symposium in which it appeared), as well as the surname of the author and date of first publication. For more details of works reference should again be made to the full bibliography. The result of this method of documentation is to reduce footnotes to a minimum. They are used only for matters ancillary to the argument of the text, whose presence there would seriously disrupt the flow of the argument. They can therefore safely be ignored without losing anything essential to the argument of the work, though they do provide clarification and justification of certain minor points if required.

Chapter six of this book was published originally in a slightly different form, with the title 'Typology and the Christian Use of the Old Testament', in the Scottish Journal of Theology 29.2, April 1976. It is included here by kind permission of Professor T.F. Torrance, co-editor of the journal.

D.L.B.

PART ONE: THE PROBLEM

0.1 INTRODUCTION

0.2 OLD TESTAMENT

0.3 NEW TESTAMENT

0.4 HISTORY OF BIBLICAL INTERPRETATION

0.5 TRANSITION TO THE MODERN PERIOD

0.6 THE TWENTIETH CENTURY

0.7 METHOD

0.1 INTRODUCTION

a. Christianity has the New Testament as the record and testimony of the life, death and resurrection of its founder, Jesus Christ, and of the formation of the Christian Church. One of the most fundamental questions which has faced theology and the Church in every age and still demands an answer today is whether or not Christianity also needs an Old Testament. Is the Old Testament to be thrown away as obsolete, or preserved as a relic from days of yore, or treasured as a classic and read by scholars, or used occasionally as a change from the New Testament, or kept in a box in case it should be needed some day? Or is the Old Testament an essential part of the Christian Bible, the eternally valid and authoritative revelation of God to man?

b. The importance of this problem has been forcibly expressed by Bernhard W. Anderson (1964) in his introduction to a symposium on the significance of the Old Testament for the Christian faith:

> 'No problem more urgently needs to be brought to a focus than the one to which the following essays are addressed: the relation of the Old Testament to the New ... it is a question which confronts every Christian in the Church, whether he be a professional theologian, a pastor of a congregation, or a layman. It is no exaggeration to say that on this question hangs the meaning of the Christian faith.' (p.1)

The complexity of the problem is shown by the vast quantity of modern literature dealing with particular aspects of the relationship between the Testaments (cf. the bibliography of the present work) and the fact that there is no comprehensive study and only a few detailed studies of the whole problem.

c. There are several levels at which the problem of the relationship between the Old Testament and the New Testament may be approached. One of the most obvious is the historical: it is indisputable that there is an historical relationship between the two Testaments, that the New Testament is historically later and to some extent derivative from the Old Testament. It would be possible also to define linguistic, literary, sociological, psychological, ethical, philosophical, and many other levels to the problem. The fact is that a comprehensive study of the problem of the relationship between the Testaments at all these levels has never been undertaken since it would be such a vast task. The present study concentrates on the theological level of the problem because, as is being increasingly recognised in modern biblical scholarship, the Old and New Testaments are first and foremost theological works, and their linguistic, historical and ethical aspects are subordinate to this central concern. Moreover, since even the theological problem of the relationship between the Testaments is too complex to be dealt with in its entirety in a work of the present scope, this thesis will not enter into detailed exegetical , historical or theological study of minor points but will concentrate on the major aspects of the problem, the major solutions proposed, and the major issues involved. Sometimes this means that a question of considerable importance is dealt with only briefly, but in such cases bibliographies of more detailed discussions are provided.

d. The first part of the work delineates the theological problem of the relationship between the Testaments by means of a biblical, historical and methodological introduction. Although it is inevitably far from comprehensive, this outline of the development of approaches to the problem is important to set the modern solutions studied in the body of the work in their context in the history of theology. The next three parts of the work are devoted to a study of eight important modern solutions to the theological problem of the relationship between the Testaments. Finally, the results and discussions of the study are summarised and some conclusions drawn.

0.2 OLD TESTAMENT

0.21 OLD TESTAMENT VIEW OF NEW TESTAMENT

It might be thought that the earliest, and therefore definitive, approach to the problem of the relationship between the Testaments would be that of the New Testament. Yet important though this is, it is necessary to go further back into history: the Old Testament has not a little to say about its relationship to future faith. A significant aspect of Old Testament faith and religion is its expectation of the future, as has been widely recognised in modern scholarship. Indeed Bultmann (1949b) and others have taken the Old Testament's 'openness to the future' to be the controlling factor in its view of God, man and history. Nevertheless this forward-looking aspect should not be overemphasised: the Old Testament is also very concerned with past and present realities.

a. On the Old Testament's 'openness to the future':
Bultmann, Primitive Christianity(1949):183 cf.15-56;
Wolff, 'The OT in Controversy'(1956),ET in EOTI:284;
von Rad, OT Theology II(1960):319-22,332,361-3,etc.

Cf. Barth, Church Dogmatics I.2(1938):70-101;
Miskotte, When the Gods are Silent(1956):207-14, cf. 283-8,295-302;
Nötscher, Gotteswege und Menschenwege(1958)
Eichrodt, 'The Problem of OT Theology'(Excursus to Theology of the OT I,1961):519;
Moltmann, Theology of Hope(1964):ch.2;
Sauter, Zukunft und Verheissung(1965);
Preuss, Jahweglaube und Zukunftserwartung(1968);
Barr, 'The Authority of the Bible',ER(1969):147-8;
Reist, 'The OT Basis for the Resurrection Faith', EQ(1971).
See also below: 4.12; 7.12; 7.24.

b. There have been several recent exegetical studies of 'hope' in the Old Testament:
Westermann, 'Das Hoffen im AT'(1952), repr. in ThB 24;
Vriezen, 'Die Hoffnung im AT', TLZ(1953);
van der Ploeg, 'L'espérance dans l'AT', RB(1954);
Zimmerli, Man and His Hope in the OT(1968).

Cf. Denbeaux, 'The Biblical Hope', Interpn(1951)
R.A.F. Mackenzie, Faith and History in the OT(1968): ch.8;
Schreiner, 'Die Hoffnung der Zukunftsschau Israels' in Kleinedam Festschrift(1969).
See also below: 7.32.

c. In contrast, on the importance of present reality in the Old Testament, see:
Berkhof, 'Over de methode der eschatologie', NedTT(1965);
Vriezen, An outline of OT theology(new edn 1966): 431-2;

Cf. Wright, 'History and Reality', OTCF(1964);
Fensham, 'Covenant, Promise and Expectation in the Bible', ThZ(1967).

0.22 DEVELOPMENT OF FUTURE EXPECTATION

a. There can be little doubt that Israel had some kind of hope for the future from early times. This is apparent from passages such as Gen.12:1-3; 49; Ex.3:8; Num.24; Deut.33; 2 Sam.7; 23:3-5; Amos 5:18 and Pss.2; 45; 68; 110. Recently Zimmerli(1968) has traced this hope of Old Testament man in great detail, and in the primeval history alone points to seven examples of his future expectation (Gen.1:26; 2:17; 3:14-20; 4:11-15; 6:5-8; 8:21-2; 11:4). It is generally an optimistic view of the future, expecting material and spiritual, political and family, blessing. Since this early salvation hope is mainly concerned with the continuation of the present order and -unlike that of the prophets -does not envisage a radical renewal, the term 'eschatology' is an inappropriate description. All the same, there are elements in common with later eschatological ideas and the distinction should not be drawn too sharply (cf. Eichrodt 1933:472-80; Vriezen 1954/66:368/457; Jacob 1955a:319-25; Preuss 1968).

b. Eschatology is best defined broadly, as 'ideas which envisage a radical change to be brought about by God in the future'. The narrower understanding of eschatology as a developed 'doctrine of the last things' is scarcely present in the Old Testament (cf. Vriezen 1953b:200-203; Jenni 1962; Bright 1963; Clements 1965a:103-6; contrast van der Ploeg 1972).

c. Various attempts have been made to explain the origin and basis of Israel's eschatology. Smend (1893) and Volz(1897) suggested nationalism as its source. Gunkel(1895) and Gressmann(1905,1929) have pointed to mythical elements and argued for an origin in ancient Eastern mythological thought. Mowinckel (1922) found the basis of the Old Testament expectation in the enthronement festival and the disappointment which ensued when the kings of Israel proved to be far different from the ideal of kingship. It can hardly be denied that there is some truth in these observations. But more recent study (e.g. Eichrodt 1933:494-9) has shown that such explanations are inadequate to account for Israel's expectation of the future. It is now clear that Old Testament eschatology has an historical and theological basis. The presupposition of the Old Testament is its belief that God is active in the history of Israel. So the Old Testament's hopes for the future are based on the certainty that God is real though life may be hard (Vriezen 1953b:228-9); on the tension between the immanence and hiddenness of God which leads to the hope that God's presence will be perfected in a future coming (Jacob 1955a:317); on the perception of the radical sin and unbelief of the people which can only be overcome by God's grace (Bultmann 1933a:27); and on the prophetic conviction that God will act in the future as he has acted in the past, though in an entirely new way (von Rad 1960:116).

Smend, Lehrbuch der atl. Religionsgeschichte(1893): 171-3,218-22,238-44;
Gunkel, Schöpfung und Chaos(1895);
Volz, Die vorexilische Jahweprophetie(1897);
Gressmann, Der Ursprung der israelitisch-jüdischen Eschatologie(1905) and Der Messias(1929);
Mowinckel, Psalmenstudien II(1922) and He That Cometh(1951);
Bultmann,'The Significance of the OT for the Christian Faith'(1933),ET in OTCF;
Eichrodt, Theology of the OT I(1933):ch.11;
Frost, 'Eschatology and Myth',VT(1952);
Vriezen, 'Prophecy and Eschatology',SVT(1953); An outline of OT theology(1954/66):ch.11/9;
Jacob, Theology of the OT(1955):317-25;
von Rad, OT Theology II(1960);
Jenni, 'Eschatology of the OT',IDB(1962);
Bright,'Eschatology',DB[2](1963);
Müller, 'Zur Frage nach dem Ursprung der biblischen Eschatologie',VT(1964);
Clements, Prophecy and Covenant(1965):ch.6;
Preuss, Jahweglaube und Zukunftserwartung(1968);
Zimmerli, Man and His Hope in the OT(1968);
van der Ploeg,'Eschatology in the OT',OTS(1972).

0.23 PROPHETIC ESCHATOLOGY

0.231 Introduction

The classical period for the development of Israel's eschatology was that of the prophets. Judgement and salvation are portrayed with unparalleled clarity in their message, as may be seen by looking at almost any page of their writings. The pre-exilic prophets attack the popular optimism of Israel and proclaim the radical judgement of God; the exilic prophets introduce a new optimism as they point to a new beginning, a new creation and a new salvation. At least four major features of the prophetic expectation of the future may be isolated: a time, a person, a place and a people.

Important modern studies of prophetic eschatology include:

Lindblom, 'Gibt es eine Eschatologie bei den atl. Propheten?', StTh(1952) and Prophecy in Ancient Israel(1962):360-75;
Vriezen, 'Prophecy and Eschatology', SVT(1953);
Jacob, Theology of the OT(1955):317-44;
Rohland, Die Bedeutung der Erwählungstraditionen Israels(1956);
Grønbaek, 'Zur Frage der Eschatologie', SEA(1959);
Knight, A Christian Theology of the OT(1959):ch.25;
Hentschke, 'Gesetz und Eschatologie', ZEE(1960);
von Rad, OT Theology II(1960);
Jenni, 'Eschatology of the OT', IDB(1962);
Clements, Prophecy and Covenant(1965):ch.6;
Preuss, Jahweglaube und Zukunftserwartung(1968);
Zimmerli, Man and His Hope in the OT(1968):86-137;
Müller, Ursprünge und Strukturen atl. Eschatologie (1969);
Schunk, 'Die Eschatologie der Propheten', SVT(1974).

See also Fohrer, 'Die Struktur der atl. Eschatologie', TLZ(1960) and Whitley, The Prophetic Achievement(1963): 199-220, which argue that there is no eschatology in the pre-exilic prophets.
Cf. Herrmann, Die prophetische Heilserwartungen im AT(1965).

0.232 Day of Yahweh

From the beginning of the prophetic period there was a belief in a day when Yahweh would intervene in the history of Israel (Amos 5:18-20). The expression 'day of Yahweh' occurs only infrequently (see also Isa.13:6,9; Ezek.13:5; Joel 1:15; 2:1,11; 3:4/ 2:31; 4:14/3:14; Obad.15; Zeph.1:7,14; Zech.14:1), but related forms are common in the prophetic writings: for example, 'day of vengeance'(Isa.34:8; 61:2; Jer. 46:10) and 'on that day' (Ezek.29.21; Amos 3:14; cf. Isa.2:11-12; Jer.3:16-18).

Among numerous studies of the 'day of Yahweh' the following are of particular interest:

Smith, 'The Day of Yahweh', AJT(1901);
Gressmann, Der Ursprung der israelitisch-jüdischen Eschatologie(1905): 141-158;
Černy, The Day of Yahweh(1948);

Mowinckel, 'Jahves dag', *NorTT*(1958; not available to me);
Bourke, 'Le jour de Yahweh dans Joël', *RB*(1959);
Largement and Lemaître, 'Le Jour de Yahweh', BETL(1959);
von Rad, 'The Origin of the Concept of the Day of Yahweh', *JSS*(1959);
Kutsch, 'Heuschreckenplage und Tag Jahwes', *ThZ*(1962);
Hélewa, 'L'origine du concept Prophétique du "Jour de Yahvé"', *EphC*(1964);
Schunk, 'Strukturlinie in der Entwicklung der Vorstellung vom "Tag Jahwes"', *VT*(1964);
Jeremias, *Theophanie*(1965):97-100;
Weiss, 'The Origin of the "Day of the Lord"', *HUCA*(1966);
Jenni, 'יום jōm Tag', *THAT*(1971);
Gray, 'The Day of Yahweh in Cultic Experience and Eschatological Prospect', *SEA*(1974);
van Leeuwen, 'The Prophecy of the Yōm YHWH', OTS(1974).

0.233 Messiah

Israel was familiar with God's provision of individuals to meet the nation's political or spiritual need, in the form of prophets, judges, priests and kings. So when her thoughts turned to the future it is not surprising that they sometimes focused on a person whom God would send. The concept of a Messiah, though hardly ever linked with the Hebrew word משיח, may be perceived in various periods, especially in connection with the figures of the Son of David (2 Sam.7; Isa.9:11; cf. Pss.89; 132) and the Servant of Yahweh (Isa.42; 49; 50; 53).

The classical studies of this important theme are:
Klausner, *The Messianic Idea in Israel*(1902-1950);
Gressmann, *Der Messias*(1929);
Mowinckel, *He That Cometh*(1951).

Others include:
Bentzen, *King and Messiah*(1948);
North, *The Suffering Servant in Deutero-Isaiah*(1948);
Rowley, 'The Suffering Servant and the Davidic Messiah'(1950) and 'The Servant of the Lord' (1952), both repr. in *The Servant of the Lord*;
Ellison, *The Centrality of the Messianic Idea for the OT*(1953);
Rigaux(ed.), *L'Attente du Messie*(1954);
Zimmerli and Jeremias, 'παῖς θεοῦ', *TDNT*(1954);
Ringgren, *The Messiah in the OT*(1956);
Fohrer, *Messiasfrage und Bibelverständnis*(1957);

Jenni, 'Jewish Messiah', IDB (1962);
Schedl, 'Die messianische Hoffnung' in Leist (1965);
Higgins, 'The Priestly Messiah', NTS (1967);
Bruce, This is That (1968): chs 6-8;
Coppens, Le Messianisme Royal (1968); 'La relève du Messianisme royal' and 'Le messianisme israélite', ETL (1971);
Rehm, Der königliche Messias (1968);
Kellermann, Messias und Gesetz (1971);
Talmon, 'Typen der Messiaserwartung um die Zeitenwende' in von Rad Festschrift (1971).

0.234 Materialistic hope

There was also a materialistic aspect to the eschatology of the prophets. This is often expressed by Utopian ideas of world renewal and has two main strands. The return of paradise is a theme which recurs in the prophetic writings (Isa.11:6-9; 25:8; 51:3; Amos 9:13; Micah 4:3). Alongside this there is the expectation of a renewed holy land (Isa.62:4 cf. 65:17; Jer.30:3; 32:6-15; Ezek.20:45; cf. Hosea 2:16-25/14-23) and a renewed holy city (Isa.60-66; Ezek.40-48; Micah 4:1-2; Zech.2).

Eichrodt, Die Hoffnung des ewigen Friedens (1920);
Gressmann, Der Messias (1929): 151-164, 171-9;
Causse; 'Le mythe de la nouvelle Jérusalem', RHPR (1938);
Hebert, The Throne of David (1941): 44-52;
K.L. Schmidt, 'Jerusalem als Urbild und Abbild', ErJb (1950);
Gross, Die Idee des ewigen und allgemeinen Weltfriedens im alten Orient und im AT (1956);
Porteous, 'Jerusalem-Zion' (1961), repr. in Living the Mystery;
Clark, 'The Origin and Development of the Land Promise Theme in the OT', Dissn (1964, not available to me);
Diepold, Israels Land (1972): 129-139.

0.235 Spiritual renewal

Finally, the prophets looked forward to a renewal of the people of God. After judgement there will be restoration (Jer.29:14; 30:3; etc.; Ezek.16:53; Zeph. 3:30; cf.Deut.30:3). The nation will be exiled but a remnant will return (Isa.7:3; 10:20-22; Jer.23:3; Micah 2:12; Zech.8; cf.1 Kings 19:18). They will take part in a new exodus (Isa.4:5; 10:24-7; 35; 51:9-11; Zech.10:8-11); a new covenant will be made (Jer.30-33; cf. Isa.55:3; Ezek.16:60; 34:25-31); and God will give them a new spirit (Ezek.11:19; 36:26; 37; Joel3:1/2:28; cf. Isa.11:2; Ezek.18:31; Hosea 6:1-3).

a. On judgement and restoration see:
Baumann, 'שוב שבות', ZAW(1929);
von Rad, OT Theology I(1957):69-84;
Ackroyd, Exile and Restoration(1968).

b. On the remnant:
Meinhold, Der heilige Rest(1903);
de Vaux, 'The "Remnant of Israel"'(1933),ET in The Bible and the Ancient Near East;
Müller, Die Vorstellung vom Rest im AT(1939; not available to me);
Herntrich, 'The "Remnant" in the OT',TDNT 4(1942);
Rowley, The Biblical Doctrine of Election(1950):ch.3;
Bright, The Kingdom of God(1953):ch.3;
Dreyfus, 'La doctrine du reste d'Israël',RSPT(1955);
Stegeman, 'Der Restgedanke bei Isaias',BZ(1969);
Hasel, The Remnant(1972).

c. On the new Exodus:
Fischer, 'Das Problem des neuen Exodus',ThQ(1929);
Stamm, Erlösen und Vergeben im AT(1940):39-44;
Zimmerli, 'Le nouvel "exode"' in Vischer Festschrift (1960);
B.W. Anderson, 'Exodus Typology in Second Isaiah' in Muilenburg Festschrift(1962).

d. On the new covenant:
Gehman, 'A Study of the New Covenant',Interpn(1955);
Miskotte, When the Gods are Silent(1956):409-15;
Wolff, 'The Understanding of History in the OT Prophets' (1960), ET in EOTI:344;
Martin-Achard, 'La nouvelle alliance',RThPh(1962);
Coppens, 'La Nouvelle Alliance',CBQ(1963);
B.W. Anderson, 'The New Covenant and the Old',OTCF (1964);
Bright, The Authority of the OT(1967):217-18;
Buis, 'La nouvelle Alliance',VT(1968);
Swetnam, 'Why was Jeremiah's new covenant new?',SVT(1974).

e. On the new spirit:
Hebert, The Throne of David(1941):58-65;
cf. Martin-Achard, From Death to Life(1956):74-86, 93-102.

0.24 APOCALYPTIC

Towards the end of the Old Testament period apocalyptic began to take the place of prophecy. The beginning of this change may be seen in Daniel, Joel, Isaiah (24-7; 56-66), Ezekiel (38-9) and Zechariah (9-14). There is a growing tendency towards transcendentalism and dualism which becomes fully developed in extra-biblical literature. The difficulty in reconciling the eschatology of the prophets with the hard realities of life caused many to look beyond the present age to a new age to be inaugurated by God. A significant feature of this expectation is the figure of the 'Son of Man'(Dan.7), which becomes so important in later Jewish and Christian thought.

a. The past few years have seen an enormous amount of literature on apocalyptic. Journal for Theology and the Church (1969,ed. Funk) and Interpretation (1971, ed. Mays) have featured symposia; see also:
von Rad, OT Theology II(1960):301-8;
Rössler, Gesetz und Geschichte(1960);
Vawter, 'Apocalyptic',CBQ(1960);
Russell The Method and Message of Jewish Apocalyptic (1964);
Schubert, 'Das Zeitalter der Apokalyptik' in Leist(1965);
Frost, 'Apocalyptic and History' in Hyatt(1966);
Murdock, 'History and Revelation in Jewish Apocalypticism',Interpn(1967);
J.M. Schmidt, Die jüdische Apokalyptik(1969);
Hamerton-Kelly, 'The Temple and the Origins of Jewish Apocalyptic',VT(1970);
Koch, The Rediscovery of Apocalyptic(1972);
Morris, Apocalyptic(1973);
Collins, 'Apocalyptic Eschatology',CBQ(1974);
Hanson, The Dawn of Apocalyptic(1975).

The earlier works of Rowley (The Relevance of Apocalyptic, 1944) and Frost (OT Apocalyptic, 1952) are still standard, and the thought of the Pannenberg group (see below: 7.32) is especially concerned with apocalyptic.

b. On the Son of Man:
Mowinckel, *He That Cometh*(1951):346-450;
Emerton, 'The Origin of the Son of Man Imagery',*JTS* (1958);
Young, *Daniel's Vision of the Son of Man*(1958);
Coppens and Dequeker, *Le fils de l'homme*(1961);
Perrin, 'The Son of Man',*BR*(1966);
Borsch, *The Son of Man in Myth and History*(1967);
Leivestad, 'Der Apokalyptische Menschensohn',*ASTI* (1968);
Colpe, 'ὁ υἱὸς τοῦ ἀνθρώπου ',*TDNT*(1969);
cf. Hill,'"Son of Man" in Psalm 80 v.17',*NovT*(1973).

0.3 NEW TESTAMENT

0.31 NEW TESTAMENT VIEW OF OLD TESTAMENT

a. Just as the Old Testament looks forward to the New, so the New Testament looks back to the Old. The writers of the New Testament were convinced that the Messiah had been born, the long awaited Son of Man had come. His message was that the day of Yahweh had dawned, and the world and the people of God were about to be renewed.

b. C.H. Dodd(1952a) has shown that the Christian Church developed a method of biblical study in which certain major passages of the Old Testament (especially from Isaiah, Psalms and the Minor Prophets) were interpreted as testimonies to Christ. The principles of this interpretation are intelligible and consistent, and all the main New Testament writers agree on the selection of passages. Sentences from these passages are quoted not as independent testimonies but to point to their context in the longer passage. These Old Testament passages and their New Testament interpretations contain the fundamental ideas about Christ and thus form the sub-structure of Christian theology.

c. Samuel Amsler(1960a) is concerned to ascertain how the New Testament writers interpreted the Old Testament. He investigates interpretation in Hebrews, 1 Peter, John, Paul, Acts and the Synoptic Gospels, deliberately starting with those in which the interpretation is most sophisticated and progressing to those where it is most simple, and concludes that the New Testament's interpretation is based on the δεῖ of the passion and resurrection announcements in the Synoptics (cf. Tinsley 1963). It is summed up in the third Gospel: 'it was necessary that all that is written about me in the law of Moses, in the prophets and in the Psalms should be fulfilled'(Luke 24:44). Amsler argues that, in spite of different emphases, there are several characteristics in their Old Testament interpretation which are common to all the New Testament authors: (a) the New Testament authors have the same basic orientation to the Old Testament, recognising that the significance of the gospel events is seen clearly only in the light of the Old Testament; (b) the New Testament authors recognise in the Old Testament a witness which corroborates their own; (c) the New Testament authors claim the Old Testament as an advance witness, a promise which shows the theological significance of events within the history of salvation prior to their occurence; (d) the New Testament authors interpret the Old Testament as a witness to God's revelation and salvation in history. This historical perspective is in contrast to the legal perspective characteristic of contemporary Judaism, and is the reason why the New Testament authors agree in their preference for citing certain parts of the Old Testament.

d. Barnabas Lindars(1961) has made a detailed study of the doctrinal significance of New Testament quotations of the Old Testament. His work is governed by two main presuppositions: the results of Dodd's research, referred to above; and the results of Qumran research, which have brought to light the _midrash pesher_ method of biblical interpretation. In this method, 'a series of significant events, more or less contemporary with the writer, is regarded as the reality to which the prophecy points forward' (p.15). Stendahl(1954) and Ellis(1957) have previously shown the influence of this method on the biblical interpretation of Matthew and Paul respectively, and

Lindars finds its influence throughout the New Testament (cf. Fitzmyer 1961; Longenecker 1970). His method is essentially that of form criticism, and he concentrates on two factors in the New Testament quotation of Old Testament passages: shift of application and modification of text. In this way he traces the apologetic of the early Church from its core in the resurrection to the passion, earthly life, birth and pre-existence of Christ.

e. There has been a wealth of study of the New Testament view of the Old Testament in recent years, much of it consolidating earlier study rather than breaking new ground. The result is to show beyond dispute that the historical and theological basis for the writing of the New Testament was the Old Testament.

Harris, *Testimonies*(1916-20);
Schrenk, 'γράφω ...',*TDNT*(1933);
Venard, 'Citations de l'AT dans le NT',*SDB*(1934);
Vis, *An Inquiry into the Rise of Christianity out of Judaism*(1936);
Goppelt, *Typos*(1939);
Sperber, 'NT and Septuagint',*JBL*(1940);
Wolff, *Jesaja 53 im Urchristentum*(1942):ch.4;
Tasker, *The OT in the NT*(1946);
Atkinson, 'The Textual Background of the Use of the OT by the New',*JTVI*(1947);
Cerfaux, 'L'exégèse de l'AT par le NT' in Auvray(1951);
Dodd, *According to the Scriptures*(1952); *The OT in the New*(1952);
Smits, *Oud-testamentische citaten in het NT*(1952-63);
Fuchs, *Hermeneutik*(1954):177-210;
Piper, 'Exodus in the NT',*Interpn*(1957);
Fitzmyer, '4Q Testimonia and the NT',*ThSt*(1957) and 'The use of explicit OT quotations in Qumran literature and in the NT',*NTS*(1961);
Wood, *The Interpretation of the Bible*(1958):ch.2;
Bruce, *Biblical Exegesis in the Qumran Texts*(1959);
Nicole, 'NT Use of the OT' in Henry(1959);
Amsler, *L'AT dans l'Eglise*(1960);
Gerhardsson, *Memory and Manuscript*(1961):225-34, 280-88;
Lindars, *NT Apologetic*(1961);
Braun, 'Das AT im NT',*ZTK*(1962);

Grelot, *Sens chrétien de l'AT*(1962);
Larcher, *L'actualité chrétienne de l'AT*(1962);
Moule, *The Birth of the NT*(1962):ch.4;
Nixon, *The Exodus in the NT*(1963);
Morris, *The NT and the Jewish Lectionaries*(1964):ch.4;
Grant, *Short History*(1965):chs 2-4;
Hanson, *Jesus Christ in the OT*(1965);
Hesse, *Das AT als Buch der Kirche*(1966):ch.3;
Grogan, 'The NT Interpretation of the OT',*TynB*(1967);
Rese, 'Die Rolle des ATs im NT',*VF*(1967);
Runia, 'The Interpretation of the OT by the NT', *TSFB*(1967);
Westermann, 'Prophetenzitate im NT',*EvTh*(1967);
Gese, 'Psalm 22 und das NT',*ZTK*(1968);
Marbury, 'OT Textual Traditions in the NT',Dissn(1968);
Moule, 'Fulfilment-Words in the NT',*NTS*(1968);
G.P. Richardson *et al.*, 'Aspects of Biblical Interpretation',*CBRFJ*(1968);
Aune, 'Early Christian Biblical Interpretation',*EQ* (1969);
D.J. Ellis, 'The NT Use of the OT' in Howley(1969);
E.E.Ellis, 'Midrash, Targum and NT Quotations' in Black Festschrift(1969);
Barrett, 'The Interpretation of the OT in the New', *CHB* I(1970);
Childs, *Biblical Theology in Crisis*(1970);
Longenecker, 'Can we reproduce the Exegesis of the NT?',*TynB*(1970); *Biblical Exegesis in the Apostolic Period*(1975);
Verhoef, 'The Relationship between the Old and the New Testaments', in Payne(1970):282-4;
Black, 'The Christological Use of the OT in the NT', *NTS*(1971);
Hahn, 'Genesis 15_6 im NT' in von Rad Festschrift(1971);
Miller, 'Targum, Midrash and the Use of the OT in the NT',*JSJ*(1971);
Sand, '"Wie geschrieben steht..."' in Ernst(1972);
D.M. Smith, 'The Use of the OT in the New' in Stinespring Festschrift(1972);
Cunliffe-Jones, *...Zechariah 9-14, the NT and Today*(1973);
Grech, 'The "Testimonia" and Modern Hermeneutics', *NTS*(1973);
Duling, 'The Promises to David',*NTS*(1974);
Holtz, 'Zur Interpretation des ATs im NT',*TLZ*(1974).

Some studies of individual New Testament passages or writers and their view of the Old Testament are listed in the relevant sections below (0.33).

0.32 JESUS AND THE OLD TESTAMENT

R.T. France (1971), arguing for the essential authenticity of the Synoptic reports (chs 1,2), describes in detail two main features of Jesus' use of the Old Testament: types and predictions (chs 3,4). In persons, institutions and experiences of Old Testament Israel Jesus sees 'types' of his own person and work (not so much explicit parallels as examples of the continuity between God's acts in past and present history). And in the Messianic predictions of the Old Testament, as well as more general eschatological hopes and passages about the work of Yahweh, Jesus finds 'predictions' which he fulfils in his life and future glory. Finally, in a study of the use of selected Old Testament passages by Jesus and his contemporaries (ch.5), France points to the revolutionary nature of Jesus' Old Testament interpretation. Thus he confirms the conclusion reached by Dodd (1952a: 109-110) that the distinctive character of the early Church's view of the Old Testament originates from Jesus himself.

The major modern work on Jesus' view of the Old Testament is France, Jesus and the OT(1971). An older one of importance is Hänel, Der Schriftbegriff Jesu(1919).

Others, apart from sections in several of the general works mentioned above (0.31), include:
Bultmann, Theology of the NT I(1948):15-18;
Manson, 'The OT in the Teaching of Jesus', BJRL(1952);
Tilden, 'The Study of Jesus' Interpretive Methods', Interpn(1953);
Marcel, 'Our Lord's Use of Scripture' in Henry(1959);
Fluster, 'Blessed Are the Poor in Spirit', IEJ(1960);
Edgar, 'Respect for Context in Quotations', NTS(1962);
Mead, 'A Dissenting Opinion...', NTS(1964);
Nielen, 'Jesus und das AT' in Leist(1965);
Jeremias, NT Theology I(1971);
Berger, Die Gesetzeauslegung Jesu I(1972);
Wenham, Christ and the Bible(1972).

0.33 NEW TESTAMENT WRITERS

It is impossible here to summarise the results of much detailed research into the way different New Testament writers view the Old Testament. Instead, a select bibliography of this research is given, concentrating on recent work. It represents only a part of the vast quantity of evidence accumulated to show the way in which the New Testament is dependent on the Old Testament.

0.331 Synoptic Gospels and Acts

a. Matthew - there are several major studies:
Stendahl, The School of St.Matthew(1954);
Gundry, The Use of the OT in St.Matthew's Gospel(1967);
McConnell, Law and Prophecy in Matthew's Gospel(1969);
Rothfuchs, Die Erfüllungszitate des Matthäus-Evangeliums(1969).

Others include:
McCasland, 'Matthew Twists the Scriptures',JBL(1961);
O'Rourke, 'The Fulfillment Texts in Matthew',CBQ (1962);
Kent, 'Matthew's Use of the OT',BS(1964);
Dupont, 'Nova et vetera(Matt.13:52)' in Leenhardt Festschrift(1968);
Senior, 'The Fate of the Betrayer',ETL(1972).

b. Mark:
Schultz, 'Markus und das AT',ZTK(1961);
Mauser, Christ in the Wilderness(1963);
Suhl, Die Funktion der atl. Zitate und Anspielungen in Markusevangelium(1965);
H. Anderson, 'The OT in Mark's Gospel' in Stinespring Festschrift(1972);
Funk, 'The Looking-Glass Tree', Interpn(1973);
Kee, 'The Function of Scriptural Quotations...' in Kümmel Festschrift(1975).

c. Luke:
Crockett, 'The OT in the Gospel of Luke',Dissn(1966);
Funk, Language, Hermeneutic and the Word of God(1966): ch.8;
Holtz, Untersuchungen über die atl. Zitate bei Lukas (1968);
Rese, Atl. Motive in der Christologie des Lukas (1969);
Bligh, Christian Deuteronomy (Luke 9-18)(1970);
Ernst, 'Schriftauslegung und Auferstehungsglaube bei Lukas' in Ernst(1972).

d. The Passion Narrative:
Bruce, 'The Book of Zechariah and the Passion Narrative', *BJRL*(1961);
Rose, 'L'influence des psaumes...' in de Langhe(1962);
Hashimoto, 'The functions of the OT quotations and allusions in the Marcan Passion narrative', Dissn(1970; not available to me).

e. Acts:
Dupont, 'L'utilisation apologétique de l'AT...', *ETL*(1953); 'L'interprétation des psaumes dans les Actes' in de Langhe(1962);
van Unnik, 'Der Ausdruck 'ΕΩΣ 'ΕΣΧΑΤΟΥ ΤΗΣ ΓΗΣ...' in Vriezen Festschrift(1966);
E.E. Ellis, 'Midraschartige Züge in den Reden der Apostelgeschichte', *ZNW*(1971).

f. Also:
Lohse, 'Hosianna', *NovT*(1963);
Banks, 'Jesus and the Law in the Synoptic Tradition', Dissn(1969);
Patience, 'The Contribution to Christology of the Quotations of the Psalms in the Gospels and Acts', Dissn(1970; not available to me);
Moule, 'Pattern of the Synoptists', *EQ*(1971).

0.332 *John*

Barrett, 'The OT in the Fourth Gospel', *JTS*(1947);
Morgan, 'Fulfillment in the Fourth Gospel', *Interpn*(1957);
Guilding, *The Fourth Gospel and Jewish Worship*(1960);
R.H. Smith, 'Exodus Typology in the Fourth Gospel', *JBL*(1962);
Glasson, *Moses in the Fourth Gospel*(1963);
Braun, *Jean le Théologien* II(1964);
Borgen, *Bread from Heaven*(1965); 'Logos was the Light', *NovT*(1972);
Freed, *OT Quotations in the Gospel of John*(1965);
Bampfylde, 'OT quotations and imagery in the Gospel according to St John', Dissn(1966 or 1967; not available to me);
Meeks, *The Prophet-King*(1967);
Richter, 'Die atl. Zitate in Joh 6:26-51a' in Ernst (1972);
Schnackenburg, 'Zur christologischen Schriftauslegung des vierten Evangelisten' in Cullmann Festschrift (1972);
Betz, 'Kann denn aus Nazareth etwas Gutes kommen?' in Elliger Festschrift(1973);
Reim, *Studien zur alt. Hintergrund des Johannesevangeliums*(1973);
Lacomara, 'Deuteronomy and the Farewell Discourse', *CBQ*(1974).

0.333 Paul

The two most important studies are:
E.E.Ellis, Paul's Use of the OT(1957);
A.T. Hanson, Studies in Paul's Technique and Theology (1974).

Others include:
Michel, Paulus und seine Bibel(1929);
Bonsirven, Exégèse rabbinique et exégèse paulinienne (1939);
Davies, Paul and Rabbinic Judaism(1948);
Bläser, 'Schriftverwertung und Schrifterklärung', ThQ(1952);
Boney, 'Paul's Use of the OT', Dissn(1956; not available to me);
Bultmann, 'Adam and Christ according to Romans 5' (1959),ET in Piper Festschrift;
von Schmid, 'Die atl. Zitate bei Paulus',BZ(1959);
Wilckens, 'Die Rechtfertigung Abrahams nach Römer 4' in von Rad Festschrift(1961);
Barrett, From First Adam to Last(1962);
Ulonska, 'Die Funktion der atl. Zitate und Anspielungen in den Paulinischen Briefen' (Dissn, not available to me);
Allen, 'The OT in Romans I-VIII',VoxEv(1964);
Ridderbos, Paulus(1966):139-170;
Conzelmann, An Outline of the Theology of the NT (1967):166-170;
Harman, 'Paul's Use of the Psalms',Dissn(1968; not available to me);
Léon-Dufour, 'Une lecture chrétienne de l'AT' in Leenhardt Festschrift(1968);
Bring, Christus und das Gesetz(1969);
Bandstra, 'Interpretation in 1 Cor.10:1-11',CTJ(1971);
Bring,'Paul and the OT',StTh(1971);
Leenhardt, 'Abraham et la conversion de Saul',RHPR (1973);
Via, 'A Structuralist Approach to Paul's OT Hermeneutic',Interpn(1974).

0.334 Hebrews

Perhaps the most important study is that of Schröger, Der Verfasser des Hebräerbriefes als Schriftausleger (1968).

See also:
Westcott, The Epistle to the Hebrews(1889):appendix;
van der Ploeg, 'L'Exégèse de l'AT...' ,RB(1947);
Katz, 'The Quotations from Deuteronomy in Hebrews', ZNW(1958);
Caird,'The Exegetical Method of the Epistle...',CJT (1959);
Synge, Hebrews and the Scriptures(1959);
Kistemaker, The Psalm Citations in the Epistle... (1961);

Köster, 'Die Auslegung der Abraham-Verheissung in Hebräer 6' in von Rad Festschrift(1961);
M. Barth, 'The OT in Hebrews' in Piper Festschrift (1962);
Fitzmyer, '"Now This Melchizedek..."(Heb.7,1)',<u>CBQ</u> (1963);
McGaughey, 'The Hermeneutic Method of the Epistle...' Dissn(1963; not available to me);
Stott, 'The Jewish Background to the Epistle...', Dissn(n.d.);
Reid, 'The Use of the OT in the Epistle...',Dissn(1964; not available to me);
Lewis, 'The Theological Logic in Hebrews 10:19-12:29 and the appropriation of the OT',Dissn(1965; not available to me);
Sowers, <u>The Hermeneutics of Philo and Hebrews</u>(1965);
Thomas, 'The OT Citations in Hebrews',<u>NTS</u>(1965);
Howard, 'Hebrews and the OT Quotations',<u>NovT</u>(1968);
Williamson, <u>Philo and the Epistle to the Hebrews</u> (1970);
Stylianopoulos, 'Shadow and Reality',<u>GOTR</u>(1972).

0.34 CONCLUSION

a. One of the results of modern biblical study has therefore been to clarify the significance of the Old Testament's future expectation. The importance of this result should be appreciated though it is unnecessary to go to the extreme of interpreting the Old Testament solely with reference to the future. It is abundantly clear that the Old Testament in itself is incomplete and looks forward to a completion by an act of God outside its limits. This act is to be performed by the same God in the context of the same history as acts described in the Old Testament. It is expected that the new act will in many respects be analogous to earlier ones, yet at the same time be radically different and more comprehensive. Thus the Old Testament looks forward to the future; and according to Christian understanding looks forward to the New Testament.

b. Another result of modern biblical study has been illumination of the extent and manner of the New Testament's dependence on the Old Testament. The New Testament proclaims the occurence of a new and unprecedented act of God in the person of Jesus of

Nazareth, but a central aspect of this proclamation is that Jesus is the fulfilment of the hopes and expectations of the Old Testament. In preaching, teaching, apologetics and ethics the Old Testament 'Scriptures' were the source and standard for the New Testament Church.

c. The material discussed in the preceding sections has been largely concerned with the explicit biblical relationship between the Testaments; in other words, the Old Testament's future expectation, the New Testament's dependence on the past, and the relationship between the two. It would also be possible, though more difficult, to analyse material concerned with the implicit relationship between the Testaments.

d. The Old Testament closes not only with certain expectations of the future but also with inner tensions which remain unresolved. There is a tension between Jewish exclusivism and universal missionary concern, deriving ultimately from the belief in both the election of Israel and the world supremacy of the one God (Bright 1960:428-32/444-8). There are also tensions in the roles of Israel's leading men: between prophet, priest and wise man (cf. Whitley 1963:ch.4; McKane 1965; Clements 1965a:ch.5; 1975: ch.6), and between charismatic leader and dynastic monarch (cf. Eichrodt 1933:441-2; von Rad 1957:93-102). Above all, there is a tension in the Old Testament between divine sovereignty and human responsibility (cf. Seeligmann 1963): on the one hand, the divine purpose and will remains unfulfilled, on the other hand, human sin and rebellion continues with neither extermination nor regeneration to realise divine sovereignty.

e. A New Testament study of the implicit relationship between the Testaments would have to consider how far and in what way such tensions have been resolved in the coming of Jesus Christ, and also what new tensions have been created and what new understanding of the meaning of the Old Testament has now become possible. One of the key issues in the early Church was the tension between Jew and Gentile, Israel and Church (cf. below:1.214,2.14); and another was the interpretation of the Old Testament which was understood by Christians to affirm the Messiahship of Jesus and by Jews to demand his execution for blasphemy. But at this point it is appropriate to turn from the biblical evidence to consider how the theological problem of the relationship between the Testaments has been understood in the history of the Christian Church.

0.4 HISTORY OF BIBLICAL INTERPRETATION

0.41 EARLY CHURCH

0.411 Introduction

The writers of the New Testament were confronted with the problem of relating the events of the life, death and resurrection of Jesus with the words and events recorded in the Hebrew Bible. It was only in the early Church, however, that the problem of the relationship between the Old Testament and the New Testament arose. Perhaps the most significant aspect of this is the change in role of the Old Testament. Jesus, Peter and Paul presupposed the Old Testament as basis of their faith and their problem was to relate the new events in which they were involved to earlier ones. The early Church, on the other hand, adopted the New Testament as the basis of its faith and the Old Testament became the problem: how far was the Old Testament to be considered valid and relevant after the completion of the New Testament, and in what way is the Old Testament related to the New?.

Westcott, The Bible in the Church(1864):chs 3-7;
Diestel, Geschichte des ATes in der christlichen Kirche(1869):book I;
Farrar, History of Interpretation(1886):chs 3-4;
Orr, 'The OT Question in the Early Church',Exp(1895);
Harnack, The Mission and Expansion of Christianity (1902):65-70,279-89;
Gilbert, Interpretation of the Bible(1908):chs 4-6;
Duff, History of OT Criticism(1910):ch.4;
Fullerton, Prophecy and Authority(1919):part I;
H.P.Smith, Essays in Biblical Interpretation(1921):ch.3;
Bugge, 'L'AT, Bible de la primitive Eglise',RHPR(1924);
Burkitt, 'The Debt of Christianity to Judaism' in Bevan and Singer(1927);

Bauer, Orthodoxy and Heresy(1934):ch.9;
Wolff, Jesaja 53 im Urchristentum(1942):chs 5-6;
Carpenter, 'The Bible in the Early Church' in Dugmore(194
Bardy, 'Interprétation II',SDB(1949);
Burghardt, 'On Early Christian Exegesis',ThSt(1950);
Daniélou, From Shadows to Reality(1950); 'The Fathers and the Scriptures',Theology(1954); Études d'exégèse judéo-chrétienne(1966); A History of Early Christian Doctrine II(1973):part 3;
Camelot, 'L'exégèse de l'AT par les Pères' in Auvray(1951
Grant, 'The Place of the OT in Early Christianity', Interpn(1951); 'History of the Interpretation of the Bible:I',IB I(1952); The Letter and the Spirit(1957);
Jacob, Theology of the OT(1955):13-16;
Wiles, 'The OT in Controversy with the Jews',SJT(1955);
Blackman, Biblical Interpretation(1957):76-108;
Alexander, 'The Interpretation of Scripture in the Ante-Nicene Period',Interpn(1958);
Kelly, Early Christian Doctrines(1958):ch.3;
Wood, The Interpretation of the Bible(1958):chs 3-6;
Sagnard, 'Holy Scripture in the Early Fathers of the Church',StEv I(1959);
Frör, Biblische Hermeutik(1961):20-22;
Chadwick, 'The Bible and the Greek Fathers', and
Kelly, 'The Bible and the Latin Fathers' in Nineham(1963)
Sundberg, The OT of the Early Church(1964);
Grant, Short History(1965):chs 5-8;
Bright, The Authority of the OT(1967):79-82;
Brown, 'Hermeneutics',JBC(1968):II.611-12;
Lampe, 'The Exposition and Exegesis of Scripture: 1. To Gregory the Great',CHB II(1969);
R.P.C.Hanson, 'Biblical Exegesis in the Early Church', CHB I(1970);
Guzie, 'Patristic Hermeneutics and the Meaning of Tradition',ThSt(1971);
Hay, Glory at the Right Hand(1973);
Hubbard, 'OT',NIDCC(1974):725-6.

0.412 Apostolic Fathers

For the Apostolic Fathers the relationship between the Testaments was scarcely a problem. Both Old and New Testaments were accepted as Scripture, though the limits of the canon had not yet been finally defined. Texts were cited frequently in exhortation and argument, with literal and allegorical meanings each having their place.

Grant, 'Scripture and Tradition in St. Ignatius', CBQ(1963);
Barnard, Studies in the Apostolic Fathers(1966):ch.9;

von Campenhausen, The Formation of the Christian Bible (1968):62-74;
Hagner, The Use of the Old and New Testaments in Clement of Rome(1973).

0.413 Marcion

The simple acceptance of the Old and New Testaments as Scripture lasted only a few decades. In the middle of the second century Marcion of Sinope issued a challenge to the Church's view of the relationship between the Testaments that has made him one of her most notorious heretics. Whether or not he should be considered a Gnostic, his thought was undoubtedly similar to Gnosticism in its dualistic emphasis. For Marcion there was a radical discontinuity between flesh and spirit, law and gospel, the god of Israel and the Father of Jesus, the Old Testament and the New Testament. Marcion followed his theory through to its logical conclusion and eliminated the Old Testament – together with unacceptable parts of the New Testament – from his Bible.

Tollinton, 'The Two Elements in Marcion's Dualism', JTS(1916);
Harnack, Marcion(1921); Neue Studien zu Marcion(1923);
Blackman, Marcion and His Influence(1948);
B.W.Anderson, 'The OT as a Christian Problem',OTCF (1964):2-5;
Bianchi, 'Marcion',VigChr(1967);
Bright, The Authority of the OT(1967):60-62;
von Campenhausen, The Formation of the Christian Bible(1968):148-167;
Aune, The Cultic Setting of Realized Eschatology... (1972):ch.6.

Cf. Wintermute, 'A Study of Gnostic Exegesis of the OT' on Stinespring Festschrift(1972).

0.414 Reactions to Marcion

Like most heretics, Marcion gained a certain following but failed to convince the majority of the Church. Nevertheless his challenge was a serious one and several of the early Church's greatest theologians devoted much energy to countering his arguments. Justin Martyr(c.100-165), a leading apologist, rejected dualism and argued for the unity of God's revelation: the Old Testament itself looks forward to the Messiah and the new covenant. Irenaeus (c.130-c.200) considered Christ to be the link between the Testaments, and the Old Testament, though subordinate in the scheme of progressive revelation, to be of real value for complete understanding of God's activity in history. Tertullian (c.160-c.220) systematically refuted Marcion's dualism, showing that even Marcion's own version of the Bible presented a Christ who was the fulfilment of the law and the prophets. Finally Origen (c.185-c.254), perhaps the greatest biblical scholar of the early Church, and Clement of Alexandria (c.150-c.220) added their voices to the defence of the Old Testament against Marcion, dealing with many of its difficult texts by means of allegorical or spiritual interpretation.

a. General:

den Boer, 'Hermeneutic problems in early Christian literature', VigChr(1947);
Armstrong, Die Genesis in der Alten Kirche(1962);
von Campenhausen, The Formation of the Christian Bible(1968):88-102,182-206,269-326.

b. Justin Martyr:

Goodenough, The Theology of JM(1923):104-122;
Barnard, 'The OT and Judaism in the Writings of JM', VT(1964);
Prigent, Justin et l'AT(1964);
Shotwell, The Biblical Exegesis of JM(1965);
Aune, 'JM's Use of the OT', BETS(1966).

c. Irenaeus:

Hitchcock, Irenaeus of Lugdunum(1914):199-210;
Lawson, The Biblical Theology of Saint Irenaeus(1948); esp. 232-40,252-4;
Markus, 'Pleroma and Fulfilment', VigChr(1954);
Benoit, Saint Irénée(1960):esp.ch.3.

d. Tertullian:
R.P.C.Hanson, 'Notes on Tertullian's Interpretation of Scripture',JTS(1961);
O'Malley, Tertullian and the Bible(1967);
Evans(ed.), Tertullian(1972);
van der Geest, Le Christ et l'AT chez Tertullian(1972);
Kuss, 'Zur Hermeneutik Tertullians' in Ernst(1972).

Cf. Fahey, Cyprian and the Bible(1971).

e. Origen:
Daniélou, Origen(1948); 'L'unité des deux Testaments dans l'oeuvre d'Origène',RevSR(1948);
de Lubac, Histoire et Esprit(1950);
R.P.C.Hanson, Allegory and Event(1959);
Wiles, 'Origen as Biblical Scholar',CHB I(1970).

f. Clement:
Camelot, 'Clément d'Alexandrie et l'Écriture',RB(1946);
Riedinger, 'Zur antimarkionitischen Polemik des Klemens von Alexandrie',VigChr(1975).

0.415 Theodore and Augustine

Orthodoxy prevailed over Marcion, and the Old Testament was preserved as part of the Church's Bible. Two of the most significant interpreters of the Bible in the succeeding years were Theodore of Mopsuestia(c.350-428) and Augustine of Hippo(354-430). Theodore was an outstanding commentator of the Antioch school of interpretation, which emphasised the importance of the literal meaning of the text in contrast to the Alexandrian school (e.g. Origen) which emphasised the allegorical meaning. He understood the relationship between the Testaments primarily in terms of historical development, although he also saw Old Testament events as types of New Testament ones. Augustine did not follow any one school but drew upon any kind of interpretation which served to illuminate the Bible, though he clearly had a liking for allegory. In a sense his work is the transition from the early Church to the Middle Ages: it is the culmination of several centuries of Christian thought and forms the foundation of theology in the West for the following centuries. He expressed his view of the relationship between the Testaments in words that have become classical: 'Multum et solide significatur, ad Vetus Testamentum timorem potius pertinere, sicut ad Novum dilectionem: quanquam et in Vetere Novum lateat, et in Novo Vetus pateat'(Quaestiones in Exodum 73).

a. Theodore of Mopsuestia:
Pirot, L'oeuvre exégétique de TM(1913):esp.chs 6-8;
Tyng, 'TM as an Interpreter of the OT',JBL(1931);
Devreese, 'La méthode exégétique de TM',RB(1946) and Essai sur TM(1948):72-8,87-93,104;
Abramowski, 'Zur Theologie TM',ZKG(1961);
Greer, TM:Exegete and Theologian(1961):ch.5;
Wiles, 'TM as Representative of the Antiochene School', CHB I(1970).

b. Augustine:
Polman, The Word of God According to St. Augustine (1955):ch.3;
Strauss, Schriftgebrauch, Schriftauslegung und Schriftbeweis bei Augustin(1959):esp.68-72;
La Bonnardière, Biblia Augustinia A.T.(1960-);
Preus, From Shadow to Promise(1969):ch.1;
Bonner, 'Augustine as Biblical Scholar',CHB I(1970);
Boundy, 'Augustine's Evangelical Use of the OT'(1972), unpublished paper.

c. Also:
Kerrigan, St Cyril of Alexandria, Interpreter of the OT (1952);
Hahn, Das wahre Gesetz(1969) - on Ambrose.

0.42 MIDDLE AGES

The Biblical interpreters of the Middle Ages generally followed closely the methods of the Fathers, and like them understood the Bible as a unity which witnesses to Christ. Those of particular interest include Bernard of Clairvaux(1090-1153), Hugh of St Victor (c.1096-c.1141), Thomas Aquinas(c.1224-74) and Nicholas of Lyra(c.1270-c.1340). A fourfold interpretation -literal, allegorical, moral and anagogical - was employed, but increasingly there was a tendency to stress the literal meaning (influenced partly by contemporary Jewish scholarship, e.g. Rashi). The New Testament was considered to be continuous with, though superior to, the Old Testament: the theological meaning of the Old Testament is seen clearly only after the coming of the New Testament (Hugh); the Old Testament is imperfect and the New Testament perfect, like a seed compared to a tree (Aquinas).

Westcott, The Bible in the Church(1864):chs 8-9;
Diestel, Geschichte des ATes(1869):book 2;
Farrar, History of Interpretation(1886):ch.5;
Gilbert, Interpretation of the Bible(1908):ch.7;
H.P.Smith, Essays in Biblical Interpretation(1921):ch.4;
Bainton, 'The Immoralities of the Patriarchs',HTR(1930);
Franks, 'The Interpretation of Holy Scripture in the Theological System of Alexander of Hales' in Harris Festschrift(1933);
Rost, Die Bibel im Mittelalter(1939);
Pepler, 'The Faith of the Middle Ages' in Dugmore(1944);
Spicq, Esquisse d'une histoire de l'exégèse latine au Moyen Age(1944);
Gribomont, 'Le lien des deux Testaments, selon la théologie de saint Thomas',ETL(1946);
Jugie and Spicq, 'Interprétation III',SDB(1949);
Leclercq, 'L'exégèse mediévale de l'AT' in Auvray(1951);
McNeill, 'History of the Interpretation of the Bible II',IB I(1952):115-123;
Smalley, The Study of the Bible in the Middle Ages (1952); 'The Bible in the Middle Ages' in Nineham(1963); 'The Exposition and Exegesis of Scripture:3. The Bible in the Medieval Schools', CHB II(1969);
Blackman, Biblical Interpretation(1957):108-116;
Wood, The Interpretation of the Bible(1958):ch.7;
McNally, The Bible in the Early Middle Ages(1959);
de Lubac, Exégèse médiévale(1959-64):esp.I.305-63;
Torrance, 'Scientific Hermeneutics According to St. Thomas Aquinas',JTS(1962);
Grant, Short History(1965):ch.9;
Winkler, Exegetische Methoden bei Meister Eckhart (1965):esp.42-9;
M.A.Schmidt, 'Zum Problem der Heilsgeschichte in der Hochscholastik' in Cullmann Festschrift(1967);
Brown, 'Hermeneutics',JBC(1968):II.612-13;
Leclercq, 'The Exposition and Exegesis of Scripture: 2. From Gregory the Great to Saint Bernard', CHB II(1969);
Preus, From Shadow to Promise(1969);
Hagen, 'The Problem of Testament in Luther's Lectures on Hebrews',HTR(1970):64-73;
Hubbard, 'OT',NIDCC(1974):726-7.

0.43 REFORMATION

0.431 Introduction

The central issue of the Reformation was the Bible. Although the primary concern was its authority and function in the Church, there was also a renewed interest in the interpretation of the Bible. A major proportion of the works of both Luther and Calvin were commentaries and expositions of biblical books. The emphasis on literal interpretation rather than allegory and the conviction that the whole Bible is Christocentric were not always easy to reconcile, and the problem of the relationship between the Testaments became a very real one.

Westcott, The Bible in the Church(1964):ch.10;
Diestel, Geschichte des ATes(1869):231-317;
Farrar, History of Interpretation(1886):ch.6;
Gilbert, Interpretation of the Bible(1908):ch.8;
Fullerton, Prophecy and Authority(1919):chs 6-7;
Carter, The Reformers and Holy Scripture(1928): esp. 58-61;
Hempel, 'Das reformatorische Evangelium und das AT', LuJ(1932);
Peel, 'The Bible and the People' in Dugmore(1944);
Thielicke, 'Law and Gospel as Constant Partners'(1948), incorporated into Theological Ethics I:117-125;
McNeill, 'History of the Interpretation of the Bible II',IB I(1952):123-6;
Jacob, Theology of the OT(1955):16-18;
Kraeling, The OT Since the Reformation(1955):chs 1-2;
Strohl, 'La méthode exégétique des Réformateurs' in Boisset(1955);
Kraus, Geschichte(1956):6-24;
Blackman, Biblical Interpretation(1957):116-127;
Wood, The Interpretation of the Bible(1958):ch.8;
Sick, Melanchthon als Ausleger des ATs(1959);
Frör, Biblische Hermeneutik(1961):23-6;
Bainton, 'The Immoralities of the Patriarchs',HTR (1930) and 'The Bible in the Reformation', CHB III(1963);
Rupp, 'The Bible in the Age of the Reformation' in Nineham(1963);
Grant, Short History(1965):ch.10;
Bright, The Authority of the OT(1967):82-4;
Stierle, 'Schriftauslegung der Reformationszeit', VF(1971);
W.Elliger, 'Müntzer und das AT' in K.Elliger Festschrift(1973);
Hubbard, 'OT',NIDCC(1974):727.

0.432 Luther

Martin Luther (1483-1546) recognised both the unity and the diversity of the Bible. For him the unity was in God who revealed himself in Christ, and the diversity in the contrast between law and gospel. It was the contrast, however, which was the dominant factor, as is shown by the summary of his position in his 'Preface to the Old Testament' (1523):

'The ground and proof of the New Testament is surely not to be despised, and therefore the Old Testament is to be highly regarded. And what is the New Testament but a public preaching and proclamation of Christ, set forth through the sayings of the Old Testament and fulfilled through Christ?' (paragraph 2)

'...the Old Testament is a book of laws, which teaches what men are to do and not to do ... just as the New Testament is gospel or book of grace, and teaches where one is to get the power to fulfil the law. Now in the New Testament there are also given ... many other teachings that are laws and commandments .... Similarly in the Old Testament too there are ... certain promises and words of grace ... Nevertheless just as the chief teaching of the New Testament is really the proclamation of grace and peace through the forgiveness of sins in Christ, so the chief teaching of the Old Testament is really the teaching of laws, the showing up of sin, and the demanding of good.' (paragraph 4)

H.P.Smith, _Essays in Biblical Interpretation_(1921):ch.5;
H.Schmidt, _Luther und das Buch der Psalmen_(1933);
Steinlein, 'Luther und das AT',_Luthertum_(1937);
Herntrich, 'Luther und das AT',_LuJ_(1938);
Ebeling, _Evangelische Evangelienauslegung_(1942);
Bornkamm, _Luther and the OT_(1948);
Ebeling, 'Die Anfänge von Luthers Hermeneutik',_ZTK_(1951);
Hahn, 'Die heilige Schrift als Problem der Auslegung bei Luther',_EvTh_(1951);
Joest, _Gesetz und Freiheit_(1951);
Gerdes, _Luthers Streit mit dem Schwärmern_(1955);
Aland, 'Luther as Exegete',_ExpT_(1957);
Heintze, _Luthers Predigt von Gesetz und Evangelium_(1958);
Pelikan, _Luther the Expositor_(1959);
Wood, _Luther's Principles of Biblical Interpretation_(1960);
Krause, _Studien zu Luthers Auslegung der Kleinen Propheten_(1962);
Albrektson, 'Luther och den allegoriska tolkningen av Gamla Testamentet',_SEA_(1967);
Preus, 'OT _Promissio_ and Luther's New Hermeneutic', _HTR_(1967) and _From Shadow to Promise_(1969);

Bernhardt, 'Gamla testamentets betydelse för Martin Luthers reformatoriska gärning', SvTK(1968);
Hagen, 'The Problem of Testament in Luther's Lectures on Hebrews', HTR(1970);
Miller, 'The Theologies of Luther and Boehme in the Light of their Genesis Commentaries', HTR(1970).

0.433 Calvin

John Calvin (1509-64) also recognised both the similarity and the differences between the two Testaments, but in contrast to Luther he stressed the former, devoting 23 sections to the similarity and 14 to the differences in his *Institutes of the Christian Religion* (1536-59). In his words:

'Christ, although he was known to the Jews under the law, was at length clearly revealed only in the Gospel.' (II.9, title)

'The covenant made with all the patriarchs is so much like ours in substance and reality that the two are actually one and the same... First, we hold that carnal prosperity and happiness did not constitute the goal set before the Jews to which they were to aspire. Rather, they were adopted into the hope of immortality ... Secondly, the covenant by which they were bound to the Lord was supported, not by their own merits, but solely by the mercy of the God who called them. Thirdly, they had and knew Christ as Mediator, through whom they were joined to God and were to share in his promises.' (II.10:2)

'I freely admit the differences in Scripture... but in such a way as not to detract from its established unity... all these pertain to the manner of dispensation rather than to the substance.'(II.11:1)

Simon, 'Die Beziehung zwischen Altem und Neuem Testament in der Schriftauslegung Calvins', RKZ(1932; not available to me);
Niesel, The Theology of Calvin(1938):ch.7;
Fuhrmann, 'Calvin, The Expositor of Scripture', Interpn(1952);
Wallace, Calvin's Doctrine of the Word and Sacrament (1953):chs 3-4;
van Ruler, The Christian Church and the OT(1955); 13n/15,25n/27-28;
Wolf, Die Einheit des Bundes(1958);
Grin, 'L'unité des deux Testaments selon Calvin', ThZ(1961);
Forstman, Word and Spirit(1962);
Vischer, 'Calvin, exégète de l'AT', ETR(1965);

Hesselink, 'Calvin and Heilsgeschichte' in Cullmann Festschrift(1967);
Atkinson, _The Great Light_(1968):174,178-9;
Kraus, 'Calvins exegetische Prinzipien',_ZKG_(1968);
Russell, 'Calvin and the Messianic Interpretation of the Psalms',_SJT_(1968);
Prins, 'The Image of God... A Study in Calvin',_SJT_(1972).

0.434 Council of Trent

The most significant feature of the Roman Catholic Counter-Reformation for interpretation of the Bible was the Council of Trent. In its fourth session (8 April 1546) the Council decreed that the purity of the Gospel

'be preserved in the Church; which (Gospel) before promised through the prophets in the holy Scriptures, our Lord Jesus Christ, the Son of God, first promulgated with His own mouth, and then commanded to be preached by His Apostles to every creature, as the fountain of all, both saving truth and moral discipline'(paragraph 1).

No doubt the Reformers would have agreed with that; but the Council differed decisively from the Reformers on two issues: scripture and tradition, and the restriction of biblical interpretation to the Church. The decree continues:

'...this truth and discipline are contained in the written books, and the unwritten tradition... (the Synod) receives and venerates with an equal affection of piety and reverence all the books both of the Old and of the New Testament... as also the said traditions'(paragraph 1).

'Furthermore, in order to restrain petulant spirits, it decrees, that no one, relying on his own skill, shall...presume to interpret the said sacred Scripture contrary to that sense which holy mother Church, - whose it is to judge of the true sense and interpretation of the holy Scriptures, - hath held and doth hold; or even contrary to the unanimous consent of the Fathers'(paragraph 5).

The implications for the understanding of the relationship between the Testaments were that the unity of the Bible -with a relationship of promise and fulfilment between the two Testaments -was recognised, but there was little room for further investigation since acceptance of the traditional interpretation was mandatory. This situation changed little until the twentieth century.

Text of 'The Canons and Dogmatic Decrees of the Council of Trent' in Schaff, The Creeds of Christendom(1877):II.79-83;
Kidd, The Counter-Reformation(1933):59-60;
Kraeling, The OT Since the Reformation(1955):33-4;
Crehan, 'The Bible in the Roman Catholic Church', CHB III(1963):199-205,236-7;
Brown, 'Hermeneutics',JBC(1968):II.613.

0.44 SEVENTEENTH TO NINETEENTH CENTURIES

0.441 Introduction

The Reformation brought a new concern for serious study of the Bible, but the correct method of interpretation and way of understanding the relationship between the Testaments was far from settled. During the next three centuries there was a polarisation between the upholders of orthodoxy and more progressive thinkers. The period may conveniently be bisected for study, with the figure of Schleiermacher standing at the juncture of the two halves.

Diestel, Geschichte des ATes(1869):317-781;
Farrar, History of Interpretation(1886):chs 7-8;
Gilbert, Interpretation of the Bible(1908):chs 9-10;
Duff, History of OT Criticism(1910):chs 6-7;
Fullerton, Prophecy and Authority(1919):chs 8-9;
H.P.Smith, Essays in Biblical Interpretation(1921):chs 6-1
Eissfeldt, 'Werden, Wesen und Wert...'(1931), repr. in Kleine Schriften I;
Robert and Vaganay, 'Interprétation IV',SDB(1949);
Terrien, 'History of the Interpretation of the Bible III',IB I(1952);
Jacob, Theology of the OT(1955):18-23;
Kraeling, The OT Since the Reformation(1955):chs 3-7;
Kraus, Geschichte(1956) and Die Biblische Theologie(1970):
Wood, The Interpretation of the Bible(1958):chs 9-11;
Frör, Biblische Hermeneutik(1961):26-31;
Betz, 'Biblical Theology, History of',IDB(1962):432-4;
Crehan, 'The Bible in the Roman Catholic Church...',
Neil, 'The Criticism and Theological Use of the Bible'and
Sykes, 'The Religion of Protestants' in CHB III(1963);

Grant, Short History(1965):chs 11-12;
Harrison, Introduction to the OT(1970):420-27;
Knight, The Traditions of Israel(1973):chs 4-5;
Hubbard, 'OT',NIDCC(1974):727-8.

0.442 Orthodoxy

The predominant characteristic of biblical study in the years immediately following the Reformation was orthodoxy. Several important creeds and confessions were formulated to define the orthodox faith more precisely and a systematic kind of study developed which was not unlike that of the Middle Ages and is often termed 'Protestant Scholasticism'. Calvin's view of the relationship between the Testaments was widely followed and the Old Testament regarded highly. This was particularly true in Britain, where the free Churches found the Old Testament congenial to their cause.

Selbie, 'The Influence of the OT on Puritanism' in Bevan and Singer(1927);
Johnston, 'The Puritan Use of the OT',EQ(1951);

0.443 Reaction to Orthodoxy

Orthodoxy was not to survive long without a reaction. In the seventeenth and eighteenth centuries an increasing number of theologians became dissatisfied with traditional ways of interpreting the Bible. The influence of grammatico-historical biblical scholarship, federal theology (developed by Cocceius, 1603-69) and rationalism (exemplified by Hobbes, 1588-1679, and Spinoza, 1632-77) brought about a more humanistic and historical approach to the Bible, and consequently a greater readiness to reject less acceptable parts such as the Old Testament. This trend was continued in the eighteenth century by the works of Lessing (1729-81) and Kant(1724-1804), but accompanied by a continuous concern for pious and scholarly biblical study (e.g. Bengel, 1687-1752).

Brown, 'Covenant Theology', _ERE_(1911);
Schrenk, _Gottesreich und Bund_(1923);
Fritsch, 'Bengel, the Student of Scripture', _Interpn_(1951);
Carpenter, 'The Bible in the Eighteenth Century' in Nineham(1963);
Reventlow, 'Die Auffassung vom AT bei Reimarus und Lessing', _EvTh_(1965);
Busch, 'Der Beitrag und Ertrag der Föderaltheologie' in Cullmann Festschrift(1967);
Willi, _Herders Beitrag zum Verstehen des ATs_(1971).

0.444 Schleiermacher

The nearest significant approach to Christian rejection of the Old Testament since Marcion, though it stopped short of the audacity of that second-century heretic, was made by Friedrich Schleiermacher (1768-1834). With a background of Pietism, Rationalism and Romanticism, he wrote voluminously and widely. In his dogmatic theology (1821) he virtually denied any theological relationship between the Old Testament and the New Testament, not disparaging the former as Marcion had done - but placing it on the same level as Heathenism (Greek and Roman thought) (§ 12). His discussion of the doctrine of Holy Scripture deals with the Old Testament only in a postscript:

'The Old Testament Scriptures owe their place in our Bible partly to the appeals the New Testament Scriptures make to them, partly to the historical connexion of Christian worship with the Jewish Synagogue; but the Old Testament Scriptures do not on that account share the normative dignity or the inspiration of the New'(§ 132).

Schleiermacher's suggestion therefore was not the elimination of the Old Testament from the Bible but the transposition of the two Testaments to show the priority of the New Testament and make the Old Testament an appendix.

The Christian Faith(1821) - Schleiermacher's major work.

Cf. Mackintosh, Types of Modern Theology(1937):esp.70-71;
Bright, The Authority of the OT(1967):62-4;
Schütte, 'Christlicher Glaube und AT bei Friedrich Schleiermacher' in Doerne Festschrift(1970).

0.445 Higher Criticism

In spite of the influence of his thought, few took seriously Schleiermacher's view of the Old Testament until a century later (as he himself had predicted, 1821:§ 132). The dominant influence in nineteenth-century biblical interpretation was higher criticism, leading to understanding of the relationship between the Testaments primarily in historical rather than theological terms: the Old Testament contains the history of the theocracy, the New Testament records the coming of Jesus Christ as the final stage of this history.

De Wette, Lehrbuch der christlichen Dogmatik I(1813); Das Wesen des christlichen Glaubens(1846):355-69;
Vatke, Die biblische Theologie(1835);
Jowett, 'On the Interpretation of Scripture' in Temple et al.(1860);
Ewald, Revelation(1871);
Mozley, Ruling Ideas in Early Ages(1874-5);
Wellhausen, Prolegomena to the History of Israel(1878);
W.R.Smith, The OT in the Jewish Church(1881); cf. 'The Attitude of Christians to the OT',Exp(1884);
Kayser, Die Theologie des ATes(1886).

Cf. Cave, 'The OT and the Critics',ConRev(1890);
Carpenter, The Bible in the Nineteenth Century(1903);
Peake, 'The History of Theology' in Germany(1914);
Lightfoot, 'The Critical Approach to the Bible in the Nineteenth Century' in Dugmore(1944);
Glover, Evangelical Nonconformists and Higher Criticism in the Nineteenth Century(1954);
Blackman, Biblical Interpretation(1957):ch.5;
Lampe, 'The Bible since the Rise of Critical Study' in Nineham(1963);
Richardson, 'The Rise of Modern Biblical Scholarship', CHB III(1963):294-305.

0.446 Conservative Reaction

The increasing acceptance of higher criticism in the nineteenth century did not prevent a number of conservative scholars from defending and developing more traditional approaches to the Bible. Their reassertion of the orthodox belief in the inspiration of the Bible was however combined with a readiness to consider new ideas and they made a lasting contribution to biblical interpretation. Von Hofmann's elaboration of 'salvation history' has influenced much later theology based on this concept (cf. below: 7.26); Hengstenberg's Christology and Franz Delitzsch's commentaries on the Old Testament are still in print a century later.

Hengstenberg, Christology of the OT(1829-35);
Beck, Die Christliche Lehrwissenschaft(1841); cf. Schlatter 1904;
Hofmann, Weissagung und Erfüllung(1841-4); also: Der Schriftbeweis(1852-3); Biblische Hermeneutik(1880); cf. Wapler 1914;Preuss 1950; Baumgärtel 1952:86-91; Hübner 1956; Steck 1959:19-35;
Trench, Hulsean Lectures(1845-6);
Schultz, OT Theology(1860);
R.P.Smith, Prophecies of Isaiah(1862); Prophecy a Preparation for Christ(1869);
Saphir, Christ and Scripture(1867); The Divine Unity of Scripture(1894);
Franz Delitzsch, OT History of Redemption(1881); Neueste Traumgesichte(1883); Der tiefen Graben(1888); Messianic Prophecies(1890);
Stoughton, The Progress of Divine Revelation(n.d.).

Cf. Sneen, 'The Hermeneutics of N.F.S.Grundtvig', Interpn(1972):esp.57.

0.5 TRANSITION TO THE MODERN PERIOD

0.51 THE DEVELOPMENTAL APPROACH

At the beginning of the twentieth century the most widely accepted way of understanding the theological relationship between the Old Testament and the New Testament was the liberal, developmental approach which may be characterised by the concept of 'progressive revelation'. Since this understanding was the primary background upon which the modern solutions examined in the major part of the present work were formulated, it will be examined in some detail now. The work of three significant British writers will first be considered, and then others will be mentioned more briefly.

Dillistone, <u>The Word of God and the People of God</u> (1948):13-15;
Kraeling, <u>The OT Since the Reformation</u>(1955):ch.9;
Richardson, 'The Rise of Modern Biblical Scholarship', <u>CHB</u> III(1963):311-18
Bright, <u>The Authority of the OT</u>(1967):96-103.

0.52 A.F.KIRKPATRICK

a. Kirkpatrick (1891) discusses the use of the Old Testament by the New Testament, its comparative neglect in his time, and the way in which it can and should be used in the contemporary Christian Church. The first and last of these are of particular interest for the problem of the relationship between the Testaments.

b. The New Testament affirms the permanent value of the Old Testament by explicit statements(e.g.

Matt.5:17; Rom.15:4; 1 Cor.10:11; 2 Tim.3:14-17) and by continually using it in expounding Christ and his work (pp. 112-116). The New Testament itself never purported to supersede the Old Testament, and yet this appeared to be an unspoken assumption of many in Kirkpatrick's time who preferred the New Testament and ignored the Old. No doubt there were good reasons for this neglect: the Church prized the New Testament as its characteristic possession, it reacted against past misuse of the Old Testament, and was understandably suspicious about its value in the light of the controversy about higher criticism. Nevertheless, Kirkpatrick argues, the Church should not on these grounds be dissuaded from use of the Old Testament but should use it properly, following the example of Jesus and the early Church (pp.116-123).

c. Kirkpatrick next considers the different ways in which the Old Testament may be used today. In itself it has a permanent value as teaching about national, social and, most of all, personal life (pp.130-133). The simplicity of its moral demands and the depth of its praise and devotion are of continuing value in the Christian era. But above all the Old Testament is needed in relation to the New Testament.

First, the Old Testament is the essential historical basis of the New Testament and Christianity, without which they cannot be properly understood (pp. 123-6). The coming of Christ did not occur in a vacuum, nor was it only related to the history of the Church which he founded, but was the consummation of a long history of God at work in human affairs. Moreover, it is not only the predictions which are relevant in considering the relationship of the Old Testament to the New: Kirkpatrick quotes with approval the opinion of an unnamed author that the Old Testament 'does not merely contain prophecies; it is from first to last a prophecy'(p.124). Fulfilment should not be understood too narrowly, as an event which has been recorded in advance by prophecy. Prophecy directs men to the future, in many different ways, and the fulfilment satisfies their hopes and longings, although not always in the way expected. Fulfilment goes far beyond expectations, and yet it is not so complete that it does not point men once more to the future, to the final goal of their redemption (pp.124-5).

Secondly, study of the language, concepts and theology of the Old Testament is essential for proper understanding of the New Testament(pp.126-130). The New Testament is written in the Hebraic Greek of the Septuagint, and many fundamental New Testament ideas such as righteousness, holiness, sacrifice and sin come from the Old Testament and can be understood only with reference to it.

Thirdly, every Christian can find encouragement in the Old Testament by looking at God's outworking of his purpose in spite of human weakness and failure (pp.127-130). Reading the Old Testament will clarify the close link between prophecy and fulfilment and strengthen the Christian hope that God will bring victory for Christ's kingdom, even though there may be much discouragement in the interim.

d. Kirkpatrick concludes with a warning not to confuse the two Testaments, a principle that the Old Testament is valid for the Church only in so far as it is fulfilled in Christ, and a reminder that in the Old Testament the Church not only has a collection of literature but is confronted by the Word of God. (1) The Old Testament has its value for the Christian, but it is clearly different in this respect from the New Testament. It must not be used as a court of appeal for Christian doctrine although support for that may well be found in it, nor may it be used to justify anything contrary to the mind of Christ (pp.133-4). (2) To interpret the Old Testament in terms of its fulfilment in Christ does not mean concern only with its prophetic aspect: rather, it demands recognition of the completion, realisation, development and universalisation in Christ of what was before incomplete and limited. Christ has given a deeper insight into God and his purpose for man, thereby enabling a new perception of his working in the Old Testament (pp.134-9). (3) The whole Bible - including the Old Testament - is inspired by God. Although revelation has taken place in many and various ways, in each case it is God who has spoken (pp.139-141).

e. A sermon of Kirkpatrick's from 1903 follows the same basic approach but defines the relationship between the Testaments more clearly and succinctly by discussing successively the unity and the distinction between the two parts of the Bible. First, the two Testaments are linked by the fact that in both God is revealing his character and purposes by words and deeds: 'the whole Bible is the history of redemption' and 'without the New Testament the Old Testament would be a magnificent failure; without the Old Testament the New Testament would be an inexplicable phenomenon' (pp.7-9). Secondly, the important distinction between the Testaments is that the Old records an incomplete, progressive revelation, but the New a complete and final one (pp.9-12). The rest of the sermon is a consideration of the nature and permanent value of the Old Testament and the way in which it should be read (pp. 12-25).

Kirkpatrick, 'The Use of the OT in the Christian Church', _The Divine Library of the OT_(1891); 'How to read the OT' in Kirkpatrick _et al_.(1903).

0.53 R.L.OTTLEY

a. In the last of his 1897 Bampton Lectures (_Aspects of the Old Testament_), Ottley discusses use of the Old Testament in the New and in the contemporary Church.

b. First, the New Testament understands the Old Testament revelation as fragmentary, varied and rudimentary. The Old Testament is the record of a developing religion and revelation, and is therefore to be interpreted historically; every part, whether type or prophecy, sign or promise, is incomplete and looks forward to God's perfect plan for the future (pp.377-8). Moreover, the New Testament recognises that much in the Old is imperfect and must be assessed by the standard of the Gospel (pp.379-80). New Testament exegesis of the Old is notable for its breadth and freedom, its concern with morals and human duty, and its Messianic nature. It represents the Old Testament as 'an organic whole, to which the Messiah and His Kingdom are the key... a shadow of good things to come'(p.396). Jesus himself, though recognising their divine inspiration and authority, treats the Scriptures with a personal authority that no one else could claim; and while using contemporary scribal methods of interpretation he modifies and adapts them for his own purposes (pp.381-9). So the key to understanding the Old Testament is for those who have the 'mind of Christ' and are guided by his Spirit (pp.389-400).

c. Secondly, the Old Testament is important in the life of the Church. Ottley points first to the historical (pp.401-5) and mystical (pp.405-12) senses of the Old Testament, warning against overestimation of the former and neglect of the latter. He defends mystical interpretation on the basis of the sacramental nature of the world assumed by the Old Testament and the close relationship between Judaism and Christianity (in view of which it is natural to find in the Old Testament types, particular events and experiences which exemplify more general moral principles and therefore are prophetic in character). He then suggests six ways in which the Old Testament may be employed by the Church. The first three concern the intrinsic value of the Old Testament: for education in morals, in the spiritual life, and in social righteousness (pp.421-33). The other three concern understanding of the Old Testament in the context of the whole Bible and merit more detailed attention here. (1) The main purpose of the Old Testament, as of the New, is to reveal the mind, character and will of God. In addition, it shows God's preparation for the coming of the Messiah and introduces the concept of suffering, the chosen tool for accomplishment of the divine purpose, the perfection of man (pp.412-16). (2) The Old Testament witnesses to Christ. Theology of the Old Testament presupposes its unity as a history of redemption, to which the coming of a redeemer is a natural climax. In the person of Christ 'all that was limited, shadowy, fragmentary, or disconnected in the writings and characters of the Old Testament, was harmonized, developed and completed' (pp.418-19). A prefiguration of Christ may be seen in law, history, prophecy, song and wisdom: in fact, the idealistic nature of much of the Old Testament is sufficient to describe it as Messianic (pp.416-21). (3) The Old Testament serves as an aid to interpretation of the New. Many of the most fundamental concepts of the New Testament are taken from the Old: Christ, kingdom of God, Son of God, to mention only three, would be virtually unintelligible without the Old Testament. Much of the content of the Christian faith is learnt from the Old Testament, and the New Testament is but the completion and formulation of these fundamental ideas and experiences (pp.433-6).

0.54 B.F.WESTCOTT

a. The appendix to Westcott's commentary on Hebrews (1899), 'On the Use of the Old Testament in the Epistle', is earlier than the works of Kirkpatrick and Ottley, but has quite a modern ring about it and has influenced at least one of the later writers (see Kirkpatrick 1891:116,124: 1903:18-19).

b. According to Westcott, the author of Hebrews represents the whole Bible as a revelation of God's way of salvation, initially 'in many and various ways' and finally 'by a Son'(pp.480-82). It is presupposed that the Old Testament has a spiritual meaning and significance, though its historical truth is also taken seriously. The Old Testament points forward to Christ, in whom alone it finds true fulfilment; so it is used in Hebrews not for discussion or proof but for understanding and illustration of the correspondences between different stages in the fulfilment of God's purpose.

'The object of the writer is not to shew that Jesus fulfils the idea of the Christ, and that the Christian Church fulfils the idea of Israel, but, taking this for granted, to mark the relation in which the Gospel stands to the Mosaic system, as part of one divine whole '(p.481).

c. God's purpose for man is entry into the divine rest, but this was never completely achieved in the Old Testament (pp.482-6).

'Each promise fulfilled brings the sense of a larger promise. The promises connected with the possession of Canaan (for example) quickened a hope of far greater blessings than the actual possession gave... and ...there remaineth a Sabbath-rest for the people of God (Hebr.iv.9)'(p.482). 'The teaching of the Old Testament as a whole is a perpetual looking forward' (p.485).

The accomplishment of God's purpose required a long preparation by discipline, to foster natural moral growth to maturity and to right the wrongs caused by the Fall. The author mentions Melchizedek as an example of natural growth, but his main interest is in the discipline through Israel and Christ. This is seen in the intimately related revelations of the two Testaments, preparatory in the Old and final in the New.

d. Westcott next discusses in more detail the work of the Messianic nation and that of the personal Messiah as interpreted by Hebrews (pp.486-91), concluding that 'the Old Testament does not simply contain prophecies, but is one vast prophecy, in the record of national fortunes, in the ordinances of a national Law, in the expression of a national hope. Israel...is a unique enigma...of which Christ is the complete solution '(p.491).

e. Finally, Westcott considers the application of the interpretative principles of Hebrews in the Christian Church (pp.492-5). He has shown that the Old Testament is an indispensable part of the Bible. It still has moral and social lessons to teach, but above all it records the history of Judaism as a type of God's action in history. This was fulfilled in Christ, but even in the Christian era it points to the future:

'Our highest joy is to recognise the divine law that each fulfilment opens a vision of something yet beyond. The Wilderness, Jordan, Canaan, necessarily take a new meaning as the experience of man extends ...as yet we do not see the end.'(p.495).

0.55 OTHER WRITERS

a. George Adam Smith (1899), in a lecture on 'The Spirit of Christ in the Old Testament', deliberately avoids the traditional approaches of typology and Messianic prophecy, as well as conventional ways of explaining Christ's sacrifice and divinity (pp.145-176). While not denying their possible validity, he points out that in practice the concepts of typology and Messianic prophecy are too vaguely defined and indiscriminately used, resulting in artificial, if not arbitrary, interpretation. Besides this, these concepts are inadequate because they fail to interpret in the light of Christ many parts of the Old Testament which unquestionably 'breathe His Spirit' (p.147). Smith believes that the sacrifice of Christ should be interpreted less in terms of Old

Testament animal sacrifices and more with reference to Israel's human sufferings and sacrifices. Moreover the divinity of Christ should be defined less on the basis of the characteristics of the Messiah and more by means of God's self-revelation found in the Old Testament. The Spirit of Christ may be perceived in the Old Testament both in its human ideals - and their enactments in Israel's heroes - and in its divine revelation.

A practical approach to the relationship between the Testaments is to consider the relationship between the social ethics of the prophets and those of the New Testament (pp.215-82). Smith argues that the political situation in the two is quite different: in the Old Testament the people of God are a nation and God's purpose for them is worked out in national life; in the New Testament, on the other hand, the 'people of God' are non-political, their only political duty being obedience to the authorities.

b. J.E.McFadyen (1903:345-64) considers that the Old Testament has a double value for the Church. In an absolute sense, it shows God's purpose in history and its prophets and psalmists can speak directly to the modern age. Apart from this, however, it has a relative value with reference to the New Testament:

' It prepared the way for the Testament by which it was transcended, though not superseded, and for Him whose coming marks a new departure, and yet was no less truly conditioned and directed by all that had gone before' (p.352).

The Old Testament is essential for the New, both historically and religiously, and in spite of obvious differences between the two, the continuity is more important than the distinction.

c. A.B.Davidson (1904:1-12) considers Old Testament theology to be a development, so that the two Testaments must neither be separated (which would remove all authority from the Old Testament) nor equated (which would imply that the Old Testament is as advanced as the New). The Old Testament describes God's activity in establishing his kingdom, which was completed only in Christ, but it does not follow that the former events and institutions are nothing more than foreshadowings of the future. Indeed most Israelites never saw beyond the immediate significance of the institutions. It was only a few of the more perceptive thinkers (e.g. the prophets) who saw the imperfection and looked deeper to the fundamental idea embodied by the institution and expressed 'their longing and certainty that the idea would yet be realised'(p.9).

d. S.R.Driver (1905) affirms that 'the Old Testament Scriptures enshrine truths of permanent and universal validity'(p.20). Without specifically discussing their relationship to the New Testament, he concludes that the Old Testament writings 'form a great and indispensable preparation for the coming of Christ. They exhibit the earlier stages of a great redemptive process, the consummation of which is recorded in the New Testament' (p.21).

e. W.H.Bennett (1893:39-40) asserts that the Old Testament 'not only prepares a way for the New, but also contains special and characteristic truths stated once and for all'. Two decades later (1914) he discusses the problem of the relationship between the Testaments in more detail, using the concept of 'progressive revelation': the Old Testament is a record of a divine revelation in two forms: history (of God and his people) and teaching (about religion and morals) (p.7). Its greatest value, according to Bennett, is in relation to Christ, witnessing to him and explaining his significance, though much in it is not surpassed by the New Testament but of continuing value in itself. The Christian should not only follow Christ's example in using the Old Testament as a guide for everyday life and religion, but should recognise in its developing revelation and religion a preparation for Christ and the New Testament (pp.25-44). There is a two-way relationship between the Testaments: just as the New Testament cannot be properly understood without the Old, so the Old Testament can be truly appreciated only when studied in the light of the New (pp.48-9).

f. W.N.Clarke (1905) offers a somewhat different solution to the problem. His concern is with the whole Bible and he believes that it is necessary in every part to distinguish between what is Christian and what is not.

'The principle is, that the Christian element in the Scriptures is the indispensable and formative element in Christian theology, and is the only element in the Scriptures which Christian theology is either required or permitted to receive as contributing to its substance'(p.50).

Theology is concerned with God, the Bible is concerned with the Hebrew and Christian religions, and the two meet in Christ who is their common possession and glory (pp.50-51). The revelation of Christ is contained within the Bible and is qualitatively different from the non-Christian matter alongside it (pp.53-4). The Christian element may be used as scripture, but not the remainder (though the latter is not entirely valueless, p.54). Clarke admits that this will lead to a smaller Bible and a smaller theological system (pp.125-6), but believes it will be 'not because we know less of God, but because we know more, and what we know is more concentrated in eternal reality' (p.126).

A few theologians and many ordinary people have made use of a similar argument and with a quick assumption that the Old Testament is non-Christian have rejected it in favour of the New. Clarke does not follow this Marcionite way but makes a division by means of the rule: 'that is Christian which enters into or accords with the view of divine realities which Jesus Christ revealed' (p.56). Although it suffers grievously through the application of this rule, the Old Testament is not reduced to nothing, nor is the New left unscathed. The result for the Old Testament is elimination of the anthropomorphisms (pp.93-4), the idea of the localisation of worship (pp.94-5), salvation by the law and works (pp.97-9), God's aloofness from men (pp.99-102), primitive eschatological ideas (pp.102-112) and sacrifice (pp.121-4). Nevertheless Clarke argues that 'the Christian element comes in from the Bible as a whole ... When the excessive influence of the Old Testament has been thrown off from theology, the Old Testament begins to be appreciated'(p.128). Christian truth is found in the prophets and psalmists, even if it is mixed with much else (pp.128-130). Moreover the Old Testament represents a history of growth of true religion and understanding of God, which is of great value to theology if read with a critical moral judgement (pp.132-4). Clarke believes that this approach will lead not to a depreciation of the Scriptures but to an appreciation of their true value, in their witness to Christ. Authority is transferred from the written word to the incarnate Word, and so 'Christian faith will rest upon a foundation that will stand forever' (p.170).

This is not the place for a general criticism of Clarke's thesis, but its implications for the problem of the relationship between the Testaments must be considered. First, the Old Testament is to be interpreted in terms of progressive revelation, according to Clarke, and its completion and perfection are found in the final revelation in Christ. Secondly, and more significantly, the two Testaments are equated - or at least put on the same level - in their <u>lack</u> of authority. The biblical writings are authoritative, inspired and normative for theology only insofar as they are 'Christian'; it is only possible therefore to conceive the unity of the Bible in terms of its very lack of inherent uniqueness. Both Testaments contain God's word, neither of them <u>are</u> God's Word.

g. C.F.Kent (1906) treats the Old Testament as the record of a varied, extended and yet incomplete revelation, which looks for the coming of one who will crystallise and perfect its teachings, and exemplify them in his own life. This coming is recorded in the New Testament which, in spite of some obvious differences, has many important similarities to the Old Testament. 'Each Testament is but a different chapter in the history of the same divine revelation. The one is the foundation on which the other is built' (p.61). So the Old Testament tells of preparation and expectation, the New Testament of a fulfilment much greater than the highest expectations (pp.60-62).

a. Bennett, 'The OT and the New Reformation',<u>Exp</u> (1890); 'OT' in <u>Faith and Criticism</u>(Essays by Congregationalists 1893); <u>The Value of the OT for the Religion of Today</u>(1914);
Sanday, <u>The Oracles of God</u>(1891):chs 8-9;
Driver, 'The Moral and Devotional Value of the OT',<u>ExpT</u>(1892); 'The OT in the Light of Today', <u>Exp</u>(1901); 'The Permanent Religious Value of the OT',<u>The Interpreter</u>(1905);
Mc Curdy, 'The Moral Evolution of the OT',<u>AJT</u>(1897);
Peake, <u>A Guide to Biblical Study</u>(1897):chs 7,10; 'The Permanent Value of the OT'(1907,1912), repr. in <u>The Nature of Scripture</u>; <u>The Bible</u> (1913):ch.18;
G.A.Smith, <u>Modern Criticism and the Preaching of the OT</u>(1899);
Davidson, 'The Uses of the OT for Edification', <u>Exp</u>(1900); <u>Biblical and Literary Essays</u>(1903): chs 1,12,13; <u>OT Prophecy</u>(1903):219; <u>Theology of the OT</u>(1904); cf.Porteous 1951:313-16;

McFadyen, OT Criticism and the Christian Church(1903);
J.A.Robinson, Some Thoughts on Inspiration(1904):41-7;
Carr, 'The Eclectic Use of the OT in the NT',Exp(1905);
Clarke, The Use of the Scriptures in Theology(1905);
Keane, 'The Moral Argument against the Inspiration of the OT',HibJ(1905);
Kent, The Origin and Permanent Value of the OT(1906);
Redpath, 'Christ the Fulfilment of Prophecy',Exp(1907);
Vernon, The Religious Value of the OT(1908);
Foakes-Jackson, 'The OT before Modern Criticism', The Interpreter(1908-9);
Jordan, Biblical Criticism and Modern Thought(1909);
Mercer, 'Is the OT a Suitable Basis for Moral Instruction?',HibJ(1909);
Knight, 'The Public Reading of the OT', The Interpreter(1911);
McNeile, The OT in the Christian Church(1913);
H.W.Robinson, The Religious Ideas of the OT(1913):ch.9.

b. There are also many works in German along similar lines to those discussed above, but it is impossible here to do more than mention a few titles:
Dalman, Das AT ein Wort Gottes(1896);
Oettli, Der gegenwärtige Kampf um das AT(1896);
Kautzsch, Die bleibende Bedeutung des ATs(1902);
Köberle, 'Heilsgeschichtliche und religionsgeschichtliche Betrachtungsweise des ATs',NKZ(1906);
Marti, The Religion of the OT(1906); Stand und Aufgabe der atl. Wissenschaft(1912);
Gunkel, 'What is Left of the OT?'(1914),ET in What Remains of the OT;
Kittel, Das AT und unser Krieg(1916): esp.49-54.

Cf. Boyer, 'The Value of the OT: A German Estimate', The Interpreter(1905);
also, originally in French, Westphal, The Law and the Prophets(1903-7).

0.56 DISCUSSION

a. The spate of works during the period around the turn of the century on the Old Testament and its relationship to the New was no doubt due largely to the uncertainties produced by the higher criticism controversy, as well as to the incentive to new study provided by its acceptance in principle (which was accompanied by many doubts about individual results of criticism). Many of the works referred to here were produced primarily to present, explain and justify criticism to ministers and laymen, and to show its positive contribution to the understanding of the

Bible. All the authors accept criticism, at least in principle, and assume the Bible to be a document which is both human and divine, an account of human history and a revelation from God.

b. The major concern of the writers is generally not the more abstract problem of the relationship between the Testaments but its practical equivalent, the use of the Old Testament in the Church (cf. below: 9.3). They are agreed that the Old Testament is indispensable for the modern Church and has two major uses. In itself, the Old Testament 'enshrines truths of permanent and universal validity'(Driver 1905:20) and may be used for instruction in social relationships, national life, and personal morality and devotion. And in relationship to the New Testament, the Old Testament is to be used in three main ways: first, the Old Testament is the most important historical basis of the New; secondly, an understanding of the language, concepts and theology of the Old Testament is essential to interpretation of the New; finally, the Old Testament is a witness to Christ (this is not always defined very closely: for example, Westcott is referring to typology, Bennett to the idealistic aspect of the Old Testament).

c. In these works a balance is generally maintained between the obvious differences of the Old Testament from the New and the belief that the two are essentially a unity. The Old Testament is incomplete, developing and imperfect, and must be judged by the standard of the final and perfect revelation in Christ; moreover, the Old Testament is concerned with a nation, the New with a supranational people of God. On the other hand, in both Testaments it is one God who speaks, and one plan of redemption which is presented. The two extremes of separation and of confusion of the two Testaments must therefore be rejected.

d. The fundamental concept underlying all the works discussed is that of 'progressive revelation' (see further, below: 0.61). The Old Testament is considered to have permanent value both as preparatory revelation and in looking beyond itself to the perfect revelation in Christ. Today the term 'progressive revelation' is outmoded, along with the optimistic evolutionary idea of history which it presupposed. Nevertheless, this was the view of the Bible which formed the basis of twentieth--century biblical interpretation. Reading these works it is interesting to discover how many so-called 'modern' ideas are to be found. The Bible is understood as a history of redemption (Ottley 1897:417; Kirkpatrick 1903:8; cf. Driver 1905:21) and the Old Testament in particular is considered to be oriented to the future. The way in which 'prophecy and fulfilment' is interpreted is not unlike modern interpretations of 'promise and fulfilment', and typology is conceived - at least by Westcott - in a similar way to many modern scholars.

e. Westcott's statement that 'each promise fulfilled brings the sense of a larger promise' (1889:482; cf. Kirkpatrick 1891:124-5) could almost have been taken from Moltmann's <u>Theology of Hope</u> (1964), and Kirkpatrick's quote that the Old Testament 'does not merely contain prophecies; it is from first to last a prophecy' (1891:124; cf. Westcott 1889:491) might have found a place in Vriezen's Old Testament theology (1954/66). Ottley takes the Bible to be the history of redemption, considers the Old Testament to point toward the future, perceives reinterpretation of texts within the Bible, and mentions typology: in fact most of the major themes of von Rad's Old Testament theology (1957-60) are in his lecture! No doubt most of these authors would have been shocked at Bultmann's views on the Old Testament; but perhaps there is a foreshadowing of that twentieth-century theologian in McFadyen's assertion that the Old Testament did not bring the redemptive purpose of God to fulfilment but 'by its repeated failures pointed men to something more strong and saving than itself (1903:347).

0.6 THE TWENTIETH CENTURY

0.61 'PROGRESSIVE REVELATION'

0.611 The majority solution

It has been shown in the preceding section that the prevailing solution to the problem of the relationship between the Testaments at the beginning of the twentieth century was that of the developmental approach, characterised by the concept of 'progressive revelation'. This solution was widely accepted during the first half of the century, at least in Britain and America. As will be shown below, even the more conservative sections of the Church, Fundamentalism and Roman Catholicism, adopted this solution and the most important voice of dissent, uttered by Neo-Marcionism, was based on an extreme interpretation of the developmental approach.

Further examples of the 'progressive revelation' approach to the relationship between the Testaments:
Malden, The OT: Its Meaning and Value(1919);
Burney, The Gospel in the OT(1921);
Box, 'The Value and Significance of the OT in Relation to the New' and
Kennett, 'The Contribution of the OT to the Religious Development of Mankind' in Peake(1925);
G.A.Smith, 'The Hebrew Genius as Exhibited in the OT' in Bevan and Singer(1927);
Berry, 'The OT: A Liability or an Asset',CRDSB(1930);
Bewer, 'The Christian Minister and the OT',JR(1930);
'The Authority of the OT',JR(1936);
Welch, The Preparation for Christ in the OT(1933);
Cook, The OT: A Reinterpretation(1936);
Burrows, An Outline of Biblical Theology(1946):e.g. 53,125; cf.Harrington 1973:265-73;
Elmslie, How Came Our Faith(1948);
Kenyon, The Bible and Modern Scholarship(1948):15-16;
Higgins, The Christian Significance of the OT(1949);
Woods, The OT in the Church(1949);
T.H.Robinson, 'The OT and the Modern World' in Rowley(19[illegible]

Hodgson, 'God and the Bible' in Hodgson(1960):6-10;
Kaufman, 'What Shall We Do With the Bible?',Interpn(1971).

Cf. Bultmann, 'The Significance of the OT for the Christian Faith'(1933), ET in OTCF:8-13; cf. below:3.121;
Manson, 'The Failure of Liberalism' in Dugmore(1944);
Wright, 'Interpreting the OT',ThTo(1946):178-185;
van Ruler, The Christian Church and the OT(1955): 25-6/27-8;
Westermann, 'Zur Auslegung des ATs'(1955),ET in EOTI: 40-44,123-4;
Reid, The Authority of Scripture(1957):182-193;
Smart, The Interpretation of Scripture(1961):79-80;
Moltmann, Theology of Hope(1964):69-76;
Bright, The Authority of the OT(1967):103-9,187-9;
Barr, The Bible in the Modern World(1973):144-6;
cf. Curr, 'Progressive Revelation',JTVI(1951).

0.612 Fundamentalism

A certain section of Protestant thought, sometimes called 'Fundamentalism' after a series of tracts entitled The Fundamentals issued in the early part of the twentieth century, rejected many of the presuppositions, methods and results of higher criticism. On the problem of the relationship between the Testaments, however, its view was not greatly different from the consensus of contemporary scholarship. James Orr (1906), for example, emphasises the predictive element of Old Testament prophecy, and considers divine guidance rather than natural evolution to be the principle of development, but accepts in general terms the concept of progressive revelation as a description of the relationship between the Testaments.

Warfield, Biblical and Theological Studies(1886-1917); The Inspiration and Authority of the Bible (1892-1915);
Green, The Higher Criticism of the Pentateuch(1895); General Introduction to the OT(1899);
Pierson, The Bible and Spiritual Criticism(1906);
Orr, The Problem of the OT(1906); The Bible under Trial(n.d.); Revelation and Inspiration(1910);
Patton, Fundamental Christianity(1926).

Cf. Margoliouth, 'Dr.Orr on the Problem of the OT', Exp(1906);
Richardson, 'The Rise of Modern Biblical Scholarship', CHB III(1963):306-11;
Pache, The Inspiration and Authority of Scripture (ET:1969):ch.11.

0.613 Roman Catholicism

Within the Roman Church at the beginning of the century there was a stronger reaction to higher criticism than that in Protestantism, since it was supported by the official maintenance of orthodox views about the Bible. As with Fundamentalism, however, its concern was mainly to defend those areas of Christian faith threatened by higher criticism, and the question of the relationship between the Testaments was not one of them. Until the present day in Roman Catholic theology the Old Testament is commonly seen as the historical and theological preparation for the New Testament. This differs from the developmental conception of revelation in that it stresses divine ordering and overruling whereas the latter stresses human evolutionary development, but the resulting views of the relationship between the Testaments are very similar.

Heinisch, Theologie des ATes(1940):esp.331-3; History of the OT(1949-50):e.g.3; cf. Harrington1973:79-81;
Courtade, 'Le sens de l'histoire dans l'Écriture', RechSR(1949);
Dubarle, 'La lecture chrétienne de l'AT' in Auvray (1951):210-23;
Voeltzel, 'Le Rôle de l'AT',RHPR(1953);
Levie, 'L'Ecriture Sainte',NRT(1956);
Grelot, Sens chrétien de l'AT(1962):21-2,196-209,275-86; cf. Alonso-Schökel 1963; Murphy 1964:353-5; Zerafa 1964; Harrington 1973:314-23;
Larcher, L'actualité chrétienne de l'AT(1962):ch.II.2; cf. Murphy 1964:352-3; Harrington 1973:323-9;
Loretz, The Truth of the Bible(1964):157-162;
McKenzie, 'The Values of the OT',Concilium 3.10(1967).

cf. Vidler, The Modernist Movement in the Roman Catholic Church(1934):ch.10;
Levie, 'Exégèse critique et interprétation théologique', RechSR(1951);
van Ruler, The Christian Church and the OT(1955):11/12;
Schulz, 'Die römisch-katholische Exegese', EvTh(1962);
Crehan, 'The Bible in the Roman Catholic Church', CHB III(1963):227-33;
Rottenberg, Redemption and Historical Reality(1964):ch.3;
Grant, Short History(1965):ch.13;
Bright, The Authority of the OT(1967):188;
Brown, 'Hermeneutics', JBC(1968):II.613-14.

0.62 NEO-MARCIONISM

0.621 Friedrich Delitzsch and Adolf von Harnack

One result of the 'progressive revelation' solution to the problem of the relationship between the Testaments was a devaluation of the Old Testament. It is indeed natural that what is imperfect and preparatory should be less highly regarded than a later superior stage of revelation. In the 1920s two well-known German scholars took this devaluation to its logical but extreme conclusion and resurrected the proposal of Marcion, only temporarily revived by Schleiermacher, that the Old Testament should be excluded from the Christian Bible. Friedrich Delitzsch's view of the Old Testament is summed up in the title of his two-volume work: The Great Deception(1920-21). Harnack concluded his standard work on Marcion(1921) with the oft-quoted thesis:

> 'To reject the Old Testament in the second century was a mistake which the Church rightly rejected; to keep it in the sixteenth century was a fate which the Reformation could not yet avoid; but to retain it after the nineteenth century as a canonical document in Protestantism results from paralysis of religion and the Church.'

Friedrich Delitzsch, Die grosse Täuschung,I(1920),II(1921);
Harnack, The Mission and Expansion of Christianity(1902);
Marcion: Das Evangelium vom fremden Gott(1921);
'Das AT in den Paulinischen Briefen', SAB(1928).

These views were naturally not received without question. See e.g.,

Eissfeldt, 'Christentum und AT'(1921),repr. in Kleine Schriften I;

König, Friedrich Delitzsch's "Die grosse Täuschung"(1920); Moderne Vergewaltigung des ATs(1921); Wie weit hat Delitzsch Recht?(1921);

Sellin, Das AT und die evangelische Kirche der Gegenwart (1921);

Theis, Friedrich Delitzsch und seine "Grosse Täuschung" (1921).

Cf. Filson, 'Adolf von Harnack and his "What is Christianity"',Interpn(1952);

Kraeling, The OT Since the Reformation(1955):ch.10;

Nicolaisen, Die Auseinandersetzung um das AT im Kirchenkampf(1966):12-18;

Bright, The Authority of the OT(1967): 64-7 ;

Kuske, Das AT als Buch von Christus(1967):14-15.

0.622 The Nazi Bible

Though their intention was explicitly theological rather than political, the works of Friedrich Delitzsch and Harnack were published about the time that anti-Semitic thought began to develop in Germany after the First World War, and they no doubt aided its growth and penetration into biblical studies. In the years between the two wars an increasingly fierce debate raged over the Old Testament, the Nazis and sympathetic theologians attacking it vehemently, those who were brave enough defending it with equal vehemence. The Nazis and 'German Christians'(Deutsche Christen) aimed to eliminate every trace of Judaism from Christianity. This involved rejection of the Old Testament and its god, and its replacement by Nordic and Aryan literature. In this they invoked the support of Luther, who they claimed would have done the same had he lived in the twentieth century. Some (e.g. Rosenberg) despised the Old Testament completely, saying that it was produced by lazy cattle-breeders who made Yahweh as a god in their own image; others (e.g. Leffler) recognised its historical and religious value but advocated that serious Germans should forget the Old Testament and study their own history and piety. It was at least consistent that those who hated and fought Jews should do the same to Jewish literature. It was also consistent that they should begin to purge the New Testament of Jewish elements, as Marcion had done eighteen centuries before. The Nazi 'Bible' was indeed a very select collection of extracts from the Christian Scriptures and it is not surprising that the Nazi 'Christ' and the German 'Christians' were very different from the usual referents of those words. Tanner (1942) comments: 'the crucifixion was only the first in a long series of devices by which the Western world has attempted to be rid of Jesus... the most subtle of these devices has been reinterpretation'(p.52).

Much of this disparagement of the Old Testament was little more than political propaganda, without theological basis or content. Mathilde Ludendorff (1939), for instance, argues that most of the Old Testament was written 300 years _after_ the time of Christ, in order to prove that it is a Jewish fabrication. An exception to this, however, is to be found in Emanuel Hirsch, a New Testament scholar who joined the German Christians and gave theological support to the Nazi programme in some of his works (cf. below:4.21).

Chamberlain, _The Foundations of the Nineteenth Century_(1899):chs 3,5,7;
Hitler, _Mein Kampf_(1925-6):60,138,278;
Rosenberg, _Der Mythus des 20. Jahrhunderts_(1930): e.g.73-6,127-134,218; _Protestantische Rompilger_(1935); cf. Künneth 1935:esp.63-74; Chandler 1945:31-5,42-4,58-9; Nicholaisen 1966:21-4;
Schairer, _Volk-Blut-Gott_(1933):113-116;
Wieneke, _Deutsche Theologie im Umriss_(1933):44-53;
Bergmann, _The 25 Theses of the German Religion_(1934);
Leffler, _Christus im Dritten Reich_(1935):esp.119-120;
Kuptsch, _Nationalsozialismus und positives Christentum_ (1937):esp.89-93;
E.and M.Ludendorff, _Die Judenmacht_(1939):esp.254-70; cf. Aland 1936; Pieper n.d.

Cf. Althaus, Die deutsche Stunde der Kirche(1933);
Schlatter, Die neue deutsche Art in der Kirche(1933): esp.23-9;
Lother, Neugermanische Religion und Christentum (1934):125-7;
MacFarland, The New Church and the New Germany(1934);
Douglass, God Among the Germans(1935):121-5;
Means, Things That are Caesar's(1935);
Shuster, Like a Mighty Army(1935):22-3,88-92;
Abramowski, 'Vom Streit um das AT',ThRu(1937): esp.68-71;
Hauer, Keim and Adam, Germany's New Religion(1937);
Tanner, The Nazi Christ(1942);
Wiener, Martin Luther: Hitler's Spiritual Ancestor (1945) and reply by Rupp 1945;
Diehn, Bibliographie zur Geschichte des Kirchenkampfes(1958):esp.197-8;
Hutten, 'Deutsch-christliche Bewegungen',RGG[3](1958);
Wolf, 'Kirchenkampf',RGG[3](1959);
Nicholaisen, Die Auseinandersetzung um das AT im Kirchenkampf(1966):esp.ch.3; 'Die Stellung der "Deutschen Christen" zum AT' in AGK(1971);
Bright, The Authority of the OT(1967):67-9;
Kuske, Das AT als Buch von Christus(1967):13-14.

0.623 Defence of the Old Testament

Naturally such attacks on the Old Testament provoked a reaction among biblical scholars, many of whom sided with the Confessing Church (Bekennende Kirche) in the German Church Struggle(Kirchenkampf). Some openly condemned the anti-Semitism of National Socialism and its adherents, but most simply reaffirmed in different ways the value of the Old Testament for the Christian faith. Wilhelm Vischer, Karl Barth, Hans Hellbardt, Helmuth Schreiner and Otto Procksch claimed the Old Testament for the Church by interpreting it as a witness to Christ, thus diverting attention from its relevance to the Jews. Emil Brunner(1930), another Dialectic theologian, argued that 'the understanding of the Old Testament is the criterion and the basis for understanding the New' (p.264). This is because of certain characteristic Old Testament ideas which are presupposed but not explicitly defined in the New: the idea of God (Creator,Lord, the one who chooses and reveals himself personally); the eschatological realism (which is necessary to appreciate properly the spirituality of the New Testament); and the importance of the community, the people of God. Volkmar Herntrich (1934) took German national thought seriously, suggesting that it should not lead to rejection of the Old Testament but give a new impetus to the search for a genuine theological understanding of it. Otto Eissfeldt, Johannes Hempel and many other Old Testament scholars continued with their work and thus implicitly defended the importance of the Old Testament.

See below on Vischer (ch.5); Barth(5.31); Hellbardt, Schreiner and Procksch (5.35).

Eissfeldt, Einleitung in das AT[1](1934):see esp.720-23; also 1919,1921,1926,1947; cf. Porteous 1951: 317-22; Hasel 1972a:15-18;
Brunner, 'The Significance of the OT for Our Faith' (1930),repr. in OTCF; Die Unentbehrlichkeit des ATes(1934);
Horst, 'Das AT als Heilige Schrift und als Kanon', ThBl(1932);
Baumgärtel, 'Das AT' in Künneth and Schreiner(1933);
Gogarten, Einheit von Evangelium und Volkstum?(1933); Ist Volksgesetz Gottesgesetz?(1934);
Herntrich, Völkische Religiosität und AT(1934);
M.Niemöller, Das Bekenntnis der Väter(1934):9-12;
Press, 'Das AT als Wort Gottes',ThBl(1934);
Schmitz, 'Das AT im NT' in Heim Festschrift(1934);
de Quervain, Das Gesetz Gottes(1935-6);
Schniewind, 'Die Eine Botschaft des Alten und des NTs' (1936), first published in Julius Schniewind(1952);
Hempel et al.(eds), Werden und Wesen des ATs(1936); cf. van der Ploeg 1962:417;
Noth, 'Zur Auslegung des ATes'(1937),repr. in Gesammelte Studien II;
Volz, 'Das AT und unsere Verkündingung',Luthertum(1937);
Hempel, Politische Absicht(1938).

Cf. Traub, 'Die Kirche und das AT',ZTK(1935);
Köhler, 'Atl.Theologie',ThRu(1935-6);
Abramowski, 'Vom Streit um das AT',ThRu(1937):71-93;
Barth, Eine Schweizer Stimme(1945);
Filson, 'The Unity of the Old and the NTs', Interpn (1951):140-141;
Kraeling, The OT Since the Reformation(1955):ch.12;
W.Niemöller, Die Evangelische Kirche im Dritten Reich (1956);

Wolf, 'Bekennende Kirche', RGG[3](1957);
Nicholaisen, Die Auseinandersetzung um das AT(1966): ch.4.

Bonhoeffer wrote and spoke much about this question (see Grunow 1955; Schulte 1962; Kuske 1967). In spite of the Third Reich, many Old Testament studies were published in Germany during the 1930s. Gerhard von Rad, for instance, published 28 books and articles on the Old Testament during the years 1933-9, and another 10 during the War, not to mention numerous reviews (see bibliography in von Rad Festschrift 1971). Eichrodt's famous Theology of the OT(1933-9) was also published in this critical period.

0.624 Implicit Marcionism

The Third Reich fell, and with it the most extreme forms of Neo-Marcionism disappeared. Open attack on the Old Testament lost its political motivation and very likely would have only brought its proponent into disrepute. A more subtle way to dispose of the Old Testament, however, is to be 'generous' and give it to the Jews. This was done in effect by Isaac G. Matthews (1947) in his presentation of Israel's religious history. Though he traces the history up to A.D.135, he virtually never refers to Christ or Christianity, assuming that Judaism is the natural continuation of Old Testament religion. He concludes:

'Judaism, the religion of the book, and of a people scattered to the four corners of the earth but united in allegiance to the one God, was well equipped to succeed in the struggle of existence. By losing its life as a nation, it saved itself as a religion. Happy was the man whose delight was in the law of the Lord, in whose law he meditated day and night.'(p.268)

A similar approach is that of the missionary who substitutes other national religions and literatures for the Old Testament as the basis for preaching Christianity (cf. Filson 1951:136). Moreover the same thing is happening in the West: often modern thought and culture are used as a 'lead-in' to presentation of the Christian message and 'modern' studies such as the social sciences are introduced to theological curricula at the expense of biblical, and especially Old Testament studies. On an even more basic level, there is in the Church a habit - not entirely new, admittedly - of simply ignoring the Old Testament. It is thought to be difficult and/or unimportant and therefore it is rarely read and expounded (or it is read in terms of the New Testament, cf. Michalson 1964:62). Evangelical Christians, who claim the Bible as their rule of faith, plead for a return to New Testament Christianity. Christians who emphasise the social element of their faith, in spite of the obvious relevance of many parts of the Old Testament to their message, are among the first to minimise the importance of Old Testament study for ordinands. Almost all the dozens of new English translations of the Bible undertaken in recent years have begun with the New Testament, and few have yet reached the Old Testament. It is clear therefore that the modern Church, in spite of its official rejection of Marcionism and Nazism, has often allowed implicit Marcionism in practice.

Phillips, The OT in the World Church(1942);
Matthews, The Religious Pilgrimage of Israel(1947);
Filson, 'The Unity of the Old and the NTs',Interpn (1951):135-7,140-141;
Wright, God Who Acts(1952):15-19;
Smart, The Interpretation of Scripture(1961):67-9;
Bright, The Authority of the OT(1967):73-6;

0.63 THE WAY AHEAD

a. The implication of neo-Marcionism is separation of the two Testaments. In other words, the Old and New Testaments are considered to belong to two different religions, so that there is no theological relationship between them. If Marcion had been right the present study would be a fruitless exercise; but among serious biblical theologians, in spite of the implicit Marcionism which often affects the Church in practice, there is virtually unanimous agreement that Marcion was not right. There are today many different evaluations of the Old Testament and interpretations of its relationship to the New, but it can at least be said that an assured result of modern scholarship is the recognition of the existence of a theological relationship between the two Testaments of the Christian Bible.

b. The task which remains to be undertaken is the definition of this relationship. While the Church was debating and digesting the results of nineteenth century scholarship - following in general its 'progressive revelation' approach to the relationship between the Testaments - and defending itself and its Bible from the anti-Semitic and anti-Christian attacks of the 1930s, twentieth-century scholars were reconsidering the results of their nineteenth century predecessors and developing a deep dissatisfaction with them. Persecution in the Church and dissatisfaction in scholarship gave a new impetus to definition of the relationship between the Testaments, and thus provided a matrix for modern study of biblical theology, which has been one of the most fruitful aspects of biblical studies in the post-War years.

c. Two of the most significant modern solutions to the problem of the relationship between the Testaments stem from the traumatic years of the 1930s; and those years were also formative for the thought of several other theologians considered here whose major works were published after the War. The name of Wilhelm Vischer has already been mentioned in connection with the defence of the Old Testament: his major work, The Witness of the Old Testament to Christ (1934), will be considered in chapter five. Rudolf Bultmann has not yet been referred to because of his ambiguous position in the German Church Struggle. In 1933, the year of the rise of National Socialism, he published an important essay on 'The Significance of the Old Testament for the Christian Faith' in which he emphasised the radical difference between the Old Testament and the New Testament; on the other hand, in the same year he warned his students about the dangers of the new movement in a lecture on 'The Task of Theology in the Present Situation'. Though scarcely an active opponent of the Nazi régime, Bultmann recognised a limited amount of value in the Old Testament for the Christian faith and his sympathies were with the Confessing Church. His view of the relationship between the Testaments will be considered in some detail in chapter three. Both Baumgärtel and von Rad, although their major works were published two decades later, were concerned in the early part of their careers with the issues raised by the Church Struggle; and probably every modern study which takes serious account of German theology has been influenced in some way by the debates of the 1930s.

0.7 METHOD

0.71 THE PROBLEM TODAY

a. Recent Old Testament research has demonstrated the importance of the concept of 'covenant' in Old Testament theology (see McCarthy 1972a; Eichrodt 1974), though Payne (1970) prefers 'testament' and some recent German scholarship (e.g. Perlitt 1969 cf. McCarthy 1972b; Kutsch 1971, 1972) advocates 'obligation' (Verpflichtung) to translate the Hebrew ברית. The concept may easily be extended to cover both Testaments: Shih (1971) presents 'covenant' as one of four major historical models for the unity of the Testaments, and Fensham (1967, 1971) considers that the covenant-idea is the most satisfactory expression of the relationship between the two (cf. Gehman 1950; Brown 1955; Kline 1972:ch.4). It would be a mistake however to think that 'covenant' offers the solution to the problem of the relationship between the Testaments. Since, as is well-known, the word 'testament' in 'Old Testament' and 'New Testament' means 'covenant', to introduce the concept of covenant to the discussion of the relationship between the Testaments does nothing more than restate the problem. The basic datum is that there are two Testaments (covenants, obligations...); the problem is to determine the theological relationship between them.

b. There is a sense in which almost any study of the Bible contributes to solving the problem of the relationship between the Testaments, but certain kinds of study are particularly important:

(1) exegetical studies of passages or themes in their whole biblical context; (2) programmatic works which set out to develop an original (or reassert a traditional) solution to the problem; (3) general works of biblical or systematic theology which present, or at least imply, a specific solution to the problem; (4) analytical studies which attempt to trace the way in which the problem has been solved in the past and present; (5) critical studies which are concerned to assess and synthesise the information and ideas accumulated by the other approaches.

c. The present study combines the fourth and fifth approaches, offering a biblical and historical survey of the problem, and analyses and criticisms of some of the major modern solutions. The results of all five kinds of research are used throughout, although the exegetical and analytic results are particularly relevant to the biblical and historical introduction, and the programmatic works are the chief concern in the major part of the study.

There are several short articles which attempt to do in brief compass what is done in detail in this study:
Filson, 'The Unity of the Old and the NTs', Interpn(1951);
Smart, The Interpretation of Scripture(1961):ch.3;
Murphy, 'The Relationship between the Testaments', CBQ(1964);
Schwarzwäller, 'Das Verhältnis AT-NT', EvTh(1969);
Verhoef, 'The Relationship between the Old and the NTs' in Payne(1970);
Hasel, OT Theology(1972):ch.4.

Relevant analytical works include:
Diestel, Geschichte des ATes in der christlichen Kirche(1869);
Kraeling, The OT Since the Reformation(1955);
The Cambridge History of the Bible(CHB,1963-70);
Kraus, Die Biblische Theologie(1970);
Laurin(ed.), Contemporary OT Theologians(1970);
Harrington, The Path of Biblical Theology(1973).

Full-length critical studies:
Amsler, L'AT dans l'Église(1960);
Barr, Old and New in Interpretation(1966);
Bright, The Authority of the OT(1967);
Shih, 'The Unity of the Testaments as a Hermeneutical Problem',Dissn(1971).

Two important symposia:
Westermann(ed.), Essays on OT Interpretation(EOTI, 1949-6
Anderson(ed.), The OT and Christian Faith(OTCF, 1964).

0.72 METHOD OF THE PRESENT STUDY

a. The aim of this study is to take account of as much and as wide a variety of the relevant material as practicable in order to reach some general but broad-based conclusions about the nature of the theological relationship between the Testaments. The author has no particular theological or denominational axe to grind but is concerned to interpret the evidence on its merits and to find a solution to the theological problem of the relationship between the Testaments which does full justice to this evidence. In particular, it is his conviction that in order to reach a satisfactory solution it is necessary to consider not only the relationship of the Old Testament to the New Testament, or that of the New Testament to the Old Testament, but the mutual relationship between the two Testaments of the one Christian Bible. This is not to presuppose any particular understanding of the nature of the Bible, but to recognise the indisputable fact that for all the nearly two thousand years of its existence the Christian Bible has contained two Testaments, and to refuse to presuppose either to be more important than the other.

b. The basic structure of the study has already been made clear: the problem is stated by means of a biblical, historical and methodological introduction; eight modern solutions are presented and discussed at length; and some conclusions are drawn. In the body of the work those modern solutions which are based more heavily on one Testament and do not take adequate account of the nature of the other Testament are considered first; and those which attempt and succeed to develop a more fully biblical understanding of the relationship between the Testaments are discussed afterwards.

c. The method employed in the study of each solution varies a certain amount to suit the subject-matter, but the basic pattern has three stages: analysis, criticism and comparison. The analysis may be a précis of one programmatic work, a study of several works of one author, or a summary of works on one theme by more than one author. The criticism may deal with specific points raised by a programmatic work, or more general issues involved in a view of the relationship between the Testaments, or may be an attempt to define more closely some ideas from the analysis. The comparison discusses solutions to the problem which are related or similar to the main solution studied in the chapter.

0.73 LIMITATIONS

a. It has been stated that this work is concerned with the theological level of the problem of the relationship between the Testaments, which explains why certain approaches to the question are not discussed. Little is said, for instance, about the linguistic relationship (on which see TDNT 1933-73 and Hill 1967; cf. von Rad 1960:352-6; Verhoef 1970a:286-7) or the conceptual relationship (cf. below: 3.213) or the historical relationship (see Noth 1950; Bruce 1969; cf. van Ruler 1955:10-11/12) between the Testaments. Although many such approaches are not without theological relevance, it has been necessary to restrict the scope of this work to specifically theological approaches to the problem.

b. It might be pointed out that some important solutions (e.g. Cullmann, Wright and Eichrodt in ch.7 below) are treated very briefly while others which are no more important (e.g. Amsler and Pannenberg in the same chapter) are given much more space. The reason for this is simply that in a study of such a vast subject a good deal of selectivity is inevitable. Several criteria of selection have been employed, so that sometimes well-known and much-discussed solutions (e.g. Bultmann,von Rad) are dealt with, sometimes those which are important though less well-known (e.g. van Ruler, Miskotte), and sometimes those which are commonly misunderstood (e.g. Vischer, typology).

c. It might also be noted that relatively more German and Dutch solutions are studied than those of any other language or country, and more Protestant than Catholic solutions. This is because, for better or worse, the Germanic spirit and the Protestant tradition of individual interpretation have led to a much greater number of original contributions to theological scholarship than have more conservative cultures and traditions.

d. It is obvious that this study cannot claim to open up virgin territory but, although it treads an area which has frequently been trod, it does so more thoroughly than any other study of its kind. There are some aspects of the subject dealt with only scantily, to be sure, but there are others discussed in greater detail than in any previous study. Another original feature of the study is the distinction between 'Old Testament', 'New Testament' and 'biblical' solutions to the problem, which reveals the strength and weakness of the various solutions: it is the very one-sidedness of the solutions of van Ruler and Bultmann, for instance, which accounts for both their brilliance and their inadequacy. Moreover, while the positive evaluation of the salvation history/'promise and fulfilment' and continuity/discontinuity solutions to the problem will occasion little surprise, the positive reinterpretation of the Christological and typical solutions points to important areas for future study of the problem.

PART TWO: 'OLD TESTAMENT' SOLUTIONS

1. The Old Testament is the essential Bible, the New Testament its interpretative glossary

1.1 ARNOLD A. VAN RULER: THE CHRISTIAN CHURCH AND THE OLD TESTAMENT

1.2 CRITICISM: THEOCRACY AND PRIORITY

1.1 ARNOLD A. VAN RULER: THE CHRISTIAN CHURCH AND THE OLD TESTAMENT

1.11 INTRODUCTION

a. In this first chapter the possibility of seeing the relationship between the Old Testament and the New Testament as a relationship of 'priority' will be investigated. It is of course obvious that the Old Testament was formed before the New Testament and no one will dispute that the Old Testament was prior to the New Testament historically. To claim that in the Christian era the Old Testament has priority over the New Testament not only historically but theologically is however a different matter. A notable Dutch Reformed scholar, the late Arnold A. van Ruler of Utrecht, has claimed this and in the following pages his claim will be examined. The second chapter will be devoted to the work of another Dutch Reformed scholar, Kornelis H. Miskotte, whose solution to the problem of the relationship between the Testaments is somewhat similar, and a number of other views and claims which imply the theological priority of the Old Testament over the New Testament will also be discussed there.

b. Van Ruler has written a great deal, but the most important elaboration of his view of the relationship between the Testaments is his book <u>The Christian Church and the Old Testament</u>, published originally in German (1955) and since translated into English (1966). He sets out to make a contribution on the part of dogmatic theology to the discussion about the interpretation of the Old Testament which arose with the preparation of the Biblischer Kommentar in the 1950s (see the preface, unfortunately omitted in the English translation; cf. below:7.31). He refers to many other writers, mostly Dutch and German, but the significance of his work lies less in the assessment or development of their ideas than in the provocative thesis which emerges from the book. Except where stated otherwise, references to van Ruler in the present chapter are to this work.

c. It is interesting to note that van Ruler, who advocates the value of the Old Testament more strongly than almost any other modern Christian scholar, is not himself an Old Testament scholar but a systematic theologian. His approach is therefore theological rather than exegetical: he does not discuss individual passages and almost never quotes the Old Testament (I counted only 22 references, mostly in the footnotes), and all but ignores historical-critical scholarship (cf. Vriezen 1956:213). Bright (1967:186-7) draws attention to van Ruler's failure to provide an adequate hermeneutic for the Old Testament since he only speaks of the Old Testament as a whole and does not deal with the problem of its 'difficult' parts. It is therefore necessary to be aware of his theological assumptions to evaluate his thesis. As van Ruler says, 'our basic theological position will decide our attitude towards the Old Testament'(p.7/9), and this is proved beyond doubt in his work. Van Ruler stands within the Reformed - especially Calvinist - tradition and so presupposes the inspiration of the Bible and reality of revelation. The historical context of his work included many negative evaluations of the Old Testament and it may be that he over-reacted to these at times (cf.Stamm 1956:204).

aa. Van Ruler's Dutch manuscript was translated into German by Herman Keller and published as Die christliche Kirche und das AT (1955). The English translation (made from the German, not the Dutch) was by Geoffrey W. Bromiley and published as The Christian Church and the OT (1966, and again 1971, an identical edition which does not mention the former). Both versions are referred to in the present work and the German and English page numbers given in that order, thus: 1955:11/13, or simply p.11/13.

The German and English versions have not been systematically compared but a number of significant translation errors have been footnoted at the relevant points in the analysis. The translation has caused some confusion by dividing the admittedly lengthy footnotes into three parts and incorporating into the text, interspersing between sections of the text or leaving as footnotes (with different numbers from the original). The result is no easier to read and is difficult to compare with the original. It is a pity that van Ruler's preface has been omitted, though a bibliography compiled from the footnotes is a useful addition. Remarkably both the notes and bibliography fail to note the translations of the important essays by Noth, von Rad and Zimmerli(1952) in Interpn(1961) and EOTI, and Vriezen's An outline of OT theology (1954/66), ET:1958[1], 1970[2].

bb. Other works by van Ruler concerned with the relationship between the Testaments include:

'De waarde van het Oude Testament', Vox Th 13(1942),113-117;

Religie en Politiek, Nijkerk 1945, 123-149 (including a reprint of the preceding article);

De vervulling van de wet, Nijkerk 1947; cf.Rottenberg 1964:162-175;

also, Reformatorische opmerkingen in de ontmoeting met Rome, Antwerp 1965.

Examples of his interpretation of the Old Testament may be found in:

God's Son and God's World, ET:Grand Rapids,Michigan 1960 (on Ps.104);

Zechariah Speaks Today,ET:London 1972 (on Zech. 1-8).

A useful survey of van Ruler's writings is given by Hesselink, 'Recent Developments in Dutch Protestant Theology', RefTR(1969),46-50.

cc. Although it is an important work and is frequently mentioned in works concerned with the relationship between the Testaments, The Christian Church and the OT has received few reviews in journals and little detailed criticism in books and articles. The following may be noted, however:

Stamm, 'Jesus Christ and the OT'(1956),ET in EOTI;
Vriezen, 'Theocracy and Soteriology'(1956),ET in EOTI;
An outline of OT theology(1954/66):-/97-8;
Velema, Confrotatie met Van Ruler(1962);
reviews by Jacob, RHPR(1963) and Fretheim, Interpn(1972);

Also, not available to me:
Hommes, 'Sovereignty and Saeculum: Arnold A.van Ruler's Theocratic Theology',Dissn(1967; abstract in HTR 1967);
Engelbrecht, 'A.A. van Ruler: moderne teokraat', NGTT(1971);
Fries, 'Van Ruler on the Holy Spirit and the salvation of the earth', RefR(1973).

1.12 THE QUESTION OF THE OLD TESTAMENT

The vital question about the Old Testament for van Ruler is how it may be recognised as the Word of God.[1] He presupposes without discussion that it *is* the Word of God since he reckons it a matter of faith to decide whether or not to submit to its authority. This presupposition is the basis for the whole book, and it is at the root of the questions as well as the answers which he discusses.

---

1. Translation (p.8/10): the first two sentences in the main text should read 'No matter how great the difficulties may be, the question of the Old Testament is, at a central point, decisive. It decides how we understand Jesus Christ...' Bromiley's paraphrase is a possible interpretation of the phrase 'the question (*Sache*) of the Old Testament', although 'the question of how the Old Testament may be recognised as the Word of God' is more likely. But better sense in the context and a more natural use of the phrase 'the question of the Old Testament' results if it simply refers to the Old Testament (as a problem).

Van Ruler points out that the Old Testament is decisively important since it determines one's understanding of Christianity, yet from the earliest times the Church has found difficulty in using it and today the question needs to be thought through once more. Before presenting his own view, van Ruler analyses into ten categories the main ways of viewing the Old Testament current when he wrote in 1955:

1. Complete devaluation	(Schleiermacher, Hirsch)
2. History of failure	(Bultmann)
3. Parallelism with paganism: both are preparation for the perfect revelation in Christ	(Heiler)
4. Historical background to New Testament	(Sellin)
5. Independent theological value	(H.W.Robinson, H.H.Rowley)[2]
6. Providential earthly preparation for heavenly salvation	(Roman Catholicism)
7. Typology	(contributors to <u>Biblischer Kommentar</u>)
8. Allegory	(-)
9. Direct and complete validity	(-)
10. Salvation History	(Reformed scholarship).

(pp.7-12/9-14)

1.13 THE OLD TESTAMENT ITSELF

In the first chapter van Ruler proposes to deal with four preliminary questions about the Old Testament. As will be seen, he does not generally give direct answers to his questions, either by logical argument or <u>a priori</u> assertion, but discusses related issues in such a way as to make his viewpoint clear without actually stating it. Although these are described

---

2. Translation (p.11/12): insert 'not' before 'controlled by the Lutheran dialectic of law and gospel'.

as 'preliminary questions' the chapter is really the most important in the book because it lays the foundation on which van Ruler's thesis is based. The form of the questions reveals immediately a number of van Ruler's presuppositions: the Old Testament is about God, it is revelation and it is a source for preaching.

1.131 Are both Testaments about the same God?
A more precise way of putting this question would be to ask whether it is Yahweh, the God of Israel, who is also the Father of the Lord Jesus Christ. It is a question which van Ruler claims is very important in determining the Church's attitude to the Old Testament: a positive attitude to the Old Testament is dependent on a positive answer to this question. Both faith and scholarship are involved here and although faith will reply first it is also the responsibility of scholarship to search for an answer. Van Ruler's answer is of course to presuppose both here and throughout the book that both Old and New Testaments are about the same God. (pp.13-16/15-18)

1.132 Revelation and scholarship.
a. The question of the identity of the God of the Old Testament leads on to the question of revelation and van Ruler asks how revelation may be perceived in the Old Testament literature. To him it is self-evident that revelation is to be found somewhere in or behind the Old Testament and the particular problem which concerns him is the extent to which scholarship is able to recognise it. He believes that the primary prerequisite for recognising revelation is faith and that the decision of faith to find revelation

in the Old Testament is not an arbitary one since Jesus Christ establishes its authority. Scholarship supports the decision of faith by demonstrating the uniqueness of the Old Testament's understanding of life. In other words, the function of scholarship is to determine what the Old Testament says and the function of faith is to decide whether or not what it says is revelation.

b. This simple distinction between the roles of faith and scholarship is nevertheless inadequate because it leaves unsolved the problem of whether the recognition of the Old Testament as revelation affects scholarly exegesis. Does scholarship study only the human aspect of revelation or can it study the revelation itself? The fundamental problem is that of the relation between revelation and the Bible: van Ruler's view is that the Bible is not only a record of revelation, nor even a witness to revelation, but is itself a means of revelation. The hermeneutical problem of relating the exegete and his scholarly method with the author and his subject is not confined to Biblical interpretation, and the tension between establishing the meaning of the text and recognising it as revelation is an aspect of that same problem. If with van Ruler it takes the step of faith and accepts that there is revelation in the Old Testament, theological scholarship will extend its investigation of the meaning of the text by attempting to penetrate to that revelation (pp.16-21/18-24).

1.133 <u>Revelation in the Old Testament</u>

a. Van Ruler considers next what the Old Testament means by 'revelation'[1]. It would be a mistake, he argues,

1. An alternative, but less likely, interpretation of van Ruler's question 'What is to be understood by revelation in the sense of the Old Testament itself?' would be 'What does it mean to say that the Old Testament

to assume some definition of revelation, such as 'communication of life'[2], and apply that definition to the Old Testament. Revelation in the Old Testament refers to the self-communication or presence of God among his people in concrete historical events. 'The dimension of history is of predominant significance for what the Old Testament understands by revelation' (p.23/25) and for van Ruler history is a vital part of the revelation itself, not just the sphere in which it takes place (p.25n./28). This understanding of revelation as God's active presence in Israel's history has at least two implications. First, although it contains religious and theological ideas, the quintessence of the Old Testament is not to be found in these but in God himself who is present in the history of Israel. Secondly, the concept of progressive revelation, which implies that man gradually

---

is revelation?' This would not greatly affect the argument of the section that revelation consists in the historical presence of God in Israel.

2. Translation (p.22/24): 8 lines from bottom, for 'This concept' substitute 'Likewise it is surely clear that also the concept of impartation of life'.

'Communication of doctrine'(ET:'impartation of teaching'): Lehrmitteilung; cf. Frör 1961:25-6.

'Communication of life' or perhaps 'living communication': Lebensmitteilung; the meaning is not entirely clear but perhaps van Ruler is referring to the collaborators of the Biblischer Kommentar who, among others, advocate the idea of revelation through God's activity in history. Or is there any connection with Bultmann's use (following Dilthey) of categories such as 'expression of life'(Lebensäusserung) for a text and 'living relationship' (Lebensverhältnis) for the relationship between the subject of the text and the interpreter (1950a:234, 240-41)? In any case, van Ruler rejects the concept as a definition of revelation in the Old Testament. Cf. Wright 1952: 'Life, reason, faith are a part of one whole and theology must deal with and attempt to communicate that whole' (p.116).

comes to know more of God, is inappropriate since revelation is not concerned with what man knows[3] but with what God does among men. Man's knowledge naturally becomes fuller with the progress of time but God's presence, and therefore revelation, cannot be said to be more or less real in different instances. It follows that the Old Testament and New Testament are equally revelation: there is no progress in revelation from the Old Testament to the New Testament[4] but God is actively present in Jesus Christ, as in Israel, and in both cases his presence needs to be authenticated and clarified by signs and witnesses.[5]

b. Van Ruler concludes his treatment of revelation in the Old Testament by asking for what purpose and in what way God is present in Israel. He answers briefly that God's purpose is not simply redemption but the establishment of his kingdom, the theocracy, and that the manner in which he is present in Israel is forceful, in contrast to his treatment of other nations to whom he gives comparative freedom.[6] This forceful aspect of God's presence among his people comes to a climax when he becomes man for them in the incarnation.(pp.22-7/24-30)

---

3. Translation (p.25/27): line 2 of main text, omit 'just'.

4. Van Ruler admits a progress in salvation history, but this is an historical, temporal progress rather than a spiritual, intellectual progress as is implied by the term 'progressive revelation'.

5. He refers to the resurrection, Spirit and apostles in the New Testament which are perhaps intended to correspond to the Exodus, the prophetic word and the historical confessions (the <u>credos</u> and the histories of which they are the core) in the Old Testament.

6. Translation (<u>CCOT</u>, 27/29): line 6 from bottom should read 'But in any case even Abraham and Israel were called and...'

1.134 Christian preaching of the Old Testament

a. So far the argument of the chapter has been that revelation in the Old Testament consists in the active presence of God in the history of Israel. But this creates a problem for the Christian who preaches from the Old Testament: how can revelation which is so inextricably tied to the history of Israel be revelation for the Christian Church? Or, in the words of Wolff (1952:97), 'What is the message that the text has for us in the name of God today if it is still to be the message of the Old Testament text, even though God has now uttered his definitive word in Jesus Christ?' If the Old Testament is to be revelation for Christians, and van Ruler assumes that it will be, they must either be Israel or be related to Israel in such a way that what happened to Israel applies to them also (e.g. typologically, by seeing Israel concentrated in Jesus Christ, so von Rad 1952). It might be suggested that 'tradition' is the key: that is, Christians stand in the same tradition as Israel. This is a view readily accepted by Jews and Roman Catholics (who more easily understand revelation in terms of tradition), and even Reformed Christians recognise that the Word of God is rooted in the history of Israel as well as in the saving event at Golgotha and may admit a place for 'tradition' in that salvation is 'passed on' from the Jews to the Gentiles. However, since the Old Testament revelation is thus rooted in the history of Israel, it can only be passed on fully if there is a 'repetition' of Israel. This takes place as 'around Christ and by the Spirit we are appointed and made Israel'.[1] It means that Christians are involved

1. pp.31-2/34. Note the translation correction: after 'Around Christ and by the Spirit we are appointed and made' insert 'Israel'.

in the sanctification of life and the world as well as in the sanctification of the Church and that the final prospect for the world is the presupposition of Israel: theocracy. It follows that a Christian nation[2] does not simply receive tradition from Israel but is its antitype.

b. Christian preaching of the Old Testament is thus not simply preaching of Christ as he may be found in the Old Testament but also preaching of the kingdom.[3] The concrete earthly things which this involves are in fact the most important since God's ultimate purpose is the sanctification of the earth. At first sight the New Testament appears more spiritual than the Old Testament but this is

---

2. Christenvolk: distinct from the Church, although the latter would naturally be the core of a Christian nation.

3. The translation is ambiguous and may imply either that Christian preaching of the Old Testament includes preaching of Christ and of the kingdom, or that Christian preaching includes preaching of Christ and of the kingdom (the former from the New Testament and the latter from the Old Testament, thus rejecting any Christological interpretation of the Old Testament).

A more precise translation of the last paragraph (p.32/34) would be: 'As I see it, one can preach from the Old Testament in the Christian Church only if one pays attention to this eschatological theocratic perspective, if the Christian preaching is not merely a preaching of Christ, but also a preaching of the kingdom. The preaching will then be dealing with the same concrete things that are also at issue in the Old Testament. The ordinary things...' This shows that the former interpretation is correct, and it is confirmed by the following chapter which demotes but does not exclude Christological interpretation of the Old Testament.

a negative rather than a positive attribute.[4] 'If the church's preaching is to be full preaching of the kingdom, in which all reality is set in the light of the Word and counsel of God, the Old Testament is quite indispensable. The New Testament is not enough.' (pp.32n./34-5). Thus the Old Testament stands as an independent source for Christian preaching, which includes preaching not only of the gospel but also of the kingdom. Van Ruler suggests that recognition of this independence of the Old Testament and the typological relationship between Israel and a Christian nation[5] will indicate the place of present-day Israel in God's plan alongside the Church (since in both he is concerned ultimately for the whole world) as well as allowing for the possibility that God may restore his people Israel. (pp.28-33/30-36)

1.14 THE OLD TESTAMENT AND CHRIST

It may seem that the problem of the interpretation of the Old Testament focuses on the idea of 'Christ in the Old Testament' (p.13/15). However, van Ruler has deliberately postponed discussing this and first established his view of the validity of the Old Testament as the Word of God quite independently of any Christological interpretation of the Old

---

4. Translation (p.32/34): penultimate line, after '...somewhat more spiritual.' insert 'However that is to be rated not as a "plus" but as a (perhaps necessary) "minus".'

5. Translation (p.33/35): penultimate paragraph, (the <u>corpus christianum</u>' should read 'a <u>corpus christianum</u>'.

Testament. Revelation in the Old Testament, he has claimed, is the active presence of the one God - who is Father of our Lord Jesus Christ - in the history of Israel, and it becomes revelation for Christians as they become Israel. Therefore preaching of this revelation will be preaching of the presence of God, and this is manifested above all in his kingdom (which is his purpose for man). Now van Ruler turns to ask whether it is also valid to use the Old Testament to preach Christ; in other words, is it possible to preach a Christian message from an Old Testament perspective? This can only be so if the Old Testament itself "sees" Christ. His method of handling this question is to consider the way Christ and the New Testament are related to the history of Israel and the Old Testament, and he concludes the chapter with criticisms of the allegorical and typological methods of Old Testament interpretation.

1.141 Jesus Christ is an act of God in his history with Israel

Van Ruler's first remark is that the Old Testament in its entirety is not a single promise of Christ but contains a history which is continually moving from promise to fulfilment, within the Old Testament itself. This is a real history, with concrete promises fulfilled in visible ways, each fulfilment pointing further into the future so that the history is never finished.[1] It is here in the history of

1. Translation (p.36/39): end of first paragraph should read 'Past and present are also described in the light of the promise, the will of God and expectation of the people, and that which is promised, and are thus described hyperbolically.'

Israel itself that the basis of typology is to be found, not only in its relationship to Christ but in the pattern of promise and fulfilment which links later events to earlier ones. Jesus Christ is one act in this history of God with his people and thus fulfils promises of the Old Testament in a similar way to the fulfilments within the Old Testament itself. In this way, and only in this way, Jesus Christ becomes theologically significant for the history of Israel, and thus for the Old Testament. (pp.34-7/37-40)

1.142 <u>This act inaugurates a new but not yet final phase of that history</u>

So far van Ruler has asserted that Jesus Christ is one act in God's history with his people. The question follows whether this is only one act among others or whether it has a special character: does it bring about a <u>new</u> phase in God's dealing with Israel or the <u>final</u> phase of ultimate fulfilment? On the one hand, the New Testament does not devalue the Old Testament, and promise and expectation are still important as Christians look into the future to the consummation of history. On the other hand, it is certain that the New Testament is more than an extension of the Old Testament since it speaks of a completely new act of God in Christ which brings the end of the law and the old covenant and inaugurates the last time in a revolutionary way by introducing Jesus Christ as the centre of history. It can only be concluded therefore that the New Testament is more than a new phase but not yet the final phase in the history of God with his people. (pp.38-40/41-3)

1.143 <u>Attempts to harmonise the Testaments</u>

a. Christian theologians, in particular those involved in the <u>Biblischer Kommentar</u>, often try to understand this integration of the New Testament events into God's history with Israel by means of the concepts of promise and expectation. They say, for instance, that since God is free to interpret and fulfil his promises, Jesus Christ may be seen as God's fulfilment of his promises to Israel in the Old Testament. There are many of these promises, some of them contradictory to others and some nebulous, but all of them are fulfilled in Christ. The expectation in the Old Testament is concerned with the coming Lord himself rather than with those to whom he will come, and he is expected as the one who comes to kill and make alive. This very pattern is fulfilled in the New Testament when God himself comes to man in Jesus Christ, whose life centres on his death and resurrection.

b. Van Ruler cannot and does not deny that there is some truth in these observations[1] but he thinks that they oversimplify the issues. The people Israel has an essential place in the Old Testament expectation, and the fulfilment of Old Testament promises is not in every case to be found in Christ by the spiritualisation of promises belonging to Israel. There is a 'plus' in the Old Testament compared with the New Testament, a remainder which is not a factor in the New Testament fulfilment. Moreover,

---

1. Translation (p.44/47): centre, before 'But it seems to me...' insert 'There is certainly some truth in this position.'

although death and resurrection are the focal point in the New Testament they are not the fundamental purpose of the revelation, which is the same as in the Old Testament: that men may live rightly to God's glory. (pp.40-46/43-9)

1.144 <u>Incongruity between the Testaments</u>
Van Ruler rejects this harmonising attempt to integrate the New Testament into God's dealing with his people Israel and argues that incongruities occur at some vital points.[1] In the first place, God himself comes as the Messiah in the New Testament, whereas in the Old Testament the Messiah is only a man. Further, the emphases of the Testaments are different since the New Testament is concerned above all with forgiveness but the Old Testament with kingship, the dominant event of the New Testament - the rejection of the Messiah by the chosen people - is not even forseen by the Old Testament, and suffering and the love of God are the keynotes of the New Testament in contrast to the wrath and glory of God in the Old Testament. Finally, there are differences with respect to salvation: the New Testament has one way of atonement but the Old Testament many, and in the New Testament the apostles are sent to the nations whereas in the Old Testament the nations have to come to Israel for salvation. (pp.49-57/46-53)

1.145 <u>Allegory</u>
a. One way of seeing 'Christ in the Old Testament' is to renew allegorising, a method that has often been popular in the history of the Church. At first

1. Translation (p.52/56): main text should begin 'We cannot master this five-fold incongruity...'

this appears to solve many problems by giving the entire Old Testament to the Church, which is therefore free to interpret it. But allegorical interpretation is arbitrary, often taking words out of context in order to find Christ in the Old Testament, and it implies that God inspired the Old Testament in a mysterious way and thus deliberately obscured the meaning. Moreover, van Ruler argues, if the Old Testament were an allegory it would not matter what it actually said since the real meaning would be something other than what it said. Its bond to the history of Israel would be irrelevant, and the Old Testament would no longer be revelation in the sense of God's presence in the history of his people. Allegorical exegesis is superficially attractive since it evades the problem of the historical reliability of the Old Testament, but in ignoring God's history with his people it inevitably fails to understand the nature of revelation and finds in the Old Testament not the historical Christ but a subjective or other-worldly Christ.

b. Van Ruler recognises a difference between intellectual knowledge and spiritual understanding of the Bible, and argues that scholarship, if it is to take the Bible seriously as God's revelation, should attempt to penetrate beyond study of the actual words to an understanding of God's purpose in revelation. This is no justification for allegorical exegesis since God has chosen to express himself in ordinary words and therefore it is only through these that his purpose will be understood. Yet although allegorising must be rejected and historico-grammatical study remains fundamental van Ruler admits that scholarship alone is insufficient to understand these words and concludes that true exegesis is only possible in and by the Holy Spirit. (pp.53-8/57-62)

1.146 Typology

a. Another way of finding 'Christ in the Old Testament' is typological interpretation, a method which is currently being revived (in the Biblischer Kommentar[1], for example). Van Ruler analyses the way the method is used today thus: earlier historical facts are related to later ones (in particular Old Testament facts to those in the New Testament), both kinds of facts being recognised as acts of God, so that features of the earlier time recur or have parallels or are continued or developed in the later time; it is stressed that typology concerns the whole Old Testament and not just the Messianic prophecies; it is asked whether the typological relationship is only perceived in retrospect or whether it is fixed by God from the beginning; it is conceded that the real meaning of a text may not originally have been understood; it is considered that Christian theologians must understand the Old Testament from the New, although this cannot be made into a strict method; and Jesus Christ is seen as 'the final goal of the way of God' with his people Israel and thus secretly present in the Old Testament. Van Ruler's critical comments on this typological method bring him right to the heart of his thesis, defining the place of Jesus

1. This is changed from text to footnote and capitals to italics in the English translation, thus obscuring its importance.

Christ in God's plan and the authenticity of the Old Testament as the canonical Word of God.

b. His first comment is concerned with the centrality of Jesus Christ in God's plan. He argues that, contrary to what is usually thought, it is less the case that God's history with Israel is directed toward Jesus Christ than that God's act in Jesus Christ is for the benefit of Israel. Similarly, God's history with Israel is for the benefit of the peoples of the earth and God's purpose in salvation is for his creation, not the other way round. 'We are not men in order that we might be Christians; we are Christians in order that we might be men' (p.65/68). It was Jesus' sacrifice that solved the problem of guilt and therefore he is the centre of God's purpose, but this is different from saying that God is concerned exclusively with him. God's concern is not only with reconciliation but with sanctification, not only with the Messiah but with the Spirit. From the beginning God's plan is for his kingdom, and 'Jesus Christ is an emergency measure that God postponed as long as possible (cf.Matt.21:33-46). Hence we must not try to find him fully in the Old Testament, even though as Christian theologians we investigate the Old Testament in orientation to God.'(p.65/69)

c. Secondly, van Ruler advocates a more cautious use of typology, limiting the types to those authenticated by God (in the New Testament, presumably). Types can be recognised only in retrospect and therefore Jesus Christ fulfils the Old Testament by putting into effect what it says, not because the Old Testament foresees what he will do and speaks about it. So the Old Testament speaks about Jesus only in the sense that he fulfils it.

d. Finally, according to van Ruler, Jesus Christ fulfils the Old Testament above all by solving its root problem, the broken relationship between God and man.[2] It follows that it is not what is typologically related to Christ that is most important but Israel, the world and God himself, the very things dealt with pre-eminently in the Old Testament. 'The Old Testament is and remains the intrinsic Bible (die eigentliche Bibel). In it God has made known himself and the secret he has with the world' (p.68/72). Thus van Ruler states explicitly the underlying theme of the whole book, that it is the Old Testament which is the original, essential and canonical Word of God and the New Testament is its interpretative glossary (erklärendes Wörterverzeichnis). So the Old Testament must not be interpreted simply in terms of the gospel of Jesus Christ: it must be interpreted in its own terms, the life of individuals and the history of the people of God. (pp.58-68/62-72)

2. Here he says that forgiveness and expiation are a fundamental part of the Old Testament, in apparent contradiction to his previous statement that forgiveness is the characteristic of the New Testament in contrast to the Old Testament (pp.48/51-2). Cf. above:1.144.

1.15 THE OLD TESTAMENT AND THE CHURCH

1.151 Six Concepts

a. In the first place, the Old Testament is necessary for the Christian Church as a legitimation of Jesus as the Christ. The Old Testament shows that Jesus is in harmony with God's relationship to his people and thus that he has been sent by God, and it witnesses to Jesus' claim to do the works of God by showing what those works are. Its attestation of Jesus' Messiahship links the Old and New Testaments as it combines the Old Testament concept of the kingdom of God and the New Testament concept of the deity of Jesus. (pp.69-71/75-7)

b. It is possible to look at the relationship between the Testaments in the opposite way: not only does the Old Testament legitimate Jesus as the Christ but Jesus himself authenticates the Old Testament, in van Ruler's terminology he is its foundation. By this he means that in Jesus Christ God's promises are fulfilled, God's relationship with Israel, man and the world has been ratified, and in his kingdom the kingdom of God has been founded on earth. Therefore the Old Testament is necessary for the Christian Church because Jesus has confirmed the validity of what it says. A corollary is that only the Christian Church can understand the Old Testament[1]: although it is indeed Israel's book, it became evident through

---

1. Translation (CCOT, 73/79): lines 10-11 should read 'Thus, rightly understood, only the Christian church can make something of the Old Testament'.

the coming of the Messiah and the Spirit that the Old Testament is not only concerned with Israel but with the whole world. The promises and the kingdom of God are passed on from Israel to the Church in the incarnation and rejection of Christ. (pp.71-4/77-80)

c. The third way in which the Old Testament is necessary for the Christian Church is for <u>interpretation</u> of the gospel, since the New Testament can be understood historically only on the basis of the Old Testament. Without the Old Testament the kingdom is lost from sight, as is the historical, worldly, theocratic element of Christianity, and so systematic theology should take the Old Testament more seriously and use it to help express the significance of Jesus being the Christ. (pp.74-7/80-82)

d. Next van Ruler refers to the Old Testament's importance for <u>illustration</u>. It is not simply that the imagery of the Old Testament has a lasting value but that Jesus Christ cannot be understood other than in terms of the Old Testament. Apart from the basic fact that Jesus is Israel's Messiah, his close involvement in the difficult situation in which Israel had got entangled, his answer to the problem of guilt (expressed in the language of Jewish 'blood-theology'), and the fact that the Church is now 'Israel' are important instances of the necessity for preaching Christ by means of Old Testament expressions and concepts. Though he does not mention the question of demythologisation, van Ruler would clearly reject any such method of using the Bible. (pp.77-9/83-5)

e. Fifthly, <u>historicisation</u>: the Old Testament shows Jesus Christ to be part of God's history with Israel and thus a genuinely historical fact. Although it is obvious to ordinary people, the fact that history is central to Christianity has been continually evaded by theology, and in this situation the Old Testament with its unmistakable concern for history is essential as a reminder that God's revelation is inextricably linked to historical facts. (pp.79-82/86-7)

f. Lastly, the Church's need of the Old Testament is expressed by the concept of <u>eschatologisation</u>, by which van Ruler means that initially, finally, and therefore all the time it is God and the world that are fundamentally important. This is seen more clearly in the Old Testament (which is positively concerned with creation, kingdom, law, sanctification, culture, marriage, the state, etc.) than in the New (where it is recognised but obscured by the details of revelation, the incarnation of the Messiah and the indwelling of the Spirit). So the Old Testament has a surplus over the New Testament not only in the cultic sphere but in its social and political ideal of the sanctification of the earth, an ideal which the Church has lost through a false deduction from the necessity for Christ's death that nothing more can be done with the earth. (pp.82-5/88-91)

1.152 <u>Some further implications</u>

Van Ruler's book ends with two questions and two problems. 'Should the Church preach only Christ?' is answered in the negative, since preaching of the kingdom - for the sake of which Christ came - is more fundamental. 'What should follow the recognition of the Old Testament as canon?' is that the Church is bound to the Old Testament, not the Old Testament to the Church as is so often the case. The problems of the relationship between the Old and New Testaments as Christian canon, and the Old Testament as Israel's book today, are outlined but not solved. What is clear is that both Old and New Testaments are to be recognised as authorities and that, although the Old Testament becomes valid for Gentiles through Jesus Christ, the people of Israel still exists and has an important part in God's history with the world. (pp.85-92/92-8)

1.2 CRITICISM: THEOCRACY AND PRIORITY

1.21 SECONDARY QUESTIONS

1.211 Contemporary views of the Old Testament

In his introduction van Ruler analyses contemporary views of the Old Testament into ten groups (1955:9-12/ 11-14; see above:1.12). These categories are neither exhaustive nor all mutually exclusive (cf. Jepsen 1958:258; Bright 1967:184n.): not all the solutions considered in the present work are included, and van Rad advocates both typology and salvation history while Schleiermacher views the Old Testament as a preparation for Christ in the same way as paganism but disparages it in itself, for example. The attributions are varied, some views being attributed to schools, some to individuals, and some to no one in particular; and whereas some are ways of evaluating the Old Testament others are ways of interpreting it. Van Ruler himself is more concerned in his work to evaluate the Old Testament, as has been seen, but this naturally has consequences for Old Testament interpretation. He gives a fair analysis of the most important views of the Old Testament, though emphases have changed in the past twenty years and today 'complete devaluation' might not be included while historical interpretations of various kinds would probably be more prominent (cf. the analyses of Bright 1967; Verhoef 1970; Shih 1971; Hasel 1972).

1.212 Are both Testaments about the same God?

Van Ruler criticises Old Testament scholars for not seeing the importance of this question, but gives only three pages to it himself and fails there to answer it explicitly (pp.15-18/13-16; see above:1.131). Since he refers to no one who advocates a negative answer to the question, he admits that those Old Testament scholars who are interested presuppose a positive answer, and his own book presupposes a positive answer without real discussion, it may be questioned whether it is really such a significant question as van Ruler suggests. At least few in the Church (to whom van Ruler directs his argument) will dispute that the one God is God of both Testaments (cf. Eissfeldt 1947; see also below:2.12a,2.21b).

1.213 <u>The quintessence of the Old Testament</u>

According to van Ruler the quintessence of the Old Testament is neither religion nor theology but God himself, the active God whose presence is encountered in the history of Israel (p.24/26; see above:1.133a). There is nothing new in the suggestion that God is the 'centre' of the Old Testament (cf.Lindblom 1936) and it is currently very popular (see below: 10.14a cf.10.15a) but it must be asked whether it is really valid. What does it mean to say that the essence of the Old Testament is God rather than theology? In what sense can God be the essence of the Old Testament other than that it speaks about him and witnesses to him, in other words that it is theology? Georg Fohrer(1966) points out that the Old Testament itself does not place God in the centre in an isolated way but always speaks of him in relationship to his activity in the life and destiny of man and creation (cf. Smend 1970; von Rad 1963:415). Perhaps it would be more consistent with van Ruler's thesis, as well as a more realistic understanding of the Old Testament, to say that it is God's relationship with Israel - and the world - that is central to the Old Testament. The Old Testament does not present God abstractly but always in terms of concrete history, in relation to man and the world (see further, below:10.16).

1.214 <u>Israel and the Church</u>

The question of the relationship of the Church to Israel is raised by van Ruler's book (pp.28-33/30-36; 89-92/95-8 see above:1.134,1.152). He argues that the Church is a repetition of Israel 'in the Spirit' and that there is a typical relationship between Israel and a Christian nation. However, although the Church is Israel, Israel is not the Church: Israel is theologically more important than the Church since the latter is dependent on the former for its self-understanding. This is perhaps a strange conclusion for a Christian writer but it is a natural corollary of van Ruler's presupposition that the Old Testament is the real Bible. He considers that Israel as a nation still has a place in God's plan, but does not make clear precisely what is that place. Recent literature on the subject generally acknowledges the Church to be the 'Israel of God' or spiritual Israel according to the New Testament though Peter Richardson (1969) argues strongly against this, claiming that the idea originated with Justin (c.160 A.D.). The question of the theological significance of the nation of Israel in the Christian era remains open, however, and will no doubt be of continuing interest in coming years.

The literature on this question is extensive and the following are of particular importance:
Campbell, Israel and the New Covenant(1954);
Torrance, 'The Israel of God',Interpn(1956);
Knight, 'Israel - A theological Problem',RefTR(1958); A Christian Theology of the OT(1959):335-43;
Martin-Achard, A Light to the Nations(1959);
Trilling, Das Wahre Israel(1959);
Ladd, 'Israel and the Church',EQ(1964); Jesus and the Kingdom(1966):239-57;
Caird, Jesus and the Jewish Nation(1965);
Cerfaux, 'Le peuple de Dieu' and 'La survivance du peuple ancien à la lunière du NT' in Ottaviani Festschrift(1966);
Küng, The Church(1967):107-150;
Huffmon, 'The Israel of God',Interpn(1969);
Clark, 'The Israel of God' in Wikgren Festschrift(1972);
Pancaro, 'The Relationship of the Church to Israel in the Gospel of St John',NTS(1975).

On the suggestion that the identification of the Church and Israel is later than the New Testament, see:
P.Richardson, Israel in the Apostolic Church(1969); 'The Israel-Idea in the Passion Narratives' in Moule Festschrift(1970);
cf.Jocz, A Theology of Election(1958):esp.102-155;
Jervell, Luke and the People of God(1972):41-74.

See also:
Phythian-Adams, The Fulness of Israel(1938);
Barth, Church DogmaticsII.2(1942):195-205;
de Lubac et al. , Israël et la foi chrétienne(1942);
Torrance, 'Salvation is of the Jews'EQ(1950);
Munck, Paul and the Salvation of Mankind(1954);
Jocz, The Spiritual History of Israel(1961);
Schedl et al., '"Da, ein Volk einsam ist es..."' in Leist(1965);
Wiesemann, Das Heil für Israel(1965);
Agus, 'Israel and the Jewish-Christian dialogue' and
Berkhof, 'Israel as a theological problem in the Christian church', JES(1969);
WCC, 'The Church and the Jewish People', symposium in Oikoumene(1974).

Many works on Rom.9-11 and Gal.6:16 are relevant.
Cf. also below:2.14;2.21a;3.26.

1.22 INCONGRUITY BETWEEN THE TESTAMENTS

a. Van Ruler draws attention to a number of incongruiti between the Old Testament and the New (pp.49-57/46-53; see above:1.144).

b. He claims, for example, that the Old Testament emphasises kingship and the New Testament guilt and atonement. Yet a dominant theme throughout the law, prophets and writings is the guilt and need for forgiveness of individuals and nations faced with a holy God, and the idea of the kingdom of God is fundamental to the teaching of Jesus (Mark 1:15) and Paul (1 Cor. 15:24-8):

E.g. חטא (sin) occurs 593 times in OT
(law 238; prophets 231; writings 124);
עון (iniquity) occurs 223 times in OT
(law 40; prophets 121; writings 62);
כפר Piel (atonement) occurs 101 times in OT
(law 77; prophets 14; writings 10);
סלח (forgive) occurs 50 times in OT
(law 20; prophets 16; writings 14);
cf. ἁμαρτία (sin) and compounds occur 149 times in NT
ἀφίημι (in the sense 'forgive') occurs 46 times in NT

And even van Ruler (p.67/71) admits that the central question of the Old Testament is that of guilt and expiation!

βασιλεία occurs 157 times in NT (Synoptics 119; John 4; Acts 8; Paul 14; rest of NT 12), usually with τοῦ θεοῦ or τῶν οὐρανῶν. Although מלך etc. occurs over 2000 times in the Old Testament it is only rarely related to God (mostly in the Psalms).

c. Van Ruler suggests that the Old Testament does not envisage the dominant event of the New Testament, the rejection of the Messiah (cf. Bright 1953:198-208; Eichrodt 1933:510-11; P.Richardson 1969). This may be countered by referring to the prophetic expectation that the Servant would be rejected (Isa.53) and the common rejection of God's messengers in the Old Testament (Isa.6:9-10; Jer.11:19; Ezek.3:7; Amos 7:12-13; cf. Steck 1967; Crenshaw 1971:94-9) but more particularly by questioning whether the rejection of the Messiah is really the dominant event of the New Testament. The resurrection is at least as important in the New Testament as the crucifixion, and the New Testament's interest in the cross is more in the fulfilment of God's plan than in man's rejection of it (Acts 2:23; cf. Mark 8:31; Luke 18:31; Acts 3:18; 4:28; 13:29; I Peter 1:19-20; Rev.13:8[1]).

d. Then van Ruler claims that whereas the Old Testament has many ways of atonement the New Testament has only one. There is some truth in this contrast but his further claim that the idea of substitution emerges clearly only in the New Testament cannot be accepted. On the contrary, substitution is an important concept in the Old Testament: 'Israel knew very well what substitution and atonement meant; what it did not know was the way of their final realization in Jesus of Nazareth' (Stamm 1956: 208; cf. Cullmann 1946:136-8; 1965:233).

e. There is also some truth in van Ruler's distinction between the Old Testament expectation of the nations coming to Israel for salvation and the New Testament apostolate which evangelises the nations. Nevertheless both Testaments recognise the fundamental point, which is that salvation is possible for the Gentiles as well as for Israel (cf. Stamm 1956:209; see also Rowley 1944b; Jeremias 1956; Martin-Achard 1959a). Although Jonah is scarcely a model missionary it is significant that he travels to Nineveh to preach his message; and further evidence that the faith of Israel had a missionary aspect is to be found in the proselytes that Paul found throughout the Roman Empire in the first century, showing that Judaism had in fact made many converts (Acts 2:10; 6:5; 13:43;

---

1. Translate: '...the Lamb slain before the foundation of the world'; so Caird 1966, Morris 1969.

cf. Matt.23:15; see Bright 1953:160-161). On the other hand, the Old Testament expectation is not entirely forgotten in the New Testament, since at the birth of Jesus 'wise men from the East came to Jerusalem, saying, "Where is he who has been born king of the Jews?"'(Matt. 2:1-2) and at Pentecost it was the 'nations' who came to Jerusalem to hear the gospel preached for the first time after the resurrection (Acts 2:5-11).

f. In conclusion, although there are obvious differences in emphasis and content between the two Testaments, the contrast is not nearly so sharp as van Ruler claims.

1.23 THE SURPLUS

a. One major aspect of the relationship between the Testaments, according to van Ruler, is that the Old Testament has a surplus over the New:

> 'To the very depths of Old Testament expectation, the people of Israel as a people, the land, posterity and theocracy play a role that cannot possibly be eliminated. This role cannot be altered by regarding Christ and his church as the fulfilment, in other words, by spiritualizing. There is a surplus (zu viel) in the Old Testament, a remnant that cannot be fitted into the New Testament fulfilment' (pp.42-3/45).

At this point Stamm (1956:206-8) criticises van Ruler, arguing that fulfilment should be seen in the context of the whole and not in terms of individual promises since Jesus - admittedly to the surprise of contemporary Jews - claimed to fulfil all the different messianic promises. But van Ruler has more to say:

> In the Old Testament 'what matters is everyone sitting under his vine and fig tree, in other words, earthly possessions and inhabiting the earth where righteousness dwells - all to God's praise. The

element of the earth is not eliminated, not even when the cross of Jesus Christ is planted in that earth. Here too is a surplus in the Old Testament as compared with the New' (p.46/49; cf. 83-5/89-91; see also below: 2.15, and Vriezen 1954/66:306-11/281-6).

b. It is indeed true that these things are characteristic of the Old Testament, perhaps more so than the New Testament. But it should not be assumed that the New Testament is disinterested in ordinary life on earth (see Matt.13; Luke 1:53a; John 10:10b; Acts 2:44-6; Rom.12-13; I Cor.7;16; Phil.4; Col.3:18-25; James; Rev.21; cf. Wilder 1955,1956; Davies 1969; also, Cullmann 1957a:89; Cranfield 1965; Houlden 1973:67-8). Nor should it be thought that the Old Testament is disinterested in spiritual things (see Gen.6:8; 15:6; Num.16:30; Deut.29:17-18/18-19; I Sam.2:26; Isa.43:1-7; Jer.31:31-4; Ezek.37; Ps.16:9-11; Job 19:25-7; Dan.12:2-3; cf. Eichrodt 1933:210-20; Vriezen 1954/66:128-147/153-175; also, von Rad 1957:368-9, 395-7). Van Ruler's mistake is oversimplification: his characterisation of the Old Testament as 'earthly' and the New Testament as 'spiritual' must be rejected (see Wolff 1956a:176-9).

1.24 JESUS CHRIST AS AN ACT OF GOD IN HIS HISTORY WITH ISRAEL

'From the Old Testament standpoint Jesus Christ is either of theological significance only as an historical fact - as an act of God in the history with his people, Israel - or he is of no significance at all' (p.37/40 cf. 34-40/37-43; also 80/86; see above: 1.141; cf. Barr 1973:167).

Indeed for van Ruler Jesus Christ is not even an essential part of this history, but an emergency measure which God delayed and eventually found necessary in order to establish his kingdom (p.65/69; see above: 1.146b). Now it is not to be disputed that Jesus Christ, as his title testifies, came as the Messiah of Israel: this is a fundamental fact for any evaluation of the relationship between the Testaments. Yet van Ruler's formulation is not only dependent on a questionable view of revelation and history (cf. Barr 1966:65-102; see also below: 7.32) but does not adequately account for the radical newness of God's act in the incarnation, life, death and resurrection of his Son (cf. von Rad 1960:382-3; Thomas 1966). To make Jesus Christ only an emergency measure, although it is true in a sense and warns against a premature Christological interpretation of the Old Testament, ignores the New Testament claim that Jesus Christ was part of God's plan from the beginning (cf. above: 1.22c).

1.25 CREATION AND SALVATION

a. Van Ruler presupposes that the doctrine of creation is more fundamental than the doctrine of salvation, and hence that sanctification is greater than reconciliation (pp.63-5/67-9; 82-5/88-91; see above: 1.146b, 1.151f). He considers that the Old Testament is concerned with creation but the New Testament with salvation, and so it follows naturally that the Old Testament has priority over the New Testament. This is apparent in his devotional study, <u>God's Son and God's World</u> (ET:1960). Unlike many books which deal first with the Old Testament and then progress to the New Testament, Part One is devoted to the New Testament (the 'I am' sayings, 28pp.)

and Part Two to the Old Testament (Ps. 104, 39pp.). 'The intention of the gospel of Christ is that we do rejoice in the world....Through the gift of Jesus Christ we are able again to love the world and be glad in it'(p.5).

b. There is indeed a certain logic in this if it is believed that God's purpose is for the world and that salvation is but a remedy to heal the world's sickness: health is obviously more important than healing. Moreover, it may be urged that 'for those who believe their God to be Lord of all, the supreme act of the past is the act of creation itself' (Foulkes 1958:31). Undoubtedly this is one aspect of the truth and may be a necessary corrective to any who are so concerned with salvation that they forget what is to be saved and for what purpose it is to be saved. In line with van Ruler, Bonhoeffer (1951) counters those who advocate Christianity simply as a religion of salvation in these terms:

'Is there any concern in the Old Testament about saving one's soul at all? Is not righteousness and the kingdom of God on earth the focus of everything...? It is not with the next world that we are concerned but with this world as created and preserved and set subject to laws and atoned for and made new. What is above the world is, in the Gospel, intended to exist <u>for</u> this world.'(pp.94-5

'Unlike the other oriental religions the faith of the Old Testament is not a religion of salvation. Christianity, it is true, has always been regarded as a religion of salvation. But isn't this a cardinal error, which divorces Christ from the Old Testament and interprets him in the light of the myths of salvation?...Is (salvation) really the distinctive feature of Christianity as proclaimed in the Gospels and St.Paul? I am sure it is not.... The Christian hope sends a man back to his life on earth in a wholly new way which is even more sharply defined than it is in the Old Testament...This world must not be prematurely written off.' (p.112 cf. 50,93)

c. Vriezen (1956:221), however, points out that

'the earth as creation cannot be truly loved without the deep confession of sin which desecrates it, and without knowledge of the power of God which has broken the power of sin and prepares a new future for the earth. Sanctification without redemption is impossible.'

The basic problem is that van Ruler does not deal adequately with the fact of sin and the theology of salvation which are fundamental to the whole Bible, not just the New Testament (see above: 1.22; cf. von Rad 1938; Festorazzi 1967; Grogan 1967a; Hill 1967; Vink 1967; Bruce 1968a:ch.3). A balanced Christian appreciation of the whole biblical message must recognise that creation and salvation are each of fundamental importance and neither exists without the other (cf. Toombs 1969:310-12). Even if it is conceded that there are different emphases in the Old and New Testaments, that 'creation' is a more dominant note in the former and 'salvation' in the latter, both Testaments have the same ideal of a sanctified earth and both acknowledge that this can only be brought about by the activity of God who not only created the world but provided for its salvation (cf. also Bonhoeffer 1951:126-7; Barr 1966:149-170; 1970).

1.26 KINGDOM OF GOD

a. The theme of the kingdom of God underlies the whole of van Ruler's book (cf. his popular exposition of Zechariah,ET:1962, of which this is also true). This is closely related to the idea that the doctrine of creation is more important than the doctrine of salvation, and van Ruler argues on this basis that the purpose of God's revelation is not only redemption but more particularly the setting up of his kingdom, the theocracy (pp.26-7/28-9, see above: 1.133b; cf. 1947:29-47; 1965:78; also, Smend 1970:33-4). Israel starts as a theocracy, the Church becomes the theocracy, and the theocracy is the final expectation for the world (p.32/34; see above: 1.134a). It follows that Israel is more important than the Church (cf. above: 1.214) and that the Old Testament is more important than the New Testament. According to van Ruler, one reason why the Old Testament is necessary for the Christian Church is because its concern for the kingdom brings out the aspect of kingship in the concept of Messiah which would be lost from sight if Jesus was understood only through the New Testament (p.75/81; see above: 1.151c). So also the Old Testament should be interpreted not Christologically but eschatologically, which for van Ruler means theocratically (pp.82-3/88-9; cf. Vriezen 1956:219-20; Plöger 1959).

b. It cannot seriously be denied that the concept of the kingdom of God is fundamental to biblical theology, and van Ruler's work provides a balance to others which stress the importance of concepts such as 'covenant', 'communion with God', 'salvation history' and 'people of God'.[1] Moreover, it is true that God saves men in order that they may live under his rule, that Jesus (the Saviour, Matt.1:21) came in order to set up God's kingdom, and that in this sense theocracy is more ultimate to the biblical message than soteriology.

---

1. These concepts are closely linked: e.g. Vatke (1835:238) and Kayser (1886:74) identify theocracy and covenant, while Fohrer (1966) considers the dual concept of the rule of God and communion between God and man to be the centre of OT theology.

c. The inadequacy of van Ruler's 'theocratic theology' (cf. Hommes 1967) is that it does not reckon adequately with the variety of biblical theology and the outstanding failure of the Israelite attempt at theocracy. Not one of the forms of statehood experienced by Israel - wilderness community, tribal league, monarchy, post-exilic community - succeed in being theocracies and it is not until Jesus comes that the kingdom of God is at last inaugurated. Van Ruler's claim that the theocracy is the presupposition of Israel must therefore be challenged (see Vriezen 1956:216-22; cf. Jacob 1963). No doubt many Israelites assumed that they lived in a theocracy and the false prophets encouraged them in their complacency, but the burden of the canonical prophets was to proclaim the eschatological kingdom of God, a theocracy to be established on the 'Day of the Lord' (Isa.9:6/7; Ezek.20:33; 37:24-8; Hosea 3:5; Obad.21; Zech.14:9, 16-17).

d. One of the stumbling-blocks of the preaching of Jesus is that the kingdom comes in an unexpected way, through the death and resurrection of the Son of God. So Vriezen (1956:218) can say:

'it had been demonstrated in Israel that theocratic preaching could not save Israel, that Israel could not be transformed into a theocracy without the suffering and sacrificial death of the Servant of God. Theocracy could become a living reality in Israel only through the cross, as in fact it can be realized in any way at all only through the cross....Jesus Christ is the locus of the breaking through of the kingdom of God in the world.'

Although the Old Testament envisages the kingdom of God it is the New Testament which portrays its coming. Thus it is a fallacy to make the Old Testament superior to the New Testament on the ground that it deals with the kingdom rather than redemption (cf. Wolff 1956a:196n.): both Testaments are vital to maintain the biblical understanding of the kingdom of God.

On the concept of the kingdom of God in biblical theology see:
Schultz, OT Theology(1860):I.56;
Hengstenberg, The Kingdom of God in the OT(1871);
Buber, Kingship of God(1932);
Bright, The Kingdom of God(1953);
Lipinski, La royauté de Yahwé(1965);
Cerfaux, 'Le royaume de Dieu' in Ottaviani Festschrift(1966);
Ladd, Jesus and the Kingdom(1966);
Bruce, This is That(1968):ch.2;
Klein, 'The Biblical Understanding of "The Kingdom of God"'(1970),ET in Interpn26;
Buchanan, The Consequences of the Covenant(1970):ch.2;
Kellermann, Messias und Gesetz(1971);
Bonsirven, 'Le règne de Dieu suivant l'AT' in Robert Festschrift(n.d.)

The isolation of the concept of theocracy as central to the OT is also not new. The word was originally coined by Josephus (Against Apion 2.164-7). Smend (Die Mitte des ATs, 1970:39-44) traces the use since the seventeenth century of theocracy as the central concept of the OT, showing that it belongs with the idea of God as the Lord (see, e.g., Wellhausen, Prolegomena 1883:411-25). On 'theocracy', see further:
Miskotte, 'Naturrecht und Theokratie' in BEvTh(1952): esp.54-6;
Vriezen, 'Theocracy and Soteriology'(1956),ET in EOTI;
Velema, Confrotatie met Van Ruler(1962):63-80.

1.27 A RELATIONSHIP OF PRIORITY

a. All these five propositions - that there are fundamental incongruities between the Testaments, that the Old Testament has a surplus compared with the New, that Jesus Christ is an act of God in his history with Israel, that the doctrine of creation is more important than the doctrine of salvation, and that the kingdom of God is the central concept of the Old Testament - are aspects of van Ruler's fundamental proposition, that the Old Testament is primarily and inherently the Bible and the New Testament is its interpretative glossary. It follows that the relationship between the Testaments is a relationship of priority: the Old Testament has historical and theological priority with respect to the New Testament. In van Ruler's words,

'The Old Testament is and remains the intrinsic Bible. In it God has made known himself and the secret he has with the world. All goodness and also all truth and beauty - the fully redemptive knowledge of being - shines out before us in this book. It is the book of humanity... Both exegetically and homiletically one must continually begin afresh and remain occupied with the text of the Old Testament itself... The Old Testament itself remains the canonical Word of God, and it constantly confronts us with its own authority' (p.68/72; cf. 1942; 1945:123-149).

b. At a number of points it has been necessary to disagree with van Ruler but although the criticism has weakened the force of his argument it has not destroyed it altogether. There _is_ a sense in which the Old Testament has priority over the New Testament. God's intentions for the salvation and sanctification of man and the world are set out first of all in the Old Testament and the New Testament records the fulfilment of those intentions. Jesus Christ is part of God's dealings in history with his chosen people and his Church is spiritually Israel. God's ultimate purpose is that his kingdom should be established over all creation.

c. This much may be learnt from van Ruler and the most fundamental criticism of his thesis is not concerned with what he says but with what he fails to say. He does not take sufficient account of the radical nature of God's act in Jesus Christ which is not simply the final stage of God's activity in Israel but also a new event that inaugurates God's kingdom. From the Old Testament point of view Jesus Christ is the final act but from the point of view of the New Testament he has become the centre of history (Cullmann 1946). The New Testament is therefore not merely a glossary to interpret the real meaning of the Old Testament but equally the record of God's activity in the history of his people Israel and thus God's self-communication or 'revelation'. Van Ruler's interpretation of the Old Testament is not to be lightly dismissed, and he draws attention to aspects of it which are often ignored. Nevertheless, for the reasons already elaborated his solution to the problem of the relationship between the Testaments is essentially an 'Old Testament' solution, and - although it may educate us - it must finally be rejected.

2. The Old Testament is an independent witness to 'the Name', the New Testament its Christian sequel

2.1 KORNELIS H. MISKOTTE: ON THE SIGNIFICANCE OF THE OLD TESTAMENT

2.2 COMPARISON: OTHER 'OLD TESTAMENT' SOLUTIONS

2.1 KORNELIS H. MISKOTTE: ON THE SIGNIFICANCE OF THE OLD TESTAMENT

2.11 INTRODUCTION

Kornelis H. Miskotte was a prolific writer in the fields of literature and philosophy as well as that of theology, but it is particularly in <u>When the Gods are Silent</u> (1956) that he expounds his view of the Old Testament. This book was called the theological book of the decade in Germany (see introduction to English edn:p.ix; cf. Kraus 1965) and was reviewed with much enthusiasm outside Germany, though strangely it has soon been forgotten and the English translation went out of print five years after publication. It remains nevertheless one of the most significant works on the Old Testament of the modern era and still awaits a more serious reaction from modern biblical scholarship. This is not the place for a full-scale study and therefore only Miskotte's view of the relationship between the Testaments will be considered here.

<u>When the Gods are Silent</u> was published in Dutch (1956), in a revised German edn (1963) and then in English (1967). The subtitle - 'On the Significance of the OT' - has been omitted in the English translation (except on the dust-cover). Among Miskotte's other works relevant to the OT and its relationship to the NT are:
<u>Het Wezen der Joodsche Religie</u>(1932);
'Das Problem der theologischen Exegese' in Barth Festschrift(1936);
<u>Edda en Thora</u>(1939);
<u>Om het levende Woord</u>(1948);
'De prediking van het OT' in Berkelbach and Abbing (1948; not available to me);
'Naturrecht und Theokratie',BEvTh(1952);
'Die Erlaubnis zu schriftgemässem Denken' in Barth Festschrift(1956);

Zur biblischen Hermeneutik(1959);
'Fragende Existenz' in Leist(1965).

Some of his OT sermons are to be found in Miskende majesteit(1969), chs 1-4,11.

The following reviews may be noted:
Kraus, VF(1965); Jacob, RHPR(1966); Clines, EQ(1968); Guersen, RefTR(1968); Brown, SJT(1969); Simon, RelSt (1970,1971); Stol, BO(1971).

2.12 A RELATIONSHIP OF PRIORITY

a. In many respects Miskotte's work implies the theological priority of the Old Testament over the New Testament and it has a number of similarities to that of van Ruler. Like him Miskotte rejects any suggestion that the New Testament is about a different God or has a different message than the Old Testament (pp.131-2,143; 1965:30-33; cf. above: 1.212) and finds the essence of the Old Testament in its testimony to God himself, to whom he refers by means of the term 'the Name' (pp.65-71,114-119, 257-64; cf. above: 1.213). He recognises that there are differences between the Testaments (p.107; cf. above: 1.22) but rejects schemata such as 'provisional' and 'definitive', 'law and gospel', 'promise and fulfilment' as inadequate descriptions of these differences (pp.108-110). The difference is not to be understood systematically but as part of the human aspect of the Scriptures: whereas the Bible is united because of its testimony to one God and one Christ, the humanity of the Scriptures means that 'though the one Word is the same in the Old Testament as in the New, it is nevertheless very decidedly different' (p.153). The unity of the Bible pervades the text, yet it is never visible or demonstrable as something 'given' (1948a:84).

b. Although he does not systematically discuss the concepts of 'theocracy' and 'kingdom of God' Miskotte assumes that the theocracy is the basis of Israel and ideal of the Church, and that the kingdom is God's ultimate purpose for the world (pp.138,207-14,216, 274-5,279,292-4,298,301,417; also, 1952; cf. above: 1.26). He is in agreement with van Ruler in accepting Bonhoeffer's use of the Old Testament to present a 'worldly Christianity' (pp.80-81, cf. 273) but he diverges on the question of the relationship between salvation and creation (cf. above: 1.25). Here Miskotte argues that salvation is part of God's plan in creation, that 'the Creation is already a part of God's redemptive history, that the existence of salvation is superior and antecedent to that of Being' (p.118, cf. 471,475; cf. also von Rad 1936a; B.W. Anderson 1955:6-10,19-20; Barr 1966:18-19). This may be compared with the statement of Nixon (1963:5): 'in the Old Testament the Exodus has pride of place even over the Creation'.

2.13 A RELATIONSHIP OF IDENTITY

a. Some of the most important links with van Ruler will be discussed below (2.14, 2.15), and it is necessary at this point to mention the relationship between Miskotte's thought and that of Vischer and Barth. There is a tension between the ideas of 'priority' (cf. van Ruler) and 'identity' (cf. Vischer) in Miskotte's solution to the problem of the relationship between the Testaments.

b. Although he will have nothing of Christological interpretation of the Old Testament (1959:119) it is clear that for Miskotte Christ is at the centre of the biblical witness:

'The testimony of the Old Testament goes out into the time of expectation, that of the New Testament into the time of recollection. Both are relative to the time of revelation itself. What they have in common is their relationship to, their orientation toward one and the same Object, one and the same Name, one and the same Event, one and the same Salvation.' (p.113; cf.143)

In other words, every part of the Bible points to the unique and definitive event of revelation in Jesus Christ though every part views it from a distance, looking forward to what God would do or back to what he had done in the past. In this way the Old Testament is an indirect witness to Christ (pp.132,144; cf. 159,467), speaking not only through the New Testament but '"for itself" as a fully valid witness of Him who has come'(p.105).

c. A further link with Vischer and Barth is Miskotte's recognition that the two Testaments have essentially the same theology (e.g. pp.131-2,257,411-12; also x,160; cf. 1948a: 80-86; Jacob 1966). But in spite of these resemblances the dominant aspect of his view of the relationship between the Testaments is the priority of the Old Testament over the New Testament, and therefore it belongs with that of van Ruler as an 'Old Testament solution'.

2.14 ISRAEL AND THE CHURCH

a. The relationship between Israel and the Church is a particularly pressing matter for those who advocate the priority of the Old Testament over the New Testament (cf. above: 1.214; below: 2.21a; Miskotte 1932, 1956a, 1965). Van Ruler views the Church as a spiritual repetition of Israel, but does not solve the problem of the relationship of the present-day nation of

Israel to that spiritual 'Israel'. Miskotte (1956a:315-18,308; 1965:33), on the other hand, affirms that in the Church Gentiles are 'grafted into the ancient tree of the Covenant people' (Rom.11:12-18) and that it is Israel's election which is the root of the salvation of Christendom. Neither Jews nor Christians alone are Israel but rather the church and synagogue together form one congregation of God. The present breach is therefore not to be removed by missions to Jews but by a call to brothers to realise their unity with each other (1956a:77-8, cf. 421). Miskotte takes up the words of Franz Rosenzweig: 'What Christ and his church mean in the world, on that we are agreed: no one comes to the Father but by him... but it is different if a person no longer needs to come to the Father, because he is <u>already</u> with him' (1956a:78). Thus Miskotte concludes that Christians must face realistically the fact that the Old Testament has two sequels, the New Testament and the Talmud. Failure to do this leads to oversimplification and misunderstanding, as in Bultmann's idea of miscarriage (Miskotte pp.165-7; cf. Horst 1932:e.g.172; Vriezen 1954/66:98/121; Childs 1964:444-9; Schofield 1964: 118-120).

b. There is of course some truth in Miskotte's argument, and it cannot be disputed that Judaism and Christianity came from the same root and still acknowledge the same God, but it seems that he does not account for the fundamental difference between the two which is that the Jews reject the one whom Christians claim was the promised Messiah (cf. above: 1.22c). Jesus' words 'no one comes to the Father, but by me'(John 14:6) were addressed to Jews, and Paul -

the missionary to the Gentiles - made a point of preaching salvation to the Jews first (Acts 13:5, 14,46,etc.). As Davies (1968a cf. 1968b) has shown, the centrality of the Torah to Judaism and Christology to Christianity means an irreconcilable dogmatic difference between the two faiths.

2.15 THE SURPLUS

a. The Old Testament has both a deficit and a surplus compared with the New Testament, but the relative importance in Miskotte's view is shown by the fact that he devotes half a page to the deficit and 132 pages to the surplus (pp.169-302; on 'surplus', cf. above: 1.23). In using the word 'surplus' Miskotte refers to elements in the Old Testament which

> 'are not surpassed in the New Testament, nor are they denied; but there they have receded into the background. We observe that when the essential substance and tendency of the Old and the New Testament are balanced there remains a margin of ideas...which includes scepticism, rebellion, erotics, politics (themes which are hardly mentioned in the New Testament).' (pp.170-171; cf. 252-7, 264-82)

He rejects the traditional disparagement of the primitive mentality of the Old Testament: according to him anthropomorphism is not a failing but a surplus (p.173 cf. 128-9; 1959:40), an idea developed by several other scholars (Vischer 1949; Jacob 1955a: 39-42; Mauser 1970,1971; Clines 1973:24-8; cf. Kuitert 1962; Gollwitzer 1963:142-161; contrast McKenzie 1972). If the New Testament is expounded without reference to the Old Testament there is the danger that naivety will be replaced by abstraction, which is really a flight from the reality of God (pp.177-9). Other aspects of the surplus are the

Torah (pp.228-46), suffering and poverty (pp.246-52), the presence of God (pp.262-3), expectation (pp.283-8) and prophetism (pp.288-95).

b. It may be cautiously conceded that these things have a more prominent place in the Old Testament than the New Testament, but it does not follow that the New Testament has nothing relevant to say. Before these things are accepted in the Christian Church they must be confronted with the message of the New Testament: only in the light of Jesus Christ's fulfilment of the Old Testament can they be valid for Christianity (Vriezen 1966:97-8).

2.16 'LET THE OLD TESTAMENT SPEAK FOR ITSELF'

a. So far Miskotte's view of the Old Testament has been seen to be similar to that of van Ruler. But there is one aspect in which Miskotte emphasises the priority of the Old Testament over the New Testament even more clearly than van Ruler and that is in his consistent plea that the Old Testament should be allowed 'to speak for itself' (pp.104-5,225-6,239, 243,262,etc.; cf. below: 2.21a; also, von Rad 1960: 333; Bright 1967:112; Porteous 1954:168-9; 1970a). 'Everything' is in the Old Testament, according to Miskotte, and it follows that the New Testament is in the Old Testament, not in detail but in the sense that the Old Testament has already said everything essential. It is therefore a mistake to read the New Testament message of Christ into the Old Testament: on the contrary, 'we need constantly to be learning from the Old Testament what is the meaning and the intent of that which we call "Christ"' (p.159; cf. Jacob 1965:48). 'The New Testament used in isolation needs to be corrected on the basis of the fundamental words of the Old Testament' (p.461). 'The testimony in the Old Testament proclaims a knowledge of salvation which, in that it becomes an event, already includes within it the fulfilled salvation as its own presupposition'(p.467).

b. Thus Miskotte views the Old Testament as an independent witness to 'the Name' and the New Testament as its Christian sequel, the Talmud being its Jewish sequel. One corollary is that the New Testament use of the Old Testament cannot be said to be binding: such a proposition is based on the false presupposition that the New Testament performs exegesis on the Old Testament. It is not that the New Testament explains the Old Testament but that the Old Testament - which speaks for itself as a witness to the Name - is used by New Testament writers to explain Christ (pp.468-9). The question arises here, however, whether the Old Testament was really accepted and understood in the early Church as easily as Miskotte implies: Acts 15, Romans 14 and similar passages suggest that it was not (so Vriezen 1966:48n).

2.2 COMPARISON: OTHER 'OLD TESTAMENT' SOLUTIONS

2.21 JAMES BARR

a. Barr's series of lectures on <u>Old and New in Interpretation</u> (1966) is his most important study of the problem of the two Testaments. He rejects formulations which understand the Old Testament 'in the light of the New Testament', arguing that 'in the minds of the apostles ... the relation was the opposite: the problem was not how to understand the Old Testament but how to understand Christ (p.139). It is often assumed that Christ is a known quantity and that it is the place of the Old Testament in the Church which is the problem. But in the early Church there was no doubt about the Old Testament, the problem was to identify the Christ. So also today, the Church's strategy should not be to take Christ as the 'key' to the meaning of the Old Testament but 'rather, taking the Old Testament as something we <u>have</u> in the Church to ask in what ways the guidance it affords helps us to understand and discern and obey the Christ more truly' (p.140). This means that a Christian formulation of the relationship must be related to the Old Testament from the beginning (p.149) and the interpretation of Old Testament texts is not automatically dependent on New Testament interpretation (pp.154-5; cf. 141-6), though Barr dismisses as naive any attempt to let 'the Old Testament speak for itself' (1962b: 145; 1966:167,170; cf. above 2.16). He sees at least five levels to the relationship between the Testaments: the religion of late Judaism (which developed out of the Old Testament and was the basis for the New Testament, 1966:134-6 cf. 159-164; 1968b; 1968c; 1974);

the text of the Old Testament (which was the authority of the New Testament, pp.136-7); the mind of Jesus (whose self-understanding was shaped by biblical patterns but who interpreted the Old Testament in an authoritative manner, pp.137-9, 157-9); the minds of the apostles (who came to understand Jesus as the Christ and used the Old Testament in their preaching, p.139; cf. Miskotte 1956a:100-101) and the relationship between Jews and Gentiles (who were made into one body in the Church, pp.164-6; cf. above: 1.214).

b. The priority of the Old Testament with respect to the New Testament, however, does not imply for Barr that the former is more important than the latter:

'The Christian faith stands equally upon the basis of the Old Testament and of the New or, more correctly, upon the basis of the God of Israel and of Jesus of Nazareth. In this sense the importance of Old and New Testaments is in principle more or less equal: and the two have a certain independence, an independence warranted by the newness of that which took place in Jesus... If for Christians Jesus is the finality and the culmination, which might place the New Testament in the higher position, Jesus himself stands under the God of Israel, which might place the Old Testament in the higher (1973: 166-7).

At the deepest level the relationship between the Testaments is not a matter of common patterns of thought or a balance of their different emphases but is an aspect of the unity of the one God (1973: 181; cf. Sanders 1974:322-3). The real basis of the relationship between the Old Testament and the New, and thus of the use of the Old in the Church inaugurated by the New Testament, is the assertion of faith that the One God of Israel is also the Father of the Lord Jesus Christ (1966:149-153; cf.above: 1.212).

c. Barr's view is evidently not nearly so extreme as that of van Ruler and Miskotte, and he indicates effectively the theological and historical priority of the Old Testament over the New Testament while demonstrating that the relationship between the Testaments is a mutual one and that neither is more important than the other.

Relevant works by Barr:
'Gerhard von Rad's Theologie des ATs', ExpT(1962);
'Taking the Cue from Bultmann', Interpn(1965);
Old and New in Interpretation(1966);
Judaism - Its Continuity with the Bible(1968);
'Le Judaïsme postbiblique', RThPh(1968);
'Themes from the OT for the Elucidation of the New Creation', Encounter(1970);
'The OT and the New Crisis of Biblical Authority', Interpn(1971);
The Bible in the Modern World(1973);
'Trends and Prospects in Biblical Theology', JTS(1974).

Barr has also made a number of other important contributions to methodology in biblical theology, mostly by means of penetrating criticisms of commonly accepted approaches.

On semantics, especially that of the TDNT, see The Semantics of Biblical Language(1961); Biblical Words for Time(1962); 'Hypostatisation of Linguistic Phenomena', JSS(1962); 'Semantics and Biblical Theology' in SVT(1972); cf. Hill 1967:1-14, 294-300 (to which Barr replies in Biblica 1968); Payot 1968; Tångberg 1973. Siertsema (1969) offers a similar but independent approach to that of Barr.

On the supposed contrast between Hebrew and Greek thought, see 1961:chs 2,4; 1966:ch.2. Barr's criticism is centred on the work of Boman (1952), and Boman replies in the fifth edition (1968:194-213). Cf. Tresmontant 1965; Ladd 1968:ch.1.

On the relationship between revelation and history, see 'Revelation Through History in the OT and in Modern Theology', Interpn(1963); 1966:ch.3 cf. ch.1.

2.22 H.WHEELER ROBINSON

a. Van Ruler (1955:11/12; see above: 1.12) refers to a type of approach to the Old Testament which accords it permanent value as an independent source of theological knowledge. He claims that this is common among Old Testament scholars and mentions, among others, H.Wheeler Robinson. That Wheeler Robinson regarded the Old Testament as an independent source for theology is clear from his proposition that the authority of revelation in the Old Testament is 'intrinsic and inherent. It is not to be sought through any testimony other than itself...' (1946:277). His view of the permanent value of the Old Testament is shown by his assertion that the authority of the Old Testament depends 'on the penetrating character of the intuition of the prophets... on the rich variety of the religious experience recorded...on the simple but searching vocabulary of worship...which remains indispensable and incomparable...' (1938:307). Moreover in exposition of the Old Testament he is concerned to show the permanent value of a text as well as its original meaning (e.g. at the end of his studies on Job, the Servant and Jeremiah, 1916-26:54,112-114,190-192).

b. The clearest expression of Wheeler Robinson's views is found in the final chapter of his early book on Israelite religious ideas (1913), 'The Permanent Value of the Old Testament'. He calls to the attention of his readers the fact that the value of the Old Testament to the early Church was obvious and unquestioned; it formed, in fact, the Bible of that Church before there was a New Testament at all (p.214; cf. Bugge 1924). In the face of contemporary doubt about the reality of revelation which resulted from critical study of the Bible, he argues that the intrinsic worth and permanent value of the ideas of the Old Testament proves them to be revelation (pp.216,222-30). The New Testament confirms this in its presupposition of the Old Testament idea of God and of human nature and of the kingly rule of God as the basis for human society (pp.224-5). So Wheeler Robinson, although he does not go as far as van Ruler in reducing the New Testament to the interpretative glossary of the Old Testament or Miskotte in emphasising the independence and surplus of the Old Testament compared to the New Testament, says in effect that theologically the Old Testament is independent of the New Testament and in that respect has a certain priority.

Works by H.W. Robinson:
The Religious Ideas of the OT(1913);
The Cross in the OT(1916-26);
'The Theology of the OT' in Robinson(1938);
'The Higher Exegesis',JTS(1943);
Inspiration and Revelation in the OT(1946).
Cf. Polley, 'H.Wheeler Robinson and the Problem of Organising an OT Theology' in Stinespring Festschrift (1972).

2.23 'SECTARIAN IMPATIENCE'

Another approach referred to by van Ruler (1955: 11-12/13; see above: 1.12) is that common among many sects, of treating the Old Testament as directly and completely valid today. He uses the term 'sectarian impatience', a very appropriate term to describe the extreme literalism that often characterises this attitude to the Old Testament. It may be seen in Seventh-Day Adventism's insistence that Saturday should be observed as the Sabbath (Bear 1956:56-64; van Baalen 1956:216-23; Hoekema 1963:161-9), Mormonism's idea of polygamy (Boyd 1956:442-3; van Baalen 1956:160-168,178) and British-Israelism's application of Old Testament prophecies to modern Britain and America (Baron 1915; van Baalen 1956:189-203). Perhaps the clearest example is that of the Jehovah's Witnesses, who retain the 'Old Testament' name for God, insist on the unity - as distinct from the trinity - of God, refuse blood transfusions on the basis of Leviticus, and forbid the use of Christmas trees on the basis of Jeremiah 10:3-4 (Stuermann 1956: 329-30; Hoekema 1963:249-50)[1] Their use of the Bible may be summarised in Stuermann's words: 'Almost everywhere they subordinate Christian and New Testament themes to those of Judaism and the Old Testament' (1956:345).

Baron, *The History of the Ten "Lost" Tribes*(1915);
van Baalen, *The Chaos of Cults*(1956[2]);
Bear, 'The Seventh-Day Adventists',
Stuermann, 'Jehovah's Witnesses' and
Boyd, 'Mormonism' in *Interpn*(1956);
Hoekema, *The Four Major Cults*(1963).

A modern sect which combines elements of Seventh--Day Adventism and British-Israelism is that headed by Herbert W. Armstrong, sometimes called the Worldwide (or Radio) Church of God. This attitude of direct application of the Old Testament is evident in their magazine, *The Plain Truth*, but more particularly in some booklets with a more limited circulation such as 'The British Commonwealth and the United States in Prophecy' (1954) and 'Which Day is the Christian Sabbath?' (1962).

2.24 OTHERS

a. There are no doubt other views of the relationship between the Testaments that fall within the category of 'Old Testament' solutions. At first sight it might be thought that the view of Wilhelm Vischer should be dealt with here: the reasons why it is not are given below (5.11a). Klaus Schwarzwäller considers the Old Testament to be the direct, critical and declaratory address of God, but although it has certain parallels with those discussed in the present section (e.g. 1966b:133), this view is closer to that of von Rad and will therefore be considered later (7.37d).

b. P.A.H. de Boer (1951) sees the New Testament as only an interpretation or application of the Old Testament, like van Ruler (so Vriezen 1954/66: 37n./48n.). Georg Fohrer (1970) agrees with van Ruler in rejecting allegory and typology, as well as 'promise and fulfilment', as ways of understanding the relationship between the Testaments. He considers that the dual concept of 'rule of God' and 'communion with God' is the centre of Old Testament theology (1966; cf. below: 10.1), and that the New Testament uses this same dual concept with reference to Christology (1970), so that the relationship between the Testaments is a relationship of 'beginning and continuation' (Beginn und Fortsetzung; 1970: 297). According to Filson (1951:135), those who advocate an extreme apocalyptic interpretation of the New Testament (e.g. Albert Schweitzer and Martin Werner) are effectively rejecting the New Testament, often in favour of the Old Testament prophets, as also do the extreme 'Jesus-of-history' school who limit themselves to parts of the Synoptics and the letter of James. Be that as it may, some of the most important views in this category have been analysed, criticised and compared, and the results are offered as 'Old Testament' solutions to the problem of the relationship between the Testaments.

de Boer, 'De functie van de Bijbel, *NedTT*(1951);

Fohrer, 'Der Mittelpunkt einer Theologie des ATs' (1966), German translation in *ThZ* 24; 'Das AT und das Thema "Christologie"',*EvTh*(1970); *Theologische Grundstrukturen des ATs*(1972); also, 'Die zeitliche und überzeitliche Bedeutung des ATs'(1950), repr. in *Studien*: 38; cf. Westermann 1974b.

PART THREE: 'NEW TESTAMENT' SOLUTIONS

3. The New Testament is the essential Bible, the Old Testament its non-Christian presupposition

3.1 RUDOLF BULTMANN: THE OLD TESTAMENT AND THE CHRISTIAN FAITH

3.2 CRITICISM: EXISTENCE AND CONTRAST

3.1 RUDOLF BULTMANN: THE OLD TESTAMENT AND THE CHRISTIAN FAITH

3.11 INTRODUCTION

Bultmann presupposes that the Old Testament is related to the New Testament. In 'The Significance of the Old Testament for the Christian Faith' (1933a:21) he affirms the Old Testament to be part of Christian history, so that it would be senseless to retain Christianity and reject the Old Testament: 'it is either-or: keep either both or neither'. He formulates the theological problem of the relationship between the Testaments by asking whether and to what extent the Old Testament can be revelation for the Christian faith, and concludes that this is possible in an indirect way. Yet it is commonly thought that Bultmann rejects the Old Testament and that part of a sentence in the same article (p.31), 'to the Christian faith the Old Testament is no longer revelation', is his view of its relationship to the New, ignoring the next few words which read: 'as it has been, and still is, for the Jews'. In spite of certain provocative and frequently misunderstood statements, Bultmann is not reviving Marcion's classical separation of the Testaments, nor has he yielded to the pressure of National Socialist antipathy to the Old Testament (cf. above:0.63). The Old Testament, though not a Christian book, is for Bultmann the presupposition of the New Testament and Christianity. It is hardly surprising that Bultmann, as a New Testament scholar, approaches the problem of the relationship between the Testaments from the perspective of the New Testament. Nevertheless, this carries the important implication that the result is a 'New Testament' solution to the problem. In the following sections Bultmann's essay mentioned above and his later essay on 'Prophecy and Fulfillment'(1949a) will be analysed in some detail.

The writings of Bultmann which most directly relate to the problem of the relationship between the Testaments are:
'The Significance of the OT for the Christian Faith' (1933), ET in OTCF;
'Christ the End of the Law'(1940), ET in Essays;
Theology of the NT I(1948);
'Prophecy and Fulfillment'(1949), ET in EOTI;
Primitive Christianity(1949);
'Ursprung und Sinn der Typologie als hermeneutischer Methode',TLZ(1950);
'The Significance of Jewish OT Tradition for the Christian West'(1950), ET in Essays;
'History and Eschatology in the NT',NTS(1954);
History and Eschatology(1957);
'Adam and Christ According to Romans 5'(1959), ET in Piper Festschrift.
A comprehensive bibliography of Bultmann's works to 1965 is given in Kegley(1966).

There is an enormous amount of critical literature on Bultmann's theology. The most important work on his view of the relationship between the Testaments is The OT and Christian Faith(OTCF, ed. B.W. Anderson 1964), which includes his 1933 essay and responses from B.W. Anderson, Cullmann, Dillenberger, McKenzie, Michalson, Richardson, J.M. Robinson, Vischer(cf.below:5.14), Voegelin, Westermann and Wright. Other studies include:

Diem, Theologie als kirchliche Wissenschaft I (1951):76-81;
Baumgärtel, Verheissung(1952):102-6;
Zimmerli, 'Promise and Fulfillment'(1952), ET in EOTI:116-120;
Kraeling, The OT Since the Reformation(1955):ch.14;
Westermann, 'Remarks on the Theses of Bultmann and Baumgärtel'(1955), ET in EOTI;
Marlé, 'Bultmann et l'AT',NRT(1956);
Malet, Mythos et Logos(1962):235-47;
Rottenberg, Redemption and Historical Reality(1964):ch.2
Barr, 'Taking the Cue from Bultmann',Interpn(1965):217-20; 'The OT and the New Crisis of Biblical Authority',Interpn(1971):30-32;
Schulte, 'The OT and its Significance for Religious Instruction' in Kegley(1966);

Young, 'Bultmann's View of the OT',SJT(1966);
Bright, The Authority of the OT(1967):69-72, 189-191, cf.177-182;
Rordorf, 'The Theology of Rudolf Bultmann and Second-Century Gnosis',NTS(1967):355-7;
Marquardt, 'Christentum und Zionismus',EvTh(1968):635-7;
Wright, The OT and Theology(1969):29-37;
Davidson, 'The OT' in Biblical Criticism(1970):157-162;
Surburg, 'The New Hermeneutic...',The Springfielder(1974).

3.12 THE SIGNIFICANCE OF THE OLD TESTAMENT FOR THE CHRISTIAN FAITH

3.121 The developmental approach

a. Bultmann points out that the developmental approach (on which, see above: 0.5) treats the Bible as a source for understanding the historical development of religion, specifically the religions of Israel and the early Church. Moreover, it regards the Old Testament as the source of Christianity, in that the 'ethical monotheism' which was perfected in Jesus originated and developed in Israel. The cultic and nationalistic elements of the Old Testament were eventually subordinated to this spiritual faith in the preaching of the prophets, and Jesus simply continued - albeit in a distinctive and unsurpassed way - their message. It follows that the relationship between the Testaments is straightforward: the only difference between the two is improvement or progression. The more sophisticated teaching in the New Testament - concerning Christology, eschatology, soteriology, etc. - is not merely unnecessary but obscures the basic message of Jesus and therefore must be rejected as mythology. (1933a:8-10)

b. The problem with this view, according to Bultmann, is that it does not fit the New Testament. Elimination of sophisticated ideas as mythology involves loss of the distinctively Christian element of the New Testament, its affirmation that God and man can meet only in the person of Jesus Christ. Moreover the basic message of Jesus cannot be used as a critical standard for eliminating mythology: it is not simply ethical teaching about the Fatherhood of God and love for others but an eschatological message which points to the dawn of the new age. Jesus' message is thus itself mythological, and is intimately connected in the New Testament with the Church's proclamation of Jesus' person. It follows that the result of the developmental approach is to remove the Christian element from Christianity, making it into a refined Judaism. (pp.10-12)

c. Bultmann refrains from forming a judgement on the developmental approach in general, however: he argues that since its concern is with the historical relationship between the religions of the two Testaments it is irrelevant to the theological problem of their relationship. A truly theological approach to the problem will ask 'whether the Old Testament still has a meaning for the faith which perceives in Jesus Christ the revelation of God'(p.12). In contrast to the objective developmental approach which does no more than analyse the relationship between historical phenomena, a subjective approach is required which will consider what is the significance of the Old Testament for the Christian faith. (pp.12-13)

3.122 <u>An existential approach</u>

a. Bultmann asks 'what basic possibility (the Old Testament) presents for an understanding of human existence (<u>Daseinsverständnis</u>)' (p.13).

This he claims is a 'genuinely historical' approach to the problem of the relationship between the Testaments because its concern is not simply to place events in the context of world history but to discover their relevance to us as human beings. (pp.13-14)

b. Such a 'genuinely historical' approach to the Old Testament leads to expression of the relationship between the Testaments in terms of law and gospel. The New Testament presupposes the Old, not in the sense of religious evolution but in the sense that it is necessary first to be under the law before it is possible to comprehend Christ as the end of the law. Moreover, even when one is no longer under the law but under grace, faith is 'a reality only by constantly overcoming the old existence under the Law'(p.15). So the law does not cease to exist for the Christian who is freed from it: only justification by the law is abolished. (pp.14-15)

c. When the Old Testament acts in this way as the presupposition of the New it loses its specifically Old Testament character. The cultic and ritual demands are now obsolete, and the moral demands - though still valid - are not unique to the Old Testament since all know the law in this general sense (Rom.1:32). (pp.15-16)

d. Further, since what is vital is that the law - rather than the Old Testament - be understood, it is not essential that the law be the Old Testament itself. Man may come to a realisation of his nothingness simply through his own relationships with others or through contemplation of some other history. The reason for using the Old Testament is expedience: its expression of the divine demand is exceptionally direct and clear. (p.17)

e. Nevertheless, although as law it is addressed to 'a particular people who stand in a particular ethnic history which is not ours' (p.17), the Old Testament confronts us with an understanding of existence that is relevant to us. This understanding of existence shows man to be subject to the unconditional moral demand of God, which is neither idealistic nor utilitarian but existential. Man is a creature living in history who is called not to a timeless ideal but to temporal and historical behaviour in obedience to God. (pp.17-20)

f. This Old Testament understanding of existence is also that of the New Testament and Christianity, in contrast to the 'humanistic or idealistic understanding of existence'[1] which characterises Greek thought. Since modern Western history has both Greek and biblical roots, the Old Testament is an important part of that history and a proper understanding of human existence today depends on serious interaction with the Old Testament. In particular, to understand the contemporary significance of Christianity the Old Testament is essential.

'If a person holds that historical reflection is necessary for gaining a clear view of himself and his contemporary world, and if he has done even a minimum of such reflection, it would be senseless for him to hold on to Christianity and at the same time discard the Old Testament .... It is either - or: keep either both or neither' (p.21).

3.123 The Old Testament as revelation

a. On an existential interpretation alone there would be no difference between the two Testaments, since both have the same understanding of existence.

---

1. Translation correction (p.20: line 10 from bottom; German: p.324).

A further question must therefore be considered: in what sense, if at all, is it right to treat the Old Testament as revelation for the Christian faith? To hear the Old Testament as Word of God is quite a different matter from the recognition that it is existentially part of Christian history. (pp.21-35)

b. In order to answer this question it is necessary first to define more precisely the relationship between law and gospel in the Old Testament. Existence under the law in the Old Testament is in the first place existence under grace since it is by grace - in election and covenant - that God called his people into being and by grace - in forgiveness and faithfulness - that God keeps sinful and unfaithful Israel as his people. If 'gospel' is understood as 'the proclamation of God's grace for the sinner' it is certainly known in the Old Testament, even if not always in an equally radical way (Pss.51; 90:7-8; 130; cf. 103: 14-16). And the divine demand in the Old Testament requires first of all not moral behaviour but trust in God's grace, that is faith (Ps.147:10-11; Jer.9:23-4; Isa.45:23-5; 30:15; 7:9; 28:16). (pp.22-7)

c. It follows that Israel's sin is unbelief, the radical nature of which is perceived by the prophets: the people deserve nothing but judgement from God. Yet in this situation eschatological hope is born, as sin and judgement release the possibility of forgiveness and salvation by God's grace (Ezek.36:22-7; 37:1-14; Jer.31:33-4). 'So far as Israel conceived the idea of God radically by grasping the ideas of sin and grace radically, the faith of the Old Testament is hope'(p.28). In other words, although they are aware of its radical nature, the prophets experience the gospel of grace only partially: the fulfilment is yet to come. That fulfilment is in fact the distinctive element of the New Testament as compared with the Old. (pp.27-9)

d. Thus the difference between the Testaments becomes clear: in Jesus Christ God has inaugurated the new age. What God has done in Jesus is not an historical event in the same sense as the events which constituted Israel as a people and benefit succeeding generations of that people. God's eschatological act in Christ has shifted the locus of divine revelation from ethnic history to personal existence. So the Christian does not look to past history for God's grace but meets it existentially in the Word proclaimed to him. In contrast to Israel, whose existence depends on its history, the Church is a community bound together by the message which it exists to proclaim. (pp.29-31)

e. The answer to the question of whether the Old Testament may be considered revelation for the Christian faith now begins to emerge. Since Israel and the Church are fundamentally different entities, Old Testament history is not Christian history. Grace in the Old Testament is specifically directed to Israel, whereas the law is an expression of God's universal moral demand on men, according to Bultmann. Therefore the Old Testament, although in itself both gospel and law, is for the Christian only law. It follows that Old Testament history is not revelation for Christians in the same way as for Jews. (pp.31-2)

f. This does not necessarily mean that the Old Testament itself, apart from its history, cannot be revelation for the Christian faith. The possibility remains open that the Christian faith should claim the Old Testament as God's Word to Christians, as an expression of what is made fully clear only in Christ. This is the approach of the New Testament and the early Church, by whom the Old Testament is interpreted eschatologically, as written for Christians and in Christ receiving its true meaning. However such 'scriptural proof' is not only inconsistent with the original meaning of the Old Testament but in any case fails to convince and cannot produce genuine faith. Moreover, this approach results in finding once more what is already known in Christ, and thus effectively denies that the Old Testament is God's Word in the true sense. (pp.32-3)

g. So the Old Testament is not revelation for Christians in the historical sense as it is for the Jews, nor in the direct eschatological sense as it is treated in the New Testament. The question still remains, however, whether there is any legitimate sense in which the Old Testament may be understood as Word of God by those who have read the New Testament. Bultmann assumes that Jesus Christ is God's Word to man, and argues that any other words which elucidate this Word are therefore indirectly (*in vermittelter Weise*) God's Word. The Old Testament contains an understanding of human existence which is normative for Christian life: man's creatureliness and sin as revealed by the law and God's grace as expressed in the gospel. Faith takes hold of the Old Testament, sees in it an image of its own existence, and claims it as God's Word. In this indirect sense the Old Testament may be considered revelation for the Christian faith. If this is done, two conditions apply: the Old Testament must be used literally - though without its original reference to Israel - and only to the extent that it really prepares for the Christian understanding of existence. (pp.33-5)

3.13 PROPHECY AND FULFILMENT

3.131 Prediction

a. The early Church understood prophecy as prediction, the foretelling of future events, and fulfilment as the occurrence of what was foretold (1949a:50-55). In the New Testament there are two aspects to this. First, the Old Testament contains Messianic prophecies, which are concerned with the eschaton that has become the present for the Church. Secondly, the Old Testament as a whole is a book of prophecy, all of its words pointing to Christ. Thus the New Testament combines the eschatological tradition of the Old Testament with the allegorical tradition of Hellistic culture.

b. Such a view of prophecy and fulfilment, Bultmann argues, is impossible today. The New Testament approach may be followed when it treats Old Testament prophecies as eschatological promises of salvation, but not when it ignores the original meaning of the biblical text. Often the New Testament writers read a Christian meaning into Old Testament texts, so that prophecy is only recognised retrospectively, after the fulfilment has occurred. No doubt this method was valuable in the apologetic of the early Church, but it has several shortcomings. It is theologically untenable, because doctrines and difficulties are not to be overcome by pointing out that they were prophesied in the Old Testament but by understanding their real significance. It is arbitrary, since the interpretation is not exegesis but eisegesis. It is unnecessary, since the texts are made to affirm Christian truths, which are known already. Moreover, in spite of its superficial value in defending the Christian faith, this method really has the effect of concealing the true stumbling-block of faith and the proper way to deal with it.

3.132 History

a. In the nineteenth century J.C.K.Hofmann advanced a view of prophecy as history: the history of Israel is prophetic history which finds its fulfilment in Christ and the Church (pp.55-8). Thus prophecy is not the foretelling of future historical events but the movement of history towards a goal. Each word and event of the Old Testament is understood in its plain historical meaning, and has prophetic significance only by virtue of its place in the prophetic history. The goal of history is Christ, and so history is a prophecy of Christ.

b. Hofmann's view, according to Bultmann, is essentially a theologically irrelevant philosophy of history. It cannot prove Christ, since Christ must be recognised as the goal of history before this view becomes possible, and in any case the real significance of Christ cannot be confirmed by a philosophical view but only by faith. The attempt to understand prophecy as history is a move in the right direction, but 'according to the New Testament, Christ is the end of salvation history ... not in the sense that he signifies the goal of historical development, but because he is its eschatological end' (p.58).

3.133 Covenant, kingdom and people of God

a. Dissatisfied with the ideas of prediction and history, Bultmann works out a conception of prophecy that relates to Christ as the eschatological end of salvation history. His method is to examine three Old Testament concepts which are eschatologically re-interpreted in the New Testament (pp.59-72).

b. God's covenant with his people is based on mutual loyalty, originated by God's election and maintained by the people's obedience, according to Bultmann. In popular thought this obedience is conceived primarily as cultic worship, a condition which can realistically be fulfilled by a people as such. If it was conceived in moral terms obedience could relate only to the individual within the people and the covenant would no longer be a relationship between God and the people as an entity. The natural consequence of this popular belief is to root the security of an individual not in his own moral behaviour but in his membership in the chosen people.

It became clear to the Old Testament prophets, as to John and Jesus, that there was a problem. They objected to assumptions that God was linked to the land and that the covenant was unbreakable. They were convinced of the necessity for a moral aspect to the covenant, though this meant that it could no longer be the relationship between God and an empirical people. 'God's covenant with a people whose individuals suffice for the moral demands of God as members of the people is an eschatological concept, because such a people is not a real empirical and historical, but an eschatological, dimension' (p.61). So the New Testament re-interprets eschatologically the Old Testament idea of covenant, affirming that the promises of Jeremiah (31:31-4) and Ezekiel (37:26-8) have been fulfilled in the Church. The Church is not an empirical and historical people: although it is inaugurated by the death of Christ and membership is linked with the sacraments, these do not have the same historical significance as the Sinai event and the cult of the Old Testament had for Israel.

The New Testament counterpart to the Old Testament covenant institutions is not to be found in any material observance but in the spiritual institution of salvation. 'The new covenant is a radically eschatological dimension, that is, a dimension outside the world, and to belong to it takes its members out of the world' (p.63).

c. Bultmann points out that it was common among Semitic peoples to represent their gods as kings, and Israel was no exception. The kingdom of God, a tenet of Israelite faith from pre-Exilic times, was celebrated every New Year in an enthronement festival. Its implications were that Yahweh expected obedience from his people, acted as their judge, and helped them in war.

The end of the monarchy and God's abandonment of his people to Babylon was naturally a crisis for the belief in the kingdom of God. In the event, however, the belief was not discarded but was made into an eschatological concept. Both during and after the Exile it was obvious that God's kingdom had not yet been established in the world, and so prophets projected their hopes further into the future while apocalyptists looked beyond the present age to a supernatural age of salvation. Jesus took up this eschatological view of the kingdom of God, 'no longer understood in the sense of Old Testament theocracy, as the dominion of the divine king in the liberated land ... but as the wonder of a new era for the world breaking in from heaven'(p.66). For Jesus and Paul the kingdom of God was a present reality, the new age was realised in the formation of the Church.

'The rule of God and so of Christ is therefore something completely different from what Old Testament prophecy had expected. It is eschatological and supramundane in its entirety; and the man who has a part in it is, as it were, already taken out of the world, so that he lives no longer "according to the flesh," however much he still lives "in the flesh"(2 Cor.10:3)' (p.67).

d. In the Old Testament, Bultmann argues, the concept of the people of God is shown to be in conflict with that of a national state. Gideon recognised the impossibility of serving more than one ruler (Judg.8:23), and the monarchy, although only temporarily opposed by the prophets, was subject to continual prophetic criticism for neglecting its responsibility to God as the true monarch. So theocracy was an ideal rather than a reality during much of the Old Testament period. Even after the Exile, when Israel might be described as a theocracy, this was possible only because it had forfeited its existence as a state and become a religious community. This community, limited to Jews and bound together by its cult, was scarcely the realisation of the people of God.

A new conception of the people of God was introduced by the New Testament claim that in Christ the new age has arrived. Now the Church has become the people of God, the true Israel, not an 'empirical historical entity' but an 'eschatological unit'. Membership of the people is no longer through birth but through individual calling and setting apart by God. So the idea of the people of God, like the ideas of the covenant and the kingdom of God, becomes in the New Testament an eschatological idea which is realised in Christ and his Church.

3.134 Miscarriage and promise

a. In the light of his study of these three concepts, Bultmann develops a view of prophecy as miscarriage and promise (pp.72-5). He argues that Old Testament Jewish history 'is fulfilled in its inner contradiction, its miscarriage (Scheitern). An inner contradiction pervades the self-consciousness and the hope of Israel and its prophets' (p.72). The miscarriage of history shows the impossibility of realising the covenant, kingdom of God and people of God within the historical community of Israel. In so doing, however, the miscarriage becomes a promise since God's grace is available only to those who recognise the complete impossibility of their situation. Thus the fulfilment is not the result of historical development, which is miscarriage, but the result of encounter with the grace of God, which is an eschatological new creation.

b. Such an interpretation of Old Testament history, Bultmann claims, follows from Paul's view of the law as a false way of salvation, which must however be known in order to understand faith as the true way (cf. Gal.3:22-4; Rom.10:4; 11:32).

'Faith requires the backward glance into Old Testament history as a history of failure, and so of promise, in order to know that the situation of the justified man arises only on the basis of this miscarriage. Thus faith, to be a really justifying faith, must constantly contain within itself the attempt to identify what happens in the secular sphere with what happens eschatologically, as something which has been overcome' (p.75).

3.2 CRITICISM: EXISTENCE AND CONTRAST

3.21 SECONDARY QUESTIONS

3.211 Myth

Bultmann rejects the liberal method of eliminating as mythology ideas inconsistent with the 'simple' prophetic message of Jesus (1933a:9-11). His own solution to the problem of myth in the Bible is developed in a programmatic essay on 'New Testament and Mythology' (1941) which provoked many volumes of debate when reprinted after the War in Kerygma and Myth. He advocates extensive demythologisation of the biblical message, retaining the essential existential meaning without the mythical framework in which it is presented. Such an approach is certainly more satisfactory than that of the liberals since it makes a serious attempt to understand and communicate the meaning of biblical theology.
As Cullmann (1964) points out, however, Bultmann's method really has the effect of dehistoricising rather than demythologising: myths in the Bible are incorporated into the history of salvation and can be properly understood not as independent existential units but only within that biblical context.

The many essays in the six German volumes of Kerygma and Myth (1948-63), some of which are translated in the two English volumes (1953,1962), are central to the debate about myth and biblical theology. A later essay by Bultmann, 'On the Problem of Demythologizing' (1961), is now readily accessible in Batey (1970).

See also:
G.E. Wright, God Who Acts (1952):116-128;
Hempel, 'Glaube, Mythos und Geschichte im AT', ZAW (1953);

van Ruler, The Christian Church and the OT(1955): 81-2/87;
Davies, 'An Approach to the Problem of OT Mythology', PEQ(1956);
Hughes, Scripture and Myth(1956);
J.S. Wright, 'The Place of Myth in the Interpretation of the Bible', JTVI(1956);
Malevez, The Christian Message and Myth(1958);
Barr, 'The Meaning of "Mythology" in Relation to the OT', VT(1959);
McKenzie, 'Myth and the OT', CBQ(1959);
Throckmorton, The NT and Mythology(1959);
Childs, Myth and Reality in the OT(1960);
Cox, History and Myth(1961);
Malet, Mythos et Logos(1962):43-57;
Good, 'The Meaning of Demythologization' in Kegley(1966);
Schmithals, An Introduction to the Theology of Rudolf Bultmann(1966):ch.11;
B.W. Anderson, 'Myth and the Biblical Tradition', ThTo(1970);
Johnstone, 'The Mythologising of History in the OT', SJT(1971);
Pinnock, 'Theology and Myth', BS(1971);
Fawcett, Hebrew Myth and Christian Gospel(1973).
Cf. also Lipinski, Essais(1970):12-14.

3.212 Prophecy

According to Bultmann (1949a), prophecy is to be understood neither as prediction - in the manner of the New Testament - nor as history - following Hofmann - but as the promise which arises from the miscarriage of Old Testament history. Now in spite of Barr's reminder about the predictive content of prophecy (1966:118-126), modern scholarship has clearly shown that there is more to prophecy than foretelling the future; and that Hofmann's view of prophecy as history is not absolutely valid is shown in chapter seven below. Nevertheless, leaving aside for the present the question of the validity of his view of the Old Testament, Bultmann's concept of 'prophecy' is not only no better than the two he rejects but scarcely related to biblical prophecy at all. It would surely have been much better to explicitly reject or ignore the idea of prophecy than to confuse the issue by using biblical terminology in a sense quite different from that of the Bible.

3.213 Concepts

An important aspect of Bultmann's work, as of the work of Baumgärtel (cf. below:ch.4), is the exegesis of concepts which embrace both Old and New Testaments (1949a:59-72; cf. Westermann 1955: 125-6). His study of the covenant, kingdom of God and people of God, although it may well be questioned in detail, is representative of an important modern trend in biblical theology. There has been an increasing awareness in recent years of the importance of studying theological concepts in their entire biblical context, as is shown by the tendency in later volumes of Kittel's _Theological Dictionary_ (1933-73) to study not only the words of biblical Greek but also the concepts which they convey, and by the concentration in biblical theology on detailed study of individual themes rather than comprehensive treatments of Old or New Testament theology.

See, for example:
Fosdick, _A Guide to Understanding the Bible: The Development of Ideas within the Old and NTs_(1938);
Snaith, _The Distinctive Ideas of the OT_(1944);
Bright, _The Kingdom of God: The Biblical Concept and Its Meaning for the Church_(1953);
Ottaviani Festschrift: _Populus Dei_(1966);
Bruce, _This is That: The NT Development of Some OT Themes_(1968);
Hillers, _Covenant: The History of a Biblical Idea_(1969);
Barr, 'Themes from the OT for the Elucidation of the New Creation', _Encounter_(1970).

Also, in Christian theology: Aulén, _Christus Victor_ (1930) and Nygren, _Agape and Eros_(1930-36).

Cf. Ramlot, 'Une décade de théologie biblique', _RThom_(1965):120-135.

3.22 EXISTENCE

a. G. Ernest Wright (1969) categorises Bultmann's approach to the relationship between the Testaments as 'existentialist Christomonism'. Thus for Bultmann the concept of existence is 'the methodological starting point of theology' (1930:92) and the central distinctive characteristic of the New Testament is the idea that 'man's relation to God is bound to the person of Jesus' (1933a:11). Of the various influences on his theology existential philosophy is undoubtedly one of the most pervasive, so it is not surprising that Bultmann frames the problem of the relationship betweeen the Testaments in terms of the possibilities for man's existence which they express.

b. There is of course no inherent objection to an existential investigation of the problem, and in Bultmann's hands the process is not without profit. He shows effectively, for example, something of the historical value of the Old Testament for modern Christendom (1933a:20-21; cf.1950c). Also, by means of the concept of 'presupposition' or 'pre-understanding' he illuminates the way in which the Old Testament embodies the divine moral demand and thus functions as preparation for the New (1933a: 15-17).

c. A fundamental limitation of the existential method, however, is its own self-limiting nature. By definition its concern is with human existence and therefore only indirectly with God. Bultmann's existential interpretation of Pauline theology, for instance, is concerned 'with God not as He is in Himself but only with God as He is significant for man', so that 'Paul's theology can best be treated as his doctrine of man' (1948a:191). It follows that existential interpretation of the Bible, however illuminating, will be inadequate to the extent that the Bible is concerned not only with man - and man's experience of God - but with God, who in the beginning created the universe (Gen.1:1) and in the end will be all in all (1 Cor. 15:28). Moreover, if the Christ-event is relevant only to the existence of the individual, as Bultmann claims, it is not the fulfilment of the promise of the Old Testament which embraced not only the individual but the people of God and the world (Westermann 1964).

d. In any case, as Bultmann (1933a:20) himself recognises, the result of an existential investigation of the problem of the relationship between the Testaments is merely to show that both have the same understanding of human existence. To determine the difference between the two it is necessary to formulate the problem in a specifically theological way: 'what is meant by saying that the Old Testament is revelation, and to what extent, if any, can the Christian proclamation really be related to the Old Testament understood as God's revelation?' (1933a:21)

Further references:
Macquarrie, An Existentialist Theology(1955);
Keller, '"Existentielle" und "heilsgeschichtliche" Deutung der Schöpfungsgeschichte',ThZ(1956);
Wolff, 'Das AT und das Problem der existentialen Interpretation',EvTh(1963);
Dreyfus, 'The Existential Value of the OT',Concilium (1967);
Young, History and Existential Theology(1969).

3.23 HISTORY

a. The nature and significance of history is one of the most fundamental issues raised by Bultmann's work (see esp. 1954, 1957a). It is not only impossible but also unnecessary to go into this in detail here, and just two points must be mentioned. First, Bultmann recognises that there is an historical (historisch) relationship between the Testaments (1949b:15-56; cf. 1933a:8; 1948a:108-121): the Old Testament is an historical document which in many ways has influenced the formation of the New Testament. Secondly, Bultmann argues that it is more profitable to consider the relationship between the Testaments as a 'genuinely historical' (echt geschichtlich) problem (1933a:13-15):

'A genuinely historical inquiry of the Old Testament is one which, prompted by one's own question concerning existence, seeks to reactualize the understanding of human existence expressed in the Old Testament, in order to gain an understanding of his own existence. ...Thus the Old Testament is the presupposition of the New. Not in the sense of a historical (historisch) view, as though the historical phenomenon of the Christian religion had become possible only on the basis of the evolving history of religion attested by the Old Testament; but rather in the material (sachlich) sense that man must stand under the Old Testament if he wants to understand the New.'

b. This is superficially convincing, but Bultmann, while emphasising the existential significance of the past, fails to grasp adequately another aim of serious historical study, namely to find out what actually happened at a particular point in time and space (cf. Wright 1964). As Voegelin (1964) points out, the implications of this method are rejection of the world and history, features which characterise Gnosticism (though cf. Rordorf 1967:355). The fault in Bultmann's approach is not to be found in what he says - which is generally unexceptionable - but in his omission from his system of the concept of reality. An important factor in both Old and New Testaments is that God acts in real history to bring about salvation (cf. Richardson 1964a).

Dodd, *History and the Gospel*(1938);
Cullmann, *Christ and Time*(1946);
Butterfield, *Christianity and History*(1949);
Eliade, *The Myth of the Eternal Return*(1949);
Löwith, *Meaning in History*(1949);
Niebuhr, *Faith and History*(1949);
von Balthasar, *A Theology of History*(1950);
Ebeling, 'Die Bedeutung der historisch-kritischen Methode',*ZTK*(1950); cf. Reisner 1952; Fuchs 1954b;
Filson, 'Method in Studying Biblical History', *JBL*(1950);
Marsh, 'History and Interpretation' in Richardson and Schweitzer(1951);
Daniélou, *The Lord of History*(1953);
Gogarten, 'Theology and History'(1953),ET in *JTC* 4;
Dentan(ed.), *The Idea of History in the Ancient Near East*(1955);
Ott, *Geschichte und Heilsgeschichte in der Theologie Rudolf Bultmanns*(1955); cf. Lieb 1955;
Westermann, 'The Interpretation of the OT'(1955), ET in *EOTI*;
Frost, 'History and the Bible',*CJT*(1957);
Gese, 'The Idea of History'(1958),ET in *JTC* 1;
Hesse, 'Die Erforschung der Geschichte Israels', *KuD*(1958);
Rylaarsdam, 'The Problem of Faith and History',*JBL*(1958)
Wolff, 'The Understanding of History in the OT Prophets'(1960), ET in *EOTI*;
Rendtorff, 'Hermeneutik des ATs',*ZTK*(1960); 'Geschichte und Überlieferung' in von Rad Festschrift (1961); 'Beobachtungen zur altisraelitischen Geschichtsschreibung' in von Rad Festschrift(1971);
Guthrie, *God and History in the OT*(1961);
Simpson, 'An Inquiry into the Biblical Theology of History',*JTS*(1961);
Malet, *Mythos et Logos*(1962):58-75;
Moltmann, 'Exegesis and the Eschatology of History' (1962),ET in *Hope and Planning*; *Theology of Hope*(1964);
Crespy, 'Une théologie de l'histoire est-elle possible?',*RThPh*(1963);
Rust, *Towards a Theological Understanding of History*(196
Albright, *History, Archaeology and Christian Humanism*(1964):272-84;

Hempel, _Geschichten und Geschichte im AT_(1964; cf. Schwarzwäller 1966c);
Richardson, _History Sacred and Profane_(1964; includes full bibliography);
Rottenberg, _Redemption and Historical Reality_(1964);
Soggin, 'Geschichte, Historie und Heilsgeschichte im AT', _TLZ_(1964);
J.M. Robinson, 'The Historicality of Biblical Language',
Voegelin, 'History and Gnosis', and
Wright, 'History and Reality' in _OTCF_(1964);
Casserley, _Toward a Theology of History_(1965);
Fuller, _Easter Faith and History_(1965); 'The Fundamental Presuppositions of the Historical Method, _ThZ_(1968);
Hoffmann, 'Kerygma and History', _JBR_(1965);
Heimann, _Theologie der Geschichte_(1966);
Ladd, 'History and Theology', _Interpn_(1966);
Ott, 'Rudolf Bultmann's Philosophy of History' in Kegley (1966);
Albrektson, _History and the Gods_(1967);
Freedman, 'The Biblical Idea of History', _Interpn_(1967);
Kraus, _Die Biblische Theologie_(1970):348-66;
Hasel, 'The Problem of History in OT Theology', _AUSS_(1970); _OT Theology_(1972):ch.2;
Johnstone, 'The Mythologising of History in the OT', _SJT_(1971);
Kraus, 'Geschichte als Erziehung' and
Westermann, 'Zum Geschichtsverständnis des ATs' in von Rad Festschrift (1971);
Goldingay, '...A study in the relationship between theology and historical truth in the OT', _TynB_(1972);
Porteous, 'OT and History', _ASTI_(1972);
Weippert, 'Fragen der israelitischen Geschichtsbewusstseins', _VT_(1973).

On the question of 'history' see especially von Rad and Pannenberg (below:ch.7); also van Ruler (above:1.141,1.151e). A bibliography of nearly one thousand items is given by North, _HT_(1973).

3.24 LAW AND GOSPEL

a. One of the classic expressions of the relationship between the Testaments is Luther's antithesis: law/gospel (cf. above:0.432). Bultmann gives his provisional approval to this, attributing its truth to the fact that the Reformation period still had 'a genuinely historical relation to the Old Testament' (1933a:14). He argues that on this basis existence under the law is the presupposition of existence under grace. Thus the Old Testament is the presupposition or 'pre-understanding' (Vorverständnis) of the New Testament, since the gospel can be understood only by one who is under the divine law, which is expressed with incomparable clarity in the Old Testament. The message of the gospel is that Christ, the end of the law, gives freedom from the law and opens up a new way to holiness by means of grace (1940).

b. It is important at this stage to remember that Bultmann is going against virtually all modern thought on the relationship between the Testaments. Siegwalt (1971), for instance, has shown that both Testaments essentially consider the law to be the consequence rather than the presupposition of the covenant. It is therefore more appropriate to treat 'gospel and law' (cf. Barth 1935; Dodd 1951a) as complementary than 'law and gospel' as antithetical.

c. Bultmann is aware of this objection to his thesis and attempts to forestall it by showing that the Old Testament contains the idea of grace as well as that of law, so that from its own point of view the Old Testament may be considered to be both law and gospel (1933a:22-31). Moreover he appears to admit the priority of grace over law in the Old Testament when he writes: 'the people are not constituted as a people by first obeying the Law but, rather, God's grace precedes, so that obedience is always to occur through faith in God's prevenient and electing grace' (1933a:23). This however is neither a contradiction of Bultmann's acceptance of the law/gospel antithesis nor a real assent to modern scholarship, since he goes on to argue that grace in the Old Testament is different from grace in the New Testament. In the first case grace is bound to the history of Israel, in the second it is eschatological, God's act in Jesus Christ having ended his gracious activity in the people of Israel. Thus from the Christian point of view the Old Testament is no longer gospel but only law (1933a:29-31).

On 'pre-understanding' see Bultmann, 'The Problem of "Natural Theology"'(1933), ET in Faith and Understanding:315-18; 'Is Exegesis without Presuppositions Possible?'(1957), ET in Existence and Faith; cf. Ott 1955:60-68; Michalson 1964; Voegelin 1964:67-9.

See also, on law and gospel,
Barth, 'Gospel and Law'(1935),ET in God,Grace and Gospel;
Schlink, Gesetz und Evangelium(1937); The Coming Christ and the Coming Church(1961):144-185;
van Ruler, De vervulling van de wet(1947);
Bornkamm, Luther and the OT(1948):ch.4.4;
Bring, 'Autorité et rôle actuels de la Bible',ETR(1948);
Thielicke, 'Law and Gospel as Constant Partners'(1948), ET in Theological Ethics I;
Dodd, Gospel and Law(1951);
Gollwitzer, 'Zur Einheit von Gesetz und Evangelium',
Wingren, 'Evangelium und Gesetz', and
Schlink, 'Gesetz und Paraklese' in Barth Festschrift (1956);
Eichrodt, 'The Law and the Gospel',Interpn(1957);
Berge, Gesetz und Evangelium(1958);
Wingren, Creation and Law(1958): 123-135;
von Rad, OT Theology II(1960):388-409;
Knight, Law and Grace(1962);
Matthias, 'Der anthropologische Sinn der Formel Gesetz und Evangelium',EvTh(1962);
G. Noth, 'Das Evangelium im AT',ZdZ(1966);
P. Brunner, 'Gesetz und Evangelium' in Schmaus Festschrift(1967);
Huffmon, 'The Israel of God',Interpn(1969);
Siegwalt, La Loi, chemin du Salut(1971);
Zimmerli, Die Weltlichkeit des ATes(1971):ch.11;
McCarthy, OT Covenant(1972):53-6;
Lawton, 'Christ: The End of the Law',TrJ(1974).

Cf. also Hirsch, see below:4.21.

3.25 MISCARRIAGE AND PROMISE

a. Possibly the most original, important and controversial aspect of Bultmann's solution to the problem of the relationship between the Testaments is his conception of prophecy as miscarriage and promise (1949a:72-5; see above:3.134). He argues that Old Testament history contains an inner contradiction between the ideal of the people of God and the reality of the empirical community; and that the failure to resolve this contradiction results in the miscarriage of history. Paradoxically however this miscarriage amounts to a promise, since it proves the impossibility of man's way and directs man to the grace of God, which alone can deal with the situation.

b. This idea is indeed not entirely original. Apart from Marcionite and neo-Marcionite rejection of the Old Testament, attention may be drawn to the remark of McFadyen (1903:347; cf. above: 0.56e), that the Old Testament 'by its repeated failures pointed men to something more strong and saving than itself'. More recently Phythian-Adams (1934) has argued that Christianity is 'the triumphant sequel' of Judaism, in which 'the tragedy of the Old Covenant is transfigured in the glory of the New'(p.5). Nevertheless Bultmann's thesis is distinctive in its radical assertion of contradiction and miscarriage and demands a serious response. Such a response is provided by Miskotte (1956a:167):

> 'The consequences of this conception are enormous and disastrous. For this means that not only is the meaning of the Old Testament history found solely in profound meaninglessness, but also that no meaningful history can be ascribed to the New Testament community; the new beginning, inaugurated

by Christ, is in no sense the beginning of a real historical development ... The inevitable result of this is a failure to appreciate the Law, a withdrawal from history, a depreciation of the world, a negation of creation, a deafness to the typical Old Testament affirmation of a god-given life. And 'desecularization' (Entweltlichung) becomes the key word, the deepest mystery, the fulfilment of human existence.'

c. Perhaps it should be said that Bultmann does not take history seriously and therefore his view of Old Testament history as a history of failure should not be taken seriously either. Since existential method involves depreciation of history it cannot be expected to deal adequately with the Old Testament, which is essentially an historical document. The conclusion must be drawn that Bultmann's thesis, perceptive and illuminating as it is, does not fit the Bible (cf. Zimmerli 1952: 117-120; Marquardt 1968:636).

3.26 PEOPLE OF GOD

a. An important element of Bultmann's thesis which must be questioned is his view of the people of God. In the Old Testament, on the one hand, he says that 'God's forgiveness is inextricably tied up with the destiny of the people' and 'so far as man belongs to this people, he can take comfort in the grace of God' (1933a:29; cf. 1957a:21-2). In the New Testament, on the other hand, 'the message of the forgiving grace of God in Jesus Christ is not a historical account about a past event, but ... addresses each person immediately as God's Word' (1933a:30; cf. 1957a:31-2). The Church is therefore 'not a sociological entity, an ethnic or cultural community bound together by the continuity of history; but is constituted by the proclaimed

Word of God's forgiveness in Christ and is the community of this proclamation' (pp.30-31). So Bultmann concludes that the Church has no history as ethnic, national, and cultural communities have their history' (p.31; cf. 1949a:62). His view is rather similar to that of the Jewish scholar Martin Buber (1951), who contrasts two types of faith: in early Israel faith (_emunah_) is trust in someone, and is an attribute of a nation; in early Christianity faith (_pistis_) is acknowledgement of the truth of something and is an attribute of individuals (for a criticism of this simplistic view, see Vriezen 1954/66:100n./123n.).

b. On some issues it is impossible to give a clear 'yes' or 'no' in response to Bultmann's proposals, but here there can be no doubt that a negative answer is required. In the Old Testament salvation was not automatic through membership of the people: it was this very presumption that was one of Israel's greatest failings. On the contrary, salvation was given to Israelites only on the condition of obedience (Deut.30:15-20), and to non-Israelites the possibility was open of joining Israel and thus finding God and salvation (Ruth; Isa.56:3-8). In the New Testament, moreover, salvation is tied to the Church in the sense that it is offered only to those who identify themselves with Christ in this particular way, though again it is not automatic but dependent on a personal relationship with God (Acts 2:37-47; Eph.2:11-22). The Church is indeed brought together by its message and exists to proclaim it, but it is not thereby prevented from being an historical and cultural community, a 'sociological entity'. Although history does not have the same significance in a spiritual community as in an ethnic one, the Church nevertheless has a history, and believes God to be at work in that history.

c. Bultmann (1949a) also claims that the covenant, kingdom of God and people of God are ideals that were shown to be unrealisable in Israel as an historical entity. However, although it is true that the reality fell far short of the ideal, it does not necessarily follow that the ideal was unrealisable. On the contrary, the people who entered into covenant with Yahweh at Sinai were given perfectly realistic moral and cultic obligations to keep as an expression of their loyalty. They broke the covenant not because they could not keep these obligations - in which case they would scarcely have been considered guilty - but because they would not keep them. So also the kingdom of God was not an unrealisable ideal: the problem was not that Israel could not be a theocracy but that she refused to be one and demanded a human king to rule her like the other nations.

d. One consequence of Bultmann's contrast between Old Testament Israel and the New Testament Church is his first condition for Christian use of the Old Testament as God's word, 'that the Old Testament is used in its original sense, although without its original reference to the Israelite people and their history...' (1933a:34). So Bultmann himself reveals an inner contradiction in his thesis: he insists on historico-critical principles of interpretation, so that the Old Testament is understood in 'its original sense'; and yet in order to fit his theory of a radical contrast between Israel and the Church he has to exclude the most fundamental aspect of that original sense, its reference to Israel and its history.

On 'people of God' see:
Dahl, Das Volk Gottes(1941) and 'The People of God',ER(1956);
Davidson, 'The OT Preparation for the NT Doctrine of the Church',RExp(1941);
Hebert, 'The Church in the Bible' in Jalland(1948);
Watts, 'The People of God',ExpT(1956);
Kraus, The People of God in the OT(1958);
Ottaviani Festschrift: Populus Dei(1966);
Cazelles, 'The Unity of the Bible and the People of God',Scripture(1966);
Bruce, This is That(1968):ch.5;
Ehrhardt, 'A Biblical View of the People of God', AER(1968);
Jannssen, Das Gottesvolk und seine Geschichte(1971).

On Israel and the Church, see above: 1.214.

3.27 A RELATIONSHIP OF CONTRAST

a. The diverse ideas about the relationship between the Testaments in Bultmann's work are not easy to bring together into a clear statement, and perhaps that is not entirely unintentional. Nevertheless, a central idea which may be drawn from his suggestions is that the New Testament in the essential Bible, the Old Testament its non-Christian presupposition. Other important aspects include his use of the law/gospel antithesis, his view of Old Testament history as miscarriage - and thereby promise - and his contrast between Israel and the Church. The dominant characteristic of Bultmann's solution to the theological problem of the relationship between the Testaments is therefore 'contrast': he assumes that the New Testament is the real Bible and categorises the Old Testament as theologically secondary, obsolete and non-Christian. Whereas for van Ruler the Old Testament has theological priority over the New Testament, for Bultmann the Old stands in radical contrast to the New.

b. It would be foolish to dismiss the work of so important a theologian as Bultmann too quickly. To accuse him of Marcionism (e.g. Surburg 1974), for example, is neither just nor effective. It is unjust since, in spite of certain similarities between his thought and that classic heresy, Bultmann neither claims to nor in fact does follow Marcionism's separation of the god of the Old Testament from the God of the New; moreover, unlike Marcion, Bultmann is happy to retain the Old Testament in the Church as an historical document and even with certain qualifications as the indirect Word of God (cf. Marlé 1956:482; Michalson 1964). The accusation of Marcionism is ineffective since, as Barr (1965; cf. 1966:183) has pointed out, it simply stereotypes the problem without really clarifying it, and in any case people today are not so afraid of heresy as in the days when it meant the loss of one's job or one's head.

c. The perceptiveness with which Bultmann has analysed certain aspects of the problem is not to be despised and his work contains valuable insights into biblical theology. Nevertheless, a number of fundamental objections to his solution have been indicated, in particular that he bases it on a depreciation of history and that, in his conceptions of law/gospel, miscarriage and the people of God, he misunderstands the Old Testament. At this stage however it is appropriate to consider some other New Testament solutions to the problem.

4. <u>The New Testament shows the Old Testament to be a witness to the promise in Christ</u>

4.1 FRIEDRICH BAUMGÄRTEL: THE EVANGELICAL UNDERSTANDING OF THE OLD TESTAMENT

4.2 COMPARISON: OTHER 'NEW TESTAMENT' SOLUTIONS

4.1 FRIEDRICH BAUMGÄRTEL: THE EVANGELICAL UNDERSTANDING OF THE OLD TESTAMENT

4.11 INTRODUCTION

a. It has been shown in the preceding chapter that Bultmann assesses the Old Testament negatively - or at least not very positively - as the non-Christian presupposition of the New Testament, which records a history of miscarriage and is to be contrasted with the New Testament by means of the Lutheran law/gospel antithesis. Baumgärtel's solution to the problem of the relationship between the Testaments has certain similarities to that of Bultmann, especially in its assumptions that the Old Testament is to be understood through the spectacles of the New and that there is an essential discontinuity between the two. Like Bultmann, he interprets the Old Testament as promise, but this is more positive and more central to his solution that to that of Bultmann, for whom the idea of promise is only an attempt to salvage something good from a history which failed (cf. above: esp.3.25).

b. Baumgärtel's major work on the relationship between the Testaments is entitled <u>Verheissung: Zur Frage des evangelischen Verständnisses des Alten Testaments</u> (1952). In a preliminary remark (p.7) he sets out the basis of his thesis, which includes three main elements. First, the Christian faith is founded on God's 'promise in Christ' (ἐπαγγελία ἐν Χριστῷ, Eph.3:6), which Baumgärtel defines by means of a creed: Jesus Christ, my Lord, has saved me, a lost and condemned man, from every sin; so that I may be his, live under him in his kingdom, and serve him in eternal righteousness, innocence and bliss. Secondly, God has authenticated his promise by the passion and resurrection of Jesus Christ. Thirdly, the Christian participates in the promise through the Gospel. This threefold basis of faith is developed and used by Baumgärtel to determine the nature of promise in the Bible, and thus to establish how the Old Testament is to be understood from the point of view of the Gospel.

The most relevant works by Baumgärtel are:
Die Bedeutung des ATs für den Christen (1925);
'Das AT' in Künneth and Schreiner (1933);
'Das Christuszeugnis des ATs', WuT (1936; not available to me);
'Zur Frage der theologischen Deutung des ATs', ZST (1938);
'Erwägungen zur Darstellung der Theologie des ATs', TLZ (1951);
Verheissung (1952);
'Das atl.Geschehen als "heilsgeschichtliches" Geschehen' in Alt Festschrift (1953);
'"Ohne Schlüssel vor der Tür des Wortes Gottes"?', EvTh (1953);
'The Hermeneutical Problem of the OT' (1954), ET in EOTI;
'Der Dissensus im Verständnis des ATs', EvTh (1954);
'Gerhard von Rad's "Theologie des ATs"', TLZ (1961);
'Der Tod des Religionsstifters', KuD (1963), cf. Koch 1962;
'Das Offenbarungszeugnis des ATs', ZTK (1967).
A bibliography of his works is given in the Baumgärtel Festschrift (1959).

Critical works include:
Köhler, 'Christus im Alten und im NT', ThZ (1953): esp. 248-51;
von Rad, 'Verheissung', EvTh (1953);
van Ruler, The Christian Church and the OT (1955): esp. 26-28nn./28-30;
Westermann, 'Remarks on the Theses of Bultmann and Baumgärtel' (1955), ET in EOTI;
Eichrodt, 'Is Typological Exegesis an Appropriate Method?' (1957), ET in EOTI: 236-41;
Hermann, 'Offenbarung, Worte und Texte', EvTh (1959);

Nicolaisen, Die Auseinandersetzung um das AT (1966):52-5;
Bright, The Authority of the OT(1967):72-3,190-192;
L. Schmidt, 'Die Einheit zwischen Altem und NT im Streit zwischen Friedrich Baumgärtel und Gerhard von Rad',EvTh(1975).

4.12 PROMISE

a. The New Testament, according to Baumgärtel (pp.7-16), conceives 'promise' as an absolutely valid pledge made by God. Its characteristic aspects are facticity (in the promise God is presently active), existence (the promise establishes and supports existence), judgement (realisation of the promise is also judgement on sin), grace (the promise is given by God's grace), universality (the promise is valid for all believers, Jews and Gentiles), and futurity (the future concept of promise is used by the New Testament to express a present gift, since the Old Testament promise has come true in Christ). This concept of promise has a double relationship to the Old Testament promise: the promise in Christ includes the promise of the Old Testament, though as promise in Christ it cannot be found in the Old Testament.

b. The Old Testament, although it lacks the New Testament concept, has its own understanding of promise, which it expresses by terms such as word, mercy, statute, covenant, speak, swear (pp.16-27). There are three groups of promises in the Old Testament: 1) pledges which are affirmed to have been realised in historical facts; 2) promises attached by God to the law, whose realisation is dependent on keeping the law; 3) prophetic promises, whose realisation is tied to the realisation of future historical events. Above all these promises, however, stands one basic promise, the statement of grace: 'I am the Lord your God'. The preaching of the Old Testament interprets this characteristically in terms of law and nation, so that in practice it is quite different from the promise in Christ. It is the basic promise - from which every promise of the Old Testament derives its essence - which is relevant for Christian faith.

c. Perhaps the most important aspect of Baumgärtel's conception of promise is its distinction from and relation to his conception of prediction (pp.28-36; cf. Westermann 1955:128-132). Prediction, he argues, stems from the basic promise, 'I am the Lord your God', and its fulfilment is closely linked with the realisation of the promise. It is communicated by the prophets and apocalyptists, though unlike soothsaying it is concerned not with detailed knowledge about the future but with the divine completion of the whole event. Baumgärtel defines the essential difference between promise and prediction by a series of contrasts:

Promise	Prediction
1.Absolute divine pledge	Conditioned human witness
2.Event	Word
3.Realisation of communion with God	Announcement of future event
4.Conditional: received by faith	Unconditional: God acts in spite of man
5.Always open to the eye of faith	Not always open, dependent on prophets
6.To be believed, because authenticated as true	To be established by fulfilment, so that its accuracy may be recognised

It is therefore promise, as the gift of God, which

is relevant for Christian faith. Christian existence is based not on scholarly insight into historical processes - prediction - but on the absolute unbreakable pledge of God. Thus Christian interpretation conceives the Old Testament word as a word of promise and incorporates it into the promise in Christ.

The idea of 'promise' is a popular characterisation of the Old Testament, as may be seen from its use by writers as diverse as:
Schniewind and Friedrich, 'ἐπαγγέλλω', TDNT(1935);
Zimmerli, 'Promise and Fulfillment'(1952), ET in EOTI;
Rowley, The Unity of the Bible(1953):ch.4;
Achtemeier, The OT Roots of Our Faith(1962);
Moltmann, Theology of Hope(1964):ch.2;
Westermann, 'The Way of the Promise through the OT', OTCF (1964);
Sauter, Zukunft und Verheissung(1965);
Hesse, Das AT als Buch der Kirche(1966):ch.4;
McCurley, 'The Christian and the OT Promise', LQ(1970);
Kaiser, 'The Promise Theme and the Theology of Rest', BS(1973); 'The Centre of OT Theology', Themelios (1974);
Premsagar, 'Theology of Promise in the Patriarchal Narratives', IJT(1974).

See also above: 0.21; 3.25; below: 7.24.

4.13 PROMISE IN CHRIST

a. The promise in Christ offers salvation which is to be appropriated in faith; and faith according to the New Testament is simply to hold on to the promise (pp.37-9; cf.1954a:151). Thus Baumgärtel defines the basis of Christian experience, and he elaborates its implications in three ways. The Christian, he argues, experiences the revelation of the existence of the transcendent God together with awareness of his own worldliness; that this divine revelation is intended for him and yet it frightens him; and that

God both judges his sin and opens the way to blessing.

b. The Old Testament is theologically understood in faith if by faith its message is conceived as promise, according to Baumgärtel (pp.39-49). Thus the experience of Old Testament man under the basic promise corresponds to that of the Christian, although the two are not identical. In the Old Testament, God is revealed as the living Lord and man as a mortal creature; this divine revelation confronts man under the law with the demand of God's will; and God reveals his will in the law and prophets to judge sin and grant blessing. So Baumgärtel, like Bultmann (see above: 3.122, 3.22), recognises an essential congruity between the conceptions of human existence in the Old and New Testaments. He considers however that there are also important differences, in particular that the Old Testament does not know the evangelical concept of eternal life, nor does it conceive an individual to be in relationship with God other than as a member of the people of Israel (p.40). Therefore, although the distinctively Old Testament character of the Old Testament experience must not be ignored, Israel under God's basic promise fundamentally experiences God as the revealed Lord just as Christians under the promise in Christ experience him as their Lord.

c. Baumgärtel has argued earlier (cf. above: 4.12a) that the promise in Christ includes the promise of the Old Testament. It follows that the Old Testament is in fact old, and therefore abolished (pp.49-53). Christ is the confirmation of God's basic promise, but not of the way in which the Old Testament conceives the realisation of the promise and the blessing which accompanies it. By faith Christians have living communion with God, something for which Old Testament men can only wait. Such waiting is abolished for Christians, whose life under the promise in Christ is based on faith in the certainty of present salvation.

d. It is questionable, however, whether it is valid to draw such a strong contrast between Old and New Testament man. Baumgärtel has to agree that there is a sense in which the Old Testament is not abolished for Christians (pp.53-64). Those within the new covenant are fellow-travellers with those of the old covenant, experiencing under the divine promise a history which with that of Israel is salvation - and disaster - history. To the Christian, as to Israel, God has revealed himself and opened the way of faith; the Holy Spirit calls, illumines and sanctifies in order to incorporate into the one Christian Church; and the cross of Christ judges sin so that freedom may be achieved.

e. The implication of Baumgärtel's argument for Christian understanding of the Old Testament is twofold. First, the Old Testament is the present word of God to Christians, those who stand under the promise in Christ (pp.64-8). Christians conceive the Old Testament witness as the witness of God's realisation of his basic promise to them through Christ, and thus the Old Testament speaks to them of Jesus Christ. It does not only judge and humble but raises up and imparts power, thus becoming gospel to the Christian.

f. Secondly, according to Baumgärtel, the Old Testament is relevant for the Christian faith only when understood as promise (pp.68-71). Prediction is irrelevant to faith, since Christian existence cannot be based on human insight but only on trust in God's grace in Christ, the realisation of the promise. Christological interpretation is inappropriate since the Old Testament does not develop a Christology, by making statements about the person, office and work of Jesus Christ. The Old Testament is related to Jesus Christ not primarily by prediction or Christology but in its basic promise - 'I am the Lord your God' - which the Christian faith affirms to have come true in Jesus Christ.

4.14 THE OLD TESTAMENT AS PROMISE

a. Having presented his analysis of promise in Christ, Baumgärtel turns next to consider the way in which the concepts of promise and prediction are understood in the New Testament and contemporary biblical theology. For the New Testament (pp.71-86) prediction is important: it cites Old Testament texts directly with reference to New Testament events, and adduces prediction to prove that Jesus is the Christ. Such procedures are neither possible nor relevant today, Baumgärtel argues. The New Testament also understands the Old Testament message as a witness of God's promise, which is over the old covenant and has come true in the promise in Christ: this alone is relevant for Christian faith.

b. In contemporary biblical theology (pp.86-128) the traditional understanding of the Old Testament in terms of prediction and fulfilment has been abandoned. Nevertheless, according to Baumgärtel, a satisfactory alternative understanding has not been found because of a failure to distinguish clearly the concepts of promise and prediction. The endeavours of Hofmann, Eichrodt, Bultmann, Vischer, Zimmerli and von Rad are on the right lines and are essentially concerned with promise rather than prediction, but are misleading or unnecessarily obscure, so Baumgärtel argues.

c. The result of the study may be summed up quite briefly (pp.128-9). The Old Testament is promissory, not predictive, in character. This conception of the Old Testament is derived from the New Testament idea of promise as promise in Christ, on the basis of the New Testament view of the Old Testament as God's promise. The relevance of the Old Testament for Christian faith is therefore found not in its prediction but only in its testimony to God's basic promise, 'I am the Lord your God'.

d. Several consequences for theology and preaching follow from Baumgärtel's argument (pp.129-159). The Old Testament word is characterised as promise (and not as prediction), a concept derived not from Old Testament promises but from the New Testament understanding of promise. Old Testament interpretation cannot be based on prediction and fulfilment nor on typology but only on the New Testament's own principle of interpretation: promise in Christ. Preaching of the promise from the Old Testament is both simple on the theological level and difficult on the practical level, since the 'holy simplicity' of the basic promise has to be communicated in a meaningful way to the ordinary man in the street.

4.15 A RELATIONSHIP OF CONTRAST

Like Bultmann, Baumgärtel considers the relationship between the Testaments to be a relationship of contrast (cf. L. Schmidt 1975:124-8). The Old Testament idea of promise is closely linked to the law and the people of Israel, he claims, in contrast to the New Testament idea which is characterised by grace and universality (chs 1,2; see above: 4.12a,b; cf. 3.24,3.26). Moreover, the Old Testament does not know the New Testament ideas of eternal life and personal relationship with God in the present (pp.40, 49-53; cf.1954a:146-7; see above: 4.13b,c;cf.3.26a). Baumgärtel's clearest expression of this contrast, however, is to be found in an article published two years later than his book: 'the Old Testament is the witness of faith from a strange religion' (1954a:147). From the perspective of the history of religions it is indisputable that Israelite religion is different from Christian religion (p.138); and in practical terms a Christian who reads the Old Testament finds he cannot understand it because it belongs to a radically different situation in the history of piety (pp.147-9). Thus for Baumgärtel the Old Testament can be understood only as Old Testament (1952:49-53; 1954a:150).

4.16 A RELATIONSHIP OF WITNESS

Another important aspect of Baumgärtel's view of the relationship between the Testaments is the idea of 'witness'. Miskotte presents the Old Testament as a witness to 'the Name' (see above: ch.2) and Vischer presents it as a witness to Christ (see below: ch.5), but for Baumgärtel the Old Testament is a witness to the promise in Christ. This is possible in two ways: the Old Testament is the witness of God's realisation through Christ of his basic promise; and the Christian affirms that Christ has realised the basic promise of the Old Testament (pp.64-71; see above: 4.13e,f). In itself, to be sure, the Old Testament would not be understood in this way; but the Christian, as he interprets it on the basis of the prior understanding given by the New Testament, can recognise the Old Testament as a witness of God's promise in Jesus Christ (1954a:134-9; cf.1954b:298-303). Thus Baumgärtel has put forward what is essentially a 'New Testament' solution to the problem of the relationship between the Testaments (cf. Köhler 1953:249-50; Westermann 1955:130-133).

4.2 COMPARISON: OTHER 'NEW TESTAMENT' SOLUTIONS

4.21 EMANUEL HIRSCH

There is a sense in which Hirsch's approach to the problem may be considered a 'New Testament' solution, alongside those of Bultmann and Baumgärtel. He takes the New Testament to be the essential Bible, and emphasises the contrast between the Testaments. However the Old Testament for Hirsch is not the presupposition of the New but its antithesis. It has no direct relevance to the Christian, although it serves to illuminate the distinctive nature of Christianity as gospel by presenting its opposite - legalistic Judaism. The characteristic theme of Hirsch's approach is 'law and gospel' (cf. above: 3.24) and he interprets it in the most radical way possible so that the two are irreconcilably contrasted. This view was particularly attractive in Nazi Germany and lent weight to contemporary anti-Semitic rejection of the Old Testament (cf. above: 0.622), although Hirsch himself did not advocate this. He recognised that the Old Testament has a limited value for Christian preaching (1936a), and asserted that in the history of Christianity it has been blessed with God's authority as a preacher of the law (1935:8). Hirsch's 'solution' to the problem of the relationship between the Testaments is indeed much more extreme than those of Bultmann and Baumgärtel: its implication is virtual dissolution of the relationship.

Relevant works by Hirsch:
'Gottes Offenbarung in Gesetz und Evangelium' in _Christliche Freiheit_(1935);
Das AT und die Predigt des Evangeliums(1936);
Das vierte Evangelium(1936):323-8.

Cf. Hempel, 'Chronik', _ZAW_(1936):296-306;
Strathmann, 'Zum Ringen um das christliche Verständnis des ATs', _ThBl_(1936);
von Rad, 'Gesetz und Evangelium im AT', _ThBl_(1937);
Kraeling, _The OT Since the Reformation_(1955):ch.15;
Smart, _The Interpretation of Scripture_(1961):73;
Nicolaisen, _Die Auseinandersetzung um das AT_(1966):90-96;
Bright, _The Authority of the OT_(1967):67-9;
Schneider-Hume, _Die politische Theologie Emanuel Hirschs_(1971).

4.22 FRANZ HESSE

a. In a critique of von Rad's Old Testament theology, Hesse (1960a) states clearly his view of the superiority of the New Testament over the Old. He argues against von Rad that the New Testament is more directly related to Christians than the Old and therefore has a higher position (p.20). Yet his judgement on the Old Testament is not entirely negative, and he recognises that it does have authority for the Christian (1959:293).

b. Perhaps the two most important concepts in Hesse's view of the relationship between the Testaments are those of 'promise' (cf. above: 4.12) and 'salvation history' (cf. below: 7.26). In a very similar way to Baumgärtel, although he does not explicitly base his argument on Baumgärtel's work, Hesse develops the concept of 'promise' as the key to Old Testament interpretation (1966:ch.4). He understands the concept to have three aspects - pledge, factic gift and eschatological blessing - and affirms that beyond the form of Old Testament promises as human predictions there is a basic promise which is determinative for the message of the whole Old Testament. He asserts moreover that in the Old Testament God's salvation history 'is seen in the first line as the history of promise, promise subsequently redeemed in Christ' (1959:294). Or, to put it in another way, since this promise has the character of a word, 'in, with, and under the Old Testament Word, witness is borne to the redemptive activity of God which finds its telos in Jesus Christ' (ibid.).

c. At this point Hesse draws attention to the problem which is raised so forcefully by the work of von Rad (cf. below: 7.22,7.26):

'The Old Testament does indeed set out to describe the redemptive activity of God which happens in, with, and under the history of Israel; but the Old Testament witnesses have a conception of the course of this history which does not agree with the actual course' (1959:295).

In contrast to von Rad, Hesse refuses to separate salvation history from 'real' history (cf. Hasel 1972a:31-4). The real course of Israel's history is more important for Christian theology than Israel's own conception of her history (1960a:24; cf.1958, 1969). It follows that 'the Old Testament can bear witness to the redemptive activity of God only in a very conditioned, very fragmented way' (1959: 295). To express it more bluntly,

'The Old Testament indeed believes that it points to God's redemptive activity, even describes it, but the redemptive activity of God attested and described by the Old Testament does not agree with God's actual redemptive activity, as little as the Old Testament conception of the course of Israelite history agrees with its actual course' (1959:296)!

There is a difference therefore between the function of history in the two Testaments. Hesse argues that in the New Testament, in contrast to the Old, history is crucially important and there are only secondary differences between what the New Testament says and what actually happened (1959:298). Thus another way in which the New Testament is superior to the Old comes to light: the witness of the New Testament, based on real historical events, is constitutive for Christian faith; the witness of the Old Testament, since its ideas often contradict the real basis of salvation history, is not constitutive for Christian faith, though it 'smooths the way for it, purifies and deepens it' (1959:299).

d. Not only does the Old Testament give an incomplete picture of the salvation history, according to Hesse, it also records human response to the activity of God, and this does not always witness to salvation history but can even go directly against it. Human listening can misunderstand or disobey God's voice: indeed,

> 'every Old Testament answer to the address of God ... must remain inadequate, often also misconceived, even perverted; this is so because the faithful people of the Old Testament live perforce in a revelatory relationship which appears from the New Testament vantage point not only as provisional and obsolete, but as insufficient, even distorted. From the viewpoint of the history of religions, one would say: The Old Testament religion is something qualitatively different from the faith of the New Testament' (1959:300).

Yet even in the error and disobedience of the Old Testament God is present, since it was he who ordered history in such a way that salvation history incorporates a history of condemnation (1959:302-3). Therefore all the Old Testament may be understood as a witness of the Word of God, which addresses Christians insofar as they are still on the way to salvation and thus Old Testament men (1959:304-13).

e. Hesse's view of the relationship between the Testaments is therefore a 'New Testament' solution. Although he does not reject the Old Testament or deny it a place in the Christian Bible, Hesse considers that it is the New Testament which is constitutive for Christian faith and that the Old Testament has only indirect authority.

Works by Hesse:

'Die Erforschung der Geschichte Israels als theologische Aufgabe', _KuD_ (1958);
'The Evaluation and Authority of OT Texts' (1959), ET in _EOTI_;
'Kerygma oder geschichtliche Wirklichkeit?', _ZTK_ (1960);
'Das AT in der gegenwärtigen Dogmatik', _NZST_ (1960);
'Wolfhart Pannenberg und das AT', _NZST_ (1965);
Das AT als Buch der Kirche (1966);
'Bewährt sich eine "Theologie der Heilstatsachen" am AT?', _ZAW_ (1969);
Abschied von der Heilsgeschichte (1971).

PART FOUR: THE SEARCH FOR A 'BIBLICAL' SOLUTION

5. The Old and New Testaments are equally Christian Scripture

5.1 WILHELM VISCHER: THE OLD TESTAMENT AND CHRIST

5.2 CRITICISM: WITNESS AND IDENTITY

5.3 COMPARISON: OTHER CHRISTOLOGICAL SOLUTIONS

5.1 WILHELM VISCHER: THE OLD TESTAMENT AND CHRIST

5.11 INTRODUCTION

a. The most important of Wilhelm Vischer's many writings is his programmatic work, The Witness of the Old Testament to Christ (1934). According to Hasel (1972a: 70), Vischer places 'primary emphasis on the OT by making it all-important theologically' and is thus in fundamental agreement with van Ruler. Vischer writes in his introduction: 'Strictly speaking only the Old Testament is "The Scripture", while the New Testament brings the good news that now the meaning of these writings, the import of all their words, their Lord and Fulfiller, has appeared incarnate' (pp.7-8; cf. 11,22,26). For all that, a study of the book shows that this is not the essence of Vischer's method. At first sight his interpretation of Noah's 'prophecy' in Gen.9:27 reaches a conclusion consistent with van Ruler's thesis (cf. above: 1.141): 'salvation is of the Jews and yet the Gentiles will also be partakers of it. For although Shem is the true root and stem, the Gentiles will be grafted on to this stem' (p.105). The fundamental difference between Vischer and van Ruler becomes apparent if we read on: 'this light Noah sees by the Holy Spirit, and although he uses obscure words, he none the less prophesies very definitely that the Kingdom of the Lord Christ will be built and planted from the tribe of Shem and not of Japheth' (p.105). Van Ruler interprets the Old Testament theocratically, Vischer Christologically. To van Ruler the meaning of the

Old Testament is clear, to Vischer there is 'a veil over the Old Testament until it is recognised that by the death and resurrection of Christ Jesus the veil is removed and the rupture and end of the old covenant unveiled' (p.208). Therefore, although he concedes the theoretical priority of the Old Testament over the New, in practice Vischer's interpretation is dominated by the New Testament. Rather than understanding the relationship between the Testaments in terms of the priority of one Testament over the other, Vischer's work implies a relationship of theological 'identity'. Whereas van Ruler finds the Old Testament to be the essential Bible and the New Testament its Christian supplement, Vischer takes the whole Bible to be equally Christian Scripture.

b. This solution to the problem of the relationship between the Testaments is naturally not new; it dates back to the earliest days of the Church. In fact it may be considered the traditional Christian approach to the Old Testament, apart from the view of Marcion and his followers, until the rise of biblical criticism in the eighteenth and nineteenth centuries (cf. Florovsky 1951:173-4; Bright 1967:79-84). In different ways the Fathers and the Reformers affirmed their basic conviction that the Old Testament is Christian Scripture and therefore to be interpreted Christologically. If not expressed explicitly, their view of the relationship between the Testaments was implicitly that the two are identical in their value, inspiration and theology (cf. above: 0.4).

c. By the twentieth century, with the general acceptance of historical criticism of the Bible, this view of the Bible was not readily acceptable. On the one hand the Bible was viewed as part of the general history of religion, and the relationship between the Testaments interpreted in terms of 'progressive revelation'; on the other hand, Marcion's idea was revived and the Old Testament thrown out of the window. These solutions did not completely satisfy either the Church or biblical scholarship, and the political situation in Europe in the thirties made the need for an answer all the more pressing (see above: 0.6).

d. Just as Barth's commentary on Romans (1918,1921) heralded the end of liberalism and the beginning of a new era in biblical interpretation, so Vischer's study of the Old Testament witness to Christ (1934, 1942) may be considered a turning-point in the history of the interpretation of the Old Testament. Although he had written on the subject in the late twenties and early thirties, and Barth's work was pointing in a similar direction (see below: 5.31), it was the first volume of Vischer's major work which started a debate in the thirties that has scarcely been resolved in the seventies. Today there is still a wide diversity of solutions to the problem of the Old Testament - which is the justification for the present thesis - and few would follow all that Vischer says, but there is fairly general agreement that a solution to the problem must be at least theological, if not Christian.

e. It is appropriate to begin an analysis of Vischer's work with his major book. In the first section the argument of the introductory essay in that book will be summarised, showing the theoretical basis of his thesis. In the following section his interpretation of the Old Testament will be considered, with reference to the rest of his major book and to certain other of his exegetical writings. The final section of the analysis will be given to another theoretical essay which he published more recently as a response to Rudolf Bultmann.

aa. Vischer's early works:
'Le Serviteur du Seigneur'(1930) and
'Job, un témoin du Jésus Christ'(1933), French translations in Valeur de l'AT;
'Das AT und die Verkündigung',ThBl(1931).
Also, not available to me:
'Das AT als Wort Gottes',ZZ(1927);
Jahweh der Gott Kains (1929);
'Der Gott Abrahams, Isaaks und Jakobs',ZZ(1930);
'Das AT und die Geschichte',ZZ(1932);
'Gehört das AT heute noch in die Bibel des deutschen Christen?',Beth-El(1932).

bb. His major work: The Witness of the OT to Christ I: The Pentateuch (1934, ET:1949). Volume II, part 1 on the Former Prophets was published in German (Das Christuszeugnis des ATs II.1,1942) but never translated into English. The rest of the work never appeared, although much material on the rest of the Old Testament was published in journal articles (see below: dd).

cc. Later theoretical discussions:
'The Significance of the OT for the Christian Life' in Edinburgh(1938);
'Le "kerygme" de l'AT',ETR(1955; not available to me);
'La méthode de l'exégèse biblique',RThPh(1960);
'Zum Problem der Hermeneutik'(1961), German translation in EvTh 24;
'Everywhere the Scripture Is about Christ Alone', OTCF(1964).

dd. Other examples of his Old Testament interpretation:
'The Book of Esther'(1937),ET in EQ 11;
Die Immanuel-Botschaft (1954);
'L'Ecclésiaste, témoin de Christ-Jésus'(1954), French translation in Valeur de l'AT;
'Return, Rebel Sons! A Sermon on Jeremiah 3:1,19-4:4', Interpn(1954);
'The Vocation of the Prophet to the Nations',Interpn (1955) - on Jer.1:4-10;
'Du sollst dir kein Bildnis machen' in Barth Festschrift (1956);
Versöhnung zwischen Ost und West(1957) - on Gen.32-3; Ezek.16;

'Perhaps the Lord will be Gracious',*Interpn*(1959) - on Amos 5;
'God's Truth and Man's Lie',*Interpn*(1961) - on Job;
'The Love Story of God',*Interpn*(1961) - on Hosea;
'Der Hymnus der Weisheit in den Sprüchen Salomos 8,22-31',*EvTh*(1962);
'Foi et Technique (Méditation sur Deutéronome 11_{10-15})', *RHPR*(1964);
'Der im Himmel Thronende lacht' in de Quervain Festschrift (1966) - on Ps.2:4;
Ils annoncent Jésus-Christ: Les patriarches(1969; not available to me);
'Nehemia, der Sonderbeauftragte und Statthalter des Königs' in von Rad Festschrift (1971).

ee. The following reviews of Vischer's major work may be noted:
E. Hermann, *RHPR*(1935); Procksch, *ThLBl*(1935);
Hertzberg, *TLZ*(1936); Daniélou, *DV*(1950);
Porter, *Theology*(1950); de Vaux, *RB*(1950,1952).

ff. Among many reactions to Vischer's work the following are particularly significant:
von Rad, 'Das Christuszeugnis des ATs',*ThBl*(1935);
Feldges, 'Die Frage des atl.Christuszeugnisses', *ThBl*(1936);
Herntrich, *Theologische Auslegung des ATs?*(1936);
R. Hermann, *'Deutung und Umdeutung der Schrift'*(1937), repr. in *Bibel und Hermeneutik*;
de Wilde, *Het probleem van het OT*(1938; not available to me);
Zimmerli, 'Auslegung des ATes',*ThBl*(1940);
Baumgartner, 'Die Auslegung des ATs im Streit der Gegenwart'(1941),repr. in *Zum AT und seiner Umwelt*;
Jacob, 'A propos de l'interprétation de l'AT', *ETR*(1945);
Thielicke, 'Law and Gospel as Constant Partners' (1948), incorporated into *Theological Ethics* I;
Congar, 'The OT as a Witness to Christ'(1949), incorporated into *The Revelation of God*;
Porteous, 'OT Theology' in Rowley(1951):337-40;
Baumgärtel, *Verheissung*(1952):91-5;
Kraeling, *The OT Since the Reformation*(1955):ch.13;
Haenchen, 'Hamans Galgen und Christi Kreuz' in Hirsch Festschrift (1963);
Thurneysen, 'Die Bedeutung der theologischen Arbeit Wilhelm Vischers',*KBRS*(1965; not available to me);
Nicolaisen, *Die Auseinandersetzung um das AT* (1966):150-174;
Kuske, *Das AT als Buch von Christus*(1967):20-21;
Kosak, *Wegweisung in das AT*(1968):E.3.

5.12 THE WITNESS OF THE OLD TESTAMENT TO CHRIST

a. 'Jesus is the Christ' (pp.7-8). This is the statement of faith of the Bible and the Christian Church. The Old Testament defines the word 'Christ' and the New Testament supplies the name 'Jesus', thus identifying Jesus as the Christ. So the Old Testament points forward to the New and the New Testament points back to the Old.

b. This close relationship between the Testaments is clear in the way Luke, for example, presents the good news that the Christ has come and that he is Jesus of Nazareth (pp.8-11). The angels who speak to Zechariah, Mary and the shepherds each announce that God is about to fulfil the promises made in the Old Testament. At his presentation in the temple Jesus is recognised by Simeon as the Christ, and when he is twelve he visits the temple again and reveals his own awareness that he is the Son of God. After baptism and temptation he commences his ministry in Galilee with the astounding claim: 'Through my presence the scripture is fulfilled'. Jesus' claim to be the Christ inevitably means a short ministry and an early death, and it might be thought that such a death disproves his claim. But the testimony of the New Testament is that this happened according to Scripture, that in his life and death Jesus was the Christ promised in the Old Testament. In their encounter with the risen Lord and in receiving the promised Holy Spirit the disciples are given the knowledge and power to witness that indeed Jesus is the Christ.

c. Jesus is the Christ of the Old Testament (pp.11-14). The intention of the apostles in their witness to Jesus as the Christ is not to give a Christian interpretation to the 'historical Jesus' but simply to proclaim that Jesus is the Christ of the Old Testament. Jesus Christ is an historical event which is the source and goal of all history, yet he is a real man whose historicity is proved by his birth and above all by his death.

d. The Bible is a witness to Jesus Christ (pp.14-17). Consistent with the historicity of Jesus Christ are the historical documents which support it. The Bible is not Holy Scripture because it fell from heaven but because it tells about Jesus Christ, the Son of God made flesh. It contains words of men rooted in history, and if this is a stumbling-block to belief that it is also the Word of God it is no more a stumbling-block than the incarnation of the Word of God. Though without the operation of the Holy Spirit the writings are dead, historical and linguistic study are essential to understand the Old Testament. So there is a logical circle: God reveals himself in Jesus Christ, Jesus Christ is attested by the Bible, and the Bible is made effective by the Holy Spirit of God.

e. Jesus Christ is the decisive event of history (pp.18-19). According to the Bible, Jesus Christ is not merely one of many historical facts but the origin and destination of history, who lived in history and died to take away the sin of the world.

f. Jesus Christ has united the Old and New Testaments (pp.19-21). The death of Christ has made the two Testaments one, and it is only if they are a unity that Jesus is really the Christ. It follows that believers before and after Christ share the same salvation through the same mediator, thus belonging to one Church of Christ. This is possible because Jesus Christ was not only a specific event in history but is eternally present (Heb.13:8) and therefore contemporary with every Christian.

g. Jesus Christ has fulfilled the Old Testament promises (pp.22-4). The essence of the unity of the Testaments, according to the New Testament, is that Jesus the Christ has fulfilled what was promised by the law and the prophets. This does not mean however that the Old Testament is now unnecessary. The promises, though fulfilled, are not dissolved: on the contrary, they are clarified and completed, and the expectation becomes even more vigorous. 'To the witness of the old covenant Jesus is near as the Coming One; to those of the new covenant as the Returning One.'

h. The Old Testament belongs to the Christian canon (pp.25-7). It is often asked whether the Church was right to bring together both Old and New Testaments into one Bible. No doubt there could be piety on the basis of the New Testament alone, but Christianity demands both Testaments as a basis since it claims that Jesus is the Christ, in the sense that the Old Testament defines 'Christ'. It was natural and essential therefore that Christians should appropriate Israel's Bible as their own.

i. Is Jesus the Christ (pp.27-33)? The unity of the Testaments is the basis of the Christian Church since without the Old Testament the Church cannot be <u>Christ</u>ian. At this point however the question arises whether the New Testament interpretation of the Old as a witness to Jesus the

Christ is correct. It is not merely a question of faith: the Bible consists of human words and these words must be examined intellectually to see if they really point to Jesus Christ. True scholarly study will not be concerned to reconstruct an 'original' meaning but will read the Old Testament naïvely (cf. above: 2.16), not knowing beforehand its content but discovering in it the meaning of 'Christ'. The ultimate decision whether or not Jesus is the Christ, although a matter of faith, is a decision based on the testimony of Scripture and intelligent study will show that it has a sound basis.

j. The Old Testament is a witness to Christ (pp.33-4). Vischer concludes his introduction by quoting J.G. Hamann's citation of Augustine: 'Read the prophetic books without reference to Christ - what couldst thou find more tasteless and insipid? Find therein Christ, and what thou readest will not only prove agreeable, but will intoxicate thee'.

5.13 OLD TESTAMENT INTERPRETATION

a. A few examples of Vischer's Old Testament interpretation are now selected for special study, not because of their unusual features - which would give an unbalanced impression of his method - but almost at random, in order to understand his view of the relationship between the Testaments in a wider context. The examples are presented in chronological order of Vischer's writing, which happens to coincide with their order in the Hebrew Bible.

b. <u>Genesis 14</u> (1934:128-133). Abraham is unaffected by the campaign of the kings but in loyalty to Lot he leads his 318 'devoted servants' into battle. On his return in triumph he is met by the priestly king of Salem (Jerusalem), the city where God's rule and presence are revealed from David to Jesus and the end of all things. The letter to the Hebrews compares the priesthood of Melchisedek with that of Christ: neither belong to a priestly family but both are accredited directly by God. Thus before God makes the covenant with Abraham, Melchisedek reveals 'the office of the Son, who is eternal and perfect' (Heb.7:28), agreeing with Jesus' declaration that Christianity is older than Judaism (John 8:58).

c. Exodus 3:13-14 (1934:169-170). Moses asks God his name and is given the name 'Yahweh', not a conventional divine name but 'an utterance in the first person in which the subject does not become an object but remains subject'. It is a revelation not of a new God but of the God of the fathers, known formerly as El Shaddai.

d. 1 Samuel 17 (1942:203-9). In the absence of any other volunteers David responds to Goliath's challenge to Israel - implicitly a challenge to the God of Israel. His only visible weapon is a staff and sling but he has the invisible armour of the panoply of God (Eph.6:13). In the name of Yahweh David defeats the giant and delivers Israel, and in his faith in that same name he is appointed king of Israel and founder of the messianic dynasty. Thus the shepherd becomes the princely witness to the promised true Shepherd, through whom God delivers and rules his people (John 10; cf. Ezek.34).

e. Jeremiah 1:4-10 (1955). The most significant aspect of Jeremiah's call is that he is appointed as prophet to the nations. Yet unlike Paul the apostle to the nations (Gal.1:15-16; cf.Jer.1:5), who travels the world to fulfil his ministry, Jeremiah stays at home and addresses most of his prophecies to Jerusalem and Judah. God speaks to the nations through Israel, and so Jeremiah's mission to superintend the destruction and rehabilitation of Israel is indirectly a mission to the world. Both Jeremiah and Paul concur in their message that not only Israel but every nation of the world is subject to God's justice and dependent on his grace.

f. Amos 5 (1959). The message of Amos is as relevant to present-day Christians as to the Israelites, though both groups are inclined to ignore it in the assumption that they have a special relationship with God. Amos does not deny this special relationship, but shows that it is this very uniqueness of God's people which makes them especially liable to God's justice (Amos 3:2; cf.Luke 12:48). Since in Jesus Christ God has given Christians even more than he gave Israel his demand on them will be correspondingly greater and their unfaithfulness will be all the more serious. Like Israel the church is condemned to death for its sin and empty religion; like Israel it is given a last chance of life if it will 'seek the Lord' (Amos 5:1-6; cf.John 5:39-40). If his people do this 'it may be that the Lord, the God of hosts, will be gracious to the remnant of Joseph' (Amos 5:15).

g. Job (1961). God's truth is Jesus Christ, man's lie is to make Jesus Christ into Christianity. The book of Job exposes this lie and points to this truth. It tells the story of a man who was upright and trusted God fully with no ulterior motives. He rejected his friends' attempts to explain life theologically and accepted only God's own solution, 'God's free, joyous goodness which is the meaning and ground of the world' (p.144). No doubt Job feared God for nought, but more important is the fact that God loves man for nought. The truth of this book is not proved by Job but by Jesus Christ, in whom God has taken the part of Job. Jesus was humiliated and tempted and he placed his life in God's hands on the Cross, but was answered by God who raised him from the dead.

h. Nehemiah (1971). As the king's minister with special responsibilities and governor of Jerusalem, Nehemiah supervises the fortification of the holy city. He is neither priest nor prophet but a politician who realises that there is a political aspect to the kingdom of God. The Jews have only a high priest at the head of their renewed state but, although the Persian regime would scarcely have tolerated its open expression, they nurture a hope for a king which is not satisfied until Jesus declares with authority that God's kingdom is at hand and is acclaimed by the crowd on his entry into Jerusalem.

5.14 EVERYWHERE THE SCRIPTURE IS ABOUT CHRIST ALONE

a. The essence of Vischer's programme for interpreting the Old Testament in relation to the New has been shown in the two preceding sections, by giving a summary of his theoretical essay and some examples of his Old Testament interpretation. A more recent theoretical essay, 'Everywhere the Scripture Is About Christ Alone' (1964), will now be discussed briefly, showing that after thirty years his position is still fundamentally the same.

b. Vischer's starting-point is Bultmann's radical claim that the Old Testament is not genuinely God's Word for Christians (see above: ch.3), and he examines this in some detail (pp.90-97). He takes issue in particular with Bultmann's distinction between the Old Testament, in which revelation is bound to the history of Israel, and the New Testament, in which revelation confronts the individual in the proclaimed Word. In the first place, Vischer admits that God's revelation in the Old Testament is bound to the history of his people, but he argues that membership of that people is not enough: faith and obedience are required to experience the grace of God. In the second place, Vischer acknowledges that in the New Testament this particularity of revelation is broken and consequently God's act in Jesus Christ is understood differently from his acts in the Old Testament: 'the New Testament asserts that <u>God's deed in Jesus Christ is not merely one but rather THE decisive event for the history of Israel</u>' (p.97).

c. The message of the New Testament is that Jesus lived, died and rose again for all who believe in him, and this message is presented by showing that Jesus is the fulfilment of the Old Testament, both its end and its goal. Therefore the New Testament points Christians to the Old, where they may see examples of God's judgement and grace toward his people. These examples are relevant because in both Old and New Testaments God's people live in time and history, and in both Testaments they encounter God in Christ within that situation. The Old Testament, however, is not simply helpful in understanding the Christian; it is essential to apprehend God's revelation in Jesus Christ, which cannot be known without the Old Testament. (pp.98-101)

5.2 CRITICISM: WITNESS AND IDENTITY

5.21 SECONDARY QUESTIONS

5.211 Method

Vischer insists on an historical and linguistic approach to the Old Testament and claims that his thesis is based on sound scholarly method (1934: 14-17,27-33; see above: 5.12d,i). Yet one of the main criticisms directed against his work is that he does not take history seriously and substitutes guesswork for scholarship in his exegesis (e.g. Thielicke 1948:105-6; Porteous 1951:339; Kraeling 1955:226; Schwarzwäller 1969:282). Now it is true, as his reviewers have pointed out at length, that some of Vischer's interpretations are open to question and others are plainly fanciful, though these are the exception rather than the rule. It is also true that he evades the question of historicity (as does von Rad in his Old Testament theology, 1957-60) and is more concerned to expound the text as it stands than to study its literary history (as is Childs in his commentary on Exodus, 1974). Moreover it could be pointed out that Vischer quotes more liberally from Luther and Calvin than from most modern authors. Nevertheless, in spite of these qualifications, Vischer's work is essentially what he intends it to be: exegesis based on the principles of modern historical and linguistic scholarship (cf. Hertzberg 1936; Jacob 1945:76; Filson 1951: 144-5; Congar 1949:11-12).

5.212 Typology and Allegory

Another common criticism of Vischer's work is that he uses unacceptable methods such as typology and allegory (e.g. Baumgärtel 1952:93; Köhler 1953:251-3; Harrington 1973:314; cf. Brunner 1941:81-2n.; Filson 1951:143-5). Yet Vischer explicitly rejects these methods and insists on scholarly study of the text (1960:120; cf. 1934:30). In fact, although his exegesis includes typology in the sense of 'example' or 'pattern' (see 1964a:99-100; cf. below: 6.21), and in spite of occasional inconsistencies in his methodology (see above: 5.211), it is unnecessary to flaw Vischer's work on these grounds. His view of the relationship between the Testaments and his exegeses of Old Testament texts depend not on allegory - nor on typology as popularly understood - but on historically based scholarship (cf. Bright 1967:86-7).

5.213 Imbalance

The first volume of Vischer's major work is perhaps somewhat unbalanced: he gives 157 pages to Genesis, 57 to Exodus, and only 47 to the other three books of the Pentateuch. But the suggestion of Baumgartner (1941:191) that Vischer picks the raisins out of the pudding, selecting those parts of the Old Testament which can more easily be shown to witness to Christ, must be rejected. If Vischer had written his whole book in as great detail as the section on Genesis it would have been more than twice its present length, so he compromises by giving a fuller exegesis of the first two books and merely a brief sketch of the last three (cf. E. Hermann 1935).

5.22 JESUS AS THE OLD TESTAMENT CHRIST

An important aspect of Vischer's interpretation of the relationship between the Testaments is his assertion that Jesus is the Christ of the Old Testament (1934:11-14; see above: 5.12c). This proposition is apparently unassailable: any Christian theology presupposes that Jesus is the Christ, and it is naturally the Old Testament which defines the concept 'Christ'. Yet it fails to account for the element of surprise in the coming of Jesus of Nazareth as the Christ. There is no doubt that Jesus, according to the testimony of the New Testament, was the fulfilment of the Old Testament promises of a Messiah; but there is equally no doubt that in many ways the fulfilment was so radically different from the expectation that Jesus can only be understood to be the Christ of the whole Bible (cf. Baumgärtel 1952:91). The New Testament does not only identify the Christ, it explains in much more detail his nature and function (Porteous 1951:337-8; cf. also Hertzberg 1936).

Cf. Brunner, Die Unentbehrlichkeit des ATes(1934); Cullmann, The Christology of the NT(1957):111-136.

5.23 NEW TESTAMENT FULFILMENT OF THE OLD TESTAMENT

Another important aspect of Vischer's interpretation of the Old Testament is that he takes seriously the way it is fulfilled in the New (cf. 1934:27-8). Following good exegetical procedure he takes account of the context of the passage in question, and for him this context is the whole Bible. Such a method lays Vischer open to the criticism that he reads the New Testament meaning into the Old Testament passage (Porteous 1951:338; cf. Baumgärtel 1952: 93,95; Kraeling 1955:223-4). But it is consistent with his presupposition of the theological identity of the Testaments which enables him to move freely in the whole Bible to find analogies and explanations for clarification of difficult passages.

5.24 CHRISTOLOGICAL OLD TESTAMENT INTERPRETATION

It follows from the two preceding points that Vischer develops a Christological interpretation of the Old Testament. He dismisses the possibility of giving a theological interpretation of the Old Testament in the Christian Church without Christ:

'The hallmark of Christian theology is that it is Christology, a theology that can affirm nothing of God except in and through Jesus Christ ... (John 1:18) ... From this it is clear that all the knowledge of God which resides in the Old Testament scriptures is mediated through Jesus Christ. Consequently, the theological exposition of these writings within the Church can be nothing other than Christology' (1934:28-9).

This does not imply that for Vischer Jesus Christ was present in Old Testament times and may be found and expounded directly in the texts of the Old Testament (contrast Hanson 1965; cf. Grelot 1962b; McAlear 1970; McCullough 1972). Immanuel, for instance, is not identical with Jesus Christ: on the contrary, Immanuel is a sign - a person, thing or event that has an essential correspondence with something greater in the future, and thus points to it and confirms it though it is not yet known (1954a: 52). Vischer's Christological interpretation means rather that every Old Testament text points toward the death of Christ and cannot be fully understood without reference to him (cf. Filson 1951:145; Bright 1967: 86-8). 'The witnesses of the Old Testament and those of the New stand facing each other like the two sections of an antiphonal choir looking towards a central point ... Immanuel' (1934:25; cf. von Rad 1952a:39; Wolff 1952:102). Not surprisingly Vischer's Christological interpretation has provoked a good deal of interest and disagreement (cf. Baumgärtel 1952:93-5); but it is a natural corollary of his view that the Old and New Testaments have the same - Christian - theology.

On Christological Old Testament interpretation see:
Volz, 'Das AT und unsere Verkündigung', _Luthertum_ (1937):338-40;
Eichrodt, 'Zur Frage der theologischen Exegese des ATes', _ThBl_(1938);
Phythian-Adams, _The Fulness of Israel_(1938):48-50;
Ducros, _La Bible et la méthode historique_(1945):49-55;
Jacob, 'A propos de l'interprétation de l'AT', _ETR_ (1945);
Glen, 'Jesus Christ and the Unity of the Bible', _Interpn_ (1951);
M. Barth, 'The Christ in Israel's History', _ThTo_(1954);
van Ruler, _The Christian Church and the OT_(1955):ch.2;
Higgins, 'The OT and Some Aspects of NT Christology', _CJT_(1960);
Frör, _Biblische Hermeneutik_(1961):129-139;
Hertzberg, 'Das Christusproblem im AT' in _Beiträge..._ (1962);
Zerafa, 'Christological interpretation of the OT', _Angelicum_ (1964);
Barr, _Old and New_(1966):99-102,151-4;
Lohfink, 'Die historische und die christliche Auslegung des ATes' in _Bibelauslegung im Wandel_(1967);
Davies, 'Torah and Dogma', _HTR_(1968):98-100;
Fohrer, 'Das AT und das Thema "Christologie"', _EvTh_ (1970);
cf. Hengstenberg, _Christology of the OT_(1829-35).
See also below: 5.3.

5.25 A TIMELESS REVELATION

a. Finally, a significant aspect of Vischer's work is its conception of a timeless revelation (cf. Thielicke 1948:100-117). On the basis of the unity of the Bible he argues that 'the events which happened in the life of Christ as temporal history form an eternal <u>now</u> ... In every generation every true Christian is contemporaneous with Christ' (1934:21; see above: 5.12f). But while it may be agreed that God himself is outside time, God's plan is enacted within history and it is there that his revelation is to be found (cf. de Vaux 1952). Vischer is in danger of obscuring the dynamic nature of divine revelation in the biblical documents by abstracting it into timelessness in this way (cf. Köhler 1935:261-2; Porteous 1951:327,339; though contrast Congar 1949:12-13). Though it starts from a very different point, the end result is akin to Bultmann's existential view of revelation (cf. above: 3.22).

b. A corollary to this view of a timeless revelation is that 'in its nature and essence <u>salvation under the old covenant was in no way different from ours</u> (1934:21; see above: 5.12f). Vischer qualifies this by indicating differences in the way salvation was administered, in earthly forms in the Old Testament and spiritual ones in the New (cf. above: 1.23b). But he virtually ignores the fundamental difference, that in the New Testament Jesus Christ has come and brought blessings, including eternal life, unknown or unexpected in the Old Testament (cf. Porteous 1951:337; Baumgärtel 1952:91-2).

5.26 A RELATIONSHIP OF IDENTITY

a. The title of the present chapter sums up Vischer's thesis: the Old and New Testaments are equally Christian Scripture. It follows that for him the theological relationship between the Testaments is a relationship involving not only 'unity' but 'identity' (cf. (Eichrodt 1938:75-6; Thielicke 1948:104; Baumgärtel 1952:93-4; Kraeling 1955:220 cf.225-6; Verhoef 1970a: 281). To be sure, Vischer is aware of the differences between the Old and the New: his starting-point ('the Old Testament tells us _what_ the Christ is; the New, _who_ He is',1934:7; see above: 5.12a) makes that clear. Nevertheless, his basic presupposition is that the two Testaments have the same theology and the same Christology. The implications of this include Christological interpretation of the Old Testament and a timeless view of revelation and salvation.

b. There is no doubt that a Christian solution to the problem of the relationship between the Testaments must take Vischer's work seriously. It must account for the fact that the New Testament identifies Jesus of Nazareth as the Christ promised in the Old Testament, though it will recognise that the full meaning of the word 'Christ' is ascertainable only from the whole Bible. It will also take into consideration the fact that the Old Testament is not a self-contained revelation but has a conclusion outside itself, in the revelation of Christ in the New Testament, though it will reject any Old Testament interpretation which forgets that the Christ is made fully known only in Jesus of Nazareth. Moreover it will be aware of the sense in which thousands of years of history can be contemporaneous to an eternal God, without neglecting the temporal nature of his revelation and salvation.

5.3 COMPARISON: OTHER CHRISTOLOGICAL SOLUTIONS

.31 KARL BARTH

; must suffice to summarise Barth's view of the ›lationship between the Testaments on the basis of few relevant passages from his works. A detailed ;udy of his position would be a formidable task, ›yond the scope of the present work. In a lecture ıring the early period of his life Barth stated his ›sition thus:

'he Old Testament mainly concerns us through its ›lation to the New Testament. If the Church is ›presented as the successor of the synagogue, then ıe Old Testament witnesses to Christ before Christ ›ut not apart from Christ). The Old and New Test-ıents are related to one another as prophecy to ;s fulfilment, and the Old Testament should always › regarded in this light ... The Old Testament, ıough a completely Jewish book, none the less refers › Christ ... The Old Testament looks forward, and the ›w Testament speaks of the future while looking ıck, and both look to Christ.' (Prayer and Preaching:93-4).

ı later works, especially Church Dogmatics, he ›ntinued to maintain that the Old Testament is a .tness to Christ (I.2:70-101,489) and that the Old ›stament points forward while the New Testament ›ints back to Christ as the centre of the Bible .2:481; IV.2:822). Like Vischer[1], Barth emphasises ıat Jesus of Nazareth is the Messiah of Israel [.2:448; II.2.198; III.1:239,276; IV.1:166) and ›cognises the 'essential identity of Old Testament

---

Although Vischer was influenced by Barth's thought, ›st of Barth's works considered here are later than .tness(1934) and he quotes Vischer with approval ›.g. I.2:80; II.2:x).

and New Testament' (I.2:74; cf.II.1:364-7; III.3:216; IV.1:167). Notwithstanding their differences, for Barth the two Testaments are one in their witness to God's revelation, in their message about God, his creation, his sovereignty and his grace (I.2:80-101; II.1:381-2; III.1:63-4,202-3; III.3:178-183; IV.2:822).

Relevant works by Barth:
Church Dogmatics: I.2(1938); II.1(1940); II.2(1942); III.1(1945); III.3(1950); IV.1(1953); IV.2(1955).
Prayer and Preaching (ET: 1964, based on lectures given when he was 'comparatively young',p.64);
'Gospel and Law'(1935),ET in God,Grace and Gospel:4 cf.16
The Knowledge of God and the Service of God(1938):64;
Christ and Adam(1952):35;
Evangelical Theology(1962):22-3/26-7.

In spite of the wealth of writing about Barth, there is no detailed study of his view of the relationship between the Testaments. The following deal briefly with the subject:
Baumgartner, 'Die Auslegung des ATs'(1941), repr. in Zum AT und seiner Umwelt:182-7;
Thielicke, 'Law and Gospel as Constant Partners'(1948), incorporated into Theological Ethics I:100-117;
Kraeling, The OT Since the Reformation(1955):168-9;
Kraus, 'Das Problem der Heilsgeschichte in der "kirchlichen Dogmatik"' in Barth Festschrift(1956); Die Biblische Theologie(1970):282-96;
Hesse, 'Das AT in der gegenwärtigen Dogmatik', NZST(1960):30-40;
Frör, Biblische Hermeneutik(1961):31-4;
Smart, The Interpretation of Scripture(1961):74-5;
Davis, 'Typology in Barth's Doctrine of Scripture', ATR (1965);
Nicolaisen, Die Auseinandersetzung um das AT(1966):55-9;
Bright, The Authority of the OT(1967):85-6;
Kuske, Das AT als Buch von Christus(1967):18-19;
Schwarzwäller, 'Das Verhältnis AT - NT',EvTh(1969):282-3.

5.32 HERMANN DIEM

Diem, like Miskotte, follows in the footsteps of Barth. In the first place, he affirms that Jesus is the Christ of the Old Testament. Moreover, he defines the unity of Scripture not as unity of doctrine but as meaning that 'in the proclamation of these witnesses Jesus Christ is to be heard proclaiming Himself; and the fact of the canon bears witness that the Church has in fact unequivocally heard in these witnesses the proclamation of Jesus Christ' (1953:234).

Diem, Theologie als kirchliche Wissenschaft I(1951):74-6; 'The Unity of Scripture' (1953) and 'Jesus the Christ of the OT' (1954), ETs in Dogmatics.

5.33 EDMOND JACOB

Although he never discusses it at length, Jacob's view of the relationship between the Testaments can be seen from a number of his works. In his Theology of the Old Testament (1955) he states, in words that could almost have been written by Vischer:

'A theology of the Old Testament which is founded not on certain isolated verses, but on the Old Testament as a whole, can only be a Christology, for what was revealed under the old covenant, through a long and varied history, in events, persons and institutions, is, in Christ, gathered together and brought to perfection ... a perfectly objective study makes us discern already in the Old Testament the same message of ... God ... which characterizes the Gospel' (p.12; cf. 15,17,328).

Christ is therefore at the centre of the Bible, and the Old Testament, although it should not be Christianised, is the road which led to Jesus Christ and can only be interpreted as such (1950:156-7; 1955b:84; cf. Smart 1961:75). Jacob recognises that there are obvious differences between the Old Testament and the New, and agrees with van Ruler and Miskotte (cf. above: 1.23,2.15) that the Old Testament supplements the New Testament message at many points. Nevertheless, the two Testaments are essentially united in their language, structure and message (1955a:31-2,61-2,112; 1966b:393; 1968b:431-2).

Works by Jacob:
'A propos de l'interprétation de l'AT', ETR(1945);
'L'AT et la prédication chrétienne', VerbC(1950);
Theology of the OT[1](1955);
'Considérations sur l'autorité canonique de l'AT' in Boisset (1955);
Grundfragen Atl.Theologie (1965);
'Possibilités et limites d'une Théologie biblique', RHPR (1966);
Théologie de l'AT[2](1968);
'La Théologie de l'AT', ETL(1968).

Like Vischer, Jacob has been criticised for inconsistencies in method (Bright, ExpT 1962) and also for giving inadequate consideration to the history of salvation (Rhodes, Interpn 1959). Perhaps in response to such criticism, Jacob has recently emphasised the importance of historical method and affirmed, while recognising the limitations of the language, that his work is a theology of the history of salvation (1966a:126n.; 1968a:vii-ix).

More general discussions of Jacob's approach to Old Testament theology include reviews by Cazelles (VT 1956) and Barr (JSS 1960); see also Laurin 1970; Harrington 1973:55-63,73-5,354-6.

5.34 GEORGE A.F.KNIGHT

Knight has the distinction of being the author of a 'Christian' Old Testament theology (1959). In it he makes no secret of his presupposition that 'the Old Testament is nothing less than Christian Scripture' (p.7; cf. 1953:51; 1962:9-10,13-14). This does not mean, however, that the Old Testament is a collection of prophecies of Christ. Rather there is a close parallel between God's acts through his Son Israel and those through his Son Jesus (1959a:8,225-47; cf. 1953:71-3). Knight's thought here has a certain similarity to the idea of typology as 'patterns' (cf. 1960a:57; see below: 6.21). Moreover, he argues, the Old and New Testaments are equally revelation and have fundamentally the same theology (1959a:8; 1953:27,36-7,66; 1962:61-5). This explains the adjective 'Christian' in the title of his theology: it is not individual passages but the Old Testament as a whole which is messianic, looking forward to Christ (1959a:286 cf.285-320; cf. also Köhler 1953: 257-8). A corollary is that there is 'an essential identity between the Israel of old and the Church which has come into existence through Christ' (1959a: 335 cf.336-43; cf. also above: 1.214).

Works by Knight:
From Moses to Paul (1949);
A Biblical Approach to the Doctrine of the Trinity(1953);
A Christian Theology of the OT (1964^{2},1959^{1});
'New Perspectives in OT Interpretation'(1960),
repr. in *BT* 19;
Law and Grace (1962).
Examples of his interpretation - which is rather similar to that of Vischer - may be found in works on Ruth and Jonah (1950), Esther, Song of Songs and Lamentations (1955), Hosea (1960) and Isaiah (1961,1966).

Three particularly important discussions of his *Theology* are by Ackroyd (*ExpT* 1962), Durham (in Laurin 1970) and Harrington (1973:34-40). The major issue raised by his reviewers is Knight's attempt to write a Christian Old Testament theology. Snaith (*SJT* 1960) acknowledges this to be the natural approach of a Christian and Richardson (*JTS* 1960) is impressed that Knight is able to do this purely by strict exegesis of the Old Testament. But others complain that he has failed to produce a distinctively Christian theology (e.g. Childs, *Interpn* 1960; Smart, *JBL* 1960) and that the result is little different from other Old Testament theologies (e.g. Rowley, *ExpT* 1959; Gehman, *ThTo* 1960). See also: Jacob 1965:14; 1968a:xii; 1968b:423; Davidson 1970:155-6.

5.35 OTHERS

a. The five solutions to the problem of the relationship between the Testaments discussed in the present chapter are of course not the only ones that might fit within the bracket of a relationship of theological identity. Miskotte, for instance, views the Bible as Christocentric and is influenced by Barth, though it was shown in the second chapter that the essence of his view is a relationship of 'priority', not of 'identity'.

b. Hans Hellbardt views the relationship non--historically in terms of 'truth and reality', and interprets the Old Testament as a witness to Christ. Helmuth Schreiner (1936) emphasises that the Word of God is both Law and Gospel, but argues that the former must be preached on the basis of the latter. For Otto Procksch (1925a:486) all theology is Christology, and S. de Diétrich's exposition of the divine plan in the Bible (1945) is explicitly dependent on Vischer's Christological exegesis (cf.p.272).

c. Christological views of the relationship between the Testaments are common in Roman Catholic scholarship. Joseph Coppens has devoted several works to the Christian interpretation of the Old Testament, while Jean Daniélou expounds and generally follows the Christological and theological biblical exegesis of the Church Fathers. C. Larcher (1962) uses the New Testament to develop a Christian theology of the Old Testament, and Hilaire Duesberg (1967) presents Jesus as the 'Object of the Scriptures'.

d. A number of works in English follow similar lines. G.S.Hendry (1948) argues that since the Bible is Christocentric it has to be interpreted Christologically, Nathaniel Micklem (1953:7-9) affirms that Christians are interested in Leviticus because of its testimony to Christ, and Ronald S. Wallace expounds the Old Testament as a witness to Christ. Finally, H.L.Ellison (1969:11) declares that 'the Old Testament is not a preparation for the New but the major part of one revelation by God'.

Procksch, 'Die Geschichte als Glaubensinhalt',NKZ(1925); 'Ziele und Grenzen der Exegese',NKZ(1925); 'Die kirchliche Bedeutung des ATs',NKZ(1931); 'Christus im AT',NKZ(1933); Theologie des ATs (1950); cf. Eissfeldt 1926:3-5; Porteous 1951: 330-33; Kraus 1970:128-130; Schofield 1970; Würthwein 1971:202-5;

Hellbardt, Abrahams Lüge (1936); 'Die Auslegung des ATs als theologische Disziplin',ThBl(1937); also, not available to me: Der verheissene König Israels (1935); 'Christos, das Telos des Gesetzes',EvTh(1936); 'Neuerscheinungen zum AT',EvTh(1937); Das AT und das Evangelium (1938); Das Bild Gottes (1939); 'Auslegung der Schrift...',DPfBl(1939); cf. Eichrodt 1938; Baumgartner 1941:188-194; Porteous 1948:140-142; Thielicke 1948:104; Nicolaisen 1966:155-160; Verhoef 1970a:297-8;

Schreiner, Die Verkündigung des Wortes Gottes(1936);

de Diétrich, Le dessein de Dieu(1945);

Hendry, 'The Exposition of Holy Scripture',SJT(1948);

Coppens, Les harmonies des deux Testaments(1948); Un nouvel essai d'Herméneutique biblique(1951); Vom Christlichen Verständnis des ATs(1952); 'Nouvelles réflexions sur les divers sens des Saintes Ecritures',NRT(1952); 'Levels of meaning in the Bible',Concilium(1967); cf. Daniélou 1950b; Harrington 1973:293-4;

Daniélou, Origen (1948); 'Les divers sens de l'Ecriture...',ETL(1948); 'L'unité des deux Testaments dans l'oeuvre d'Origène',RevSR(1948); From Shadows to Reality (1950); 'The Fathers and the Scriptures',Theology(1954); Études d'exégèse judéo-chrétienne(1966); 'Patristic Literature' in Historical Theology (1969);

Micklem, 'Leviticus',IB (1953);

Wallace, 'The Preaching of the OT',TSFB(1953); Elijah and Elisha(1957); The Ten Commandments(1965);

Ellison, The Centrality of the Messianic Idea for the OT(1953); The Message of the OT(1969);

Larcher, L'actualité chrétienne de l'AT(1962); cf. Alonso-Schökel 1963; Harrington 1973:323-9;

Duesberg, '"He opened their minds to understand the Scriptures"',Concilium(1967).

6. <u>The Old and New Testaments correspond to each other</u>

6.1 TYPOLOGY IN RECENT STUDY

6.2 SYNTHESIS: A NEW LOOK AT TYPOLOGY

6.3 CRITICISM: THE NATURE OF TYPOLOGY

6.1 TYPOLOGY IN RECENT STUDY

6.11 INTRODUCTION

a. It is necessary first of all to consider what is meant by the word 'typology', There is a world of difference between the use of τύπος ('type') in the Bible and many of the fanciful interpretations of the early Church, or between the use of typology in modern biblical scholarship and in modern Church life. Two main conceptions of typology are to be found today. Recently a number of biblical scholars have used the term 'typology' for the interpretation of history involved in the 'promise-fulfilment' approach to the relationship between the Testaments. Alongside this there are those who perpetuate fanciful forms of biblical interpretation closely related to allegory and symbolism, referring to them as typology. The place of typology in the theological relationship between the Old Testament and the New Testament depends entirely therefore on what is meant by 'typology'.

b. A term with such diverse connotations stands in need of replacement or more precise definition. Of those scholars who have chosen the former alternative, some have rejected the idea of typology for the modern Church (see below: bb), while others have suggested substitutes. W.J. Phythian-Adams (1944:11), for example, has developed the idea of 'homology', and this is taken up by A.G. Hebert (1947a:218-22). The concept of 'analogy' is important for Barth (Smart

1961:125-9; cf. von Balthasar 1951:93-181; Pannenberg 1953; Pöhlmann 1965), as also for von Rad (1960: 363-4) and Wolff (1956a:167-181; cf.below:6.15). Rowley (1953:19-20; cf.below: 8.223) rejects the term 'typology' but recognises common patterns in the two Testaments (cf. Hooke 1961), and A.T. Hanson (1965:162) writes of 'parallel situation'.

c. On the other hand, although there are problems in retaining the term 'typology', a term originating in the Bible and well-recognised in modern scholarship cannot be dropped so easily simply because it has been misused in some periods of history and is popularly misunderstood today (cf. Wolff 1956a:181n.; also, von Rad 1952a:38-9). Like it or not the term 'typology' is firmly established in theological vocabulary and in the present chapter the latter alternative is chosen in an attempt to define the word more precisely. After an analysis of modern study of biblical typology, a synthesis will be attempted on the basis of the meaning of τύπος and its cognates in biblical Greek and the meaning of 'type' in modern English. It will be seen that this results in a more satisfactory understanding of typology, which is consistent with the nature of the biblical literature and illuminates the theological relationship between the Old and New Testaments.

aa. Calmet, 'Type' in Calmet's Dictionary(1837[6]);
Fairbairn, The Typology of Scripture(1864[4]);
Davidson, OT Prophecy(1903);
Lambert, 'Type',HDAC(1918);
Moorehead, 'Type',ISBE(1939);
Goppelt, Typos (1939);
Fritsch, 'Biblical Typology',BS(1946-7);
'ΤΟ 'ΑΝΤΙΤΥΠΟΝ' in Vriezen Festschrift(1966);
Edsman, 'Gammal och ny typologisk tolkning av G.T.', SEA(1947);

Richardson, Christian Apologetics(1947): 188-193;
Sailer, 'Über Typen im NT',ZKT(1947);
Walvoord, 'Christological Typology',BS(1948-9);
Berkhof, Principles of Biblical Interpretation (1950):142-8;
Hebert, 'The Interpretation of the Bible',Interpn(1950);
Daniélou, From Shadows to Reality(1950); 'Qu'est-ce que la typologie?' in Auvray (1951);
Miller, 'Zur Typologie des ATs',BenM(1951);
Coppens, Vom Christlichen Verständnis des ATs(1952);
Wright, God Who Acts(1952):61-66;
Amsler, 'Où en est la typologie de l'AT?',ETR(1952); 'Prophétie et typologie',RThPh(1953); L'Ancien Testament dans l'Eglise(1960):141-7, 215-27, cf. below: 7.33e;
von Rad, 'Typological Interpretation of the OT' (1952),ET in EOTI; OT Theology II(1960),part 3; cf. below: 7.23;
Ellison, 'Typology',EQ(1953);
Ramm, Protestant Biblical Interpretation(1953):ch.9;
Lampe, 'Typological Exegesis',Theology(1953); 'The Reasonableness of Typology' in Lampe and Woollcombe (1957); 'Hermeneutics and Typology', LQHR(1965);
Wolff, 'The Hermeneutics of the OT'(1956),ET in EOTI; 'The OT in Controversy'(1956),ET in Interpn 12;
Eichrodt, 'Is Typological Exegesis an Appropriate Method?'(1957),ET in EOTI;
Marcus, 'Presuppositions of the Typological Approach to Scripture',CQR(1957);
Woollcombe, 'The Biblical Origins and Patristic Development of Typology' in Lampe and Woollcombe(1957);
Ridderbos, 'Typologie',VoxTh(1961);
Verhoef, 'Some Notes on Typological Exegesis', OTWSA (1962);
Mickelsen, Interpreting the Bible(1963):236-64;
Bläser, 'Typos in der Schrift',LTK[2](1965);
Lys, The Meaning of the OT(1967):esp.54-75;
Gundry, 'Typology as a Means of Interpretation', BETS(1969);
Friederichsen, 'The Hermeneutics of Typology', Dissn (1970; not available to me);
Stek, 'Biblical Typology Yesterday and Today', CTJ(1970);
Röhr, '...Untersuchung zur Typologie zweier Welt-Religionen',ZRG(1973).

bb. Those who reject the idea of typology include:
Bultmann, 'Ursprung und Sinn der Typologie',TLZ(1950);
Irwin, 'The Interpretation of the OT',ZAW(1950); cf. 'A Still Small Voice...',JBL(1959);
Baumgärtel, Verheissung(1952):78-85,138-143; 'The Hermeneutical Problem of the OT'(1954), ET in EOTI:143; cf. Eichrodt 1957a:236-41;

van Ruler, The Christian Church and the OT(1955): 58-68/62-73, cf. above: 1.146;
Smart, The Interpretation of Scripture(1961):129-133;
Barr, Old and New(1966):ch.4;
Fohrer, 'Das AT und das Thema "Christologie"', EvTh(1970):esp.293-4.

6.12 MODERN DEFINITIONS OF TYPOLOGY

a. In modern scholarship many definitions of typology have been proposed, and they fall into two main categories. The first category comprises definitions centring on the idea of 'prefiguration', and these date mainly from more than twenty years ago. An example is the definition given by C.T. Fritsch (1947:214): 'a type is an institution, historical event or person, ordained by God, which effectively prefigures some truth connected with Christianity' (cf. Lambert 1918; Goppelt 1939:18-19; Moorehead 1939; Amsler 1952:80; 1953:139; R.P.C. Hanson 1959:7).

b. The second category comprises definitions centring on the idea of 'correspondence', and these date mainly from the past twenty years. An example is G.W.H. Lampe's definition (1953:202) of typology as 'primarily a method of historical interpretation, based upon the continuity of God's purpose throughout the history of his covenant. It seeks to demonstrate the correspondence between the various stages in the fulfilment of that purpose' (cf. Ellison 1953b:161; Woollcombe 1957:39-40; von Rad 1960:272,329; Wolff 1960:344; Mickelsen 1963:237; France 1971:40).

c. Both kinds of definition have in common an historical basis and both are clearly distinguished from fanciful interpretation. It is true that these definitions, like the term 'typology' itself, are theological rather than biblical (cf. Lambert 1918), but the Bible's general lack of abstraction makes this inevitable (cf. Hummel 1964:40). There seems to be general agreement among modern scholars that typology is a form of historical interpretation, based on the Bible itself.

Stek (1970) contrasts the use of 'typology' in Fairbairn's Typology of Scripture (1864[4]) with that in volume two of von Rad's OT Theology (1960). He characterises the former as 'a divine pedagogical instrument for progressive revelation of a system of spiritual truths about heavenly and earthly realities', and the latter as 'a useful theological method by which men appropriate for themselves and proclaim to others their experiences of the self-revelation of God in history'.

6.13 TYPOLOGY IN THE OLD TESTAMENT

a. A number of scholars claim that typology originated in the Old Testament itself, especially in the prophetic writings (though contrast Rohland 1956:284-7, who considers typology to be characteristic of apocalyptic, not of prophecy): Isaiah uses the garden of Eden as a type for the new paradise (Isa.9:1/2; 11:6-9), Hosea predicts another period in the wilderness (Hosea 2:16-17/14-15; 12:10/9; cf. Jer.31:2), Second Isaiah expects a new exodus (e.g. Isa.43:16-21; 48:20-21; 51:9-11; 52:11-12; cf. 11:15-16; Jer.16:14-15), and many of the prophets see David as typical of the king who is to come in the future (Isa.11:1; 55:3-4; Jer.23:5; Ezek.34:23-4; Amos 9:11). Eichrodt (1935-9:277; 1957a:235) and von Rad (1957:282,294) also see typology within the Pentateuch, so that Abraham is a type of the faithful (Gen.15:6), Moses a type of the prophets (Deut.18:15,18), and even the story of the manna has the typological significance that God gives to each according to his need (Ex.16: 9-27).

b. Francis Foulkes (1958) sets out to show that the 'theological and eschatological interpretation of history' which is called typology originates in the Old Testament (p.7). He argues that, since the prophets assumed that God would act in the future in the same way that he had acted in the past (e.g. call of Abraham; Exodus; reign of David), the concept of God's acts in history being repeated is fundamental to the Old Testament. However, Israel hoped not simply for a repetition of God's acts but for a repetition of an unprecedented nature (e.g. new Temple; new covenant; new creation). This hope was fulfilled in the New Testament and was the basis of the New Testament's typological interpretation of history.

c. Horace Hummel (1964) asserts even more emphatically that typology is based in the Old Testament, stating that 'the <u>typical</u> is a dominant concern of the O.T., its historiography, its cultus, its prophecy, etc.'(p.40). He surveys 'typical' thinking - which he identifies with typological thinking - in the Old Testament, and finds examples in the presentation of historical events (e.g. Exodus), individuals (e.g. Abraham; Moses; David), groups (e.g. the righteous; Israel; the wise man), laws (e.g. Pss.15, 24), nations (e.g. Israel; Edom; Babylon; Gog and Magog), places (e.g. holy land; Jerusalem; temple), legends (creation; flood; Jonah) and the cult (in its very nature: re-enaction of God's redemptive acts). Thus Hummel defends his proposition that 'Israel's fundamental concern behind all the personages, events, and scenes of her history was typical, and intended to point to the basic realities of all existence' (p.47).

Eichrodt, Theology of the OT II(1935-9):244,277-8; 'Is Typological Exegesis an Appropriate Method?' (1957),ET in EOTI:234-5; 'Vom Symbol zur Typos',ThZ(1957);
Elliger, 'Der Jakobskampf am Jabbok',ZTK(1951):29-31;
Amsler, 'Où en est la typologie de l'AT?',ETR(1952): 80-81;
Rohland, Die Bedeutung der Erwählungstraditionen Israels (1956):284-7;
Lampe, 'The Reasonableness of Typology' in Lampe and Woollcombe (1957):26-7;
von Rad, OT Theology I(1957):282,294,351; II(1960): 272 cf.323;
Foulkes, The Acts of God(1958);
Smart, The Interpretation of Scripture(1961):102-3;
B.W. Anderson, 'Exodus Typology in Second Isaiah' in Muilenburg Festschrift (1962);
Daube, The Exodus Pattern in the Bible(1963);
Hummel, 'The OT Basis of Typological Interpretation', BR (1964);
Uhlig, 'Die Typologische Bedeutung des Begriffs Babylon',AUSS(1974);
Wifall, 'David - Prototype of Israel's Future?', BThB (1974).

6.14 TYPOLOGY IN THE NEW TESTAMENT

a. In the New Testament the typical element is even clearer than in the Old, especially in its interpretation of the Old Testament. The standard work on the subject is still Leonhard Goppelt's *Typos: Die typologische Deutung des Alten Testaments im Neuen* (1939). Goppelt examines in detail those passages of the New Testament which involve a typological use of the Old Testament, against the background of the contemporary Jewish understanding of Scripture and in contrast to the 'typology' of the letter of Barnabas. His conclusion is simple and important: typology is the dominant and characteristic method of interpretation for the New Testament use of the Old Testament (pp.239-49; cf. Richardson 1947:190; Wright 1952:61; Grant 1965:ch.4; contrast Hanson 1965:8,172-7). It is not only when the Old Testament is actually cited that this is apparent but in all the New Testament allusions to the Old, many of which do not refer to specific texts. The New Testament writers recall Old Testament parallels to Jesus and the salvation which came through him, depicting both the similarity and the difference.

b. The purpose of this, according to Goppelt, is not primarily to expound the meaning of an Old Testament text. Typology is not a system for interpretation of the Old Testament but a way of thinking. It is primarily directed to the understanding of the New Testament, both with respect to individual passages and to theological ideas. It is an aspect of the New Testament's own awareness of being part of the history of salvation: the New Testament is both a typological fulfilment of the Old Testament salvation history and a typological prophecy of the consummation to come. In contemporary Jewish biblical interpretation typology is relatively unimportant, and where it does occur it is comparatively superficial. In the letter of Barnabas 'typology' is used to make the Old Testament a collection of Christian teaching, instead of the New Testament's view of the Old Testament as a unity which is valid in its own right. So the New Testament views the Old Testament by means of typology, according to Goppelt, in an historical and not a mystical sense.

As well as his major work, Goppelt has written two important articles on this question: 'Apokalyptik und Typologie bei Paulus', TLZ(1964), repr. as appendix to the reissue of Typos (1969); 'τύπος', TDNT(1969).

Among other studies of New Testament typology, the following are particularly important:
Ellis, Paul's Use of the OT(1957):126-135;
Woollcombe, 'The Biblical Origins and Patristic Development of Typology' in Lampe and Woollcombe(1957);
Amsler, L'AT dans l'Église(1960):esp.141-7,215-27;
France, '...A Study of Jesus' Typology', TSFB(1970); Jesus and the OT (1971):ch.3.

Studies of individual aspects of this subject include:
R.P.C. Hanson, 'Moses in the Typology of St Paul', Theology(1945);
Guillet, 'Thème de la marche au désert', RechSR(1949);
Sahlin, Zur Typologie des Johannesevangeliums(1950);
Goulder, Type and History in Acts (1964);
Wood, 'Isaac Typology in the NT', NTS(1968);
Dahlberg, 'The Typological Use of Jer.1:4-19 in Matt. 16:13-23', JBL(1975).

6.15 TYPOLOGY IN THE RELATIONSHIP BETWEEN THE TESTAMENTS

a. Hans Walter Wolff (1956a:167-181) develops the idea of typology as the analogy between the Old and New Testaments, centring his argument on the special starting-point of Old Testament interpretation.

b. First, he rejects any suggestion that ancient near Eastern religion is this starting-point. The Old Testament is quite distinct from its ancient near Eastern environment: in spite of parallels in detail, the substance is essentially different. Its distinctive characteristics - including its divine law and prophecy, which are more important than the cult, and especially the unique nature of Yahweh, the God of Israel - show that the Old Testament is a stranger in the ancient Orient. It follows that the essence of the Old Testament cannot be understood by analogy to its religious environment.

c. Secondly, he asks, if studies of the ancient near East are not the key to the Old Testament, will Rabbinic studies unlock its meaning? There is an apparent continuity between the Old Testament and Judaism (cf. above: 2.14a), but the fact is that from the Christian standpoint Judaism has not properly understood the Old Testament. Whether the synagogue reads its Bible as law or as the source of all wisdom, the full meaning of the Old Testament is to be sought elsewhere.

d. Thirdly, the question of whether the New Testament can show the meaning of the Old Testament remains for consideration. Wolff points out that Paul addresses the Church as the Israel of God (Gal. 6:16) and throughout the New Testament Israel is a type of the Church of Jesus Christ (e.g. Mark 3:14; Rom.11:17ff.; James 1:1; Rev.21:12-14). Here he says is a fundamental analogy: 'the Church of Jesus Christ can understand itself aright only as the eschatological Israel of God' (p.174; cf. above: 1.214). There is also an analogy between the basis and method of salvation in the two Testaments. Although there are obvious differences, the fundamental pattern is the same: the people of God is formed through God's saving activity, the covenant is kept intact only through the forgiveness of sins, and God's kingship over the members of his people demands their obedience to his law. Finally, there is a third analogy between God's gifts in the Old and New Testaments. In both cases there are material and spiritual gifts, and although there are differences the analogy is dominant: 'the new covenant in Christ corresponds to the covenant will of Yahweh as its fulfilment in the same way that marriage corresponds to engagement' (pp.179-180). Wolff concludes in these words: 'the old Oriental environment and the Jewish successors of the Old Testament Israel, while presenting us with numerous aids to understanding details, still do not provide anything comparable to the essential total meaning of the Old Testament. Only the New Testament offers the analogy of a witness of faith to the covenant will of God - a witness founded on historical facts - who chooses out of the world a people for himself and calls it to freedom under his Lordship' (p.180; cf. Davidson 1903a:239-40). This analogy he calls 'typology'.

e. Wolff gives a number of examples of how this idea of analogy can be used in biblical interpretation, and some will mentioned here. The Sermon on the Mount and Paul's exhortations give insight into the Old Testament law as God's covenant gift, the concept of 'witness' in Luke and John illuminates that in Ezekiel, and God's salvation of his people by the judges may be seen as one aspect of his continual saving activity throughout their history. Moreover, the primeval history witnesses to God's intention for the world, without which Jesus Christ would not be properly understood; the day of Atonement ritual shows God's principles in dealing with sin, which are the presupposition for the coming of Jesus and apart from which his death would be inexplicable; and Exodus 14 and Ezekiel 37 show the nature of the divinely-constituted people of God, and thus the self-understanding of the Church (pp.181-199).

f. To sum up, the conclusion of not a few modern scholars is that typology is far from being a fanciful method of interpretation to be dismissed as an illegitimate way of understanding the Bible. On the contrary, it is historically based and originates in the Bible itself. In order to define its place in understanding the relationship between the Testaments, the basis and nature of typology will be considered in the synthesis and criticism which follow.

6.2 SYNTHESIS: A NEW LOOK AT TYPOLOGY

6.21 EXAMPLE AND PATTERN

a. A more precise definition of the biblical meaning of 'typology' necessitates an examination of the biblical use of the word τύπος ('type') and its cognates τυπικός ('typical'), ἀντίτυπος ('antitype') and ὑποτύπωσις ('type'). There is no biblical equivalent to 'typology' for the simple reason that the biblical authors did not analyse or systematise types. For the same reason, 'typical' is a more appropriate translation of τυπικός than 'typological'. 'Type' is a common word in modern English, but in the Septuagint and New Testament τύπος is used only 17 times. In both cases however there is one basic meaning.

b. The word τύπος in the Bible usually means 'example' or 'pattern' (12 times); and the occasional meanings 'mark' (John 20:25, twice), 'image' (Amos 5:26; Acts 7:43) and 'to this effect' (Acts 23:25) are closely related in meaning. Its cognates also relate in every case to the meaning 'example' or 'pattern'. To show this clearly the biblical occurrences of τύπος and its cognates are set out in full. The basic text is the RSV and the translations in brackets are from the RSV, NEB and NIV respectively (except for the Septuagint: RSV, NEB and Bagster).

c. The use of the τύπος word-group in the Septuagint (Old Testament) and New Testament:

τύπος

Ex.25:40 'the (pattern,design,pattern)...shown you on the mountain'

Amos 5:26 'your (images,images,images)'

John 20:25 '(print,mark,marks) of the nails'

John 20:25 '(mark,place,where(the nails)were) of the nails'

Acts 7:43 '(figures,images,idols) which you made to worship'

Acts 7:44 'the (pattern,pattern,pattern) that he had seen'

Acts 23:25 'a letter (to this effect,to this effect,as follows)

Rom.5:14 'Adam, who was a (type,foreshadows,pattern)'

Rom.6:17 'obedient...to the (standard,pattern,form) of teaching'

1 Cor.10:6 'these things are (warnings,symbols to warn, examples) for us'

Phil.3:17 'as you have an (example,model,pattern) in us'

1 Th.1:7 'an (example,model,model) to all the believers'

2 Th.3:9 'an (example,example,model) to imitate'

1 Tim.4:12 'set the believers an (example,example,example)'

Titus 2:7 'show yourself...a (model,example,example) of good deeds'

Heb.8:5 'the (pattern,pattern,pattern)...shown you on the mountain'

1 Pet.5:3 'being (examples,an example,examples) to the flock'

τυπικός

1 Cor.10:11 'happened to them as (a warning,symbolic,examples)

ἀντίτυπος

Heb.9:24 'a (copy,symbol,copy) of the true one'

1 Pet.3:21 'Baptism, which (corresponds) to this' (RSV)
'This water (prefigured,symbolizes) baptism'(NEB,N

ὑποτύπωσις

1 Tim.1:16 '(example to,typical of,example for) those who...believe'

2 Tim.1:13 'Follow the (pattern,outline,pattern) of the sound words'

d. The τύπος word-group is closely related in meaning to the word-group which includes δεῖγμα (Jude 7) and its cognates δειγματίζω (Col.2:15), παράδειγμα (Ex.25:9; 1 Chron.28:11,12,18,19), παραδειγματίζω (Matt.1:19; Heb.6:6) and ὑπόδειγμα (John 13:15; Heb.4:11; 8:5; 9:23; James 5:10; 2 Peter 2:6). Here again, apart from Heb.6:6 where the meaning of παραδειγματίζω is 'to hold up to contempt', the meaning is 'example' or 'pattern' in every case.

e. In no case is any member of either of these word-groups used as a technical term. It is sometimes thought that the word τύπος has a technical sense in 1 Cor.10:6 (cf.v.11) and Rom.5:14 (e.g. Goppelt 1969:251-3). However, translators generally agree that the meaning is 'foreshadow'(NEB), 'prefigure'(JB) or 'pattern'(NIV) in Rom.5:14 and 'example'(NIV) or 'warning'(RSV,JB) in 1 Cor.10:6,11. In both cases the usual biblical meaning 'example, pattern' is entirely appropriate and it is unnecessary to suggest a technical use. It is presumably to prevent any implication of a technical term that the English versions avoid the translation 'type' for τύπος. KJV, NIV, Moffatt do not use the word 'type' at all, RSV does so only at Rom.5:14. Vischer (1960:120) rejects 'typology' partly because it has poorly understood the meaning of τύπος, which he argues is 'example'. The conclusion is straightforward: the evidence of biblical terminology suggests the meaning 'example, pattern' for 'type'.

6.22 ANALOGY AND CORRESPONDENCE

a. Typological thinking is part of all human thought, arising out of man's attempt to understand the world on the basis of concrete analogies, as von Rad (1952a:17; 1960:364) points out.[1] It follows that there is nothing surprising about the application of this method to the biblical world. Archbishop Trench (1870:12-14) once wrote:

'the parable or other analogy to spiritual truth appropriated from the world of nature or man, is not merely illustration, but also in some sort proof. It is not merely that these analogies assist to make the truth intelligible ... Their power lies deeper than this, in the harmony unconsciously felt by all men, and which all deeper minds have delighted to trace, between the natural and the spiritual worlds, so that analogies from the first are felt to be something more than illustrations, happily but yet arbitrarily chosen ... They belong to one another, the type and the thing typified, by an inward necessity; they were linked together long before by the law of a secret affinity.' (cf. Dodd 1935:21-2/20)

It is the conviction that there is such a 'secret affinity' within God's created order, shared by the biblical writers and many of their interpreters throughout the centuries, which lies at the root of the idea of typology. Some use typology cautiously, others use it extravagantly, but all base their use of typology on the conviction that there is a 'secret affinity' between the natural and spiritual orders, as well as between different events in the same order.

---

1. Contrast Bultmann (1950b) who rejects typology because it is based on the idea of repetition. According to him this is derived from the cyclic view of history of the ancient near East and classical Greece, whereas the Old Testament has a linear view of history, a history whose course is divinely-directed and moves toward a definite conclusion. Von Rad (1952a:20) disputes the validity of this view.

b. Thus it is natural for those in biblical times to see an analogy between the tabernacle and the heavenly pattern shown to Moses (Ex.25:40; Acts 7:44; Heb.8:5), between the life of Christ or a Christian leader and the way Christians ought to live (1 Tim.1:16; Phil.3:17; 1 Peter 5:3), between events in Israel's history and events in the life of the Church (1 Cor.10:6,11; 1 Peter 3:21), between an idol and the spiritual reality it symbolises (Amos 5:26; Acts 7:43), and between the man who brought sin into the world and the man who took it away (Rom.5:14). In each case the presupposition is that God acts consistently so that there are correspondences between different parts of his created order. Typology rests on the basic assumption that 'the history of God's people and of his dealings with them is a single continuous process in which a uniform pattern may be discerned' (Lampe 1953:201; cf. Fritsch 1946:293; Marcus 1957:448; Wolff 1960:344n.; Hummel 1964:41).

There are two main kinds of correspondence here: vertical (archetype and antitype, i.e. the relationship between heavenly and earthly realities) and horizontal (prototype and antitype, i.e. the relationship between earlier and later historical facts). In practice however the Bible is more interested in horizontal than vertical typology, as is most modern writing on the subject. On this distinction, see Hummel 1964:39; Fritsch 1966.

On analogy and correspondence, see further: Mildenberger, Gottes Tat im Wort(1964):78-83; Sauter, Zukunft und Verheissung(1965):184-207.

6.23 ILLUSTRATION

a. It has been shown that understanding of the relationship between the Testaments in terms of typology is based on the biblical meaning of τύπος ('example, pattern') and the consistency of God which leads to analogies and correspondences within creation and history. Yet there is something even more basic about the idea of typology: it is the way in which almost any biblical text - Old Testament or New Testament - addresses the Church. The Bible contains, in general, not propositions but stories, and these can only be relevant in the sense of being typical (see Miskotte 1956a:199-207 cf.388-404; cf. Sanders 1974:329). What significance would Abraham or Moses have if they were not typical? That a frog can hop or a snake can bite is hardly of Christian significance. It is because Abraham and Moses were men 'of like nature with ourselves' (James 5:17) and as such encountered the same God as the Christian does, in other words because they were typical, that their experiences are directly relevant to the Church.

b. At the end of John's Gospel it is noted that 'Jesus did many other signs in the presence of the disciples, which are not written in this book; but these are written that you may believe that Jesus is the Christ...'(John 20:30-31). The implication is that certain signs were recorded because they were typical. In Chemistry a 'type' is a 'compound whose structure illustrates that of many others' (Concise Oxford Dictionary). Hydrochloric acid, for example, is a type of the acids. It is no more an acid than any other but is typical because it shows clearly the essential nature of an acid in its structure: HCl. Sulphuric acid (H_2SO_4) and acetic acid (CH_3COOH) have the same basic structure but it is not so clear. The structure of hydrochloric acid is also a pattern for such compounds as $NaCl$ and HBr and so it may be termed a type of the haloids too. In a similar way certain signs are recorded in John because they illustrate some aspect or aspects of the gospel message especially well and thus can serve as types (cf. above: 1.151d).

c. This provides at least one reason why so much is made of the affair between David and Bathsheba. There is no question of revelling in the sins of others: it is rather that the temptation, sin, attempt to conceal, rebuke, repentance, forgiveness, punishment and restoration are recorded because they are typical of what happens frequently in the life of a believer. Jonah may be chosen as a type of the Christian because like so many he was led from sin through despair to eventual salvation. He is also a type of Christ who bore the sins of the world, was brought to the point of despair and descended to the lowest state possible before he was raised from death to life.

On typology as study of what is typical, see Röhr, '...Untersuchung zur Typologie zweier Weltreligionen', ZRG(1973):290; cf. Bozzo,'Jesus as a Paradigm for Personal Life',JES(1974).

6.3 CRITICISM: THE NATURE OF TYPOLOGY

6.31 FALSE IDEAS OF TYPOLOGY

Before attempting a precise definition of the nature of typology it is necessary to distinguish a number of incorrect uses of the word.

a. Typology is not exegesis (Goppelt 1939:19-20; Amsler 1952:77-9; von Rad 1952a:37-8; Wolff 1956b:285; France 1971:41; contrast Woollcombe 1957:39-40). The biblical text has only one meaning, its literal meaning, and this is to be found by means of grammatico-historical study. If the author intended a typical significance it will be clear in the text. And if we see a typical significance not perceived by the original author it must be consistent with the literal meaning. Typology is not an exegesis or interpretation of a text but the study of relationships between events, persons and institutions recorded in biblical texts.

b. Typology is not prophecy (Amsler 1953; Wolff 1956a: 188-9; Eichrodt 1957a:229; Woollcombe 1957:41-2). The two are related since both presuppose continuity and correspondence in history, but typology is retrospective whereas prophecy is prospective. It is true that recognition of the fulfilment of prophecy is retrospective, but this is concerned with the fulfilment of <u>words</u> in the Old Testament whereas typology discerns a relationship between the <u>events</u>, <u>persons</u> and <u>institutions</u> recorded in the Bible.

c. Typology is not allegory (Goppelt 1939:19; Richardson 1947:190; Florovsky 1951:173-6; Amsler 1952: 77; Eichrodt 1957a:227; Lampe 1957:29-35; Woollcombe 1957: 40-42; Nixon 1963:11; Lys 1967:54-75; cf.de Lubac 1947). The distinction between typology and allegory was formulated as early as 1762 by J. Gerhard: 'Typology consists in the comparison of facts. Allegory is not so much concerned in facts as in their assembly, from which it draws out useful and hidden doctrine' (quoted by Goppelt 1939:8, ET by Wright 1952:61). Modern scholars have generally accepted this distinction, laying stress on the historical nature of typology in contrast to the fanciful nature of allegory which often entirely ignores the historical situation. A few scholars disagree: Barr (1966:103-111) denies the validity of the distinction; Jewett (1954) thinks they are much the same thing; and Bright (1967:79) points out that it is difficult to distinguish between the two in the Fathers. But they have not invalidated the fundamental distinction that typology is generally historical, whereas allegory is fanciful. Typology requires a real correspondence between the events, persons and institutions in question, but allegory can find 'spiritual' significance in unimportant details or words.

d. Typology is not symbolism (Goppelt 1939:19). Symbolic interpretation involves understanding objects as expressions of a general truth but typical interpretation is concerned to see relationships between historical facts.

e. Typology is not a method or a system (Goppelt 1939:243-4; Eichrodt 1957a:229-31; France 1971:76-7; cf. Amsler 1960a:141,144). In the Church Fathers an elaborate typological method was developed, but in the Bible the typical approach is so unsystematic that it does not even have a fixed terminology. The Bible gives no exhaustive list of types and implies no developed method for their interpretation. On the contrary, there is great freedom and variety in the outworking of the basic principle that the Old Testament is a model for the New.

6.32 SUGGESTED CHARACTERISTICS OF TYPES

There have been numerous attempts to define the characteristics of types, many of which make the mistake of treating typology as a fixed system of interpretation rather than a basic approach to the Bible.

a. It is suggested, for instance, that an essential characteristic of a type is that it is designed by God (Goppelt 1939:18-19; Moorehead 1939; Fritsch 1947:214; Berkhof 1950:145; Amsler 1952:79). At first sight this is very plausible and it may be thought that it is self-evident. But surely Christian faith affirms that the whole Bible was designed by God? 'If David could have been placed where he was, and been what he was, without God's design, he would still have been typical. But, of course, without God's intervention, neither he nor his dispensation could have come into existence' (Davidson 1903a:237). Cf. Calmet (1837:II.769): 'Whether certain histories which happened in ancient times were designed as types of future events, it is not easy to determine: but observe, (1.) it is likely that such histories are recorded (being selected from among many occurrences) as might be useful lessons, &c. to succeeding ages. (2.) That there being a general conformity in the dispensations of providence and grace, to different persons, and in different ages, instances of former dispensations may usefully be held up to the view of later times, and may encourage, or may check, may direct or may control, those placed in circumstances, &c. similar to what is recorded, though their times and their places may be widely separated. We have New Testament authority for this.'

b. Another suggestion is that the limits of typology should be defined by giving a series of standards to which a type must conform (Moorehead 1939; Amsler 1952:81; cf.Eichrodt 1957a:244), or by limiting types to those found in the New Testament (Wright 1952:66; cf.France 1970:16; an early advocate of this was Bishop Marsh, see Fairbairn 1864:32-44). But although it is possible to describe what is meant by 'typical', it is arbitrary to limit its occurrence in the Bible by a set of rules. The New Testament gives guidelines but does not pretend to give a definition or exhaustive list of types (Fritsch 1947:220). Since typology is not concerned only with certain parts of the Old Testament but with the whole Bible there are an unlimited number of possible types (von Rad 1952a:36; cf. Sailer 1947). It is not a matter of finding types in a fixed system: rather, many events and persons may usefully serve as typical for one purpose or another.

c. It is sometimes suggested that types are always concerned with Christ (Amsler 1952:79; 1960a:144) or with God's redemptive activity (Fritsch 1947:220; Woollcombe 1957:75; Payne 1962:357). But then much of the Bible is concerned with God's redemptive activity and thus with Christ! It is not surprising that this is the dominant concern of types in the Bible; but the Bible is interested in creation and the kingdom of God as well as redemption (see above: 1.25,1.26) and these have typical aspects too (cf. Verhoef 1962:63).

d. A further suggestion is that types prefigure something future (Moorehead 1939; Berkhof 1950:145; cf. von Rad 1952a:36). But this implies that they have some meaning other than that which is apparent at the time. It is only in retrospect that an event, person or institution may be seen to be typical (von Rad 1960:384; Bright 1967:92-3; Lys 1967:71). The existence of types necessitates there being other events, persons or institutions - earlier or later - of which they are typical.

e. It is often suggested that there is an 'increase' (<u>Steigerung</u>, Goppelt 1939:19,244) or 'progression' (Davidson 1903a:240; Amsler 1960a:145; Verhoef 1962: 64; France 1971:78; cf. von Rad 1952a:37) from the type to its antitype. But this is simply an aspect of the progression from Old Testament to New Testament and not a necessary characteristic of a type. The essence of a type is that it is exemplary, and it would be theoretically possible for something which is more advanced to be typical of something which is less advanced. Moreover it is possible for one thing to be a type of its opposite: for example, the entry of sin into the world by the first Adam and the entry of grace by the second (Amsler 1952:80).

6.33 CONFUSION OF TYPOLOGY WITH FANCIFUL INTERPRETATION

a. One of the basic issues mentioned in the introduction was that typology in Church history and today has frequently been taken to be a fanciful kind of biblical interpretation. Sometimes, for instance, the word 'typology' has been used for what is really symbolism or allegory. Sometimes typology has been used as a method of exegesis (cf. above: 6.31a): there is all the difference between finding the real meaning of Genesis 37-50 to be a prefiguration of Christ ('exegesis'), and seeing Joseph as a typical character whose life reveals basic principles of God's activity which are also true for the life of Christ and Christians ('typology').

b. The most common failing however is to find correspondences in trivial details. There is no historical or theological correspondence between Rahab's scarlet cord and the death of Christ, nor between the axe Elisha retrieved from the river and the cross (1 Clement 12; Justin, Dialogue: 86). There is a consistency in God's created order which makes it possible for there to be red or wooden objects in both Old and New Testaments; but that does not mean that these things have any typical or exemplary importance for the Christian! Nevertheless the fact that the term 'typology' has been applied to trivial correspondences, confused with allegory and symbolism, amd misused in the exegesis of the Old Testament does not invalidate it as a principle if properly used. And although the modern Church should certainly not adopt such exegetical methods, neither should it despise those who used them; it was the allegorical school in the early Church who preserved the Old Testament for the Christian Church (cf. Grant 1965:ch.5).

6.34 A NOTE ON THE 'FULLER MEANING'

a. During the past thirty years, encouraged particularly by the encyclical 'Divino afflante Spiritu' (1943) of Pius XII, a deep interest in the interpretation and theology of the Bible has developed in the Roman Catholic Church. An important aspect of this has been the discussion and use of the concept of a 'fuller meaning' (sensus plenior), introduced in 1927 by Andrés Fernández but widely used only after the Second World War. It is defined by Brown (1968) as 'the deeper meaning, intended by God but not clearly intended by the human author, that is seen to exist in the words of Scripture when they are studied in the light of further revelation or of development in the understanding of revelation'. Its implication for understanding the relationship between the Testaments is that the Old Testament is considered to have a deeper meaning of which the human authors were not aware but which becomes clear in the light of the New Testament. In the pages of the Old Testament 'God so directed the human author's choice of language that future generations should see there "the mystery of Christ" ... This choice of language, the secret of which is revealed in the New Testament, shows in a very clear manner the unity of the two Testaments' (Sutcliffe 1953:343).

b. The fuller meaning should not be confused with the 'spiritual meaning' (sensus spiritualis), which is essentially a mystical idea based on the interpretation of the Fathers. It should also be distinguished from typology, at least as the latter is defined here. There is indeed a certain resemblance between the fuller meaning and typology in that both consider words in the Old Testament to be related to Christ, but there is also an essential difference. The fuller meaning considers the reference to Christ to be part of the 'real' meaning of the text, though the author was unaware of it. Typology, in contrast, does not claim to elucidate the meaning of a text but adduces it as a description of a 'type' (example, pattern) of God's activity in the history of his people, and the author may well have been aware of this.

aa. On recent Roman Catholic biblical interpretation:
Bonnard, 'L'encyclique Divino afflante Spiritu...', RThPh(1950);

Levie, 'A la lumière de l'encyclique "Divino afflante Spiritu"' in Auvray (1951);
Grelot, 'L'interprétation catholique des livres saints' in Robert and Feuillet (1957);
McKenzie, 'Problems of Hermeneutics in Roman Catholic Exegesis', JBL(1958); 'The Significance of the OT for Christian Faith in Roman Catholicism' in OTCF (1964);
H.H. Miskotte, Sensus spiritualis (1966);
Scharleman, 'Roman Catholic Biblical Interpretation' in Gingrich Festschrift (1972).

bb. The theory of the 'fuller meaning' has generated a vast quantity of literature, from which only a few works can be mentioned here:

Fernández, 'Hermeneutica' in Institutiones Biblicae (1927[2]; not available to me);
Coppens, Les harmonies des deux Testaments(1948); 'Le problème d'un Sens biblique plénier' in ALBO (1950); Le Problème du Sens Plénier(1958);
Sutcliffe, 'The Plenary Sense', Biblica(1953);
Brown, The Sensus Plenior of Sacred Scripture (1955; not available to me); 'The History and Development of the Theory of a Sensus Plenior', CBQ (1953); 'The Sensus Plenior in the Last Ten Years', CBQ(1963); 'The Problems of the Sensus Plenior', ETL(1967); 'Hermeneutics', JBC(1968):II.615-18;
Benoit, 'La plénitude de sens des Livres Saints', RB(1960);
Grelot, La Bible, Parole de Dieu(1965); 'La lecture chrétienne de l'AT' in Weber and Schmitt(1968).

Some Catholic scholars have rejected the fuller meaning, e.g.:

Bierberg, 'Does Sacred Scripture Have a Sensus Plenior?', CBQ(1948);
Courtade, 'Les Écritures ont-elles un sens "plénier"?', RechSR (1950);
Vawter, 'The Fuller Sense', CBQ (1964).

See also:

Gribomont, 'Sens plénier, sens typique et sens littéral' in ALBO (1950);
Braun, 'Le sens plénier et les encycliques', RThom(1951);
Temiño, 'En torno al problema del "sensus plenior"', EstB (1955);
von Schmid, 'Die atl. Zitate bei Paulus und die Theorie vom sensus plenior', BZ(1959);
Amsler, L'AT dans l'Église(1960):183-6;
J.M.Robinson, '...A Protestant Study in Sensus Plenior', CBQ(1965);
Harrington, The Path of Biblical Theology(1973):293-304.

cc. On 'spiritual meaning' see:
Dubarle, 'Le sens spirituel de l'Écriture', RSPT(1947);
de Lubac, '"Sens spirituel"', RechSR(1949); Histoire et Esprit(1950); L'Écriture dans la tradition (1966):24-47;
McKenzie, 'A Chapter in the History of Spiritual Exegesis', ThSt(1951).

6.35 PRINCIPLES AND DEFINITIONS

a. So far the argument has taken the form of negative criticism. It has been argued that typology is not exegesis, prophecy, allegory, symbolism or a system. The suggestions that divine design, specific limits, connection with Christ and redemption, prefiguration of the future and progression from type to antitype are necessary characteristics of typology have been rejected. Typology has also been distinguished from fanciful interpretation and the Roman Catholic theory of a 'fuller meaning'. On the positive side there are two basic principles of typology which must be adhered to if it is not to result in fanciful or trivial biblical interpretation.

b. First, typology is historical (Goppelt 1939:18; Florovsky 1951:175; Amsler 1952:80; Lampe 1953:202; 1965:24; Woollcombe 1957:75; Wolff 1956a:344; cf. von Rad 1952:36-7; contrast Barr 1966:ch.4). Its concern is not with words but with historical facts: events, people, institutions. It is not a method of philological or textual study but a way of understanding history.

It follows that typology does not imply any particular doctrine of the inspiration of the Bible: its basis is God's direction of history (so Amsler 1952:78; but contrast Gundry 1969). The question may be raised whether Jonah or Job, for instance, must be historical in order to be typical. It may be suggested that although typology is essentially historical it is possible to have correspondences between an imaginary person and a real person. Even if such a type is somewhat artificial it could still have educative value. There is an undoubted correspondence between Macbeth or Hamlet and real people: the significance of these characters is not lessened by the fact that they are merely fictional. Likewise, whether or not they ever lived, there remains a fundamental correspondence between the lives of Jonah and Job as portrayed in the biblical story and those of Christians.

The fundamental conviction which underlies typology is that God is consistently active in the history of this world - especially in the history of his chosen people - and that as a consequence the events in this history tend to follow a consistent pattern. One event may therefore be chosen as typical of another, or of many others.

c. Secondly, typology implies a real correspondence (Berkhof 1950:145; Amsler 1952:79; Woollcombe 1957:75; France 1971:41; Hasel 1972a:73). It is not interested in parallels of detail but only in an agreement of fundamental principles and structure. There must be a correspondence in history and theology or the parallel will be trivial and valueless for understanding the Bible.

d. On the basis of these two principles some working definitions may be suggested:
a _type_ is a biblical event, person or institution which serves as an example or pattern for other events, persons or institutions;
typology is the study of types and the historical and theological correspondences between them;
the _basis_ of typology is God's consistent activity in the history of his chosen people.

6.36 A RELATIONSHIP OF ANALOGY

a. It has been argued that typology is not a method of exegesis or interpretation but the study of historical and theological correspondences between different parts of God's activity among his people in order to find what is typical there. The function of typology is therefore not to give a procedure for using the Old Testament but to point to the consistent working of God in the experience of his people. Thus parallels may be drawn between different events, persons and institutions, and individual events may be seen as examples or patterns for others. Typology cannot be used for exegesis, because its concern is not primarily with the words of the text but with the events recorded in it. This means also that Old Testament exegesis is freed from the pressure to be relevant: often the narrator has recorded only a bare event, but in this very lack of interpretation it may have typical and thus theological significance (von Rad 1952a:38). The exegete has to find the meaning of the text and its witness to an event, and for this the tool is grammatico-historical exegesis. To relate it to other events recorded in the Bible is the task of the biblical theologian and historian; to relate it to modern Christian experience is the task of the preacher. For these typology has its value but it must be used judiciously and in accordance with the principles previously outlined.

b. The contribution of typology to understanding the relationship between the Testaments is to point to the fundamental analogy between different parts of the Bible. Every part of the Bible is an expression of the consistent activity of the one God. This means that the Old Testament illuminates the New and the New Testament illuminates the Old. It is not the New Testament's use of the Old or parallels in detail which are in question but a fundamental analogy between the Old and New Testaments as witnesses to God's activity in history. In this way, although it is not a method of exegesis, typology supplements exegesis by throwing further light on the text in question. The most closely related discipline to the study of the Old Testament is therefore that of the New Testament: ancient Oriental and Jewish studies clarify details of the Old Testament but lack the intrinsic analogy of New Testament studies to Old Testament studies. The corollary is that the most closely related discipline to the study of the New Testament is that of the Old Testament: Jewish and Hellenistic studies are important but do not have a fundamental analogy to New Testament studies in the way that Old Testament studies do. This shows a double aspect to the relationship between the Testaments: on the one hand, correct understanding and use of the Old Testament depends on the New Testament; and on the other hand, one of the primary uses of the Old Testament is to be the basis for correct understanding and use of the New Testament.

c. A corollary to this is that typology is an aid to interpretation of the Bible in the Christian Church. It has been shown that the essence of the biblical concept of 'type' is 'example, pattern', and one of the primary values of the Bible for the Christian is that it presents examples and patterns of the experience of men and women with God which correspond to the experience of modern men and women. Events, persons and institutions present types for the Christian life. The flood (cf. 1 Peter 3:20-21), the oppression and exodus (cf. 1 Cor.10), and the exile and restoration (cf. Jer.23:7-8) are typical of God's saving activity among his people, and thus patterns of the salvation which the Christian experiences in Christ. Noah and Job (cf. Ezek.14:14,20), Moses (cf. Heb.3:2) and David (cf. 1 Kings 3:14; 15:3,11) are examples of how the believer should live. Balaam (cf. 2 Peter 2:15; Jude 11; Rev.2:14) and Jeroboam (cf. 1 Kings 15:26,34; 16:2-3,19,26,31), in contrast, are examples of how he should not live. These instances could easily be multiplied (cf. Heb.11). The correspondence between Israelite and Christian institutions (e.g. Passover and Lord's Supper; psalms and hymns) and the spiritual application of Old Testament material realities (e.g. the temple and the Christian Church as divine dwelling-places, cf. 1 Cor.3:16; sacrifices and offerings, and the Christian's 'living sacrifice', cf.Rom.12:1) are further ways in which typology may aid practical use of the Bible. All these examples - and many others which could be adduced - apply to the Christian, but most apply also and especially to Christ himself, which is why typology is often thought to be concerned with types of Christ. But what is more important is that Jesus Christ himself is the supreme example and pattern for Christians (Matt.11:29; John 13:15; Phil.2:5; 1 Peter 2:21). Perhaps the concern of typology is less to look for types <u>of</u> Christ than to present Christ <u>himself</u> as the supreme type for Christians and the world.

7. The Old and New Testaments form one salvation history

7.1 GERHARD VON RAD: THE OLD TESTAMENT AND THE NEW

7.2 CRITICISM: SALVATION HISTORY AND ACTUALISATION

7.3 COMPARISON: OTHER SALVATION HISTORY SOLUTIONS

7.1 GERHARD VON RAD: THE OLD TESTAMENT AND THE NEW

7.11 INTRODUCTION

a. Historians and prophets are important people, according to von Rad. The first volume of his massive Old Testament Theology (I:1957; II:1960) is given to 'The Theology of Israel's Historical Traditions', while most of the second volume is concerned with 'The Theology of Israel's Prophetic Traditions'. There are at least two reasons for surprise at such a plan for an Old Testament theology. First, the word 'theology' refers usually to a systematic treatment of the doctrines of God, man and their interrelations, and this is in fact what is provided by the majority of Old Testament theologies (e.g. Eichrodt, Vriezen, Jacob, Knight). In von Rad's _Theology_, however, the titles of the major sections refer not to 'God' or 'man' but to 'history','prophecy' and 'tradition' (words associated more with study of Israelite religion than with theology). Secondly, it seems that von Rad attaches such importance to the historical and prophetic traditions that their theology can be taken to constitute a theology of the whole Old Testament. The law, psalms, wisdom writings and Pentateuchal narratives are evidently either of little theological importance, or to be categorised as historical or prophetic traditions.

b. An analysis of the space which von Rad allocates in his theology to different parts of the Old Testament will clarify further his distinctive approach to Old Testament theology.

I. The Theology of Israel's Historical Traditions:

Introduction: History of Yahwism	130pp.
Hexateuch	175pp.
Deuteronomic History	40pp.
Chronicler's History	7pp.
Psalms	15pp.
Wisdom Literature	80pp.

II. The Theology of Israel's Prophetic Traditions:

Introduction: Prophecy	130pp.
Classical Prophets	190pp.

It is obvious from this analysis that von Rad's theology is not a systematic treatment of doctrine but a study of the theologies of each strand of the Old Testament. The analysis also shows that von Rad attaches particular significance to the Hexateuch (cf.175pp. for this, with the total of 47pp. for the other two historical works) and the Prophets.

c. The key to von Rad's new exposition of Old Testament theology is found in the preface, where he explains that study of the history of traditions has made his work possible. In fact traditio-historical interpretation of the Old Testament, based on the literary analyses of Gunkel and the historical criticism of Alt and Noth, forms the foundation of his theology. He starts from the premise that 'the Hexateuch is built upon a very few ancient credal statements which became constitutive for the Israel of all ages' (1957:vi), the most important of which is that found in Deut.26:5-9 (cf. below: 7.25). These credal statements were developed and interpreted by means of further traditions until eventually the 'history' of the Hexateuch was formed. In a similar way the Deuteronomic and Chronicler's histories have certain fundamental bases - going back originally to the Hexateuchal traditions - which have been expanded to form the present works. Israel's history as found in the Old Testament is therefore 'confessional', since essentially it is confession of the saving acts of God: Israel's origin in the patriarchs, oppression in and redemption from Egypt, the gift of the promised land. The whole of von Rad's theology is founded on this 'salvation history', which is therefore the predominant theme in his interpretation of the Old Testament. Cullmann (1965) sums up von Rad's approach thus:

'The progressive reinterpretation of Israel's old traditions is continually awakened by new events in the present. This development of the traditions is itself salvation history and stands in continuity with the original event basic to the traditions' (p.54).

d. The reason for the structure of von Rad's book now becomes clear. It has been shown that the core of his theology is the saving history, presented and developed in Israel's historical traditions. Under these 'historical traditions' are subsumed the primeval history, patriarchal stories, law, psalms and wisdom literature, the first three being integrated into the 'canonical' saving history and the last two forming Israel's response to Yahweh. There is one major element of Old Testament thought which does not fit into this structure: the prophetic traditions. The prophets rejected the efficacy of past saving acts for their own time and looked to a new salvation in a new history (1957:vii). Nevertheless, the theology of Israel's prophetic traditions is also based on 'salvation history' and forms a complement to that of the historical traditions.

e. While much of his writing has implications for the relationship between the Testaments, the most important elaboration of von Rad's solution to the problem is the final section of his Old Testament Theology II (1960). An analysis of this section, which von Rad calls 'The Old Testament and the New', will now be made.

aa. Von Rad's major work is his OT Theology (I:1957; II:1960). Other works concerned with the relationship between the Testaments include:
'There still remains a rest for the people of God' (1933),ET in Problem of Hexateuch;
'Das Christuszeugnis des ATs',ThBl(1935);
'Sensus Scripturae Sacrae duplex?',ThBl(1936);
'Gesetz und Evangelium im AT',ThBl(1937);
'Grundprobleme einer biblischen Theologie des ATs',TLZ(1943);
'Typological Interpretation of the OT'(1952), ET in EOTI;
'Kritische Vorarbeiten zu einer Theologie des ATs' in Hennig(1952);
'Verheissung',EvTh(1953);
'Ancient Word and Living Word',Interpn(1961);
'Offene Fragen im Umkreis einer Theologie des ATs' (1963),ET as 'Postscript' to OT Theology II;
'Antwort auf Conzelmanns Fragen',EvTh(1964);
'Christliche Weisheit?',EvTh(1971).
A full bibliography of von Rad's works is given in his Festschrift (1971).

bb. Several recent theses have been concerned with von Rad's approach to Old Testament theology:
Nesbit, 'A Study of Methodologies in Contemporary OT Theologies'(1969);
Spriggs, 'Towards an Understanding of OT Theology' (1971), abridged version published as Two Old Testament Theologies(1974);
Greig, 'Geschichte und Heilsgeschichte in OT Interpretation'(1974).
Also, not available to me,
Jones, 'The Exegetical Method of Gerhard von Rad'(1966);
Bell, 'An examination of the presuppositions and methodology of Gerhard von Rad in his OT Theology' (1970).

cc. The following are important reviews of von Rad's OT Theology:
Baumgärtel, TLZ(1961); Murphy, CBQ(1961);
Barr, ExpT(1962); Hempel, BO(1962);
de Vaux, RB(1963); Zimmerli, VT(1963);
B.W.Anderson,Interpn(1965,1969); Cazelles,BO(1969).

dd. Other critical works include:

Baumgärtel, *Verheissung*(1952):115-127; 'Der Dissensus im Verständnis des ATs',*EvTh*(1954);
van Ruler, *The Christian Church and the OT*(1955);
Hermann, 'Offenbarung, Worte und Texte',*EvTh*(1959);
Hesse, 'Kerygma oder geschichtliche Wirklichkeit?', *ZTK*(1960);
von Rad Festschrift: *Studien zur Theologie der atl. Überlieferungen*(1961) - articles by Köster, Wilckens, Rössler and others;
Eichrodt, 'The Problem of OT Theology'(1961) in *Theology of the OT* I;
Frör, *Biblische Hermeneutik*(1961):part II,*passim*;
Pannenberg, 'Kerygma and History'(1961),ET in *Basic Questions* I;
van der Ploeg, 'Une "Théologie de l'AT" est-elle possible?',*ETL*(1962):430-34;
C. Barth, 'Grundprobleme einer Theologie des ATs', *EvTh*(1963);
Mildenberger, *Gottes Tat im Wort*(1964);
Clements, 'The Problem of OT Theology',*LQHR*(1965);
Conzelmann, 'Fragen an Gerhard von Rad',*EvTh*(1964);
Ramlot, 'Une décade de théologie biblique',*RThom*(1965);
Vriezen, 'Geloof, openbaring en geschiedenis',*KT*(1965);
Barr, *Old and New*(1966):chs 3-4;
de Vaux, 'Is It Possible to Write a "Theology of the OT"?'(1967),ET in *The Bible and the Ancient Near East*;
Jacob, 'La Théologie de l'AT',*ETL*(1968);
Hesse, 'Bewährt sich eine "Theologie der Heilstatsachen" am AT?',*ZAW*(1969);
Schwarzwäller, 'Das Verhältnis AT - NT',*EvTh*(1969);
Wright, *The OT and Theology*(1969):ch.2;
Kraus, *Die Biblische Theologie*(1970):133-9;
Davies, 'Gerhard von Rad, *OT Theology*' in Laurin(1970);
Smend, *Die Mitte des ATs*(1970);
Wagner, 'Zur Frage nach dem Gegenstand einer Theologie des ATs' in Doerne Festschrift(1970);
Carrez, 'La méthode de G.von Rad' and
Fruchon, 'Sur l'herméneutique de Gerhard von Rad', *RSPT*(1971);
Harvey, 'The New Diachronic Biblical Theology of the OT',*BThB*(1971);
Porteous, 'Magnalia Dei' in von Rad Festschrift(1971);
Hasel, *OT Theology*(1972);
W.H. Schmidt, '"Theologie des ATs" vor und nach Gerhard von Rad',*VF*(1972);
Harrington, *The Path of Biblical Theology*(1973): 63-77, 273-6,285-8,362-3;
Wolff *et al.*,*Gerhard von Rad*(1973);
L.Schmidt, 'Die Einheit zwischen Altem und NT im Streit zwischen Friedrich Baumgärtel und Gerhard von Rad',*EvTh*(1975).

7.12 ACTUALISATION

a. Von Rad begins by considering 'The Actualisation of the Old Testament in the New' (1960:319-35). He limits himself to a traditio-historical approach to the problem of the relationship between the Testaments, already taken as the basis for understanding Old Testament theology. He argues that 'the way in which the Old Testament is absorbed in the New is the logical end of a process initiated by the Old Testament itself, and that its "laws" are to some extent repeated in this final reinterpretation' (p.321). Thus von Rad does not begin with the New Testament use of the Old but attempts to show how the Old Testament points forward to the New.

b. The Old Testament, according to von Rad, is oriented towards the future: it 'can only be read as a book of ever increasing anticipation' (p.319). It presents a dynamic religion, which is never complete or satisfied but continually looks to the future for improvement, fulfilment, or re-formation. At any particular point in time the religion is part of a continual appropriation, reinterpretation and actualisation of more primitive forms of the religion. This is seen in the way Yahwism adopts and adapts the pre-Mosaic religion; the way in which the prophets take the election traditions and reinterpret them with reference to the coming day of the Lord; and in the way the New Testament writers take the Old Testament traditions, accepting, rejecting or revising them in much the same way that the Old Testament writers themselves interpreted and used the traditions at their disposal.(pp.319-28)

c. Central to the New Testament is the idea that a new saving event has taken place. It announces the inauguration of the kingdom of God in the person and work of Jesus, the promised Christ. Old Testament traditions are cited as promises which are now fulfilled, and correspondences are noted between God's earlier saving acts and the supreme saving act which has occurred in Christ. There is both contrast and continuity between the Old and the New: on the one hand, the newness of the Christ-event is emphasised; on the other, Old Testament prophecies and parallels are pointed out. The New Testament exhibits great freedom in the way it takes over the Old, showing sometimes the contrast and at other times the continuity between the Testaments. 'Proof from Scripture' is therefore inadequate to describe this method: the Old Testament is used not so much for proof as because the New Testament needs the Old to express its message. The approach of the New Testament is ad hoc, presupposing a general understanding of the relationship between the Testaments and on that basis actualising Old Testament texts by citation or allusion. (pp.328-35)

7.13 THE WORLD AND MAN

a. The most difficult problem raised by the continued Christian use of the Old Testament is whether or not it was only of temporary value and should have been given to Israel when the Church separated from her. No doubt study of New Testament use of the Old may provide an answer to this question, and that is a task for New Testament theology. Christianity, however, is based not only on the New Testament but on the whole Bible, and it is therefore important to consider the Old Testament's view of the matter. This von Rad elaborates in the next three chapters, starting with a study of the relationship between 'The Old Testament's Understanding of the World and Man, and Christianity' (pp.336-56).

b. Does the Old Testament remain revelation now that Christ has come? Or, to rephrase the question in a more penetrating way, is the real meaning of the Old Testament brought to light only with the coming of Christ? The Church has always recognised the theoretical equality of revelation in the Old and New Testaments, but in practice has usually found interpretation of the Old Testament in relation to the New to be a problem. It has rarely achieved the New Testament's freedom and insight in biblical interpretation, though even the New Testament does not contain an exhaustive account of its relationship to the Old. Von Rad's attempt to deal with the problem is based on the proposition 'that it is in history that God reveals the secret of his person' (p.338), a proposition which is admittedly very general and requires closer definition by means of concrete examples. (pp.336-8)

c. A study of the Old Testament's understanding of the world, man and death follows. In each case von Rad concludes that Israel's view was decidedly secular, in contrast to the mythological views of contemporary nations. Yahweh is not limited to the realms of myth or the sacred but is active in the world, in history, in everyday life. (pp.338-50)

d. The same is true of Christianity, according to von Rad. The message of the New Testament is not mythological, nor primarily didactic, but descriptive of God's action in history by which he renews his relationship with Israel and the world. This similarity between Israel's secular view of the world and Christianity is of course not coincidental: rather, the language and thought of the Old Testament are fundamental to the expression of the New Testament saving event. Israel's unique experience of Yahweh prepared her quite specifically for the supreme experience of Yahweh made possible in Jesus Christ. (pp.350-56)

7.14 THE SAVING EVENT

a. There is naturally more to the relationship between the Testaments than a conception of the world and man. Von Rad proceeds to consider 'The Old Testament Saving Event in the Light of the New Testament Fulfilment' (pp.357-87).

b. 'The Old Testament is a history book' (p.357[1]). This history, which extends from the creation to the end of the world and includes Israel, the nations and the world, is saving history since every part is presented as the activity of God whose will and purpose is to save. In this history God reveals himself by words and acts, and in the Old Testament there are two corresponding kinds of account: theological, where the event is put in a wider interpretative context, and pre-theological, where the account concentrates on the event itself, without interpretation. It is these pre-theological accounts which make the Old Testament characteristically a history book, although they are fewer

---

1. Cf. 1952a:25. This sentence is also the title of the abridgement of this article in the German version of EOTI.

in number than those accounts which give a theological interpretation to the events they describe. Even the pre-theological accounts, it is true, received new interpretations as they were placed by redactors in wider contexts or adapted to suit the style of a particular strand of the Old Testament, for example in the Priestly Document or the Deuteronomic History. Nevertheless, this continual reinterpretation did not do violence to the stories since 'their intrinsic openness to a future actually needed such fresh interpretations on the part of later ages' (p.361). (pp.357-62)

c. Theologians such as Bengel, Beck and Hofmann (cf. above: 0.44) explained the relationship between the Testaments in terms of a detailed and connected divine plan or 'economy' of salvation. Modern biblical theology, on the other hand, emphasises the discontinuity both within the Old Testament and between the Old Testament and the New. Von Rad rejects such extreme views of continuity and discontinuity and suggests a unity in the sense that 'the true goal of God's relationship with Israel is the coming of Jesus Christ' (p.363). He argues first of all that there is a 'structural analogy' between the saving events in the Old and New Testaments (although not ideal, the term 'typology' may be used to describe this, cf. above: ch.6). Old Testament events are to be understood in the context of God's action in history, which comes to fulfilment in Jesus Christ. Indeed it is only in the Christ-event that analogies and correspondences with earlier events become truly meaningful. (pp.362-74

d. 'The coming of Jesus Christ as a historical reality leaves the exegete no choice at all; he must interpret the Old Testament as pointing to Christ, whom he must understand in its light' (p.374). This raises a double question: how far can Christ elucidate the Old Testament and how far can the Old Testament elucidate Christ? Von Rad answers simply that Christ is necessary to understand the Old Testament and the Old Testament is necessary to understand Christ (pp.384-7). This proposition, he argues, has the support of Church history and the Old and New Testaments themselves. Without the New Testament saving event, the Old Testament would be understood only incompletely; without the Old Testament, the New Testament witness to Christ would have to be radically reinterpreted.

e. Von Rad's previous chapter was concerned with the Old Testament's language and thought about the world and man, and its relationship to Christianity, but there is more to the relationship between the Testaments than this. 'The chief consideration in the correspondence between the two Testaments does not lie primarily in the field of religious terminology, but in that of saving history' (p.382). In the Old Testament there is a close relationship between divine words and historical acts as means of revelation (cf.p.358; see above: b), and in Jesus Christ this dual form of revelation comes to its highest expression. Thus von Rad affirms that the central theme of his whole theology, God's salvation in history, is also the fundamental factor in the relationship between the Testaments. There are two aspects to this: first, the New Testament saving event appears as the prolongation and conclusion of Israel's history with God' (cf. van Ruler, see above: 1.141,1.24); secondly, 'the New Testament saving event has at the same time to be understood in the sense of a repetition, though ... on the basis of an entirely new saving event' (p.383).

7.15 THE LAW

a. There are two reasons why biblical studies cannot ignore the question of the relationship between the Testaments. On the one hand, according to von Rad, the most essential characteristic of the Old Testament is that it points forward, and it is naturally important to know what it points forward to; on the other hand, the New Testament explicitly refers back into the past, so that it is important to consider what is its origin. To understand 'The Law', the third aspect of the relationship between the Testaments considered by von Rad, it is therefore necessary to take full account of its meaning in both Old and New Testaments (pp. 388-409).

b. First, the significance of the law in early Israel is considered. Von Rad rejects the idea that the law was the primary or essential aspect of the relationship between Israel and Yahweh. Israel's relationship to Yahweh was not dependent on the law; on the contrary, it was the law's presupposition. (pp. 390-95)

c. Secondly, von Rad considers attitudes to the law in the preaching of the prophets. In early Israel the law was understood as something which was quite capable of being fulfilled: if it was not fulfilled, the reason was not Israel's inability but her unwillingness to obey. This conception of the law, as also of Israel's relationship to Yahweh as a whole, was transformed by the prophets. The early prophets took the law and applied it to Israel in a new way, showing that since disobedience to the law demonstrated the radical failure of her relationship with Yahweh, judgement and death were coming to her. Jeremiah and Ezekiel penetrated the situation more deeply still, realising that Israel was unable to keep the law and announcing that Yahweh himself would make possible a new obedience. This process of renewing the law may be understood by means of von Rad's fundamental approach to Old Testament theology, the reinterpretation of earlier traditions: 'confronted with the eschatological situation, the prophets were set the task of taking the old regulations and making them the basis of an entirely new interpretation of Jahweh's current demands upon Israel' (p.400). (pp.395-402)

d. Thirdly, even after the Exile the law was not central to Israel's faith. Although the first steps may be recognised in parts of the Old Testament (e.g. the Chronicler's history), the transition from salvation based on grace to a legalistic religion was not made within the Old Testament.

'There is no basis in the Old Testament for the well-known idea which early Lutheranism exalted to almost canonical status, that Israel was compelled by God's law to an ever greater zeal for the Law, and that it was the Law and the emotions it evoked which prepared the way for true salvation in Christ' (p.405; contrast Bultmann, see above: 3.24). (pp.402-7)

e. Finally, von Rad turns to the question of the early Church's understanding of Old Testament law. He argues that the same principle is found here as in the Old Testament prophets: 'reinterpretation in the light of a new saving event'(p.407). There is no normative interpretation of the Old Testament, but many charismatic interpretations, among which that of Paul is central. According to him, the Old Testament law is radically fulfilled in Christ, who himself lived a perfect life before God, took the punishment for other men's disobedience to the law, and made possible a more personal relationship between men and God than existed under the old covenant. (pp.407-9)

7.2 CRITICISM: SALVATION HISTORY AND ACTUALISATION

7.21 SECONDARY QUESTIONS

7.211 Inconsistencies

Spriggs (1974) asserts that von Rad's chapters on the relationship between the Testaments 'betray a lack of integration with the rest of the book and with one another. Indeed, they show an alarming confusion of thought, self-contradiction, and ambiguity' (p.74). This is certainly a serious allegation, but closer examination shows it to be unfounded. It may be that von Rad does not define the Old Testament's orientation to the future as clearly as one might wish, but Spriggs' description of 'confusion' (p.78) is a misrepresentation of von Rad, based on a failure to take into account the context of the statements quoted. Moreover Spriggs' claim that at one point von Rad (1960:371) denies this future orientation of the Old Testament must be rejected, since the statement in question refers only to ancient Israel's view of the texts - which von Rad explicitly contrasts to the Church's view - and in any case it is omitted in the most recent edition of the book. Possibly von Rad overstates his case when he writes (1960: 319): 'All these writings of ancient Israel ... were seen by Jesus Christ ... as a collection of predictions which pointed to him' (Spriggs: 79-80). However von Rad's argument does not depend on whether Jesus saw 'all', 'many' or only 'some' of ancient Israel's writings in this way: rather, he introduces Jesus' predictive view of the Old Testament in order to contrast it with the fact that the Old Testament never explicitly mentions Jesus Christ and to resolve the paradox by explaining that the Old Testament is to be read as 'a book of ever increasing anticipation'. These and other such criticisms scarcely accord with Spriggs' claim to have restricted his comments to 'the most important of the central issues' (p.117). None of them invalidate any of von Rad's major points.

7.212 Presuppositions

Greig (1974) suggests six major formative factors in von Rad's theology: a) Barth's separation of revelation from history; b) Bultmann's non-historical kerygma theology; c) Troeltsch's principles of analogy and correlation; d) Alt and Noth's historical scepticism; e) Dilthey's philosophy of history; f) Otto's charismatic elevation of secondary interpretations. To these might be added: g) the Graf--Wellhausen documentary theory; h) Gunkel's traditio-historical research. It is neither fair nor necessarily effective to prejudge a work on the basis of its presuppositions. It is in any case impossible to work without some presuppositions and to imply that presuppositions dominate his theology would be to underestimate the great originality of von Rad's work. Nevertheless, as Greig has pointed out, several of von Rad's presuppositions are open to question, even if they are not to be lightly dismissed. This must naturally be taken into account in an assessment of his solution to the problem of the relationship between the Testaments (see,e.g.,below: 7.22,7.25).

7.213 Old Testament theology

A detailed criticism of von Rad's approach to Old Testament theology is here neither possible nor, in view of the many studies available (see above: 7.11), necessary. The most characteristic feature of von Rad's work is its choice of a diachronic rather than a cross-sectional organisation (cf. Harvey 1971). Whereas Eichrodt, Vriezen, Jacob and Knight consider the subject-matter of an Old Testament theology to be various aspects of the Old Testament doctrine of God and his relationship to man, von Rad is concerned to trace the development of ideas of God and his relationship to man found in the several strands of the Old Testament. These approaches are however not mutually exclusive. Cross-sectional theologies often treat the historical development of individual ideas, and Vriezen (1954/66: ch.3) in particular devotes forty pages to a diachronic study of 'The spiritual structure of the Old Testament and of the Old Testament writings'. Von Rad, on the other hand, includes in his diachronic theology systematic treatments of Old Testament ideas of the world and man (1957:336-56), righteousness (1957:370-83) and time (1960:99-125), as Barr (1962b) points out, and explicitly approves conceptual studies of Old Testament theology, emphasising that 'he does not consider what he offers to be a complete and comprehensive theology of the Old Testament' (1960:vi).

7.214 The centre of the Old Testament

It follows from his approach to Old Testament theology that von Rad rejects the idea of a 'centre' of the Old Testament (cf. Jacob 1968b:424; Smend 1970:9,18-21). 'Unlike the revelation in Christ, the revelation of Jahweh in the Old Testament is divided up over a long series of separate acts of revelation ... It seems to be without a centre which determines everything' (1957:115; cf. 1960:362). Nevertheless the Old Testament writings are united in their orientation to the future, shown in their characteristic re-actualisation of historical saving events (1963; cf. Smend 1970:21-5). On this question, see further above (1.213) and below (10.1).

7.215 Witness to Christ

Von Rad (1952a:39) writes:

'One must therefore ... really speak of a witness of the Old Testament to Christ, for our knowledge of Christ is incomplete without the witness of the Old Testament. Christ is given to us only through the double witness of the choir of those who await and those who remember' (cf. Vischer 1934:25, see above:5.24).

So Schwarzwäller (1969:285) claims that von Rad has realised the intention of Vischer but avoided his mistakes. It is clear at least that von Rad's intention, like that of Vischer, is to find a biblical solution to the problem of the relationship between the Testaments by taking seriously the testimony of both Old and New. Von Rad has also taken more seriously than many the possibility that the Old Testament should be understood as a witness to Christ (see also 1960:374), although it should be noted that he mentions this rather infrequently. Moreover he avoids one of Vischer's mistakes by taking fuller account of the historical nature of the Bible, although his conception of 'history' is open to question (cf. below:7.22). As will emerge in the following pages, von Rad - like Vischer - has made a significant contribution to finding a biblical solution to the problem of the relationship between the Testaments, and thus to understanding the Old Testament as a witness to Christ.

7.216 Old Testament interpretation

Von Rad shows effectively the way in which traditions are continually reinterpreted throughout the Bible, but he fails to deal adequately with interpretation of the Old Testament in the modern world. He has indeed produced a number of examples of Old Testament interpretation, among which his commentary on Genesis (1956) is outstanding, but he refuses to lay down any principles or guidelines for such interpretation (cf. Köster 1961:108). He argues that the New Testament's interpretation of the Old Testament is charismatic and does not provide an absolute norm for Christian interpretation (1960:409). Yet only a few pages earlier he has written: 'the coming of Jesus Christ as a historical reality leaves the exegete no choice at all; he must interpret the Old Testament as pointing to Christ, whom he must understand in its light' (1960:374 cf. 386). Surely this is the statement of an absolute norm? There is undoubtedly considerable diversity in the Old Testament interpretation of the different New Testament writers, but that is not to exclude altogether basic principles and consistency of method (cf. above:0.3). A 'charismatic' approach to Old Testament interpretation - which in practice means not a divinely-inspired approach but an individualistic one - may produce helpful results and give existential satisfaction, but it is too superficial to solve the problem of interpreting the Old Testament today.

7.22 HISTORY

As a starting-point in considering von Rad's solution to the problem of the relationship between the Testaments it is important to look at his view of history (cf. Honecker 1963; Greig 1974). Like Bultmann, von Rad distinguishes between history with a meaning (Geschichte) and history as it happened at a point in time and space (Historie). He takes up some of the insights of existential 'kerygma theology', understanding the Bible not as a presentation of general truths or a source for historical research but as a witness to God's saving activity in history (Pannenberg 1961b; cf. Eichrodt 1961: 515). Thus he expounds the significance of the canonical saving history of election, oppression, Exodus and the gift of a new land (Geschichte), though he can say very little about what actually took place in those 'events' since he accepts the critical reconstruction of Alt and Noth which denies that most of Israel was ever in Egypt! One of the most fundamental criticisms of von Rad's thesis is therefore its failure to provide a real foundation for the 'history' it describes (Eichrodt 1961: 516; de Vaux 1963). Von Rad (1963: 423-5) claims that Israel's view of history has a real historical basis, it is true, but in his actual exposition he gives little content to this 'reality' (cf. Davies 1970: 73-7; Pannenberg 1973).

On the Alt - Noth reconstruction of Israel's history see Alt, Kleine Schriften (1913-56) and Noth, The History of Israel (1950; cf. 1949, 1953). Criticisms of this include Bright, Early Israel in Recent History Writing (1956) and Wright, 'History and the Patriarchs', ExpT (1960). Von Rad replies to Wright's criticism of his work in 'History and the Patriarchs', ExpT (1961).

See further:

von Rad, 'Theologische Geschichtsschreibung im AT', ThZ (1948);

Rendtorff, 'Geschichte und Überlieferung' in von Rad Festschrift (1961);

Honecker, 'Zum Verständnis der Geschichte in Gerhard von Rads Theologie des ATs', EvTh (1963).

On 'history', see above: 3.23.

7.23 TYPOLOGY

Von Rad's programmatic essay on 'Typological Interpretation of the Old Testament' (1952) has been one of the most influential factors in the revival of typology in recent years. In it he argues that

'we see everywhere in this history brought to pass by God's Word, in acts of judgement and acts of redemption alike, the prefiguration of the Christ--event of the New Testament ... This renewed recognition of types in the Old Testament is no peddling of secret lore, no digging up of miracles, but is simply correspondent to the belief that the same God who revealed himself in Christ has also left his footprints in the history of the Old Testament covenant people' (p.36).

Von Rad has been criticised by Baumgärtel (1952: 115-127), Barr (1966: ch.4) and van Ruler, whose important book, <u>The Christian Church and the Old Testament</u>(1955), was written partly in response to von Rad's essay (see especially pp.58-68/62-74; cf. above: 1.146). However this approach to the problem of the relationship between the Testaments has already been discussed in detail above (ch.6), and little more needs to be said here. In spite of Eichrodt (1961: 514-5), von Rad does not define the relationship between the Testaments primarily in terms of typology: rather, he holds a complex view of the relationship which includes typology and 'promise and fulfilment' but is dominated by 'salvation history'.

7.24 PROMISE AND FULFILMENT

a. It was shown above (3.13) that Bultmann (1949a) rejected the popular idea of 'prophecy and fulfilment' as an expression of the relationship between the Testaments, at least if prophecy is to be understood as prediction (the traditional view) or history (Hofmann's view). Today the closely related idea of 'promise and fulfilment' has taken the place of 'prophecy and fulfilment' as probably the most popular expression of the relationship between the Testaments, and this is due especially to the works of von Rad and the Biblischer Kommentar group.

b. Von Rad does not dispute the importance of prophecy, nor deny its predictive element, but he prefers the concept of 'promise' which embraces more readily the historical traditions of the Old Testament as well as the prophetic traditions. The Hexateuch, according to von Rad, is spanned by a 'massive arch leading from promise to fulfilment' (1957: 170); the Deuteronomic history presents a course of history 'determined by a whole pattern of corresponding prophetic promises and divine fulfillments' (1952a: 27; cf.1947:ch.7); the several Old Testament historical works are united in their understanding of history as 'a continuum of events determined by Jahweh's promise, which flows forward to the fulfilment intended by him' (1963: 426-7); and the Old Testament as a whole is to be seen as 'the ceaseless saving movement of promise and fulfilment' (1960: viii). Von Rad shows that this pattern of promise and fulfilment found in the Old Testament is also an aspect of the relationship between the Old Testament and the New: the Old Testament is oriented to the future and 'can only be read as a book in which expectation keeps mounting up to vast proportions' (1960: 321); and the New Testament is concerned not only with the newness of the Christ-event but also with the way in which it fulfilled promises and predictions of the Old (1960:328-35).

c. Von Rad's argument is impressive, convincing and to a certain extent right. In the light of modern scholarship it can scarcely be disputed that the Old Testament points forward to the New and that the New Testament claims to fulfil the Old, though this in itself is not a new insight (cf. above: ch.0). This must be balanced, however, with another indisputable fact, namely that both Old and New Testaments are interested not only in the future and past, respectively, but in past, present and future. It is true that the Old Testament contains many divine promises, and as a whole may be considered a promise of the New; but it is equally true that the Old Testament is concerned with the immediate reality of life in Palestine in the first and second millenia B.C. Moreover, the New Testament does not simply fulfil the promises of the Old, it is also the fulfilment of law, piety and wisdom, and the resolution of inner tensions of the Old Testament. Perhaps the formula 'reality and fulfilment' would therefore be more appropriate than 'promise and fulfilment'.[1] The realities of the Old Testament point forward to the New in the sense that they are imperfect, though not necessarily in the sense that they promise something better in the future.

d. Yet this is not to deny the validity of the concept of 'promise and fulfilment' as a description of one aspect of the relationship between the Testaments. Although like typology (see above: 7.23) it is only a secondary aspect of his solution to the problem of the relationship between the Testaments, von Rad has made one of the most important contributions to modern understanding of 'promise and fulfilment'.

---

1. I owe this suggestion to Mr D.J.A.Clines.

In addition to von Rad's major works on the relationship between the Testaments, see his essay: 'The Deuteronomistic Theology of History in the Books of Kings' in Studies in Deuteronomy(1947).

On 'prophecy and fulfilment':
Hofmann, Weissagung und Erfüllung(1841-4);
Eichrodt, Theology of the OT I(1933):501-511;
Schildenberger, 'Weissagung und Erfüllung', Biblica (1943);
Allis, Prophecy and the Church(1945);
Bultmann, 'Prophecy and Fulfillment'(1949), ET in EOTI;
Baumgärtel, Verheissung(1952);
Childs, 'Prophecy and Fulfillment', Interpn(1958);
Payne, Encyclopedia of Biblical Prophecy(1973).
Cf. Dodd, The Apostolic Preaching(1936);
Bentzen, King and Messiah(1948).
Also, many works on NT use of the OT (see above: 0.3); cf. below: 8.221.

On 'promise and fulfilment':
Lofthouse, 'The OT and Christianity' in Robinson(1938);
Kümmel, Promise and Fulfilment(1945);
Dillistone, The Word of God and the People of God (1948):15-22;
Baumgärtel, Verheissung(1952);
Rowley, The Unity of the Bible(1953):ch.4;
Ridderbos, 'Oud en Nieuw Verbond' in Kampen(1954):9-18;
van Ruler, The Christian Church and the OT(1955): 34-7/37-40, see above: 1.141;
Gross, 'Zum Problem Verheissung und Erfüllung', BZ(1959);
Larcher, L'actualité chrétienne de l'AT(1962):esp. 399-488;
Bruce, 'Promise and Fulfilment in Paul's Presentation of Jesus' in Hooke Festschrift(1963);
Sauter, Zukunft und Verheissung(1965): esp. 251-62;
Schniewind, 'Die Beziehung des NTs zum AT', ZdZ(1966);
Verhoef, 'The Relationship between the Old and the NTs' in Payne(1970):289-92;
Harrington, The Path of Biblical Theology(1973):282-7;
Ohler, Gattungen im AT II(1973):171-6.
Cf. Delling, 'πλήρης, πληρόω ...', TDNT(1959);
Fensham, 'Covenant, Promise and Expectation in the Bible', ThZ(1967).

See further above: 4.12 and below: 7.3, esp.7.31.

7.25 TRADITION HISTORY

a. One of the most important contributions to modern study of Old Testament tradition history is von Rad's monograph, 'The Form-Critical Problem of the Hexateuch' (1938). His argument is essentially that the Hexateuch is an elaboration of one simple idea, namely God's grace to Israel shown in election of the patriarchs, Exodus from Egypt and settlement in Palestine. This idea is expressed in Israel's earliest creeds, among which Deut.26:5b-9, Deut.6:20-24 and Josh.24:2b-13 are the most important, and forms the basis of Israel's 'salvation history'. One of the most revolutionary features of von Rad's study is his claim (disputed by Davies 1970:71-3) that these creeds do not mention the events of Sinai, and that therefore the Sinai tradition was originally independent of the Exodus tradition proper. The combination of these two traditions was the work of the Yahwist, who was largely responsible for the formation of the Hexateuch by gathering together many scattered traditions around the central coordinating conception of the ancient creeds. Subsequent redaction added many other elements to the Hexateuch, but always in subjection to the central idea of the Settlement.

b. This reconstruction of the origin of the Hexateuch naturally provoked considerable interest and reaction (see Huffmon 1965). It is mentioned here however not in order to contribute to that debate but because this understanding of the Hexateuch is the basis of von Rad's conception of Old Testament theology and its relationship to that of the New Testament. In the preface to the first volume of his Old Testament theology von Rad (1957) writes:

'if there is any truth in the recognition that the whole of the Hexateuch is built upon a very few ancient credal statements which became constitutive for the Israel of all ages, then this is so important that a theology of the Old Testament would practically have to start out from this fact'. On this basis von Rad develops his theology, using the methods of form criticism and tradition history.

c. Von Rad's use of the traditio-historical method is particularly significant in his presentation of the relationship between the Testaments. He considers that the Bible contains a few basal traditions which are continually reinterpreted to make them relevant to the contemporary situation. Repeatedly Israel is addressed as the people of God and claims the old saving history as her own (1963: 413): 'Not with our fathers did the Lord make this covenant, but with us, who are all of us here alive this day' (Deut.5:3; cf. 1957:193; 1960: 109,268). In the Deuteronomic and Chronicler's histories the same traditions are taken up and applied to the election of David and his throne (1957: 306-54; cf. Rost 1947). The message of the prophets does not belong to the basic theology of the Old Testament, according to von Rad; but understood in terms of tradition history it is seen to be a reinterpretation of the salvation history, initially as condemnation and later as a new salvation (1957: 66; 1960: 3-5). This new salvation, although it contains the implication that the old salvation has come to an end, is expressed in the language of the old: there is to be 'a new David, a new Exodus, a new covenant, a new city of God' (1960: 323, cf. 239-40; cf. above: 6.13a). Such continual reinterpretation is made possible and valid by the fact that the Old Testament traditions are 'open to the future' (1960: 319-21,360-62; cf. 1961a:

10-11; see above: 0.21, 7.12). Moreover the same fact makes possible a traditio-historical approach to the relationship between the Testaments (1960: 321-33, 367-9, 384-6; cf. above: 7.12):

'We said earlier that the prophets do not improvise, that they show themselves to be bound to definite traditions, that they move about within the realm of older witnesses to Jahwism in an extraordinarily dialectic fashion, that they take their own legitimation from these and at the same time, because of new content which they give them, go beyond them and even break them up, that, while they certainly select from among the traditions, at the same time they keep them as the broad basis of their arguments - does not this also describe the relationship of the Apostles and the writers of the Gospels to the Old Testament?' (1960: 327)

d. Tradition history is therefore an important clue to understanding von Rad's solution to the problem of the relationship between the Testaments. Even more important, however, is a conception which in von Rad's theology is closely related to tradition history and sometimes hardly distinguishable from it (cf. Knight 1973: 133-6): the conception of salvation history.

Von Rad's monograph, 'The Form-Critical Problem of the Hexateuch' (1938) has been translated in _The Problem of the Hexateuch_. For recent discussions of some of the issues raised see:

Beyerlin, _Origins and History of the Oldest Sinaitic Traditions_(1961);
Vriezen, 'The Credo in the OT' in _OTWSA_(1963);
Wolff, 'Das Kerygma des Jahwisten',_EvTh_(1964);
Huffmon, 'The Exodus, Sinai and the Credo',_CBQ_(1965);
Rost, _Das kleine Credo_(1965):11-25;
Schreiner, 'The Development of the Israelite "Credo"', _Concilium_(1966);
Richter, 'Beobachtungen...' in Schmaus Festschrift(1967);
Hyatt, 'Were There an Ancient Historical Credo in Israel and an Independent Sinai Tradition?' in May Festschrift(1970);
J.M. Schmidt, 'Erwägungen zum Verhältnis von Auszugs- und Sinaitraditionen',_ZAW_(1970);
Steck, 'Genesis 12:1-3 und die Urgeschichte des Jahwisten' in von Rad Festschrift(1971);
Nicholson, _Exodus and Sinai in History and Tradition_ (1973).

D.A. Knight has made a valuable survey of traditio-historical study of the Old Testament: Rediscovering the Traditions of Israel(1973; pp.97-142 on von Rad). See also:

Jacob, 'La tradition historique en Israël',ETR(1946);
Rost, 'Sinaibund und Davidsbund',TLZ(1947);
Noth, A History of Pentateuchal Traditions(1948);
Wright, 'Recent European Study in the Pentateuch', JBR(1950);
Barr, 'Tradition and Expectation in Ancient Israel', SJT(1957);
von Rad Festschrift: Studien zur Theologie der atl. Überlieferungen(1961);
Fohrer, 'Tradition und Interpretation im AT',ZAW(1961);
Childs, Memory and Tradition in Israel(1962);
Porteous, 'Actualization and the Prophetic Criticism of the Cult' in Weiser Festschrift (1963);
Mildenberger, Gottes Tat im Wort(1964):17-43;
Geyer, 'Zur Frage der Notwendigkeit des ATes', EvTh(1965);
Sauter, Zukunft und Verheissung(1965):208-18;
Grelot, 'Tradition as Source and Environment of Scripture',Concilium(1966);
Hesse, Das AT als Buch der Kirche(1966):ch.2;
Bruce, 'Tradition and Interpretation in the NT' in Holy Book and Holy Tradition(1968);
Gese, 'Erwägungen zur Einheit der biblischen Theologie',ZTK(1970);
Berger, 'Zum traditionsgeschichtlichen Hintergrund christologischer Hoheitstitel',NTS(1971);
Vesco, 'Abraham: actualisation et relectures', RSPT(1971);
Zimmerli, 'Atl.Traditionsgeschichte und Theologie' in von Rad Festschrift(1971);
Rendtorff, 'Die atl.Überlieferungen als Grundthemen der Lebensarbeit Gerhard von Rads' in Wolff et al.(1973);
Clements, Prophecy and Tradition(1975).

7.26 SALVATION HISTORY

a. It was mentioned above (0.446) that von Hofmann's idea of 'salvation history' has influenced modern studies of this theme, and this is true in particular of von Rad's theology (see e.g. 1960:vi). Both of these theologians were concerned to find a genuinely theological way to understand the Old Testament, in contrast to the widespread 'history of religions' approach (Greig 1974: ch.1). The major difference between the two is that von Hofmann was interested in an objective saving history, von Rad in an existential one (cf. Pannenberg 1961b:91). Today the question of salvation history remains the topic of lively debate, as may be seen from the selection of literature below. In the present work it is impossible to enter into this debate and discussion will be limited to two or three aspects of von Rad's use of salvation history to express the relationship between the Testaments.

b. First of all, it may be asked whether salvation history is an adequate structuring concept for a theology of the Old Testament and its relationship to the New.

Does it do justice to the creation story, sagas, laws, poetry and wisdom literature of the Old Testament to fit them into the (Procrustean?) category of historical traditions? Barr (e.g. 1963; 1966: 72-6) has repeatedly argued that it does not, that the Old Testament contains more than salvation history (cf. Spriggs 1974: 40-42). Christoph Barth (1963: 368-9) has challenged von Rad's treatment of the psalms and wisdom literature as Israel's answer to God's history of salvation: he considers the whole Bible to be both God's word and Israel's answer. David Burdett (1974), on the other hand, has recently attempted to show that the wisdom literature is an integral part of the history of redemption, as a demonstration of the ideal character of a citizen in the messianic kingdom.

Be that as it may, a more fundamental question still demands an answer: is the creed of 'salvation in history' (cf. Deut.26: 5-9) really the kernel of Old Testament theology? Barr (1962b: 144) claims:

'There is no evidence that von Rad treats this concept critically, and it is obvious that he feels he can use it as an ace of trumps against all other ideas of the planning of an Old Testament theology, or of the treatment of certain details within it.'

It should be noted however that von Rad does recognise at least some of the limitations of his work. In the introductions to both volumes he emphasises that he does not consider his work to be a complete and comprehensive Old Testament theology (1957:vii; 1960:vi). He points out that the idea of salvation history was lost in the legalism and apocalyptic of the post-exilic period (1957:91; 1960:303-4). Moreover his fundamental proposition, 'the Old Testament writings confine themselves to representing Jahweh's relationship to Israel and the world in one aspect only, namely as a continuing divine activity in history' (1957: 106), is immediately qualified by reference to the obvious fact that it is apparently not true of some parts of the Old Testament. In some cases (e.g. some of the Psalms) von Rad argues that they presuppose God's historical activity, in others (e.g. Job, Ecclesiastes) he suggests that the failure to relate to the salvation history'is closely connected with the grave affliction which is the theme of both these works'.

It is not to be expected that any one concept will be completely satisfactory as the 'centre' of an Old Testament theology (cf. below: 10.6), or as an expression of its relationship to New Testament theology. Nevertheless the concept of 'salvation history' has the merit of effectively grasping and organising the material of the Old Testament in such a way as to stress the centrality of elements which are undoubtedly central and the secondary nature of others which are not. Even Barr (1963: 201), while emphasising that there are other important axes through the biblical material, admits that

'there really is a Heilsgeschichte ... we have been generally right in saying that this can be taken as the central theme of the Bible, that it forms the main link between Old and New Testaments, and that its presence and importance clearly marks biblical faith off from other religions'.

c. Another problem in von Rad's use of the concept of 'salvation history' is the nature of the 'salvation' and the 'history'.

First, is this 'salvation' real, or merely a product of Israel's imagination? Like a pure mathematician who analyses concepts and their interrelationships without asking whether or not they have any connection with the real world, von Rad evades the question. He separates the 'objective' picture of Israel's history obtained by historical criticism on the basis of Troeltsch's principle of analogy from the kerygmatic picture given by Israel's confessions which understood history in terms of God's activity (1957: 107-8; cf. C.Barth 1963: 368). Yet the question remains: did God choose and deliver Israel and give them a new land in fulfilment of his promise, or is salvation history an invention or misapprehension? The Old Testament is based on the belief that God really acts in history to save his people, and von Rad's existential presentation is inadequate to the extent that it fails to take account of this (cf. above: 7.22; Pannenberg 1961b: 94n.; Spriggs 1974: 57,81).

Secondly, a closely related question concerns the reality of this 'history' (cf. Hasel 1970). The crux of the matter is that von Rad expounds the saving history not on the basis of the modern scholarly reconstruction of Israel's history but on Israel's own understanding of her history (1957: vi; cf. above: 7.22). Undoubtedly such an exposition may be illuminating, and if Israel rather than modern scholarship were right it would be the best kind of exposition; but since von Rad believes that modern scholarship is right, the validity of his approach is questionable. Logic and honesty demand a theology based on either the historico-critical reconstruction of Israel's history (if that is considered to be correct; cf. Hesse 1960a: 24-6) or Israel's own account of her history (if that is considered to have a real historical basis; cf. Eichrodt 1961: 516). It may well be true that von Rad has drawn too sharply the contrast between the two pictures of Israel's history (cf. Soggin 1964), but the fact that he bases his theology on what he considers to be an invalid foundation remains a fundamental weakness in his work.

Fritsch, 'Biblical Typology: The Bible as Redemptive History', BS(1946);
Bultmann, 'History of Salvation and History'(1948), ET in *Existence and Faith*;
Baumgärtel, 'Das atl.Geschehen als "heilsgeschichtliches Geschehen' in Alt Festschrift(1953);
Stoebe, 'Der heilsgeschichtliche Bezug der Jabbok--Perikope', EvTh(1954);
Kraus, 'Das Problem der Heilsgeschichte in der "Kirchlichen Dogmatik"' in Barth Festschrift(1956);
Miskotte, *When the Gods are Silent*(1956):279-80;
Ott, 'Heilsgeschichte', RGG³(1959);
Steck, *Die Idee der Heilsgeschichte*(1959);
Schnackenburg *et al.*, 'Heilsgeschichte', LTK²(1960);
Frör, *Biblische Hermeneutik*(1961):86-103;
Soggin, 'Atl.Glaubenszeugnisse und geschichtliche Wirklichkeit', ThZ(1961); 'Geschichte, Historie und Heilsgeschichte im AT', TLZ(1964);
Barr, 'Revelation Through History in the OT and Modern Theology', Interpn(1963);
Sekine, 'Vom Verstehen der Heilsgeschichte', ZAW(1963);
Fohrer, 'Prophetie und Geschichte', TLZ(1964);
Malevez, 'Les dimensions de l'histoire du salut', NRT(1964);
Richardson, *History Sacred and Profane*(1964):133-9;
J.M. Robinson, 'The Historicality of Biblical Language', OTCF(1964);

Rottenberg, Redemption and Historical Reality (1964): ch.1;
Feiner and Löhrer (eds), Mysterium Salutis: Grundriss heilsgeschichtlicher Dogmatik (5 vols, 1965-);
Braaten, History and Hermeneutics (1966): ch.5;
Braun, 'Heil als Geschichte', EvTh (1967);
Bright, The Authority of the OT (1967): 192-201;
Cullmann Festschrift: Oikonomia: Heilsgeschichte als Thema der Theologie (1967);
Greidanus, Sola Scriptura (1970): ch.4;
Hasel, 'The Problem of History in OT Theology', AUSS (1970);
Peter, 'Salvation History as a Model for Theological Thought', SJT (1970);
Porteous, 'A Question of Perspectives' in Eichrodt Festschrift (1970);
Hesse, Abschied von der Heilsgeschichte (1971);
Klein, 'Bibel und Heilsgeschichte', ZNW (1971);
Burdett, 'Wisdom Literature and the Promise Doctrine', TrJ (1974).

See also below: 7.3, esp. 7.34.

7.27 A RELATIONSHIP OF ACTUALISATION

a. It has been shown that von Rad offers a complex solution to the theological problem of the relationship between the Testaments which includes the aspects of salvation history, tradition history, promise and fulfilment, and typology. While it would be a mistake to oversimplify what is essentially a complex relationship, it may be asked whether behind these different aspects there is a unifying factor or distinctive concept by which von Rad's solution can be usefully characterised. A concept mentioned by von Rad only comparatively infrequently and yet of great importance is that of 'actualisation' (Aktualisierung; closely related to the idea of 're-presentation', Vergegenwärtigung, used by Noth 1952, see below: 7.31b; cf. Westermann 1963; Dreyfus 1967). If it were necessary to summarise in one word von Rad's view of the relationship between the Testaments, 'actualisation' would be the most appropriate word to choose.

b. An example of actualisation in the Old Testament itself is to be found in the cult, according to von Rad (1960: 103-110). In the great festivals, for instance, which though originally agricultural were historicised by Israel, the saving events connected with the festivals were 'actualised' in the cultic celebration. Another example of a somewhat different nature is the book of Deuteronomy, which von Rad (1960: 394) considers to be 'a unique actualisation of God's will designed to counter specific dangers which appeared at a definite hour in the already lengthy history of Jahwism'. The concept is elaborated further in the postscript to von Rad's theology (1963: 413-16):

'In each specific case, Israel spoke in quite a different way about the "mighty acts" of her God ... Israel constantly fell back on the old traditions connected with the great saving appointments, and in each specific case she actualised them in a very arbitrary, and often novel, way ... This continual actualisation of the data of the saving history, with its consequence that every generation saw itself anew on the march towards a fulfilment, occupies such a prominent position in the Old Testament that a "Theology of the Old Testament" must accommodate itself to it'.

The concept of 'actualisation' is therefore very suitable to express the relationship between the Old Testament and the New (1960: 319-35; see above: 7.12):

'the way in which the Old Testament is absorbed in the New is the logical end of a process initiated by the Old Testament itself (1960: 321) ... The history of tradition showed us how old material could suddenly be put on a new basis and into new theological horizons, and the question therefore is whether the reinterpretation of Old Testament traditions in the light of Christ's appearance on earth is not also hermeneutically perfectly permissible ... The Apostles clearly take the view that the texts of the Old Testament only attain their fullest actuality in the light of their fulfilment' (p.333).

c. That there are some fundamental weaknesses in von Rad's work - especially in his view of history and the reality of salvation history - has been shown above (esp. 7.22, 7.26) and discussed at length by his critics. It is moreover obvious that many of his other propositions are not beyond criticism. Nevertheless, it has become clear in the course of the preceding discussion that von Rad has made a very significant contribution to solving the theological problem of the relationship between the Testaments, a contribution possibly greater than any other modern scholar. Despite all necessary qualifications, he has demonstrated the essential truth of his solution, which may be summarised by means of the concepts of typology, promise and fulfilment, tradition history, salvation history and, above all, actualisation. Since 1960, therefore, no serious consideration of the relationship between the Testaments can ignore the important outlines sketched by von Rad. The final section of the present chapter will be concerned with a number of other solutions to the problem which are related to or dependent on von Rad, and which may be subsumed under the general heading of 'salvation history solutions'.

7.3 COMPARISON: OTHER SALVATION HISTORY SOLUTIONS

7.31 BIBLISCHER KOMMENTAR GROUP

a. Since the launching of the project by a series of essays in 1952, the collaborators of the *Biblischer Kommentar Altes Testament* have made a major contribution to the theological understanding of the Old Testament in relation to the New. In many respects their conception of the relationship between the Testaments is similar to that of von Rad, who was in fact one of those to launch the project though he did not contribute to the commentary itself. The theoretical essays of the group of collaborators have dealt with the questions of actualisation/re-presentation, typology, promise and fulfilment, salvation history and tradition. The commentaries follow an original pattern for the systematic interpretation in five stages of each biblical passage, a pattern first set out by Wolff (1952): (Literature), *Text* (translation and textual criticism), *Form*, (historical) *Ort*, *Wort* (Exegesis), *Ziel* (Kerygma). The most interesting and important stage for the question of the relationship between the Testaments is the final one, in which is considered the theological significance of the passage in the context of the whole Bible, including the New Testament. An interesting piece of research, which cannot be undertaken here, would be to compare the principles set out in the theoretical essays with the interpretations of the commentaries, in order to see how far it has been possible to employ the principles to produce consistent and convincing interpretations of biblical texts. It is possible here only to consider briefly the theoretical implications of the project, and this will be done with reference to the programmatic essays of Noth and Zimmerli.

b. Noth's contribution to the 1952 symposium is concerned with 'The "Re-presentation" of the Old Testament in Proclamation'. In order to deal with the problem of transition from exegesis to proclamation Noth turns to the Old Testament, in which he finds a process of re-presentation of historical events. The festivals of Passover and Tabernacles, for instance, came to be understood as re-enactments of events related to the Exodus. The proclamation of the law took place 'in such a way as to make Israel hear the law as if it were for the very first time' (p.82). Such cultic re-presentation is not entirely unrelated to the ancient Oriental cyclic view of history, Noth admits, but there is also a fundamental difference: 'the "re-presentation" at the periodical feasts of ancient Israel does not involve some timeless myth, but something which by nature is a unique historical event ... the Exodus from Egypt' (p.85). The Old Testament's re-presentation is distinctive in its historical nature, being concerned not with myth but with the saving acts and moral demands of God. From a brief survey of the Old Testament evidence Noth draws three conclusions for a legitimate re-presentation of the Old Testament: it cannot use historical individuals, nor can it use specific historical situations, since both of these are unrepeatable; it can only re-present the saving acts of God by 'telling' them. 'Re-presentation' is therefore much the same as von Rad's concept of 'actualisation' (cf. above: 7.12, 7.27).

c. Zimmerli (1952) points out that the formulation 'Promise and Fulfillment' is New Testament language and devotes the first part of his essay on this theme to a discussion of whether or not it corresponds to genuine Old Testament ideas. After considering evidence in the Pentateuch, prophets and elsewhere he concludes that in the whole Old Testament 'we find ourselves involved in a great history of movement from promise toward fulfillment' (pp.111-112; cf. above: 7.24). Within the Old Testament fulfilments are always incomplete and continually raise the question of deeper fulfilment in the future, but in the New Testament a definitive fulfilment is attested in the person of Christ, who is both the end and the consummation of the Old Testament.

aa. The essays which first set out the principles for the Biblischer Kommentar (BK) and which provoked a heated debate about the interpretation of the Old Testament were published in EvTh 12,July/August 1952:
von Rad, 'Predigt über Ruth 1' and 'Typologische Auslegung des ATs';
Noth, 'Die Vergegenwärtigung des ATs in der Verkündigung';
Zimmerli, 'Verheissung und Erfüllung';
Kraus, 'Gespräch mit Martin Buber';
Wolff, 'Der grosse Jesreeltag (Hosea 2,1-3)'.
ETs of the essays by Noth and Zimmerli, and von Rad's second essay were published in Interpn(1961) and again in EOTI.

bb. The most important replies to these programmatic essays came from Friedrich Baumgärtel and Arnold A. van Ruler. Baumgärtel produced several works dealing with issues raised: Verheissung (1952): 106-127; 'Das atl. Geschehen als "heilsgeschichtliches" Geschehen' in Alt Festschrift (1953); '"Ohne Schlüssel vor der Tür des Wortes Gottes"?', EvTh(1953); 'Das hermeneutische Problem des ATs', EvTh(1954; ET in EOTI); 'Der Dissensus im Verständnis des ATs',EvTh(1954); cf. above: ch.4. Van Ruler was provoked by the essays to write his important work: Die christliche Kirche und das AT(1955; ET: 1966); cf. above: ch.1.

cc. Some collaborators of the BK replied to their critics and further elaborated their programme in EvTh 16, August/September 1956:
Wolff, 'Zur Hermeneutik des ATs';
Kraus, 'Zur Geschichte des Überlieferungsbegriffs in der atl. Wissenschaft';
Stamm, 'Jesus Christus und das AT';
Vriezen, 'Theokratie und Soteriologie';
Wildberger, 'Israel und sein Land'.
There are ETs in EOTI of the essays by Wolff (also in Interpn 1961), Stamm and Vriezen.

dd. In the same year (1956) BK commenced publication with a slim volume on Lamentations (by Kraus). To date the volumes on Psalms (Kraus 1960), Ruth and Song of Songs (Gerleman 1965), Ezekiel (Zimmerli 1969) and Esther (Gerleman 1973) have been completed; part volumes on Genesis 1-11 (Westermann 1974), 1 Kings 1-16 (Noth 1968), Isaiah 1-12 (Wildberger 1972), Hosea (Wolff 1961), Joel and Amos (Wolff 1969) and Job 1-19 (Horst 1968) have appeared; and fascicles of Exodus (W.H.Schmidt), Second Isaiah (Elliger), and the next part-volume of Isaiah (Wildberger) have begun to appear.

ee. Further theoretical works by members of the 'BK group' concerned with the relationship between the Testaments include:
von Rad, 'Verheissung', EvTh(1953);
Wolff, 'The OT in Controversy'(1956), ET in Interpn 12; 'Das Geschichtsverständnis der atl. Prophetie', EvTh(1960, ET in EOTI);
Wildberger, 'Auf dem Wege zu einer biblischen Theologie', EvTh(1959);
Zimmerli, 'Das AT in der Verkündigung der christlichen Kirche' in Das AT als Anrede(1956); 'Das Gesetz im AT', TLZ(1960); The Law and the Prophets(1965);
Westermann, 'Zur Auslegung des ATs' in Vergegenwärtigung (1955, abridged ET in EOTI); 'Vergegenwärtigung der Geschichte in den Psalmen' in Kupisch Festschrift (1963); 'The Way of the Promise through the OT', OTCF(1964); The OT and Jesus Christ(1968); 'Zur Auslegung des ATs' in Loretz and Strolz(1968);
Kraus, Die Biblische Theologie(1970):193-395.

ff. The group have also produced many studies and expositions of OT passages apart from BK. Some are by-products of work on BK (e.g. Zimmerli's essays on Ezekiel, repr. in Gottes Offenbarung), while others are independent works important in their own right (e.g. von Rad's Genesis, 1953; and Westermann's Isaiah 40-66, 1966).

7.32 PANNENBERG GROUP

a. In the year following the completion of von Rad's Old Testament theology was published a programmatic work by a group of younger Heidelberg scholars entitled Revelation as History (1961). It was edited by Wolfhart Pannenberg, who has since become the chief spokesman of the group, and included essays by him, Rolf Rendtorff, Ulrich Wilckens and Trutz Rendtorff. The programme is well summed up in Pannenberg's seven dogmatic theses (ch.4):

1. God's self-revelation in the Bible is indirect, being mediated through historical acts.
2. Revelation is understood fully only at the end of revelatory history.
3. Revelation is universal, being open to anyone who has eyes to see.
4. Revelation is first realised in the fate of Jesus, insofar as the end of all events in anticipated in that event.
5. The Christ-event is revelation insofar as it is part of God's history with Israel.
6. The universality of the Christ-event is expressed in the Gentile Christian understanding of revelation.
7. The Word relates itself to revelation as foretelling, forthtelling, and report.

A lively debate on the relationship between revelation and history ensued. It is however Pannenberg's view of the relationship between the Testaments which requires particular attention here.

b. The close link between God's history with Israel and the Christ-event is implied in Pannenberg's fourth and fifth theses. Like von Rad, Pannenberg uses the categories of salvation history and promise and fulfilment to express the relationship between the Testaments (cf. J.M.Robinson 1964: 127-9), but he rejects von Rad's separation of salvation history from history as it 'really' happened. For Pannenberg

> 'the connection between the Old and New Testaments is made understandable only by the consciousness of the one history which binds together the eschatological community of Jesus Christ and ancient Israel by means of the bracket of promise and fulfillment' (1959:25; cf.1967:179-181).

But this 'history' is not simply salvation history as believed and confessed by Israel (von Rad): it is 'reality in its totality' (1959: 21), which includes not only salvation history but the Creation and the Consummation as well. Thus Pannenberg establishes the relationship between the Testaments in real history, which he conceives as God's characteristic sphere of self-revelation. This history, to be sure, is completely intelligible only from the perspective of its end, but in the Christ event this end is anticipated, so that at least in an anticipatory sense the meaning of the revelation in history recorded in the Old Testament becomes clear.

c. In this universal understanding of revelation apocalyptic has an important place. According to Koch (1970: 14), Pannenberg (1959) reintroduced the apocalyptic concept of history into systematic theology, but it was Käsemann who effectively brought the concept out of obscurity into the forefront of theological discussion. The latter, in his programmatic essay 'The Beginnings of Christian Theology' (1960), argued that apocalyptic was 'the mother of all Christian theology' (p.40). It follows from this that apocalyptic is seen to be the chief link between the Testaments. Koch (1970) concludes his study of apocalyptic in these words:

> 'Our survey has shown sufficiently that late Israelite and early Christian apocalyptic is not one branch of the literature of the ancient world among others, a sector which one may consider philologically and exegetically or leave alone, according to taste.

Does the apocalyptic world of ideas not represent the change-over between the Testaments, i.e., does it not reflect that religious movement which, under the impression of the person of Jesus and his destiny, permitted a part of late Israel to merge into early Christianity?'

d. This positive evaluation of apocalyptic stands in sharp contrast to that of von Rad (1960: 301-8). Moltmann (1964: 136) argues however that both evaluations 'have their ground in the recognition of the fact that apocalyptic applies cosmological patterns to history, with the result that either "history" comes to a standstill' (von Rad) or '"history" becomes intelligible as a summary representation of reality in its totality' (Pannenberg). He suggests a third way of looking at apocalyptic, by seeing its significance not in 'cosmological interpretation of eschatological history' but in 'eschatological and historic interpretation of the cosmos'. Just as in the message of the prophets Israel's 'hope for history' became concerned with world history, so in apocalyptic this hope became concerned with cosmology. Thus apocalyptic points theological eschatology beyond national history and individual existence to the world as a whole; and thus in effect it is one way in which the Old Testament points forward to the New.

aa. Pannenberg's two most important works are his Christology, Jesus - God and Man (1964) and his collection of theological essays, Basic Questions in Theology (1967). Works particularly relevant to the problem of the relationship between the Testaments are:
'Redemptive Event and History'(1959),
'Kerygma and History'(1961),
'The God of Hope'(1965) and
'On Historical and Theological Hermeneutic'(1967),
all reprinted in Basic Questions;
'Appearance as the Arrival of the Future', JAAR(1967);
'Weltgeschichte und Heilsgeschichte' in von Rad Festschrift(1971).

Cf. Osborn, 'Pannenberg's Programme', CJT(1967);
Berten, Geschichte . Offenbarung . Glaube(1969);
Dressler, 'The Authority of the Holy Scriptures', Dissn(1972):ch.6;
Galloway, Wolfhart Pannenberg(1973);
Tupper, The Theology of Wolfhart Pannenberg(1974).

bb. The extensive literature which documents the debate evoked by Revelation and History(1961) includes a symposium in the series New Frontiers in Theology (ed. Robinson and Cobb) entitled Theology as History(1967), with essays by Pannenberg, Robinson, Cobb and three other American scholars; and also the following:
Bornkamm, 'Geschichte und Glaube im NT',
Zimmerli, '"Offenbarung" im AT: Ein Gespräch mit R.Rendtorff' (+ reply by
Rendtorff, 'Geschichte und Wort im AT'),
Moltmann, 'Exegesis and the Eschatology of History',
Bohren, 'Die Krise der Predigt' and
Geyer, 'Geschichte als theologisches Problem', all in EvTh(1962);
Althaus, 'Offenbarung als Geschichte',TLZ(1962);
Steiger, 'Revelation-History and Theological Reason'(1962),ET in JTC 4;
Barr, 'Revelation Through History',Interpn(1963); Old and New(1966):ch.3;
Fuchs, 'Theologie oder Ideologie',TLZ(1963);
Gollwitzer, The Existence of God(1963):143-7;
Schnackenburg, 'Zum Offenbarungsgedanken in der Bibel',BZ(1963);
Klein, Theologie des Wortes Gottes(1964);
Loretz, The Truth of the Bible(1964):22-42;
Moltmann, Theology of Hope(1964):esp.76-84 (cf.below:d);
Muschalek and Gamper,'Offenbarung in Geschichte', ZKT(1964);
Braaten, 'The Current Controversy on Revelation', JR(1965);
Hesse, 'Wolfhart Pannenberg und das AT',NZST(1965);
Fuller, Easter Faith and History(1965):177-187; 'A New German Theological Movement',SJT(1966);
Vriezen, 'Geloof, openbaring en geschiedenis', KT(1965):210-12; An outline of OT theology (1966):188-205;
O'Collins, 'Revelation as History',HeyJ(1966);
Vawter, 'History and the Word',CBQ(1967);
Obayashi, 'Pannenberg and Troeltsch',JAAR(1970);
Harder and Stevenson, 'The Continuity of History and Faith in the Theology of Wolfhart Pannenberg',JR(1971);
Knierim, 'Offenbarung im AT' in von Rad Festschrift(1971
North, 'Pannenberg's Historicizing Exegesis',HeyJ(1971);
Hasel, OT Theology(1972):40-47;
Erickson, 'Pannenberg's Use of History',JETS(1974).

cc. On the understanding of apocalyptic as the bond between the Testaments, see
Pannenberg, 'Redemptive Event and History' (1959), repr. in Basic Questions;
Rössler, Gesetz und Geschichte(1960);
Käsemann, 'The Beginnings of Christian Theology'(1960), ET in JTC 6 - some replies to this essay are printed in the same issue of JTC;
Koch, 'Spätisraelitisches Geschichtsdenken',HZ(1961); The Rediscovery of Apocalyptic(1970).
Cf. Wolff, 'The Understanding of History in the OT Prophets'(1960),ET in EOTI: 352n.24;
Sauter, Zukunft und Verheissung(1965):239-51;
Betz, 'The Concept of Apocalyptic in the Theology of the Pannenberg Group',JTC(1969);
Sand, 'Zur Frage nach dem "Sitz im Leben" der Apokalyptischen Texte des NTs',NTS(1972);
Hamerton-Kelly, Pre-Existence, Wisdom and the Son of Man(1973): esp.276-9.
For general literature on apocalyptic, see above:0.24.
A bibliography of more than 200 items related to this question is given by North, HT(1973): 86-103.

dd. On Moltmann and his Theology of Hope(1964) see:
Fries, 'Spero ut intelligam' in Schmaus Festschrift (1967);
Geyer, 'Ansichten zu Jürgen Moltmanns "Theologie der Hoffnung"',TLZ(1967);
Hedinger, 'Glaube und Hoffnung',EvTh(1967);
O'Collins, 'Spes Quarens Intellectum', Interpn(1968); 'The Theology of Hope',The Way(1968);
Connell, 'Review Article: Theology of Hope',VoxEv(1969);
Macquarrie, 'Theologies of Hope',ExpT(1971);
Park, 'The Christian Hope',WTJ(1971);
Kayayan, 'Théologie de l'espérance',EtEv(1971);
Thils, '...La théologie de l'espérance de J. Moltmann',ETL(1971);
Mondin, 'Theology of Hope',BThB(1972);
O'Grady, 'The Theology of Hope',DL(1972);
Stadtke, 'Die Hoffnung des Glaubens',KuD(1972);
cf. Miskotte, When the Gods are Silent(1956):295-302.

7.33 SAMUEL AMSLER

a. Amsler's published thesis, L'Ancien Testament dans l'Église (1960), is probably the most important French Protestant work on the relationship between the Old Testament and the New. Its aim is not to show if or to what extent Jesus has fulfilled the Old Testament but to attempt a definition of principles for reading the Old Testament in the Christian Church (p.11). Amsler presupposes that Jesus is the Christ, claiming that this presupposition, although obviously not from the Old Testament itself, is not alien to the Old Testament because it affirms that it is the God who revealed himself in the Old Testament who has done the same decisively in Jesus of Nazareth. He argues, using a play on words, that his approach is the only genuinely objective one since the object of the Old Testament witness is God's revelation and it is impossible to take proper account of this object without recognising God's supreme revelation in Jesus (pp.10-11). Amsler's method is first to analyse what the Bible itself says about Christian reading of the Old Testament (cf. above: 0.31c), and secondly to relate this to the results of contemporary Old Testament scholarship. His argument centres on the fact that the Old Testament was the Bible of the primitive Church: the early Christians used the Old Testament not simply because in a Jewish context it was convenient to do so but because they were convinced that the advent, life, death and resurrection of Jesus Christ were the fulfilment of the old covenant, and therefore inextricably related to it. The ultimate reason for Christian use of the Old Testament is therefore quite simply that Jesus is the Christ promised by the Old Testament (p.10).

b. For the present study it is the second main section of Amsler's book, a normative investigation of interpretative principles appropriate for the modern Church, which is of greater importance. Amsler rejects a simple adoption of New Testament methods, choosing rather to go beyond them to the fundamental principle by which they are governed. Their value lies not in themselves but in their expression of the early Church's faith in Jesus Christ, and this faith implies a theological relationship between the old and new covenants which alone can validate Christian reading of the Old Testament. Amsler admits that such a synthetic approach has the danger of generalisation, but points out that a certain generalisation is necessary in order to advance beyond the problems of individual texts (pp.103-4). In the first half of the second section, 'Why read the Old Testament in the Church?' (pp.105-151), Amsler considers specifically the problem of the relationship between the Testaments, and this half-section will therefore be considered at length here (see below: c-e).

c. The central aim of the New Testament is to witness to an historical event, the birth, ministry, death and resurrection of Jesus Christ. It is a unique event, since in it God himself has intervened in the world to save men; but it is not an isolated event, since it is to be viewed as the centre of a history which extends from creation to the end of time. In so saying, Amsler takes up Cullmann's view that Jesus is the final and definitive meaning of both salvation history and universal history. On the one hand, according to the New Testament, the last days have come in him and the whole history of men and creation is henceforth determined by him; on the other hand, the New Testament relates Jesus to past history, showing him to be the final outcome of God's activity in creation and in the history of Israel. To separate the central event of history from the events which lead up to and follow on from it robs both the centre and the context of their full significance for revelation and salvation. (pp.105-7)

The question arises whether this New Testament perspective of salvation history corresponds to that of the Old. Recent Old Testament study leads to the reply: the Old Testament bears witness to the living God who revealed himself to Israel by intervening in her secular history (p.108). According to the Old Testament, God encounters his people in historical events, and these events are significant not as a succession of incidental facts but as a sequence of interlinked occurrences which together make a history. The historical works organise the material into a connected narrative, the prophets declare that past and future events play a role in the present, the Psalms and liturgical writing concentrate history into the present by means of the cult, the law expresses the practical consequences of God's historical action in making a covenant with his people, and the wisdom literature shows in a negative fashion that the result of abandoning the historical perspective is to lose the key to the biblical revelation (cf. above: 7.26b). In order to interpret the Old Testament, therefore, it is vital to place every event in its historical context, which includes both events that precede it and those that result from it. This orientation to history, Amsler claims, is apparent in the attitude of the Old Testament prophets to time: one stations himself beyond the event (e.g. Ezek.20:42), another describes a future event as though it had already taken place (e.g. Amos 5:2), while another describes past events as though they had yet to happen (e.g. Dan.7:23 - is Daniel also among the prophets?). It is not only the prophets, however, which interpret events with reference to the future: the whole Old Testament bears witness to a history which is incomplete in itself and is open to the future. So for the Old Testament the interpretation of historical events will be truly possible only at the end of time (cf. Pannenberg, above:7.32). (pp.107-119)

The New Testament affirms that the end of time has already been inaugurated in Jesus Christ, who thus shows the full significance of the events of the old covenant by giving them their complete context. So Christian interpretation of the Old Testament is the direct consequence of faith in Jesus Christ. Every event of the old covenant receives in him the eschatological context by which its full meaning becomes clear, and at the same time contributes to elucidate the central event of salvation history. Here Amsler finds the real theological basis for Christian reading of the Old Testament: without the Old Testament salvation history is curtailed and disfigured, and the Christ-event loses its authentic significance. (pp.119-121)

d. Amsler's argument up to this point has been directed toward establishing that there is an integral relationship between the old covenant and Jesus Christ, and he next proceeds to define this more precisely. The central fact is that in the Christ-event God has realised the promises and fulfilled the demands of the Old Testament, so that the relationship between the two covenants is characterised by the concept of fulfilment. It is therefore an historical relationship which is in question, not a doctrinal one; a relationship between two complementary series of events in the plan of salvation history, not between two collections of timeless truths. There are two main aspects to this relationship of fulfilment:
a) God's historical activity in Jesus Christ finishes and goes beyond all his words and acts in the history of Israel (p.122) and b) the new covenant confirms

the promises and demands of the old covenant to be those of God (p.123). Moreover, it is not just specific texts but the old covenant as a whole which is fulfilled in Jesus Christ, according to the New Testament. (pp.122-5)

It may be asked how far this New Testament idea of fulfilment is appropriate to the Old Testament. Amsler claims that the faith of the Old Testament, in clear contrast to the religions of Babylon and Egypt whose gods acted in an arbitrary way (disputed by Albrektson 1967), discerned a divine plan behind historical events. The focal point of this plan of salvation history is Israel's election, which is shown above all in deliverance from Egypt, theophany at Sinai and settlement in Canaan. These events are at once the fulfilment of the promise to the patriarchs and promises of a covenant which will govern subsequent relations between God and his people. In a similar way, Amsler argues, every event in the salvation history is both fulfilment and promise (cf. Zimmerli 1952). This Old Testament promise consists not of predictions, which describe future events in detail, but of prophecy, which is concerned with immediate historical events and only secondarily with the future. In the Old Testament God's revelation in history is not yet complete but is 'ouverte sur la révélation finale' (p.130); in the New Testament God's revelation is final and definitive. (pp.125-130)

The New Testament adopts the Old Testament idea of the salvation history as a chain of events linked by promise and fulfilment, but introduces a new aspect to the concept of fulfilment: Jesus Christ does not simply prolong the old covenant but replaces it by another, that of the eschatological kingdom of God. This decisive fulfilment is not alien to the Old Testament; on the contrary, in it the prophetic linking of events by promise and fulfilment finds its goal. Moreover, Christian interpretation of the Old Testament must be based on this understanding of fulfilment since only then can it be true to the prophetic interpretation of history.

e. Amsler has argued that Jesus Christ is an integral part of the salvation history inaugurated in the Old Testament and that his role is primarily to fulfil the promises and demands of the Old Testament. He proceeds finally to consider the witness of the Old Testament to its relationship with the Christ-event. Jesus' fulfilment of the old covenant has two consequences: not only does Jesus Christ show the real revelatory significance of the old covenant but the events of the old covenant display clearly particular aspects of the event in which they are fulfilled, God's revelation in Christ. This circular argument does not prove rationally that Jesus is the Christ but it secures the Old Testament in its role as a witness to God's saving activity in history. Since the climax of history occurred in Jesus Christ, it is only in the Church - among those who believe that Jesus is the Christ - that the Old Testament can play its authentic role as witness to that salvation history. This witness takes two forms, words and events, and according to the New Testament each is fulfilled in Jesus Christ. (pp.135-6)

First, certain revelatory words in the Old Testament are fulfilled in the Christ-event. Amsler admits that the New Testament often applies a text which originally referred to God, David, Israel, a prophet, etc. to Jesus Christ or the Church; but he notes a striking agreement between the New Testament authors in their interpretation of such Old Testament passages - for example in the Christological use of individual psalms of lament by the Synoptics, Acts and Hebrews - and suggests that these transpositions are based on the belief that the text of Scripture finds its real meaning only with reference to Christ and the Church. This does not mean however that Old Testament texts are pure prediction, having no referent within the old covenant: every event has its own significance in the salvation history, as well as being a witness to its fulfilment in Christ. (pp.136-140)

Secondly, the New Testament writers often refer to historical events within the old covenant without specifically citing any Old Testament text, and thus they implicitly or explicitly employ the principle of typology (cf. 1952, 1953; see above: ch.6). Amsler tabulates typological references to Old Testament persons, events and institutions, and concludes that the chief features of the typological method as employed in the New Testament are that it is occasional, it is centred on Christ, and it involves progression from the old covenant to the new: 1) the analysis shows the occasional nature of the typology in that one element in the new covenant may be prefigured by various types in the old and equally one element in the old covenant may have various antitypes in the new and may also be cited without any typological interpretation; 2) the types prefiguring Jesus Christ are by far the most common and the significance of many other types is dependent on their Christological reference; 3) the typological connection is progressive since the types belong to God's provisional revelation in Israel whereas the antitypes belong to his definitive revelation in Jesus Christ, and the antitypes always surpass the types. (pp.141-6)

Behind this New Testament use of Old Testament words and events lies the principle that directly or indirectly the words and events of the Old Testament, in their witness to God's provisional revelation in the old covenant, bear witness to God's definitive revelation in Jesus Christ. Further, the New Testament affirms that the true meaning of the Old Testament is in God's intervention in history to reveal himself and save men, which makes every part of this salvation history more or less important - though never unimportant - as it bears witness in advance to the way God would later reveal himself in Jesus Christ. (pp.146-7)

At this point Amsler raises a question: is this New Testament typological use of the Old consistent with the Old Testament's self-understanding, or is it alien to the texts and therefore inauthentic? His answer is that the salvation history, according to the prophets, is a development which opens out toward the final salvation yet to come. On the one hand, prophetic testimony is concerned not only with past and present events but also with the final revelation for which these events prepare; on the other hand, the historical events attested by the Old Testament, as understood in terms of the dynamic nature of revelation, take on a wider significance as announcements of future revelatory events. (pp.147-9)

Finally, Amsler considers how the Old Testament can function as a witness to God's revelation in Jesus Christ. It is only from the perspective of the New Testament, according to which Jesus Christ completes the salvation history of the Old Testament, that Old Testament words and events can be recognised as promises and prefigurations of Jesus Christ. This is legitimate, according to Amsler, because the Old

Testament is aware of an eschatological aspect to both word and event. The New Testament shows the Church both the reason and the method for reading the Old Testament: since it has been fulfilled in Jesus Christ all the events of the Old Testament prefigure that definitive revelation in some way and its words bear indirect witness to its meaning.

f. The second half of the second section, 'How should the Old Testament be read in the Church?' (pp.151-227), brings Amsler's work to a close. Having presented the relationship between the Testaments as one which demands continued reading of the Old Testament in the Church today, Amsler advances to a discussion of methodology for such reading. He has already shown the fundamental principle to be that of 'fulfilment', and he considers the application of this principle to modern Old Testament interpretation. An important presupposition is a correct understanding of the relationship between word and event: confusion of these leads to allegory while separation leads to historicism or symbolism. Authentic reading of the Old Testament demands distinction but not separation between text and event in the Bible (p.161). To interpret an Old Testament text it is important to establish its literal meaning and to avoid spiritualisation of the sort which perceives a 'fuller meaning' (_sens plénier_) behind its words. To interpret an Old Testament event it is important to establish what really happened, from which it follows that historical criticism is an essential part of Old Testament interpretation, though Christian preaching is not a history lesson but a declaration of the theological truth of salvation history (p.199).

g. It is evident that Amsler's solution to the problem of the relationship between the Testaments is somewhat similar to that of von Rad (both were published in the same year, 1960). Both of them consider salvation history, promise and fulfilment, and typology to be central aspects of the relationship. This is all the more significant since they approach the problem from quite different angles: von Rad from that of Old Testament tradition history, Amsler from that of New Testament interpretation of the Old Testament. Amsler's work gives additional support to this understanding of the relationship between the Testaments, therefore, though it is also subject to some of the criticisms applied to von Rad's work; for example, the fact that it fits some parts of the Old Testament better than others. Amsler, to be sure, stresses the importance of 'text' as well as 'event' in the Bible (pp. 135-163; cf. 1960b; Barr 1966: ch.3), but his concern to interpret the whole Old Testament in terms of salvation history is such that like von Rad he is led to a negative evaluation of all that does not fit this perspective (e.g. the wisdom literature, p.111). Moreover it may be asked whether there is not more to the Bible than text and event. Life and personality involves three main aspects: thought, word and deed. Perhaps more attention should be given to the thoughts of God and man recorded in the Bible, as well as their words and deeds. God does not only speak and act, according to the Old Testament, he chooses, plans, loves, delights, hates and is faithful and true. So also man is not limited to word and deed, but frequently engages in worship, obedience or disobedience, love, delight, hate, unfaithfulness and hardness of heart.

In addition to his major work, L'AT dans l'Église (1960), the following works by Amsler are relevant:
'Où en est la typologie de l'AT?', ETR(1952);
'Prophétie et typologie', RThPh(1953);
'Texte et événement' in Vischer Festschrift(1960);
David, Roi et Messie (1963).

Cf. reviews of Amsler's book by Jacob (RThPh 1961), Soggin (Protestantesimo 1961), Westermann (TLZ 1962), Tinsley (JTS 1963) and Ringgren (Interpn 1964).

7.34 OSCAR CULLMANN

In a recent book Oscar Cullmann (1965) develops further his view (first propounded in 1946) of the centrality of salvation history to New Testament faith. He argues that 'New Testament man was certain that he was continuing the work God began with the election of the people of Israel for the salvation of mankind, which God fulfilled in Christ, which he unfolds in the present and which he will complete at the end' (p.13). Although his main concern is to expound New Testament theology, not to solve the problem of the relationship between the Testaments, Cullmann's work is nevertheless an important contribution to the understanding of the latter question.

Works by Cullmann:
Christ and Time (1946);
'La nécessité et la fonction de l'exégèse philologique et historique de la Bible', VerbC(1949);
'The Connection of Primal Events and End Events with the NT Redemptive History' in OTCF(1964);
Salvation in History (1965).

Cf. Bultmann, 'History of Salvation and History' (1948), ET in Existence and Faith;
Steck, Die Idee der Heilsgeschichte(1959):43-51;
Frisque, Oscar Cullmann (1960);
Ladd, 'History and Theology in Biblical Exegesis', Interpn (1966);
Harrington, The Path of Biblical Theology(1973): 197-201.

7.35 G. ERNEST WRIGHT

One of the most significant contributions to understanding the theological relationship between the Testaments has been made by the American scholar, G. Ernest Wright. Although he has since (1969) qualified his view in certain respects, Wright's programmatic monograph - God Who Acts (1952) - remains the most important statement of his solution to the problem. He maintains that 'Biblical theology is the confessional recital of the redemptive acts of God in a particular history, because history is the chief medium of revelation' (p.13). It follows that Jesus Christ is not to be understood primarily as a teacher; rather, 'his coming was a historical event which was the climax of God's working since the creation. All former history had its goal in him because God had so directed it' (p.56). Thus Wright's study of biblical theology leads to conclusions similar to those of von Rad and other scholars considered in the present chapter: the relationship between the Testaments is to be understood in terms of salvation history, and important aspects include the framework of promise and fulfilment (pp.56-7) and typology (pp.61-6).

Works by Wright:
The Challenge of Israel's Faith (1944);
'Interpreting the OT', ThTo(1946);
'The Christian Interpreter as Biblical Critic', Interpn(1947);
The OT Against Its Environment (1950);
'The Unity of the Bible', Interpn(1951);
'From the Bible to the Modern World' in Richardson and Schweitzer (1951);
God Who Acts (1952; cf. review by Eichrodt, JBL 1954);
'The Unity of the Bible', SJT(1955);
'History and Reality' in OTCF(1964);
'Reflections concerning OT Theology' in Vriezen Festschrift (1966);

The OT and Theology (1969);
'Historical Knowledge and Revelation' in May Festschrift (1970);
'The Theological Study of the Bible',IOVCB(1972).
Cf. Gilkey, 'Cosmology, Ontology and the Travail of Biblical Language',JR(1961).

7.36 WALTHER EICHRODT

It may seem strange to mention Eichrodt in a subsection of a chapter concerned primarily with von Rad. There is of course a world of difference, with many important implications, between the approaches to Old Testament theology of the two great masters of that art (or science?); but it is unnecessary to enter into that here since it receives detailed discussion in the hands of Nesbit (1969) and Spriggs (1974). What is of particular significance in the present context is that Eichrodt - like Pannenberg, Cullmann and Amsler - starts from a different point and proceeds with a different methodology than von Rad and yet reaches strikingly similar conclusions. Though less enthusiastic than von Rad, Eichrodt explicitly accepts as partial expressions of the relationship between the Testaments the concepts of typology (1957a) and actualisation (1961: 519-20), and propounds a view of 'prophecy and fulfilment' (1933:501-11; 1961:518-20) not unlike von Rad's view of 'promise and fulfilment'. Moreover it would not be an injustice, even if an oversimplification, to suggest that the key concept in Eichrodt's understanding of the relationship between the Testaments is 'salvation history' (cf. Miller 1956).

Works by Eichrodt:
'Die atl. Theologie',ZAW (1929);
Theology of the OT(1933-9):esp.I:26-8,472-511;
Das AT und der christliche Glaube(1936; not available to me);
'Zur Frage der theologischen Exegese des ATes',ThBl(1938);
'Offenbarung und Geschichte im AT',ThZ(1948);
'The Right Interpretation of the OT',ThTo(1950);
Gottes Ruf im AT (1951);
'Les rapports du NT et de l'AT' in Boisset(1955);
'Heilserfahrung und Zeitverständnis im AT',ThZ(1956);
'Is Typological Exegesis an Appropriate Method?' (1957), ET in EOTI;
'The Law and the Gospel',Interpn(1957);
'The Problem of OT Theology',Excursus to ET of Theology of the OT I(1961);
'Covenant and Law'(1965),ET in Interpn 20.

Cf. Porteous, 'OT Theology' in Rowley(1951):322-8;
Baumgärtel, Verheissung (1952):95-102;
Nesbit, 'A Study of Methodologies in Contemporary OT Theologies',Dissn(1969);
Gottwald, 'W.Eichrodt, Theology of the OT' in Laurin (1970);
Kraus, Die Biblische Theologie(1970):127-8;
Würthwein, 'Zur Theologie des ATs',ThRu(1971):195-9;
Hasel, OT Theology(1972):18-22;
Harrington, The Path of Biblical Theology(1973): 41-50,71-2,279-81,289-91;
Spriggs, Two OT Theologies(1974).

7.37 OTHERS

a. The salvation history solution to the problem of the relationship between the Testaments, often linked with the 'promise and fulfilment' scheme, is undoubtedly that most widely accepted in modern scholarship. Apart from the work of von Rad himself, six other major solutions to the problem which fall within the general category have been considered in the present chapter. In this concluding section it is possible only to mention briefly a number of other important solutions which follow similar lines.

b. During the period of the German Church Struggle Emil Brunner persistently maintained that the Church stands and falls with the Old Testament, just as it stands and falls with Jesus Christ, since without the Old Testament there is no Jesus Christ (1934:7). He argued that the Old Testament is a beginning, the New Testament its completion (1930:263); revelation is promise in the old covenant, fulfilment in the new (1941: chs 7-8). This idea of promise and fulfilment has been taken up in many quarters (cf. above: 7.24), as may be instanced by the works of the Dutch Reformed theologian, G.C.Berkouwer (1952:113-152), the American Roman Catholic scholar, Roland E. Murphy (1964), and the British evangelical Rylands Professor, F.F. Bruce (1955, p.4: 'the specifically Christian approach to the Old Testament ... sees the relation of the Old Testament to the New as that of promise to fulfilment'). Likewise Norman W. Porteous, who approves with reservations the approaches to Old Testament theology of both Eichrodt and von Rad, asserts that the Christian believes 'that the Old Testament and the New Testament correspond to each other as promise to fulfilment' (1954:168). And even John L. McKenzie (1974), who devalues salvation history (p.325) and typology (pp.28,324) as expressions of the relationship between the Testaments, affirms the importance of promise and fulfilment (1964; 1968:766-7; cf. 1974: 139-144).

c. Another work written in Germany in the 1930s was Ethelbert Stauffer's <u>New Testament Theology</u>(1941), a work based materially on the concept of salvation history. About the same time, W.J. Phythian-Adams in England wrote several studies of biblical theology structured around the concept of 'sacred history'.

More recently Alan Richardson (1964a) has declared that 'the essential and differentiating factor' in both Testaments is 'a kerygma concerning God's saving action in the history of his people (p.44; though cf. 1964b:133-9). And in various studies of biblical theology George Eldon Ladd has argued that 'the entire Bible finds its unity in what can best be called holy history - Heilsgeschichte' (1968:110; for further literature on salvation history, see above: 7.26).

d. This is by no means an exhaustive survey, but it would be exhausting and perhaps not very profitable to attempt such a survey. The extent to which the 'salvation history' solution to the problem of the relationship between the Testaments is widespread today may be indicated by reference to the work of a Polish scholar, Józef Kudasiewicz (1971). He takes salvation history as the basis of his study and elaborates three principles for relating the Testaments: unity and continuity; announcement and fulfilment, and typology. Finally, the works of Jacob and Schwarzwäller should be mentioned again. Jacob has been discussed in conjunction with Vischer (see above: 5.33), but attention must be drawn here to the fact that he considers the unity of the Testaments to be a function of salvation history (1968a:ix; cf. 1965:ch.4). Schwarzwäller's view has a certain similarity to the Old Testament solutions discussed above (see: 2.24), but is closer to those of von Rad, the Biblischer Kommentar group and Amsler, which he assesses positively in his survey of recent study (1969). His formula for the relationship between the Testaments is 'demonstration (Erweis) and result (Ergebnis)', so that Jesus is recognised as the

Christ, that is as the result of God's salvation history, only in the recognition of this history of divine self-demonstration (1966a:55).

Brunner, 'The Significance of the OT for Our Faith' (1930), ET in OTCF; Die Unentbehrlichkeit des ATes (1934); Revelation and Reason(1941): chs 7-8; Dogmatics II(1950): chs 7-9; cf.Filson 1951:142-3; Hesse 1960b:25-30;
Phythian-Adams, The Call of Israel(1934); The Fulness of Israel(1938); The People and the Presence (1942); The Way of At-one-ment(1944); 'Shadow and Substance',Interpn(1947); cf. Hebert, The Throne of David(1941), The Authority of the OT(1947), Scripture and the Faith(1947) and 'The Interpretation of the Bible',Interpn(1950);
Stauffer, NT Theology(1941); cf. Filson 1951:148-9; Harrington 1973:169-178,188,281;
Wilder, 'NT Theology in Transition' in Willoughby(1947);
Bentzen, 'The OT and the New Covenant',HervTS(1950);
Bruce, The Books and the Parchments(1950):ch.6; Approach to the OT(1955); This is That(1968);
Porteous, 'Semantics and OT Theology',OTS(1950); 'The OT and Some Theological Thought-Forms', SJT(1954); 'The Theology of the OT',PCB(1962); 'Actualization' in Weiser Festschrift(1963); 'The Present State of OT Theology',ExpT(1963); 'The Relevance of the OT' in Vriezen Festschrift (1966); 'A Question of Perspectives' in Eichrodt Festschrift(1970); 'Magnalia Dei' in von Rad Festschrift(1971); 'OT and History', ASTI(1972); cf. Harrington 1973:32-4,356-8;
Berkouwer, The Person of Christ(1952):113-152; cf. van Ruler 1955:12/13-14;
Richardson, 'Is the OT the Propaedeutic to Christian Faith?',OTCF(1964); History Sacred and Profane(1964
McKenzie, 'The Significance of the OT for Christian Faith in Roman Catholicism',OTCF(1964); 'Aspects of OT Thought',JBC(1968); A Theology of the OT(1974); cf. Harrington 1973:86-8,281-2;
Murphy, 'The Relationship between the Testaments', CBQ (1964); cf. Harrington 1973:308-9;
Ladd, 'History and Theology in Biblical Exegesis', Interpn(1966); Jesus and the Kingdom(1966); The Pattern of NT Truth(1968); 'The Search for Perspective',Interpn(1971).
Schwarzwäller, Das AT in Christus(1966); 'Das Verhältnis AT-NT im Lichte der gegenwärtigen Bestimmungen',EvTh(1969); also, 'Probleme gegenwärtiger Theologie und das AT' in von Rad Festschrift (1971);
Kudasiewicz, 'Jedność dwu Testamentów',RBL(1971).

8. The Old and New Testaments are continuous and discontinuous

8.1 TH. C. VRIEZEN: THE CHRISTIAN CHURCH AND THE OLD TESTAMENT

8.2 H.H.ROWLEY AND C.H.DODD: TWO BRITISH CONTRIBUTIONS

8.3 COMPARISON: OTHER CONTINUITY/DISCONTINUITY SOLUTIONS

8.1 TH.C. VRIEZEN: THE CHRISTIAN CHURCH AND THE OLD TESTAMENT

8.11 INTRODUCTION

a. Vriezen's Old Testament theology (1954/66) is based on the view that 'both as to its object and its method Old Testament theology is and must be a (Christian) theological science' (p.121/147; cf. 9/19). He admits that the Old Testament may be either the subject or the object of theology, so that Old Testament theology is respectively either an historical study of theology contained in the Old Testament - like the older biblical theologies - or a dogmatic theological study of the Old Testament (p.118/143). Nevertheless, it is the latter approach which he considers to be the more important. Old Testament theology, for Vriezen, is a branch of systematic theology which deals with the Old Testament on the basis of the Christian faith, and interprets its theological concepts in the light of the fuller understanding made possible by the coming of Christ (ch.5). It is quite distinct from history of the religion of Israel (on which Vriezen has written a separate book, 1963) both in its object, the Old Testament rather than Israelite religion, and in its method, which is kerygmatic rather than historical.[1]

---

1. See pp.121-3/148-150 cf. 12-16/22-6; see Porteous 1963c; Clements 1970: 125; cf. Steuernagel 1925; Eissfeldt 1926; Rendtorff 1963; Barr 1957a; 1974: 275-8; Harrington 1973:88-106.

b. Although he calls his subject a 'Christian theological science' and considers the Old Testament to be the Word of God (ch.4), Vriezen is fully aware that the Old Testament is an ancient oriental book (pp.15/25, 80/92) and affirms that the methods of historical and literary criticism are both applicable and essential in its study (pp.8-10/18-20). Indeed, in practice, it is the historical rather than the 'Christian theological' perspective which dominates Vriezen's work (cf. Clements 1970:134-5). Historical criticism, he argues, neither determines nor alters a particular view of the Old Testament, but helps to root the Old Testament in human history (p.92/115).

c. This insistence on an approach which is both Christian and historico-critical distinguishes Vriezen's Old Testament theology (as also those of Jacob and Knight, see above: 5.33,5.34) from the major works of Eichrodt and von Rad. Eichrodt's theology is based on historical criticism and is systematic in structure, but it is limited to empirico-historical study and therefore is essentially phenomenological in approach, according to Vriezen (p.120/146; though see Eichrodt 1933:33n.; cf. Würthwein 1971:206-7). Von Rad explicitly rejects both systematic method and historical criticism as a basis for Old Testament theology, in the sense that he treats individual Old Testament writings separately and - although accepting the results of historical criticism - bases his theology on Israel's own view of her history (cf. above: 7.213). Vriezen's work is therefore quite distinct from that of von Rad, though in chapter three he does very briefly what is for von Rad the whole of his theology (see pp. -/146-7; cf.1965).

d. The first third of Vriezen's Old Testament theology is devoted to introductory matters, among which the problem of the relationship between the Testaments is central, and the remainder is a study of 'The content of Old Testament theology'. One of the most serious criticisms of Vriezen's work is that there is a certain lack of harmony between the principles he enunciates in part one and their outworking in his exposition of Old Testament theology in part two (cf. Childs 1959; Ellison 1959; Clements 1970:126,134-5). His exposition does not reflect the influence of the New Testament and Christian theology nearly so much as his insistence on a 'Christian theological' approach leads one to expect. Nevertheless, Vriezen is not the first to find difficulty in putting what he preaches into practice, and this deficiency in his work does not in itself invalidate his principles. His failure is not to relate the Testaments differently in practice than in theory, but simply to make comparatively little use of his principles in practical exposition. In any case, in the present work it is only possible to consider the problem in theoretical terms. Since he does not deal with the problem systematically it is impossible to give a précis of Vriezen's argument: instead, the following sections will focus on some aspects of the problem as treated in his Old Testament theology.

A full bibliography of Vriezen's works is given in his Festschrift (1966). The most important for the present study are:
An outline of OT theology (1954/66);
'Theocracy and Soteriology'(1956),ET in EOTI;
'Geloof, openbaring en geschiedenis',KT(1965).

Significant reviews of his theology:
Childs, JBL(1959); Ellison, EQ(1959);
Knight, SJT(1959); Mauchline, JSS(1959);
Myers, Interpn(1959); Alonso-Schökel, Biblica(1961);
G.W. Anderson, ExpT(1962); Porteous, JTS(1963).

See also:
Barr, Old and New (1966):168-9;
Clements, 'Theodorus C. Vriezen, An Outline of OT Theology' in Laurin (1970);
Kraus, Die Biblische Theologie(1970):131-3;
Würthwein, 'Zur Theologie des ATs',ThRu(1971):205-8;
Harrington, The Path of Biblical Theology(1973): 50-55,72-3,276-9.

8.12 HISTORY AND REVELATION

The historical character of the Old Testament revelation is 'the most difficult and the most disputed question of present-day theology', according to Vriezen (p.12/22). It was shown in the previous section that Vriezen presupposes historical criticism, and it follows that his reference to God's activity in history (e.g. pp.29-30/39,136-7/162-3) is concerned, unlike that of von Rad, with real history as reconstructed by scholarship (though the authority of the Bible depends not on historical accuracy but on theological truth, p.86/99). The corollary of his acceptance of 'real' history as the locus of God's activity is that Vriezen considers this activity also to be real. Though he does not explicitly defend it, the reality of divine activity is an assumption of Vriezen's work, so that he frequently makes God the subject of a verb (e.g. pp.4/13,12-13/22-3, 37/48) and writes of the encounter between God and man as something which really happened (pp.10/19-20). On the question of the relationship between history and revelation (on which, cf. above: 7.32), Vriezen affirms that history is the place rather than the organ of revelation, and becomes revelatory only as it is declared to be such by God's word (pp. -/188-190)

8.13 COMMON PERSPECTIVES

Vriezen considers that both Old and New Testaments have certain common perspectives, among which the concepts of communion, prophecy and kingdom are particularly important. He takes the certainty of immediate communion between God and man not only as the unifying factor of his Old Testament theology (cf. pp.-/150-152) but to be 'the underlying idea of the whole of the Biblical testimony' (p.131/157; cf. -/204-5; see Harrington 1973:73). In contrast to von Rad (1952a:25), for whom the Old Testament is a 'history book', Vriezen asserts that prophecy is the basis of the witness of the Old Testament[1]: only the vision and testimony of the prophets can account for Israel's awareness of God's activity in history (pp.40/51; -/101-3; 90-91/113-114; cf.Sanders 1972:55). Moreover the prophetic message is continued in the New Testament, which preaches the same God (pp.-/104-6; cf. above: 1.212), expects the same kingdom (pp.-/104,106-8; cf. above: 1.26), and demands the same life of faith (pp.-/104-5,108-9) as the Old Testament. In particular, the eschatological prospect of the kingdom of God is for Vriezen not only 'the most profound leading motif in the Old Testament' (p.91/114), but also the 'true heart' of the message of both Testaments (pp.100/123; cf. 91-2/114-115).

---

1. In spite of its obvious importance (cf. also above: 7.11), it is an exaggeration to make prophecy as central to the Old Testament as Vriezen does. Clements (1970) points out that from an historical and theological point of view the law has priority over the prophets in the Old Testament canon (p.136).

8.14 A RELATIONSHIP OF TENSION

a. It is clear that according to Vriezen the Old and New Testaments have a good deal in common; but there is also a decisive discontinuity: the disciples of Jesus were convinced that he was the Messiah (pp.-/106,109). This tension between continuity and discontinuity is the essence of Vriezen's view of the relationship between the Testaments (p.98/121).

b. In the thought of Jesus (pp.2-4/11-13) and Paul (pp.81-3/93-5), Vriezen argues, there is a tension between acceptance of the Old Testament as the word of God and reinterpretation in the conviction that it is superseded with the coming of Christ. This tension has continued through the history of the Church and remains unresolved today (pp.83-5/95-9). On the one hand, there are various attempts to overcome the tension: some (e.g. Vischer, von Rad) have revived the traditional ideas of allegory and typology in an attempt to reconcile unity and diversity in the Bible, while others (e.g. van Ruler, Miskotte) have replied to the threat to the Old Testament's authority by affirming its independent theological significance. On the other hand, some (e.g. Bultmann, Baumgärtel) have stressed the tension so strongly that the Old Testament is understood to be a non-Christian book. None of these attempts have provided a satisfactory solution, according to Vriezen, who argues that the tension is not to be overcome but to be recognised as central to an understanding of the relationship between the Testaments (cf. Childs 1959).

c. It follows that there is a double relationship between the Testaments: organic spiritual unity, and historical difference and distance (pp.87/100, 98/120-121). A balanced solution to the problem must take account of both the fundamental theological agreement between the two Testaments and the radical inward renovation of Israel's religion accomplished by Jesus Christ (pp.77/89,-/110). In this the person of Jesus has a double role: not only is he the decisive difference between the Testaments but also, paradoxically, the essential unity of the Bible becomes evident in him. 'Jesus Christ is the end of God's self-disclosure to Israel and at the same time He is the man through whom God made the world share in His redeeming work in Israel' (p.-/28; cf. 99-101/122-4).

8.15 OLD TESTAMENT INTERPRETATION

Vriezen distinguishes two main aspects to Christian interpretation of the Old Testament: exegesis and preaching (pp.97-117/120-142; cf. Smart 1961: 40-44).

Exegesis cannot be limited to use of New Testament principles, which are not only separated by nineteen centuries from modern thought but concerned with a different task than that of present-day exegesis; it must go beyond the New Testament to use all the tools of twentieth-century scholarship in understanding the Bible as the revelation of God (pp.103-5/126-8). Unlike exegesis in other branches of scholarship, theological exegesis presses deeper than the literal meaning to consider the spiritual import of a biblical passage, and it does this by means of a threefold method: historico--critical study of the text, hermeneutical study of the message of the author and theological study of the text in the light of the whole biblical message (pp.105-111/129-138). In discussing the third stage of exegesis, which is expecially dependent on understanding of the theological relationship between the Testaments, Vriezen indicates four main ways in which a text may be understood in its biblical context: typology, preparation, similarity and contrast. Only by such a multiplex method, he argues, can the organic and historical relationship between the Testaments be expressed without forced interpretation of the texts (pp.110-111/135-8).

Preaching differs from exegesis in that it involves proclamation - not just explanation - of the Word of God (pp.111-112/138). Though he must base his message on thorough critical examination of the text, the preacher's prophetic task is to declare the divine word from the Bible to man. The focus of preaching is the gospel of Jesus Christ, but this is not to be understood in isolation from the law and the prophets. Thus Vriezen argues that in preaching, as in exegesis, the Old and New Testaments should be neither identified nor separated, nor should one be overemphasised at the expense of the other, but both should be recognised as part of one witness to God's communion with man from creation to consummation (pp.112-115/138-141).

For examples of Vriezen's interpretation of the OT see the bibliography in his Festschrift (1966). Also, more recently: 'Exodusstudien Exodus I', VT(1967); 'Erwägungen zu Amos 3,2' in Galling Festschrift(1970); 'The Exegesis of Exodus xxiv 9-11',OTS(1972).

8.2 H.H. ROWLEY AND C.H. DODD: TWO BRITISH CONTRIBUTIONS

8.21 INTRODUCTION

In many respects the outstanding British Old and New Testament scholars of the present century were respectively H.H. Rowley and C.H. Dodd. Their work is an important part of the foundation of modern biblical scholarship in this country, and their contribution to understanding the relationship between the Testaments has been built upon rather than replaced in more recent years. As with British scholars generally, their solutions to the problem are complex and attempt to achieve a balance without over-stressing any one aspect of the relationship. Possibly the most dominant feature of their solutions, however, is their expression of a tension between a relationship of continuity and one of discontinuity.

Relevant works by Rowley:
Israel's Mission to the World (1939);
The Relevance of the Bible (1941);
The Re-Discovery of the OT (1946);
'The Unity of the OT', BJRL(1946);
'The Relevance of Biblical Interpretation', Interpn (1947);
'The Authority of the Bible'(1949),repr. in revised form in From Moses to Qumran;
'The Gospel in the OT' in Smith (1950);
The Unity of the Bible (1953); cf. Boyd 1955, Harrington 1973:260-65;
The Faith of Israel (1956).
A 'select' but nevertheless detailed bibliography of his writings is given in the Rowley Festschrift (1955).

Relevant works by Dodd:
<u>The Authority of the Bible</u> (1928); cf.Hebert 1947:33-7;
<u>The Parables of the Kingdom</u> (1935);
<u>The Apostolic Preaching and its Developments</u> (1936);
<u>History and the Gospel</u> (1938);
<u>The Bible Today</u> (1946); cf. Porteous 1951:340-43;
'Natural Law in the NT'(1946),repr. in his <u>NT Studies</u>;
'Autorité et rôle de la Bible',<u>ETR</u>(1948);
<u>Gospel and Law</u> (1951);
'The Relevance of the Bible' in Richardson and Schweitzer (1951);
<u>According to the Scriptures</u> (1952);
<u>The Founder of Christianity</u> (1971).
A bibliography of Dodd's works up to 1961 is given by Wolfzorn, 'Realized Eschatology',<u>ETL</u>(1962):63-70.

8.22 AN OLD TESTAMENT APPROACH

8.221 <u>Prophecy and fulfilment</u>

a. One of the central ideas in Rowley's approach to the problem is that of 'prophecy and fulfilment' (cf. above: 3.13,7.24). He points out that the unfashionable idea of'prediction', although undoubtedly not all that is involved, is nevertheless a vital element of prophecy (1946a:203). The essence of prediction - in spite of the fact that some predictions were neither intended nor expected to be fulfilled literally (e.g. Isa.40:4), some were not fulfilled because they provoked a change of heart (e.g. Jonah 3) and for some the fulfilment was delayed or different from what was expected (e.g. Jer.4:23-8; 51:28-9) - is that it expects the fulfilment of what is predicted (1946a:203-6). According to the New Testament, this fulfilment occurred in Jesus Christ, who applied the term 'Son of Man' to himself and accepted the title 'Christ' from his followers, so linking himself directly with Old Testament hopes for the future (1946a:210 cf.ch.11). Sometimes prophecies, such as the Immanuel oracle, which do not refer directly to Jesus are 'taken up and filled with new meaning in Him' (1946a:207), while others, such as the Servant Songs, 'so deeply influenced our Lord that he entered into their spirit, and so embodied their mission and message in Himself, and became their fulfilment' (1946a:208). In Jesus Christ 'the hopes of the prophets were not so much realized as transmuted, and given a higher realization than their authors dreamed' (1946a:211). There is however more to be said than that Christ fulfils the predictions and prophecies of the Old Testament.

b. The Old Testament 'constantly points to something beyond itself' (1949:17), it 'looks forward to something which should follow it' (1953:94); and the New Testament looks back to the Old Testament, offering the answer to its expectation (1949:17), the response to its faith and hope (1953:117; 1949:28), and the fulfilment of its promise (1953:106). Thus we find the fulfilment of the Old Testament in the New, even though fulfilment is not complete here but awaits consummation in the more distant future (1953:109-110). Not only does the New Testament discharge the promises of the Old but it takes up the mission and message of the former covenant and makes them its own. Israel was called to be a light to the nations, and Jesus Christ as the Suffering Servant takes this task upon himself (John 8:12) and passes it on to his followers (Matt.5:14) (1946a:215; cf.1939:89-94).

8.222 <u>Continuity and discontinuity</u>

a. It has been shown that Rowley makes use of the ideas of prophecy and fulfilment to express the relationship between the Testaments. It is also evident that he perceives a tension between continuity and discontinuity in this relationship (1949:20n.). For instance, certain aspects of the Old Testament such as primitive ideas (1953: 14-16), much of the old law (1953:102-3) and sacrifice (1953:103-8,129-130) are superseded by the New Testament, but this does not mean that the Old Testament as a whole is superseded (1953:2). Both old and new revelations are real and valid in their own right (1953:98) but 'the two Testaments belong to one another and neither is complete without the other' (1949:17).

b. On the one hand, there is no doubt that for Rowley the Old Testament belongs in the Christian Bible. It is there not simply as the preparation for the New Testament, a function which other religious literature may serve without thereby securing a place in the Bible, but as an integral part of the Christian Scriptures (1946a:9-10). The two Testaments are complementary and belong together so that neither can be fully understood without the other (1956:45; 1949:17; 1953:94,112).

c. On the other hand, although it is essential to the Christian Bible, the Old Testament is not a Christian book but an early stage of growth towards the whole (1956:14). The two Testaments are related not by their similarity but because they are different. 'The most significant bond between the two Testaments ... is to be found ... in the fundamental differences between the Testaments' (1953: 89). Prophecy and fulfilment are two quite different things, yet they are intimately linked.

d. Rowley's view of the relationship between the Testaments may therefore be characterised by the idea of 'continuity and discontinuity' (cf. 1941:ch.4; 1947:15; 1950c:35). Smart (1961:90) asserts that Rowley does not take the discontinuity seriously enough, but this must be rejected in view of Rowley's conclusion that the differences between the Testaments provide the most important link between them (see above: c), his warning of the danger of equating the two Testaments (1953:90), and his rejoinder to Smart which reaffirms that he recognises fully both continuity and discontinuity between the Testaments (1949:20n.).

8.223 Theological unity

The continuity and discontinuity between the two Testaments are brought together in the essential theological unity of the Bible. It is a dynamic unity (1956:14), the unity of development (1953:7), process (1953:27) and growth (1953:63), and therefore it is manifested not in uniformity but in diversity (1946b:358; 1953:1-29). Rowley rejects understanding of this unity in terms of a typological foreshadowing of the new revelation in the old, since he considers that such an approach tends to ignore the value of the Old Testament in its own right within its own context.[1] Instead, he finds the

---

1. His criticism that it 'treats the essential meaning and purpose of the Old Testament as a prefiguring of the experience of Christ or of the Church' (1953:19-20 cf.98) is a too narrow understanding of typology. Although this is no doubt true of some so-called 'typology', the views of Amsler and von Rad - whom he quotes as representatives of the typological method of interpretation - do not fit this description. Amsler (1960a) says that every event of the old covenant is significant

unity of the Testaments in their common divine origin (1953:96-7,118,121), common teaching about God and man (1953:62-89), common patterns (1949: 18-25; 1953:10-13 cf.20,97), and common ethical and liturgical principles (1953:77-8,139-140,166).

8.23 A NEW TESTAMENT APPROACH

8.231 Realized eschatology

a. The Old Testament is not final, according to C.H. Dodd. The prophets believe that God is at work in Israel's history and is revealing his purpose there, though this purpose is not completely revealed within the Old Testament. Many questions are raised in the Old Testament, such as the relationships between nationalism and universalism, righteousness and grace, and divine justice and the human situation, which are left unanswered (cf.above: 0.34d). The Old Testament for Dodd is

---

for revelation in its own right (p.140), emphasises the importance of the literal meaning of the text (pp.178-183) and the historical reality of the event (pp.192-4), rejects spiritualisation (pp.183-6), and advocates primarily a theological rather than a typological interpretation of the Old Testament (pp.200-227). Von Rad (1952a) accepts that typology must be bound by the historical sense (p.21) and not separated from exegesis (pp.37-8), that the Old Testament had a real meaning for Israel (pp.35-6) and must 'first of all be heard in its witness to the creative Word of God in history'(p.39), although it is true that he sees the theological significance of the Old Testament for the Christian to lie primarily in its prefiguration of Christ (p.36).

Rowley is therefore criticising only his own misunderstanding of typology. His idea of 'common patterns' in the Old and New Testaments - for example, in the Exodus and the deliverance by Christ - is in fact not very different from the understanding of typology proposed in the present study (cf. above: ch.6).

a process, not a completed whole, and it is pervaded by a sense of inconclusiveness (1928:189-190/182-3, 206-7/195-6; 1938:32-5/24-6; 1951b:158). This process is set in the context of a history which moves forward, but whose goal is not seen clearly within the Old Testament since there are different strands pointing forward in different directions which are not yet resolved (1928:190/183,283/261; 1951a:26; 1951b:158; 1971:82-4). Now that the goal has been reached it is possible to look back and see that the Old Testament was really looking forward to the centre of history, the cross and resurrection of Christ (1951b:160).

b. Dodd argues that the New Testament - in contrast to the Old Testament - is final, or at least it inaugurates the finale of history. It announces that the time is fulfilled and the expected event has taken place. The coming, death and resurrection of Christ fulfil the whole complex drama of judgement and redemption which made up the history of Israel. God has established a new covenant, which does not simply supplement, amend or supersede the old covenant but is its fulfilment.[1] The New Testament writers assert that the 'Day of the Lord', anticipated by the prophets and apocalyptists, has been realised in Jesus Christ; and this leads Dodd to describe the ministry of Jesus, in a phrase that has since become famous, as 'realized eschatology' (1935:51/41,198-9/148; 1936:195-214/79-87). In the face of some criticism he later admitted that the term was 'not altogether felicitous'

1. 1928:ch.10,-/260; 1935:198-9/148; 1936:18/13, 38/21,96-7/43,107/47,119-120/52-3,165-7/69-70; 1938:35/26,138-145/96-101; 1946a:10,74-5,151; 1946b:129; 1951b:158; 1952a:72,88,102-3,129-130.

and referred approvingly to the suggested emendations 'inaugurated eschatology' and 'eschatology that is in process of realization' (*sich realisierende Eschatologie*). He did not adopt either in later works, however, but maintained his basic thesis that in Christ's coming the crucial event of history anticipated by the prophets had taken place (cf. 1951a:25-32; 1971:115-116).

Cf. Jeremias, 'Eine neue Schau der Zukunftsaussagen Jesu', *ThBl* (1941); *The Parables of Jesus* (1962):230;
Florovsky, 'Revelation and Interpretation' in Richardson and Schweitzer (1951):179-180;
Wolfzorn, 'Realized Eschatology', *ETL* (1962);
Ladd, *Jesus and the Kingdom* (1966):19-20.

8.232 Continuity and discontinuity

It has been alleged that Dodd tends to eliminate the differences between the Old and New Testaments (Verhoef 1970a:281[1]), but in fact it is quite clear that he recognises the differences as much as the continuity between the two (cf. Filson 1951:149). Although he admits there is some truth in the idea of evolution of religion he denies that it is a sufficient account of the growth of the Bible. There is indeed a certain continuity in the sequence of events from the early nomads, through the monarchy and dispersion, to the Church, but the biblical narrative depicts a series of crises rather than a smooth development, and the conclusion is radically different from the beginning. The New Testament writers are aware of being in continuity with the

1. He does not cite any work of Dodd's for this, but adduces W. Schweitzer as an authority.

older traditions, but their experience is revolutionary and their interpretation of those traditions original and creative, following the example of Jesus himself. The Church is simultaneously the 'Israel of God' (Gal.6:16) and a 'new creation' (2 Cor.5:17); it perpetuates the old and inaugurates the new. Moreover there is a difference between the Testaments in that the subject in the Old is a community, Israel, whereas in the New it is a person, Jesus Christ (1946a:73; on this, see above: 3.26). The statement 'the writers of the New Testament and of early Christianity in general are clearly aware both of continuity and of newness' (1928:263/244) is without doubt Dodd's assessment of the relationship between the Testaments (1928: 205-7/194-6,ch.12; 1938:138-142/96-8; 1946a:3-4, 73; 1951b:157; 1952a:109-110).

8.233 Historical unity

The unity of the Bible is, for Dodd, not based on the identity or similarity of the two Testaments but on the common origin of every part of the Bible in a 'community conscious of a continuous history' (1946a:3). This history, recorded in the Bible as the inner core of world history, may be called 'sacred history' (Heilsgeschichte) since it understands history as a process of redemption and revelation. It culminates in the death and resurrection of Christ, though it does not end at that point but is reconstituted in the history of the Church. Since God is the creator and sovereign of all men, the meaning of this sacred history is also the ultimate meaning of all history. All history is therefore ultimately sacred, as is shown by the way the Bible puts sacred history into the context of a world history with a real beginning and end. Thus Dodd, like Rowley, shows that the continuity and discontinuity between the Old and New Testaments is consistent with an essential unity within the Bible, which he believes stems from the history of one community in which God has revealed himself (1928:-/10; 1938: 166-182/114-125; 1946a:2-3; 1946b:129; 1951b:161-162).

8.234 Israel, Jesus, Church and Bible

a. Dodd's view of the relationship between the Testaments has several implications. First, Jesus in the Messiah of Israel (cf. above: 5.22): his mission is primarily to Israel, he claims to be the answer to their hopes of a coming king and 'representative', and it is in Jerusalem that his career comes to its climax (1938:130-138/90-96; 1952a:114-123; 1971:99-103).

b. Another implication is that Christians live within the new covenant (cf. above: 0.235): the prophets - in particular Jeremiah - proclaim the renewal of the old covenant with a covenant under which God will write his laws on men's hearts. In the same way in which God's deliverance of the Israelites at the Exodus is the foundation of the old covenant, the New Testament affirms that in his deliverance of mankind through the death and resurrection of Christ God has established a new covenant (1946b:129-130,141; 1951a:67-8; 1951b:158; cf. 1952a:124).

c. The Church is the new Israel (cf. above: 1.214) Jesus' claim to be their Messiah is rejected by Israel, so he institutes a new people of God to fulfil the mission which had been entrusted to Israel. He founds this new community with the twelve apostles, symbolising the twelve tribes, and it is confirmed as the Israel of God by the gift of the Spirit. Jesus and the New Testament authors apply Old Testament texts concerning Israel to the Church, thus forming the basis for use of the Old Testament in the life and worship of the Church (1928:-/260; 1938:134-8/93-6; 1946a:4-5, 70,76; 1951b:158; 1952a:88,111-114; 1971:91-2).

d. Finally, the Old Testament and the New Testament together, and only together, constitute the Christian Bible: the Old Testament contains difficulties and incongruities and can be properly understood only in the light of its fulfilment; the New Testament, on the other hand, has its background in the Old Testament and is liable to be interpreted in a distorted manner if isolated from that background. The Church grew up in dependence on the Old Testament and soon recognised the New Testament to have an equal authority: neither are to be rejected now (1946a:9-12,15).

8.3 COMPARISON: OTHER CONTINUITY/ DISCONTINUITY SOLUTIONS

8.31 JOHN BRIGHT

a. For John Bright (1967:ch.2) the 'classical' solutions to the problem of the relationship between the Testaments - Marcionism, Christianisation of the Old Testament, progressive revelation - are to be rejected. He affirms that the Old Testament records real history, in conjunction with a theological interpretation of that history, which is understood to be moving toward a destination but which does not reach it. The Old Testament is therefore theologically incomplete, describing a salvation history in which salvation is not yet achieved (pp.136-8). Fulfilment and completion occur only outside the limits of the Old Testament, in the New Testament. At the centre of the New Testament message stands one central fact: Jesus Christ has come, God has acted decisively in human history to fulfil his promises and achieve salvation (pp.138-140).

b. The Bible is a theological book, and it follows that the unity of the Bible depends on there being unity in biblical theology. According to Bright, there exists such a unity: the 'overarching structure of theology, which in one way or another informs each of its texts, constitutes the essential and normative element in the Old Testament, and the one that binds it irrevocably to the New Testament within the canon of Scripture' (p.143).

c. Such a general expression of the relationship between the Testaments demands further definition. Bright draws attention to various modern schemata for understanding the relationship - parity (involving Christological Old Testament interpretation), continuity (historical and theological preparation for the gospel), dialectic (subjective preparation) and salvation history (promise-fulfilment) - but argues that in spite of a certain validity none of them contains the whole truth (pp.184-196). The only way to a satisfactory solution to the problem is to recognise that the relationship is a complex one (p.197). Bright attempts to sum up his solution in one sentence: 'The Old Testament is the history of our own heritage of faith - but before Christ; it is the record of the dealings of our God - but before Christ' (p.201). As Bright admits, any formulation of something as complex as the theological relationship between the Testaments inevitably leaves something to be desired; but this formulation at least makes clear the dual nature of his solution, which defines the relationship to be one both of continuity and of discontinuity:

'The continuity lies in the obvious fact that Christianity is historically a development out of Judaism; the discontinuity in the equally obvious fact that Christianity is not a continuation, or even a radical reform, of Judaism, but an entirely separate religion. The continuity lies in the fact that the theological structure of the two Testaments is fundamentally the same, with the major themes of the theology of the Old carried over and resumed in the New; the discontinuity lies in the fact that these themes receive radical reinterpretation in the light of what Christ has done. Above all, continuity lies in the New Testament's affirmation that Jesus is the Christ (Messiah), who has fulfilled the law and the prophets; the discontinuity lies in the fact that this fulfillment, though foreshadowed in the Old Testament, is not necessarily deducible from the plain sense of the Old and was in fact so surprising that the majority of Israelites could not see it as fulfillment. The New Testament, while unbreakably linked with the Old, announces the intrusion of something New and, therewith, the end of the Old. It affirms the fulfillment of Israel's hope - and pronounces radical judgement on that hope as generally held. It announces the fulfillment of the law - and the abrogation of the way of the law. In a word, the two Testaments are continuous within the unity of God's redemptive purpose; but their discontinuity is the discontinuity of two aeons.' (p.201)

The most important of Bright's works on this problem is The Authority of the OT (1967); see also:
'Faith and Destiny', Interpn(1951);
The Kingdom of God (1953);
A History of Israel(1960):esp.446-53/461-7;
Jeremiah (1965):esp.cxi-cxviii;
cf. Harrington 1973:309-13,358-60.

8.32 BERNHARD W. ANDERSON

In his own contribution to the symposium he edited on the significance of the Old Testament for Christian faith, Anderson (1964) presents a study of the relationship between the new covenant and the old. The study centres on the prophecy of Jeremiah 31: 31-34, and concludes that in this oracle 'the relation between the old and new covenants is characterised by both continuity and discontinuity' (pp.238-9). On the one hand, the new covenant will be 'not like' the old in that it will bring about a radically inward relationship to Yahweh, mark the end of all tradition and be based on divine forgiveness (pp.232-6). On the other hand, it is one God who is author of both covenants, which are continuous in that they are based on one torah, directed toward the establishment of a relationship between God and the people, and made with 'the house of Israel' (pp.236-8). The New Testament declares that the new covenant has been realised in Jesus

Christ, though this is a fulfilment beyond all prophetic expectation. 'Yet manifest within this deepest discontinuity is the continuity of the same almighty grace which had called Israel into existence and had directed her toward the future' (p.242).

B.W.Anderson, 'The New Covenant and the Old' in <u>OTCF</u> (1964). See also his introduction to <u>OTCF</u>, <u>'The OT as a Christian Problem'</u>; and
<u>The Living World of the OT</u> (1958);
<u>'The Problem of OT History'</u>, <u>LQHR</u> (1965).

8.33 BREVARD S. CHILDS

The New Testament's quotation of Old Testament texts is used by Childs (1970) to develop an appr-oach to biblical theology. Such quotation, he argues, demonstrates the continuity between the Testaments in three ways: the Christian God is identified with the God of Israel, the Old Testament idea of God is understood to be consistent with faith in the person of Jesus Christ, and attempts to separate Christ and the Old Testament are rejected by affirming the dynamic personal and practical unity between God and Christ (pp.202-9). It might be asked whether this continuity is really representative of the relationship between the Testaments as a whole, whether there is not an essential discontinuity in the tension between monotheism and trinity, old crea-tion and new creation, old covenant and new covenant. Childs admits the force of such an objection, but considers that even in this undeniable discontinuity there is a fundamental continuity of divinity, crea-tion and covenant (pp.211-16). Thus Childs, although he tends to stress the former more than the latter, conceives the relationship between the Testaments as a relationship of continuity and discontinuity (cf. 1958:268-70).

Childs, Biblical Theology in Crisis (1970); cf. Vawter 1971; also,
'Prophecy and Fulfillment', Interpn(1958);
'Interpretation in Faith', Interpn(1964);
'A Tale of Two Testaments', Interpn(1972);
Exodus (1974).
Cf. Hasel 1972a: 25-8; Sheppard 1974.

8.34 OTHERS

The tension between continuity and discontinuity in the relationship between the Testaments has been recognised by several other scholars. F.W. Dillistone (1948), for instance, in a study of the word and the people of God, finds that 'through the action of the Divine Word there came to be a recurring discontinuity within the continuity, a recurring creativity within the settled order' (p.68). Herbert H. Farmer (1952) considers the theme of continuity - discontinuity to be fundamental to the structure of the whole Bible, being an expression not only of the relationship between the Testaments but also of tensions within the Old Testament (between Israel and the rest of the world) and in the person of Christ (between humanity and divinity). Geoffrey W. Grogan (1967a) is concerned with the continuity and discontinuity of spiritual experience in the two Testaments, while Peter Richardson (1969) analyses the aspects of continuity in the relationship between Israel and the Church. Hans-Joachim Kraus (1970) discusses the balance of biblical theology and history, showing that it includes both continuity in the history of revelation and discontinuity between Old Testament and New. Anthony Tyrrell Hanson (1974) concludes his study of Paul's theological approach to the

Old Testament with a discussion of the relationship between the Testaments: for him it is the revelation of God's character that provides the link between the Testaments (p.276 cf. 269) and this involves tension between the ideas of continuity and transcendence (p.260).

Dillistone, The Word of God and the People of God (1948);
Farmer, 'The Bible', IB 1(1952):8-11;
Grogan, 'The Experience of Salvation', VoxEv(1967);
P. Richardson, Israel in the Apostolic Church(1969): e.g.5-8,14-21;
Kraus, Die Biblische Theologie(1970):309-21;
A.T. Hanson, Studies in Paul's Technique and Theology (1974):esp.ch.12.
Cf. Eichrodt 1933:501-11; Verhoef 1970a:293-5; Kline 1972:94-6.

CONCLUSION

9.1 THE THEOLOGICAL RELATIONSHIP BETWEEN THE TESTAMENTS

9.1 THE THEOLOGICAL RELATIONSHIP BETWEEN THE TESTAMENTS

9.11 THE PROBLEM

a. The theological problem of the relationship between the Testaments is stated in Part One by means of a biblical, historical and methodological introduction. In a survey of early hopes for the future, the eschatology of the prophets and the apocalyptic of the later Old Testament writings, we are reminded that expectation is an important factor in the Old Testament. Since much of this expectation remains unfulfilled at the end of the period, and also because of fundamental tensions - for example, between nationalism and universalism - which are not resolved, the Old Testament is an incomplete book. The New Testament, on the other hand, affirms the fulfilment of Old Testament hopes and is substantially dependent on the Old Testament for the understanding and expression of that fulfilment. Moreover there is evidence to suggest that this attitude toward the Old Testament is not an innovation of the early Church but derives from Jesus himself.

b. After this biblical survey, the problem is traced through the history of biblical interpretation from the early Church to the nineteenth century. During that time it became universally recognised that a satisfactory interpretation of the Bible must be historically based, on literal understanding of the text, though in the nineteenth century the importance of theological understanding - which had been central in other periods - was all but forgotten. At the end of the nineteenth and the beginning of the twentieth century biblical studies were dominated by the developmental approach, which understood the relationship between the Testaments in terms of 'progressive revelation'. This concept is therefore the basis for understanding modern solutions to the problem, though it was more dissatisfaction with it than development from it that provoked new consideration of the matter. Aside from the radical depreciation of the Old Testament in neo-Marcionism, and the perpetuation of the developmental approach in certain other circles, the trend since the first - and even more since the second - World War has been towards a more distinctively theological solution to the problem. Eight such modern attempts at a solution have been isolated for analytical and critical study in this thesis.

9.12 THE NEED FOR A 'BIBLICAL' SOLUTION

a. All the views of the relationship between the Testaments considered in Part Two have in common that in one way or another they regard the Old Testament to have a certain theological priority and independence with respect to the New Testament. Van Ruler's view may be summarised in words from the title of the first chapter: the Old Testament is the essential - real, intrinsic, true - Bible and the New Testament is its - Christian - interpretative glossary. Miskotte and Barr reject the idea that the Old Testament should be interpreted in the light of the New, because it is based on the false presupposition that Christ is the known and the Old Testament is the unknown; they argue that the reverse is the case, that Christian faith must have the Old Testament as its basis from the beginning. Miskotte carries the argument further by pointing to the surplus which the Old Testament has over the New, and by urging that the Old Testament must be allowed to speak for itself. Wheeler Robinson emphasises the independent and permanent theological value of the Old Testament, and the sects do fundamentally the same but apply the principle in a very literal manner, often to trivial rather than essential parts of the Old Testament.

b. These 'Old Testament' solutions do not depreciate the New Testament in itself, in contrast to the Jewish view, according to which the Old Testament is naturally the Bible and the New Testament its (false) Christian supplement. The solutions considered here ascribe theological priority to the Old Testament but acknowledge the New Testament as its true and necessary Christian supplement without which the Bible would be incomplete. Nevertheless the most fundamental criticism of these 'Old Testament' solutions is that they take inadequate account of the radical newness of the event which occurred in Jesus Christ. The works of van Ruler and Miskotte in particular are valuable for their powerful expression of certain central issues, such as the importance of God's creation and kingdom, as well as for their penetrating insights into many aspects of biblical interpretation. But the final judgement on their solutions to the problem of the relationship between the Testaments can only be negative: they are 'Old Testament' solutions and thus fundamentally unsatisfactory.

c. Although there are not a few differences between the two, the solutions of Bultmann and Baumgärtel discussed in Part Three agree in recognising both an existential similarity and a theological contrast between the Testaments. In other words, the understanding of existence in the Old Testament is essentially the same as that in the New Testament, though there are differences in detail; but the theology of the

Old Testament, with its national and legal concern, stands in clear contrast to the New Testament theology of 'grace' or 'promise in Christ'. For Bultmann the Old Testament is the presupposition of the New Testament, recording a miscarriage of history which in its very failure becomes a promise. For Baumgärtel the Old Testament stems from one basic promise - 'I am the Lord your God' - which is also at the root of the New Testament promise in Christ. For both of them, however, the Old Testament is a non-Christian book and the New Testament, at least from the Christian point of view, is the essential Bible. It is only when understood in the light of the New Testament that the Old Testament has meaning for Christians. Other important New Testament solutions are offered by Hirsch, who is more radical than either Bultmann or Baumgärtel, and Hesse, who follows Baumgärtel rather closely.

d. Like the 'Old Testament' solutions, these 'New Testament' solutions must be reluctantly rejected. The argument of Bultmann, and to a lesser extent that of Baumgärtel, is presented with such force and contains such patent truth that it is possible to overlook its serious inadequacy. And it is the simple fact that they are 'New Testament' solutions - not in the sense that what they suggest conforms more nearly to the New Testament than do other suggestions, but rather that for them it is the New Testament which is important and the Old Testament is only of secondary value in relation to the New - which makes them inadequate. The result of the studies undertaken in Parts Two and Three, therefore, apart from the great deal of information and ideas analysed, criticised and compared, is to point to the need for a 'biblical' solution to the problem.

9.13 THE SEARCH FOR A 'BIBLICAL' SOLUTION

9.131 Christology: witness and identity

The highest common factor of the approaches to the theological problem of the relationship between the Testaments considered in chapter five is their recognition of both Old and New Testaments as equally Christian Scripture. They do not deny that there are differences between the two, but affirm that in terms of theology and revelation the two Testaments are one. Vischer has presented this solution especially clearly and the main features are: Jesus is the Christ of the Old Testament; the New Testament is to be taken seriously in interpreting the Old Testament, leading to Christological interpretation of the latter; salvation is the same in both Testaments and revelation is timeless. It may be summed up in words from the title of his major work: the Old Testament is a witness to Christ. Barth follows Vischer closely, Diem to a lesser extent. Jacob and Knight accept in principle that the Old and New Testaments are equally Christian Scripture but in practice their Old Testament interpretation is less influenced by the New Testament than that of Vischer.

Of the four 'biblical' solutions considered in Part Four, the Christological solution of Vischer, Barth, Diem, Jacob and Knight is the one which has attracted the most disagreement. There can be no unequivocal rejection, because any Christian approach to the problem will recognise the truth of much that they say. Christ is the centre of the Christian faith, and if the Old Testament is to remain in the Christian Bible - and virtually every Christian agrees that it should, in theory if not in practice - it can only be as Christian Scripture and thus as a witness to Christ. It is not surprising if the two

Testaments are united in their theology: the New Testament bases itself explicitly on the Old Testament and claims that it is Yahweh - the God of Israel who gave the law to Moses and spoke to the prophets - who has sent his Son to be Christ and Lord. On the other hand, while there is much truth in this, it would be a mistake to forget the glaring differences between the Old and New Testaments or to let either dominate the interpretation of the other. At times some of the writers considered in chapter five have been liable to this lapse of memory, though perhaps not often. But there is in the work of Vischer and the others mentioned in this chapter a concern to allow each Testament to speak for itself - though never in isolation from the other - which makes it essentially a 'biblical' solution to the problem. It is not necessary to surrender the historico-critical approach to the Bible, nor to follow the occasional wrong paths that appear along the way, to recognise the central truth that the Bible revolves around the person of Jesus Christ and therefore the relationship between the Testaments inevitably involves the concept of Christology. As well as this, however, there are other complementary ways of seeking a 'biblical' solution to the problem.

9.132 Typology: example and analogy

In chapter six the recent revival of interest in biblical typology is surveyed and critically evaluated. There is found a good deal of scholarly agreement that typology is an historically-based way of understanding the Bible, not a fanciful kind of interpretation to be rejected with allegory and other over-imaginative kinds of biblical study. Beyond this, however, the concept is not understood satisfactorily, and so a new approach to typology is developed here by means of a reconsideration of the meaning of τύπος in Greek and 'type' in English. Two fundamental principles for interpretation of types in the Bible are given, namely that they must be historical and that a real correspondence between two events, persons or institutions is implied, not simply a superficial resemblance or coincidence of detail. A 'type' is thus defined as an 'example' or 'pattern', and 'typology' as the study of historical and theological correspondences between types, on the basis of God's consistent activity in history.

The implication of typology for the problem of the relationship between the Testaments, hinted at by Wolff in his essay on Old Testament hermeneutics, is that there is a relationship of analogy between the two. There are, for example, analogies between the people of God, salvation and God's gifts in the Old and New Testaments. In contrast to ancient near Eastern and Rabbinic literature, which illuminate the Old Testament but are essentially different from it, the New Testament is fundamentally analogous as a witness to God's covenant. In the present work this idea has been developed further in conjunction with the idea of typology as the study of examples and patterns within God's consistent activity in history. Thus alongside the aspect of theological identity, expressed by Vischer's Christological solution to the problem, may be set the aspect of analogy, as expressed in the typical approach to the relationship between the Testaments.

9.133 <u>Salvation history and actualisation</u>

A third 'biblical' solution to the problem is that of the popular 'salvation history' approach to the Bible (chapter seven). It takes different forms in the hands of its varied proponents, but essentially expresses the same conviction that the two Testaments are bound together by divine revelation which occurs in the history of the people of God. Von Rad makes use of the ideas of typology and 'promise and fulfilment', and the method of tradition history, to interpret the relationship between the Testaments in terms of 'actualisation'. Thus the relationship is a progressive one, in the sense that historical events are continually actualised or re-presented in the Old Testament and above all in the New Testament. The Biblischer Kommentar group follow von Rad fairly closely, the Pannenberg group less so. In the latter group, although salvation history, actualisation, 'promise and fulfilment' are important aspects of the relationship, it is apocalyptic eschatology which is central. Amsler, Cullmann, Wright and Eichrodt each affirm in different ways the centrality of salvation history to the relationship, though like the Pannenberg group they are aware of the unsatisfactory separation between salvation history and reality in von Rad's thought and attempt to find a solution which does justice to both.

In spite of a number of reservations, the 'salvation history' solution is generally well-founded, being consistent with the character of the biblical documents and expressing clearly many of the central issues. It is broad enough to include the important ideas of 'promise and fulfilment', 'typology', tradition history and actualisation. The idea of salvation in history is clearly important, though not unique, as a unifying concept in biblical theology; but some of its proponents, especially von Rad, must be challenged with respect to the reality of both the 'salvation' and the 'history'.

9.134 Continuity and discontinuity

The final 'biblical' solution considered (in chapter eight) is that which draws attention to the aspects of continuity and discontinuity between the Testaments. One of the most important expressions of this is in the first part of Vriezen's Old Testament theology.

He finds a tension between recognition of the Old Testament as Scripture and critical reinterpretation in the light of Jesus Christ, who might well be thought to have made the Old Testament obsolete. This approach to the relationship between the Testaments has been particularly popular among British and American scholars, Rowley uses the concepts of prophecy and fulfilment, and Dodd that of realized eschatology, but both conceive a unity within the Bible which includes elements of continuity and discontinuity. Bright and, to a lesser extent, Anderson and Childs, show the importance of recognising both the continuity and the discontinuity but point beyond it to the theological unity which binds together the two Testaments in one Bible.

There is no doubt that a biblical solution to the problem must recognise this tension between continuity and discontinuity. On the one hand, the two Testaments have a number of common perspectives and patterns: they centre on the concepts of communion and kingdom, their concern is with the people of God, and they are united in their history and theology. There is moreover a fundamental continuity in the distinctive claim of the New Testament that Jesus is the Christ, the fulfilment of the law and the prophets. On the other hand, there are not a few differences between the Testaments: many Old Testament ideas and practices are primitive and are superseded by the New Testament; the Old Testament is characterised by prophecy and is a provisional revelation, in contrast to the final revelation of the New Testament which is characterised by fulfilment; and the new covenant is marked by a more personal relationship with God than was experienced by most who lived under the old covenant. Paradoxically, however, the most radical discontinuity lies in the New Testament's claim that Jesus is the Christ, for it presents him not only as the Christ of the Old Testament but as a Christ who surpasses expectations, completely renews the religion of Israel and inaugurates the new aeon. Thus in the person of Jesus Christ, who stands at the centre of Christian faith as both God and man, the continuity and discontinuity between the Testaments are both distinguished and brought together.

9.14 CENTRAL ISSUES

9.141 Incongruity?

A recurring feature in the Old and New Testament solutions is the isolation of supposed incongruities between the Testaments. Creation/salvation, theocracy/soteriology, earthly/spiritual, law/gospel, community/individual, wrath/love, glory/suffering, human Messiah/divine Messiah, and other contrasts are adduced as evidence of incongruity between the Old Testament and the New. But it has been shown here that these contrasts have either been drawn too sharply or they represent genuine biblical categories which are important throughout the Bible as contrasts, and not to be divided so that one half characterises Old Testament thought and the other half that of the New Testament. The existence of contrasts and paradoxes in the Bible is not to be denied, but they are subordinate to the essential theological unity of the Bible, which centres on Jesus Christ, who is not merely the difference between the New Testament and the Old but in his person brings together the two Testaments into one Bible.

9.142 History

Another central question which has arisen in connection with the relationship between the Testaments is the nature and importance of history in the Bible. For van Ruler, Jesus Christ is an act of God in his history with Israel. Von Rad would agree, but his understanding of salvation history and tradition history provoke questioning about the reality of the history he claims is so important. Vischer, in contrast, does not appreciate adequately the historical character of the Bible but views it as a timeless revelation. Likewise Bultmann, though in a quite different way, depreciates the historical aspect of the Bible by concentrating on its existential significance. A satisfactory solution to the problem of the relationship between the Testaments will give due consideration to the centrality of 'real' history in the Bible, without neglecting its other aspects.

9.143 Promise and fulfilment

It has been shown that the formula 'promise and fulfilment' is the most popular way of expressing the relationship between the Testaments today. Sometimes the old formula 'prophecy and fulfilment' is still used, often with much the same meaning as 'promise and fulfilment', and occasionally other terms such as 'expectation' and 'announcement' are substituted for 'promise'. Baumgärtel and Bultmann have elaborated approaches to the Old Testament as 'promise', though they attach idiosyncratic meanings to the word; while Vischer and Dodd, among others, have demonstrated the significance of 'fulfilment' in the message of the New Testament. In general terms this understanding of the relationship has been accepted, though it has been pointed out that there is more to the Old Testament than promise, and that the New Testament's fulfilment goes far beyond the expectations of the Old.

9.15 POSTSCRIPT

These conclusions have important consequences for theology and the Church. They raise questions such as the possibility of a 'biblical theology'; the authority of the Old Testament for doctrine and ethics, and the related issues of the canon and the nature of revelation; and the way in which the Old Testament should be understood by the Christian today. It is beyond the scope of the present work to enter into these questions, although a short bibliography is given in an appendix (see below: 10.2). There is a need for these issues to be pursued, however, so that the Old Testament may be given its rightful place in the Christian Bible.

APPENDICES

10.1 THE DEBATE ABOUT THE 'CENTRE' OF THE OLD TESTAMENT

10.2 THE OLD TESTAMENT IN THEOLOGY AND THE CHURCH: A BIBLIOGRAPHICAL NOTE

0.1 THE DEBATE ABOUT THE 'CENTRE' OF THE OLD TESTAMENT

0.11 THE DEBATE

. There has recently been a good deal of riting which has attempted to define the 'centre' f the Old Testament. Rudolf Smend (1970) traces the istory of ideas about the centre of the Old Testament rom the nineteenth century view of a 'basic idea' or principle' to the twentieth century loss of confidence n postulating a centre. Less definitive terms such s 'essence' and 'central concept' were gradually ubstituted and this development culminated in Gerhard on Rad's rejection of the whole conception of a centre f the Old Testament (cf. above: 7.214). Smend considers hat it is possible to locate a centre of the Old estament but finds commonly suggested concepts - alvation and redemption, monotheism and the holiness f God, theocracy and covenant - to be inadequate. is own suggestion is that this centre may be expressed ost satisfactorily in Wellhausen's formula, 'Yahweh he God of Israel, Israel the people of Yahweh'.

. Werner Schmidt (1969:51-2) finds the unity - or at east the characteristic idea - of the Old Testament in he first commandment, with its demand for exclusiveness. eorg Fohrer (1966; cf. 1964:500; 1970) argues that this s too narrow and that the theology of the Old Testament as a double centre, found in the concepts of 'the rule f God' and 'communion between God and man' (Gottesherrschaft, ottesgemeinschaft). Siegfried Herrmann (1971) suggests hat Deuteronomy is the centre of Old Testament theology, ince the basic questions of Old Testament theology are oncentrated in it. Gerhard Hasel (1972/74) surveys any views and concludes that the centre of the Old

Testament is God, and Alfons Deissler (1972) comes to a similar conclusion, considering the fundamental message of the Old Testament to be the message of God (cf. van Ruler, above: 1.213). Walter Kaiser (1974) claims that the texts themselves give a centre for Old Testament theology, namely the theme of 'promise'.

c. One thing is clear: there is widespread disagreement about the question of the centre of the Old Testament. In this appendix an analysis of the debate is offered together with some suggestions for its resolution.

Literature relevant to the question of a 'centre' of the Old Testament is voluminous, including many of the works on biblical theology referred to in the present study. Some studies more specifically concerned with the question are:

Hänel, Die Religion der Heiligkeit (1931);
Lindblom, 'Zur Frage der Eigenart der atl. Religion' in BZAW (1936);
Dentan, 'The Unity of the OT', Interpn (1951);
Bright, The Kingdom of God (1953);
Ellison, The Centrality of the Messianic Idea for the OT (1953);
Rowley, The Unity of the Bible (1953):chs 1-3;
Reventlow, 'Grundfragen der atl. Theologie', ThZ (1961);
Seebass, 'Der Beitrag des ATs zum Entwurf einer biblischen Theologie', WuD (1965);
Cazelles, 'The Unity of the Bible and the People of God', Scripture (1966);
Fohrer, 'The Centre of a Theology of the OT', NGTT (1966); German translation in ThZ 24;
Prussner, 'The Covenant of David and the Problem of Unity in OT Theology' in Rylaarsdam (1968);
W.H. Schmidt, Das erste Gebot (1969);
de Vaux, 'God's Presence and Absence in History', Concilium (1969);
Gese, 'Erwägungen zur Einheit der biblischen Theologie', ZTK (1970);
Klein, 'The Biblical Understanding of "The Kingdom of God"', (1970), ET in Interpn 26;
Smend, Die Mitte des ATs (1970);

Wagner, 'Zur Frage nach dem Gegenstand einer Theologie des ATs' in Doerne Festschrift (1970);
Herrmann, '...Das Deuteronomium als Mitte biblischer Theologie' in von Rad Festschrift (1971);
Deissler, Die Grundbotschaft des ATs (1972);
Hasel, OT Theology (1972):ch.3; revd version published as 'The Problem of the Center in the OT Theology Debate', ZAW (1974);
Kaiser, 'The Centre of OT Theology', Themelios (1974);
Zimmerli, 'Zum Problem der "Mitte des ATes"', EvTh (1975).

The concurrent debate about the 'centre' of the New Testament cannot be discussed here; see, e.g.,
Fröhlich, 'Die Mitte des NTs' in Cullmann Festschrift (1967);
Kümmel, 'Mitte des NTs' in Leenhardt Festschrift (1968);
Baumann, Mitte und Norm des Christlichen (1969);
Luz, 'Theologia crucis als Mitte der Theologie im NT', EvTh (1974);
cf. Lohse, 'Die Einheit des NTs als theologisches Problem', EvTh (1975).

10.12 TERMINOLOGY

a. A significant aspect of literature concerned to isolate a unifying factor for the Old Testament is the variety of terms used to describe that unifying factor. The title of this appendix simply uses the commonest term, 'centre' (= Mitte, Zentrum). These terms may be classified into two main categories:

1) centre (Fohrer 1966; Jacob 1968a:ix; Ladd 1968:45; Prussner 1968; Hasel 1972/74; Kaiser 1974; cf. Brunner 1941:88; van Ruler 1955:65/68; Rowley 1956:48);

Mitte (von Rad 1947:37; 1952c:30; 1957:115; 1960:362; 1963:405n.; Baumgärtel 1961:896n.; Reventlow 1961:94-6; Zimmerli 1956; 1963b:105; 1972:10-11; 1975; Smend 1970; Wagner 1970:406-11; cf. Jacob 1965:18; Gese 1970:418);

Zentrum (Herrmann 1971:156; cf. Reventlow 1961:98);

central point (de Vaux 1969:8);

Mittelpunkt (Fohrer 1966; cf. Reventlow 1961:98; Jacob 1965:26);

focal point (Vriezen 1966:150; Ellison 1969:12);

heart (Ladd 1968:40);
central element (Vriezen 1966:150);
essential and normative element (Bright 1967:143);
quintessence (van Ruler, cf. above: 1.213);
vantage-point (Barr 1966:19);
subject (Wright 1969:44; cf. Heschel 1951:ch.14);
object (Miskotte 1956a:114);

2) unity (Rowley 1953:chs.1-3; Cazelles 1966; W.H. Schmidt 1969:51-2);
unifying principle (Ellison 1953a:6; von Rad 1957:118);
unifying theme (H.W. Robinson 1946:148; Bright 1953:10-11
central theme (Dentan 1951:163; Barr 1963:201; Knight 1959a:9; cf. Jeremias 1965:1);
central concept (Sellin 1933:19; Eichrodt 1933:13; cf. Wildberger 1959:77);
primary structuring concept (Wright 1972:986);
essential root idea (Vriezen 1954/66:134/160);
essence (Hänel 1931:8-22);
basis (Lindblom 1936:131; cf. Köhler 1936:30,35);
fundamental principle (Schultz 1860:I.55);
fundamental message (Deissler 1972).

b. Some of the writers are interested in the centre of the Old Testament, some in the centre of Old Testament theology and one or two in the centre of Israel's faith or the whole Bible. But these will be treated together, since they overlap and the differences do not appear to be significant, there being little correlation between the subject and the term used for 'centre' or the nature of the proposed centre. The Old Testament is the most common subject - rather more than half the works considered - and therefore 'the centre of the Old Testament' is used as a general term in the present discussion.

10.13 IS THERE A CENTRE?

a. Thirty-nine writings, some of composite authorship, might be expected to display such a wide variety of viewpoints that the possibility of a centre of the Old Testament would be excluded. It is no surprise therefore when Barr (1966:ch.1), von Rad (1952c:30; 1957:115; 1960:362; cf. Gese 1970:418; see above: 7.214) and Vriezen (1956:220) deny the concept of a centre or focus.

b. Yet most of the literature considered here assumes that the Old Testament has a centre and sets about finding it, and even the three writers just mentioned do not completely exclude the idea. Barr (1966:18-19; 1963:201) accepts that the creation story is a 'starting-point' for understanding the Old Testament, although he will not make it a vantage-point for viewing the Bible, and concedes that _Heilsgeschichte_ - alongside others - can be taken as the central theme of the Bible. Von Rad refers to 'the typical element of Israel's faith' (1963:415) and in an early work designates Deuteronomy as the middle point (_Mitte_) of the Old Testament (1947:37). And Vriezen in the second edition of his Old Testament theology (1966:150) says that God is the focal point of the Old Testament. Thus the literature surveyed shows a consensus of opinion that the Old Testament is a unified whole and that the attempt to determine its centre is a viable one. Since there are two main kinds of 'centre' in question each will be given separate attention.

10.14 SUGGESTED OLD TESTAMENT FOCI

a. Most of the works which define the focus of the Old Testament find it to be outside the Old Testament itself. The most common suggestion is that God is its focus, advocated by van Ruler (cf. above: 1.213), Miskotte (cf. above: 2.12a), Rowley (1956:48), Baumgärtel (1961:896n.), Reventlow (1961:96), Ladd (1968:40), Wright (1969:44), Jacob (1965:18 cf. 26, 50; 1968a:ix) and Hasel (1972/74; cf. also: Heschel 1951:129; Vriezen 1965:215; Bright 1967: 141, 143). Zimmerli (1963b:105; 1972:10-11; 1975) and Vriezen (1966:150; cf. also: Brunner 1941:88-90) suggest that the focus is Yahweh, while for Ellison (1969:12) it is Christ, even further outside the Old Testament (cf. also: Gerleman 1956; van Ruler 1955:65/68). Others argue that the Old Testament centres on the relationship between Yahweh and Israel, though they use different formulae to express the relationship: for example, rule of God and communion between God and man (Fohrer 1966); election and covenant (de Vaux 1969:8; cf. Prussner 1968); 'Yahweh the God of Israel, Israel the people of Yahweh' (Smend 1970; cf. Zimmerli 1956:79).

b. Something rather different is meant when the focus is found within the Old Testament documents themselves. Von Rad (1947:37) and Herrmann (1971) set Deuteronomy at the centre of Old Testament theology, Barr (cf. above: 10.3) recognises the creation story as the starting-point for understanding the Old Testament, and G.W. Anderson (1963:281) says that 'the Psalter is representative of practically the whole range of Old Testament literature'. And Kaiser (1974), although he uses the term 'centre', is concerned not with a focal point but with a unifying theme, which places his work in the second category.

10.15 SUGGESTED OLD TESTAMENT UNIFYING THEMES

a. The unifying theme of the Old Testament is understood as a concept which is dominant or significant throughout. In spite of Ellison (1953a:6), who considers the witness of the Old Testament to Christ to be its unifying principle, there is general agreement that this unifying theme is to be found in the Old Testament's presentation of the relationship between God and Israel. Sometimes the emphasis falls on one partner in the relationship, on God (Lindblom 1936:131; H.W. Robinson 1946:148-150; Jeremias 1965:1; Deissler 1972; cf. Köhler 1936:30,35) or on Israel (von Rad 1957:118).

b. More often it is one or more aspects of God's relationship with Israel which are considered to be dominant. Election (Dentan 1951:163; Wildberger 1959:77-8); promise (Kaiser 1974); covenant (Eichrodt 1933; Wright 1972; cf. Barth 1953:3); kingdom of God (Schultz 1860:I.56; Bright 1953; van Ruler 1955:27/28 cf. above: 1.26; cf. Seebass 1965; Klein 1970); communion with God (Vriezen 1954/66); God's demand for exclusive worship (W.H. Schmidt 1969:51-2); holiness of God (Hänel 1931; Sellin 1933:18-22); the revelation of God's redemptive activity (Knight 1959a:9; cf. Barr 1963:201; Festorazzi 1967) and Israel's experience of God in history (Rowley 1953:65; Cazelles 1966); have all been suggested as the central or unifying theme of the Old Testament.

10.16 RESOLUTION OF THE DEBATE

a. The debate about the centre of the Old Testament has now been outlined. It can be seen that there are a wide variety of terms used to describe the unifying factor and a wide variety of proposals as to what that factor is. There would be little value here in rehearsing and evaluating the arguments in favour of one or another opinion since this has been done only too frequently in the literature surveyed. The analysis above is an attempt to clarify the diverse ideas involved in the debate and a few general suggestions about its resolution will now be made.

b. In the quest for the centre of the Old Testament it is assumed that the goal is clearly defined. It may be suggested, however, that the main reason for the diversity of propositions advanced in the debate is that the proponents have different intentions. Apart from the basic distinction between a focus and a unifying theme there are many differences even within the use of one term. The importance of a 'centre' is dependent on one's interest in the object: the centre of an apple is thrown away if it is to be eaten, but for a market gardener who plans to extend his orchard the core is the vital part. The centre may be the same as the focus or it may be quite different: in a circle the two are identical but in an ellipse there are two foci, both different from the centre. Moreover, there may be more than one centre: an eccentric wheel has a geometric centre and an effective centre (the axle); and in a ring of electric flex there is a centre of the flex (its core) and also a centre of the ring. In the latter case the centre is not even part of the object itself.

c. To say that God is the centre of the Old Testament is quite different from saying that Deuteronomy is the centre. Yet both are valid within their own terms of reference. God may legitimately be considered the centre of the Old Testament in the sense that he is its origin and focus, though obviously not part of it; and Deuteronomy may be considered the centre in the sense that it is a part of the Old Testament which is especially representative of the whole and around which the rest resolves, since what it says helps to determine the character of the other documents. It is different again, but equally valid, to say that concepts such as election, promise, covenant and kingdom are central to the Old Testament. Undoubtedly they pervade the Old Testament like rails in a railway tunnel and in that sense may be considered centres, though to isolate any one as <u>the</u> centre is precarious, as is shown by the lack of agreement on which concept is most important.

d. The fundamental assumption underlying the debate about the centre of the Old Testament is that the Old Testament is a unity and has some unifying factor which makes it such. It is particularly significant, therefore, that one of the results of the debate has been to show that no one unifying factor can adequately embrace the whole. Unwittingly the search for a simple key to understanding the unity of the Old Testament has ended by proving the complexity of this unity and pointing to numerous unifying factors (cf. Barr 1974:272)! A brief outline of these will be given in conclusion.

e. The most general unifying factor is that the Old Testament is all part of the national literature of Israel. The Torah presents the origin and constitution of Israel, the Former Prophets its history, the Latter Prophets its prophecy and the Writings its other literature - poetry, philosophy, history, historical novel, ethics, futurology. A basic unifying factor of the Old Testament is therefore 'Israel'. This nation was characteristically religious, having a unique understanding and experience of God since he had revealed himself to them by his name Yahweh, so two foci of the Old Testament literature may be identified: God (Yahweh) and the people of God (Israel). The core of Israel's religion was the special relationship with God which was characterised by themes running through the whole Old Testament such as election, promise, covenant, kingdom, communion, exclusiveness and redemption. The ideals and hopes of the Old Testament are never satisfied within the Old Testament itself and are only fulfilled with the coming of Jesus Christ. In the Old Testament the relationship between God and his people remains imperfect but in the New Testament Christ stands between the two parties, restoring and renewing the relationship. Christians may therefore look back and see that the missing climax - or 'centre'? - of the Old Testament is Jesus Christ. There is indeed a unity in the Old Testament but it cannot be expressed by a single concept.

f. This understanding of the Old Testament might be expressed diagrammatically by an elliptical cylinder. The centre is Christ; the foci are God (Yahweh) and people (Israel); concentric layers of the cylinder are election, promise, covenant, kingdom, etc.; and the length of the cylinder is the time in which Israel experienced God in history.

10.2 THE OLD TESTAMENT IN THEOLOGY AND THE CHURCH: A BIBLIOGRAPHICAL NOTE

10.21 BIBLICAL THEOLOGY

Craig, 'BTh and the Rise of Historicism', JBL(1943);
Burrows, An Outline of BTh(1946);
Haroutinian, 'The Bible and the Word of God', Interpn (1947);
Vos, Biblical Theology (1948);
Spicq, 'L'avènement de la théologie biblique', RSPT (1951);
Gamble, 'The Nature of BTh', Interpn (1951); 'The Literature of BTh', Interpn (1953); 'The Method of BTh', Interpn (1955);
Wright, God Who Acts: BTh as Recital (1952);
Braun, 'La théologie biblique', RThom (1953);
Ebeling, 'The Meaning of BTh', JTS (1955);
Wildberger, 'Auf dem Wege zu einer biblischen Theologie', EvTh(1959);
Bauer (ed.), EBT (1959);
Betz, 'BTh, History of' and
Stendahl, 'BTh, Contemporary', IDB (1962);
Watson, 'The Nature and Function of BTh', ExpT(1962);
Wallace, 'BTh: Past and Future', ThZ (1963);
Ramlot, 'Une décade de théologie biblique', RThom(1964-5);
Seebass, 'Der Beitrag des ATs zum Entwurf einer biblischen Theologie', WuD (1965);
Jacob, 'Possibilités et limites d'une Théologie biblique', RHPR (1966);
Stendahl and Dulles, 'Method in the Study of BTh' in Hyatt (1966);
Bright, The Authority of the OT (1967): ch.3;
Childs, BTh in Crisis (1970);
Gese, 'Erwägungen zur Einheit der biblischen Theologie', ZTK (1970);
Verhoef, 'Some Thoughts on the Present-Day Situation in BTh', WTJ (1970);
Harrington, The Path of BTh (1973);
Barr, 'Trends and Prospects in BTh', JTS(1974).

Cf. above: 1.212; 7.213; 8.11; 8.223, 8.233.

10.22 THE AUTHORITY OF THE OLD TESTAMENT

Cunliffe-Jones, The Authority of the Biblical Revelation (1945);
Hebert, The Authority of the OT (1947);
van Veenen, 'La signification de l'AT pour les questions sociales et politiques',
Richardson, 'Autorité et rôle actuels de l'éthique de l'AT', and
Eichrodt, 'Le message social et économique de l'AT' in ETR (1948);
Rowley, 'The Authority of the Bible' (1949), repr. in From Moses to Qumran;
Dinkler, 'Bibelautorität und Bibelkritik', ZTK (1950);
Richardson and Schweitzer (eds), Biblical Authority for Today (1951);
Langford, 'Gospel and Duty: A Study of the Unity of Biblical Ethics', Interpn (1951);
Kühl, The OT (1953): 1-9;
Jacob, 'Considérations sur l'autorité canonique de l'AT' and
Leenhardt, 'La Bible et le message de l'Eglise au monde' in Boisset (1955);
Reid, The Authority of Scripture (1957);
Hesse, 'The Evaluation and Authority of OT Texts' (1959), ET in EOTI;
Jocz, 'Law and Grace', Judaica (1965);
Meyer zu Uptrup, Die Bedeutung des ATs für eine Transformation der Kirche heute (1966);
Bright, The Authority of the OT
Huffmon, 'The Israel of God', Interpn (1969);
Nineham, 'The Use of the Bible in Modern Theology', BJRL (1969);
Barr, 'The Authority of the Bible: A Study Outline', ER (1969); 'The OT and the New Crisis of Biblical Authority', Interpn (1971); 'Man and Nature - The Ecological Controversy and the OT', BJRL (1972); The Bible in the Modern World (1973);
Dressler, 'The Authority of the Holy Scriptures', Dissn (1972);
Kline, The Structure of Biblical Authority (1972);
Sanders, Torah and Canon (1972).

Cf. above: 1.132, 1.133; 3.123; 8.12; 1.214.

10.23 OLD TESTAMENT INTERPRETATION

Wright, 'Interpreting the OT', ThTo (1946);
WCC, 'Guiding Principles for the Interpretation of the Bible', ER (1949);
Jacob, 'L'AT et la prédication chrétienne', VerbC (1950);
Lerch, Isaaks Opferung christlich gedeutet (1950);

Hertzberg, 'Ist Exegese theologisch möglich?'(1952), repr. in *Beiträge...*;
Wallace, 'The Preaching of the OT', *TSFB* (1953);
Jepsen, 'Probleme der Auslegung des ATs', *ZST* (1954);
Gerleman, 'Gamla testamentet i förkunnelsen', *SvTK* (1956);
Wolff, 'The Hermeneutics of the OT'(1956), ET in *EOTI*; 'The OT in Controversy'(1956), ET in *Interpn* 12;
Ferré, 'Notes by a Theologian on Biblical Hermeneutics', *JBL* (1959);
Piccard, 'Réflexions sur l'interprétation chrétienne de trois récits de la Genèse' in Vischer Festschrift (1960);
Frör, *Biblische Hermeneutik* (1961);
Rössler, 'Die Predigt über atl. Texte' in von Rad Festschrift (1961);
Smart, *The Interpretation of Scripture* (1961); *The OT in Dialogue with Modern Man* (1965);
Balchin, 'Biblical Hermeneutics', *TSFB* (1961-2);
Clowney, *Preaching and Biblical Theology* (1962);
Mildenberger, *Gottes Tat im Wort* (1964); cf. Schmid 1965;
Bright, *The Authority of the OT* (1967): chs 4-5;
Gunneweg, 'Über die Prädikabilität atl.Texte', *ZTK*(1968);
Kosak, *Wegweisung in das AT* (1968);
Toombs, 'The Problematic of Preaching from the OT', *Interpn* (1969);
Hicks, 'Form and Content' in May Festschrift (1970);
Porteous, 'The Limits of OT Interpretation' in Davies Festschrift (1970);
Cole, 'Are You Bleached in the Belly of the Whale?', *Interchange* (1973);
Clines, 'Expounding the OT'(1974), unpublished paper.

Cf. above: 1.134; 2.16; 5.13; 5.24; 7.216; 8.15.

ABBREVIATIONS AND BIBLIOGRAPHY

Abbreviations are generally used for serials, standard works, symposia and Festschriften which are referred to twice or more in the thesis. The bibliography consists substantially of works referred to in the thesis, although a few others consulted but not specifically cited are included. It does not claim to be an exhaustive survey of literature on the theological problem of the relationship between the Testaments, though it is the most comprehensive available and mentions most of the important works on the subject. A few works which have not been available to me but appear to be important are marked with an asterisk*. ET = English translation; Fs = Festschrift.

11.1 SERIALS AND STANDARD WORKS

AER	*The American Ecclesiastical Review*
AGK	Arbeiten zur Geschichte des Kirchenkampfes
AJT	*The American Journal of Theology*
AK	*Ateneum Kapłańskie*
ALBO	Analecta Lovaniensa Biblica et Orientalia
AnaB	Analecta Biblica
ASTI	*Annual of the Swedish Theological Institute*
AT	Altes, Ancien Testament
ATR	*Anglican Theological Review*
AUSS	*Andrews University Seminary Studies*
BenM	*Benediktinische Monatsschrift*
BETL	Bibliotheca Ephemeridum Theologicarum Lovaniensum
BETS	*Bulletin of the Evangelical Theological Society*
BEvTh	Beiträge zur evangelischen Theologie
BFChTh	Beiträge zur Förderung christlicher Theologie
BGBH	Beiträge zur Geschichte der biblischen Hermeneutik
BHTh	Beiträge zur historischen Theologie
BJRL	*Bulletin of the John Rylands Library* (from volume 55, 1972-3: *Bulletin of the John Rylands University Library of Manchester*)
BK	Biblischer Kommentar Altes Testament
BO	*Bibliotheca Orientalis*

BR Biblical Research

BS Bibliotheca Sacra

BT The Bible Translator

BThB Biblical Theology Bulletin

BThom Bibliothèque thomiste

BWANT Beiträge zur Wissenschaft vom Alten und Neuen Testament

BZ Biblische Zeitschrift

BZAW Beihefte zur ZAW

CBQ The Catholic Biblical Quarterly

CHB The Cambridge History of the Bible, 3 volumes:
I. From the Beginnings to Jerome (ed. P.R. Ackroyd and C.F. Evans, 1970);
II. The West from the Fathers to the Reformation (ed. G.W.H. Lampe, 1969);
III. The West from the Reformation to the Present Day (ed. S.L. Greenslade, 1963)

CJT Canadian Journal of Theology

ConRev The Contemporary Review

CQR Church Quarterly Review

CRDSB Colgate Rochester Divinity School Bulletin

CTJ Calvin Theological Journal

DB[2] Dictionary of the Bible[2] (originally ed. by J. Hastings, revised by F.C. Grant and H.H. Rowley), Edinburgh 1963

DL Doctrine and Life

DPfBl Deutsches Pfarrerblatt

DV Dieu vivant

EBT Encyclopedia of Biblical Theology (ed. J.B. Bauer), ET: London/Sydney 1970 (German 1967[3], 1959[1]), 3 volumes

EOTI Essays on Old Testament Interpretation: see below, Westermann (1949-60)

EphC	*Ephemerides Carmeliticae*
EQ	*The Evangelical Quarterly*
ER	*Ecumenical Review*
ERE	*Encyclopædia of Religion and Ethics* (ed. J. Hastings *et al.*), Edinburgh 1908-26
ErJb	*Eranos - Jahrbuch*
EstB	*Estudios Bíblicos*
EtEv	*Études Évangéliques*
ETL	*Ephemerides Theologicae Lovanienses*
ETR	*Études théologiques et religieuses*
EvTh	*Evangelische Theologie*
Exp	*The Expositor*
ExpT	*The Expository Times*
FGLP	Forschung zur Geschichte und Lehre des Protestantismus
GOTR	*Greek Orthodox Theological Review*
HDAC	*Dictionary of the Apostolic Church* (ed. J. Hastings), Edinburgh I:1915; II:1918
HervTS	*Hervormde Teologiese Studies*
HeyJ	*The Heythrop Journal*
HibJ	*The Hibbert Journal*
HT	*History and Theory*
HTR	*Harvard Theological Review*
HUCA	*Hebrew Union College Annual*
HZ	*Historische Zeitschrift*
IB	*The Interpreter's Bible* (ed. G.A. Buttrick *et al.*), New York/Nashville 1952-7
IDB	*The Interpreter's Dictionary of the Bible* (ed. G.A. Buttrick *et al.*), New York/Nashville 1962

IEJ	*Israel Exploration Journal*
IJT	*The Indian Journal of Theology*
Interpn	*Interpretation*
IOVCB	*The Interpreter's One-Volume Commentary on the Bible* (ed. M. Laymon), London/Glasgow 1972
ISBE	*The International Standard Bible Encyclopaedia* (ed. J. Orr *et al.*), Grand Rapids, Mich. 1939 (revd edn, originally 1925 or 1929?)
JAAR	*Journal of the American Academy of Religion* (originally *JBR*)
JB	The Jerusalem Bible (1966)
JBC	*The Jerome Biblical Commentary* (ed. R.E.Brown *et al.*), London 1968
JBL	*Journal of Biblical Literature*
JBR	*The Journal of Bible and Religion* (now *JAAR*)
JCBRF	*The Journal of the Christian Brethren Research Fellowship*
JES	*Journal of Ecumenical Studies*
JETS	*Journal of the Evangelical Theological Society*
JR	*The Journal of Religion*
JSJ	*Journal for the Study of Judaism*
JSS	*Journal of Semitic Studies*
JTC	*Journal for Theology and the Church*
JTS	*The Journal of Theological Studies*
JTVI	*Journal of the Transactions of The Victoria Institute*
KBRS	*Kirchenblatt für die reformierte Schweiz*
KJV	The King James Version (Authorised Version, 1611
KT	*Kerk en Theologie*
KuD	*Kerygma und Dogma*

LCP Latinitas Christianorum Primaeva

LQ The Lutheran Quarterly

LQHR The London Quarterly and Holborn Review

LTK[2] Lexikon für Theologie und Kirche[2] (ed. J. Höfer and K. Rahner), Freiburg 1957-68 (1930-38[1])

LuJ Luther = Jahrbuch

NEB The New English Bible (1970)

NedTT Nederlands theologisch Tijdschrift

NGTT Nederduitse Gereformeerde Teologiese Tydskrif

NIDCC The New International Dictionary of the Christian Church (ed. J.D. Douglas), Exeter 1974

NIV The New International Version (NT: 1973)

NKZ Neue kirchliche Zeitschrift

NorTT Norsk Teologisk Tidsskrift

NovT Novum Testamentum

NRT Nouvelle revue théologique

NT New, Neues, Nouveau, Nieuwe Testament

NTS New Testament Studies

NZST Neue Zeitschrift für systematische Theologie (und Religionsphilosophie, since volume 5)

OT Old, Oude Testament

OTCF The Old Testament and Christian Faith: see below, Anderson (1964)

OTS Oudtestamentische Studiën (occasionally OTS, for some earlier volumes which were published as a journal rather than a series)

OTWSA (Papers read at Meetings of) Die Ou Testamentiese Werkgemeenskap in Suid-Afrika

PCB Peake's Commentary on the Bible (ed. M. Black and H.H. Rowley), London 1962

PEQ	*Palestine Exploration Quarterly*
RB	*Revue Biblique*
RBL	*Ruch biblijny i liturgiczny*
RechSR	*Recherches de science religieuse*
RefR	*The Reformed Review*
RefTR	*The Reformed Theological Review*
RelSt	*Religious Studies*
RevSR	*Revue des sciences religieuses*
RExp	*The Review and Expositor*
RGG^{3}	*Die Religion in Geschichte und Gegenwart*^{3} (ed. K.Galling *et al.*), Tübingen 1957-65 (1913^{1}, 1927-32^{2})
RHPR	*Revue d'histoire et de philosophie religieuses*
RKZ	*Reformierte Kirchenzeitung*
RSPT	*Revue des sciences philosophiques et théologiqu*
RSV	The Revised Standard Version (OT: 1952; NT: 1971^{2})
RThom	*Revue thomiste*
RThPh	*Revue de théologie et de philosophie*
SAB	*Sitzungsberichte der Preussischen (Deutschen) Akademie der Wissenschaften*, Berlin
SBL	Society of Biblical Literature
SBT	Studies in Biblical Theology
SDB	*Supplément au Dictionnaire de la Bible* (ed. L. Pirot *et al.*), Paris 1928-
SEA	*Svensk Exegetisk Årsbok*
SJT	*Scottish Journal of Theology*
SNovT	Supplements to *NovT*
SNTS Mon	Society for New Testament Studies Monograph Series

StEv	Studia Evangelica (published in TU)
StTh	Studia Theologica
SVT	Supplements to VT
SvTK	Svensk Teologisk Kvartalskrift
TDNT	Theological Dictionary of the New Testament (ed. G. Kittel and G. Friedrich), ET: Grand Rapids, Mich. 1964- (German 1933-)
THAT	Theologisches Handwörterbuch zum Alten Testament (ed. E. Jenni and C. Westermann) Munich/Zürich I:1971; II: not yet published
ThB	Theologische Bücherei
ThBl	Theologische Blätter
ThEx	Theologische Existenz heute
ThLBl	Theologisches Literaturblatt
ThQ	Theologische Quartalschrift
ThRu	Theologische Rundschau
ThSt	Theological Studies
ThSt	Theologische Studien
ThStKr	Theologische Studien und Kritiken
ThTo	Theology Today
ThZ	Theologische Zeitschrift
TLZ	Theologische Literaturzeitung
TrJ	Trinity Journal
TSFB	The Theological Students' Fellowship Bulletin
TU	Texte und Untersuchungen
TynB	Tyndale Bulletin
VerbC	Verbum Caro
VF	Verkündigung und Forschung
VigChr	Vigilae Christianae

VoxEv	*Vox Evangelica*
VoxTh	*Vox Theologica*
VT	*Vetus Testamentum*
WMANT	Wissenschaftliche Monographien zum Alten und Neuen Testament
WTJ	*The Westminster Theological Journal*
WuD	*Wort und Dienst*
WuT	*Wort und Tat*
ZAW	*Zeitschrift für die alttestamentliche Wissenschaft*
ZdZ	*Die Zeichen der Zeit*
ZEE	*Zeitschrift für evangelische Ethik*
ZKG	*Zeitschrift für Kirchengeschichte*
ZKT	*Zeitschrift für katholische Theologie*
ZNW	*Zeitschrift für die neutestamentliche Wissenschaft*
ZRG	*Zeitschrift für Religions- und Geistesgeschicht*
ZST	*Zeitschrift für systematische Theologie*
ZTK	*Zeitschrift für Theologie und Kirche*
ZZ	*Zwischen den Zeiten*

A number of serials with short titles are not abbreviated, although they are referred to more than once: *Angelicum*, *Beth-El*, *Biblica*, *Concilium*, *Encounter*, *Interchange*, *The Interpreter*, *Judaica*, *Luthertum*, *Oikoumene*, *Protestantesimo*, *Scripture*, *The Springfielder* *Themelios*, Théologie, *Theology*, *The Way*.

11.2 SYMPOSIA AND FESTSCHRIFTEN

Achtemeier (1962) *The Old Testament Roots of Our Faith* (P. and E. Achtemeier), London 1964 (USA: 1962).

Alt Fs (1953) *Geschichte und Altes Testament: Aufsätze* (Festschrift for A. Alt), Tübingen (BHTh 16).

Anderson (1964) *The Old Testament and Christian Faith: Essays by Rudolf Bultmann and others* (*OTCF*, ed. B.W. Anderson), London.

Auvray (1951) *L'Ancien Testament et les chrétiens* (P. Auvray *et al.*), Paris.

Barth Fs (1936) *Theologische Aufsätze: Karl Barth zum 50. Geburtstag* (ed. E. Wolf), Munich.

Barth Fs (1956) *Antwort: Karl Barth zum siebzigsten Geburtstag*, Zollikon-Zürich.

Bartsch (1948-63) *Kerygma and Myth: A Theological Debate* (ed. H.W. Bartsch), ET: two volumes of selections, London 1953, 1962 (6 volumes in German: 1948-63).

Batey (1970) *New Testament Issues* (ed. R. Batey), London.

Baumgärtel Fs (1959) *Festschrift: Friedrich Baumgärtel zum 70. Geburtstag* (ed. L. Rost), Erlangen (Erlanger Forschungen A.10).

Berkelbach and Abbing (1948) *Handboek voor de prediking* (ed. S.F.H.J. Berkelbach van der Sprenkel and P.J. Roscam Abbing), Amsterdam.*

Bevan and Singer (1927) *The Legacy of Israel* (ed. E.R. Bevan and C. Singer), Oxford.

Black Fs (1969) *Neotestamentica et Semitica: Studies in Honour of Matthew Black* (ed. E.E. Ellis and M. Wilcox), Edinburgh.

Boisset (1955) *Le Problème Biblique dans le Protestantisme* (ed. J. Boisset), Paris (Les Problèmes de la Pensée Chrétienne 7).

Bossey (1947) 'Résumé de la discussion de la Conférence de Bossey' (5-9 January 1947), *ETR* 23(1948):107-146.

Congregationalists (1893) *Faith and Criticism* (Essays by Congregationalists), London.

Coppens and Dequeker (1961) *Le Fils de l'homme et les Saints du Très Haut en Daniel, VII, dans les Apocryphes et dans le Nouveau Testament* (J. Coppens and L. Dequek Louvain.

Cullmann Fs (1967) *Oikonomia: Heilsgeschichte als Thema der Theologie* (ed. F. Christ Oscar Cullmann zum 65. Geburtstag gewidmet), Hamburg-Bergstedt.

Cullmann Fs (1972) *Neues Testament und Geschichte: Historisches Geschehen und Deutung im Neuen Testament: Oscar Cullmann zum 70. Geburtstag* (ed. H. Baltensweiler and B. Reicke), Zürich.

Davies Fs (1970) *Proclamation and Presence: Old Testament Essays in Honour of Gwynne Henton Davies* (ed. J.I.Durha and J.R.Porter), London.

Dentan (1955) *The Idea of History in the Ancient Near East* (ed. R.C. Dentan), New Haven/London.

Dodd Fs (1956) *The Background of the New Testament and its Eschatology: Studies in Honour of C.H. Dodd* (ed. W.D.Davies and D.Daube), Cambridge.

Doerne Fs (1970) *Fides et communicatio: Festschrift für Martin Doerne zum 70. Geburtsta* (ed. D. Rössler *et al.*), Göttingen.

Dugmore (1944) *The Interpretation of the Bible: Edward Alleyn Lectures 1943* (ed. C.W. Dugmore), London.

Edinburgh (1938) *Proceedings of the Fourth Calvinist Congress, held in Edinburgh 6th to 11th July 1938*, Edinburgh.

Eichrodt Fs (1970) *Wort - Gebot - Glaube: Walther Eichrodt zum 80. Geburtstag* (ed.H.J. Stoebe), Zürich (Abhandlungen zur Theologie des Alten und Neuen Testaments 59).

Elliger Fs (1973) — Wort und Geschichte: Festschrift für Karl Elliger zum 70. Geburtstag (ed. H. Gese and H.P. Rüger), Neukirchen (Alter Orient und Altes Testament 18).

Ernst (1972) — Schriftauslegung: Beiträge zur Hermeneutik des Neuen Testamentes und im Neuen Testament (ed. J. Ernst), Paderborn.

Evans (1972) — Tertullian: Adversus Marcionem (ed. E. Evans), Oxford.

Feiner and Löhrer (1965-) — Mysterium Salutis: Grundriss heilsgeschichtlicher Dogmatik (ed. J. Feiner and M. Löhrer), Einsiedeln, Switzerland 1965- (5 volumes, 4 published so far).

Funk (1969) — 'Apocalypticism', JTC 6 (ed. R.W. Funk).

Galling Fs (1970) — Archäologie und Altes Testament: Festschrift für Kurt Galling, Tübingen.

Gingrich Fs (1972) — Festschrift to Honor F. Wilbur Gingrich: Lexicographer, Scholar, Teacher, and Committed Christian Layman (ed. E.H. Barth and R.E. Cocroft) Leiden.

Harder and Stevenson (1971) — 'The Continuity of History and Faith in the Theology of Wolfhart Pannenberg: Toward an Erotics of History', JR 51: 34-56 (H.G. Harder and W.T. Stevenson).

Harris Fs (1933) — Amiticiae Corolla: A Volume of Essays Presented to James Rendel Harris, D.Litt. on the Occasion of His Eightieth Birthday (ed. H.G. Wood), London.

Hauer (1937) — Germany's New Religion: The German Faith Movement (W. Hauer et al.), London.

Heim Fs (1934) — Wort und Geist: Studien zur christlichen Erkenntnis von Gott, Welt und Mensch: Festgabe für Karl Heim zum 60. Geburtstag (ed. A. Köberle and O. Schmitz), Berlin.

Hempel (1936) — Werden und Wesen des Alten Testaments (ed. J. Hempel et al.), Berlin (BZAW 66).

Hennig (1952) — Theologie und Liturgie: Eine Gesamtschau der gegenwärtigen Forschung in Einzeldarstellungen (ed. L. Hennig), Kassel.

Henry (1959) — Revelation and the Bible: Contemporary Evangelical Thought (ed. C.F. Henry), London.

Hertzberg Fs (1965) — *Gottes Wort und Gottes Land: Hans-Wilhelm Hertzberg zum 70. Geburtstag* (ed. H.G. Reventlow), Göttingen.

Hirsch Fs (1963) — *Wahrheit und Glaube: Festschrift für Emanuel Hirsch zu seinem 75. Geburtstag* (ed. H. Gerdes), Itzehoe.

Hodgson (1960) — *On the Authority of the Bible: Some Recent Studies* (L. Hodgson *et al.*), London.

Hooke Fs (1963) — *Promise and Fulfilment: Essays Presented to Professor S.H. Hooke* (ed. F.F. Bruce), Edinburgh.

Howley (1969) — *A New Testament Commentary* (ed. G.C.D. Howley), London.

Hyatt (1966) — *The Bible in Modern Scholarship* (ed. J.P. Hyatt), London.

Jalland (1948) — *The Israel of God* (ed. T.G. Jalland), Exeter.

Job (1972) — *Studying God's Word: An Introduction to methods of Bible study* (ed. J.B. Job), London.

Jugie and Spicq (1949) — 'Interprétation (histoire de l'): III. Exégèse médiévale', *SDB* 4: 591-627

Kampen (1954) — *De Apostolische Kerk: Theologische Bijdragen ter Gelegenheid van het honderdjarig Bestaan der theologische Hogeschool van de Gereformeerde Kerken in Nederland aangeboden door de Hoogleraren*, Kampen.

Kegley (1966) — *The Theology of Rudolf Bultmann* (ed. C.W. Kegley), London.

Kirkpatrick (1903) — *Critical Questions* (A.F. Kirkpatrick *et al.*), London.

Kleinedam Fs (1969) — *Sapienter ordinare: Festgabe für Erich Kleinedam* (ed. F. Hoffmann *et al.* Leipzig (Erfürter theologische Studien

Kümmel Fs (1975) — *Jesus und Paulus: Festschrift für Werner Georg Kümmel zum 70. Geburtstag* (ed. E.E. Ellis and E. Grässer), Göttingen.

Künneth and Schreiner (1933) | Die Nation vor Gott: Zur Botschaft der Kirche im Dritten Reich (ed. W. Künneth and H. Schreiner), Berlin 1934[3], 1933[1].

Kupisch Fs (1963) | Zwischenstation: Festschrift für Karl Kupisch zum 60.Geburtstag (ed. E. Wolf et al.), Munich.

Lampe and Woollcombe (1957) | Essays on Typology (G.W.H.Lampe and K.J.Woollcombe), London (SBT 22).

de Langhe (1962) | Le Psautier (ed. R. de Langhe), Louvain.

Largement and Lemaître (1959) | 'Le Jour de Yahweh dans le contexte oriental' in Sacra Pagina (ed. J.Coppens et al.),Gembloux (BETL 12-13): I.259-66 (R. Largement and H. Lemaître).

Laurin (1970) | Contemporary Old Testament Theologians (ed. R.B. Laurin), London.

Leenhardt Fs (1968) | L'Évangile, hier et aujourd'hui: Mélanges offerts au Professeur Franz-J. Leenhardt, Geneva.

Leist (1965) | SEINE Rede geschah zu mir: Einübung in das Alte Testament (ed. F. Leist), Munich.

London (1946) | 'Résumé des discussions de la Conférence de Londres' (10-12 August 1946), ETR 23(1948):41-55.

Loretz and Strolz (1968) | Die hermeneutische Frage in der Theologie (ed. O. Loretz and W. Strolz), Freiburg.

de Lubac (1942) | Israël et la foi chrétienne (H. de Lubac et al.), Fribourg.

Ludendorff (1939) | Die Judenmacht - ihr Wesen und Ende (E. and M. Ludendorff), Munich.

May Fs (1970) | Translating & Understanding the Old Testament: Essays in Honor of Herbert Gordon May (ed. H.T.Frank and W.L.Reed), Nashville.

Mays (1971) | Interpn 25: 419-501 - various articles on apocalyptic.

Montpellier (1948) | 'De la Bible au monde moderne', ETR 23: 3-152 (Faculté libre de Théologie Protestante, Montpellier; papers from conferences in London and Bossey).

Moule Fs (1970) — The Trial of Jesus: Cambridge Studies in honour of C.F.D. Moule (ed. E. Bammel), London (SBT 2.13).

Muilenburg Fs (1962) — Israel's Prophetic Heritage: Essays in honor of James Muilenburg (ed. B.W. Anderson and W. Harrelson), London.

Muschalek and Gamper (1964) — 'Offenbarung in Geschichte', ZKT 86: 180-196 (G. Muschalek and A. Gamper).

Netherlands Reformed Church (1969) — The Bible Speaks Again: A Guide from Holland, commissioned by the Netherlands Reformed Church, London.

Nineham (1963) — The Church's Use of the Bible: Past and Present (ed. D.E. Nineham), London (lectures given in the University of London, 1960).

Ottaviani Fs (1966) — Populus Dei: Studi in onore del Card. Alfredo Ottaviani, Rome.

Pannenberg (1961) — Revelation as History (ed. W. Pannenberg), ET: New York 1968 (German 1961)

Payne (1970) — New Perspectives on the Old Testament (ed. J.B. Payne), Waco,Texas/London.

Peake (1925) — The People and the Book (ed. A.S. Peake), Oxford.

Piper Fs (1962) — Current Issues in New Testament Interpretation: Essays in honor of Otto A. Piper (ed. W. Klassen and G.F. Snyder), London.

de Quervain Fs (1966) — Freude am Evangelium: Alfred de Quervain zum 70. Geburtstag (ed. J.J. Stamm and E. Wolf), Munich (BEvTh 44).

von Rad Fs (1961) — Studien zur Theologie der alttestamentlichen Überlieferungen (ed. R. Rendtorff and K. Koch), Neukirchen (Gerhard von Rad unserem Lehrer zum 60. Geburtstag)

von Rad Fs (1971) — Probleme biblischer Theologie: Gerhard von Rad zum 70. Geburtstag (ed. H.W. Wolff), Munich.

Richardson and Schweitzer (1951) — Biblical Authority for Today: A World Council of Churches Symposium (ed. A. Richardson and W. Schweitzer),London.

Richardson (1968) 'Aspects of Biblical Interpretation', *JCBRF* 17: 3-19 (G.P. Richardson *et al.*).

Rigaux (1954) *L'Attente du Messie* (ed. B. Rigaux), Bruges/Paris.

Robert and Vaganay (1949) 'Interprétation (histoire de l'): IV. Exégèse moderne et contemporaine', *SDB* 4: 627-46 (A. Robert and L. Vaganay).

Robert Fs (n.d.) *Mélanges bibliques: rédigés en l'honneur de André Robert*, Paris (n.d., after 1955).

Robert and Feuillet (1957) *Introduction à la Bible* (ed. A. Robert and A. Feuillet), Tournai, volume I: 1957.

Robinson (1938) *Record and Revelation: Essays on the Old Testament by Members of the Society for Old Testament Study* (ed. H.W. Robinson), Oxford.

Robinson (1972) *Religion and the Humanizing of Man* (ed. J.M. Robinson), Waterloo, Ontario.

Robinson and Cobb (1967) *New Frontiers in Theology, Volume III: Theology as History* (ed. J.M. Robinson and J.B. Cobb), New York/Evanston/London.

Rowley (1951) *The Old Testament and Modern Study: A Generation of Discovery and Research* (ed. H.H. Rowley), Oxford.

Rowley Fs (1955) *Wisdom in Israel and in the Ancient Near East* (ed. M. Noth and D.W. Thomas), Leiden (SVT 3).

Rylaarsdam (1968) *Transitions in Biblical Scholarship* (ed. J.C. Rylaarsdam), Chicago/London.

Schedl (1965) '"Da, ein Volk einsam ist es..."' in Leist (1965): 511-93 (C. Schedl *et al.*).

Schmaus Fs (1967) *Wahrheit und Verkündigung: Michael Schmaus zum 70. Geburtstag* (ed. L. Scheffczyk *et al.*), Paderborn.

Schniewind and Friedrich (1935) 'ἐπαγγέλλω, ἐπαγγελλία, ἐπάγγελμα, προεπαγγέλλομαι', *TDNT* 2: 576-86.

Smith (1950) *The Enduring Gospel* (ed. R. Gregor Smith), London.

Stendahl and Dulles (1966) 'Method in the Study of Biblical Theology in Hyatt (1966): 196-216 (paper by K. Stendahl with response by A. Dulles).

Stinespring Fs (1972) — *The Use of the Old Testament in the New and Other Essays: Studies in Honor of William Franklin Stinespring* (ed. J.M. Efird), Durham,N.C.

Temple (1860) — *Essays and Reviews* (F. Temple *et al.*), London.

Vischer Fs (1960) — **maqqél shâqédh, La branche d'amandier: *Hommage à Wilhelm Vischer* (ed.D.Lys), Montpellier.**

Vriezen Fs (1966) — *Studia Biblica et Semitica: Theodoro Christiano Vriezen dedicata* (ed. W.C. van Unnik and A.S. van der Woude), Wageningen.

Weber and Schmitt (1968) — *Où en sont les Études Bibliques?* (ed. J.J. Weber and J. Schmitt),Paris.

Weiser Fs (1963) — *Tradition und Situation: Studien zur alttestamentlichen Prophetie: Artur Weiser zum 70. Geburtstag* (ed. E. Würthwein and O. Kaiser), Göttingen.

Westermann (1949-60) — *Essays on Old Testament Interpretatio* (*EOTI*, ed. C.Westermann),ET: London 196 (German 1960; a collection of essays originally published 1949-60).

Wikgren Fs (1972) — *Studies in New Testament and Early Christian Literature - Essays in Honor of Allan P. Wikgren* (ed.D.E. Aune),Leiden (SNovT 33).

Willoughby (1947) — *The Study of the Bible Today and Tomorrow* (ed. H.R. Willoughby),Chicag

Wolff (1973) — *Gerhard von Rad: Seine Bedeutung für die Theologie* (H.W. Wolff *et al.*),Munic

WCC (1949) — 'Guiding Principles for the Interpretation of the Bible',*ER* 2: 81-6 (from ecumenical study conference in Oxford, July 1949).

WCC (1974) — 'The Church and the Jewish People', symposium in *Oikoumene: World Council of Churches Newsletter*, 1974: no.1.

Zimmerli and Jeremias (1954) — 'παῖς θεοῦ', *TDNT* 5: 654-717 (an earlier ET was published as *The Servan of God*, London 1957, SBT 20).

11.3 MONOGRAPHS

Aalen, L.

1948 'Les deux Testaments', _ETR_ 23: 71-7.

Abramowski, L.

1961 'Zur Theologie Theodors von Mopsuestia', _ZKG_ 72: 263-93.

Abramowski, R.

1937 'Vom Streit um das Alte Testament', _ThRu_ 9: 65-93.

Ackroyd, P.R.

1962 'G.A.F. Knight's "A Christian Theology of the Old Testament"', _ExpT_ 73: 164-8.

1963a 'The Old Testament in the Christian Church', _Theology_ 66: 46-52.

1963b 'The Place of the Old Testament in the Church's Teaching and Worship', _ExpT_ 74: 164-7.

1968 _Exile and Restoration: A Study of Hebrew Thought of the Sixth Century BC_, London.

Agus, J.

1969 'Israel and the Jewish-Christian dialogue', _JES_ 6: 18-36.

Aland, K.

1936 _Wer fälscht? Die Entstehung der Bibel: Zu den "Enthüllungen" E. und M. Ludendorffs_, Berlin=Steglitz.

1957 'Luther as Exegete', _ExpT_ 69: 45-8,68-70.

Albertz, M.

1947-57 _Die Botschaft des Neuen Testamentes_, Zollikon-Zürich, 2 volumes.

Albrektson, B.

1967a _History and the Gods: An Essay on the Idea of Historical Events as Divine Manifestations in the Ancient Near East and in Israel_, Lund.

1967b 'Luther och den allegoriska tolkningen av Gamla Testamentet', SEA 32: 5-20.

Albright, W.F.
1964 History, Archaeology and Christian Humanism, New York/Toronto/London: 272-84 (expansion of review article in JBL 77,1958: 244-8; 'Rudolf Bultmann on history and eschatology').

Alexander, J.N.S.
1958 'The Interpretation of Scripture in the Ante-Nicene Period: A Brief Conspectus', Interpn 12:272-80.

Allen, L.C.
1964 'The Old Testament in Romans I-VIII', VoxEv 3: 6-41.

Allis, O.T.
1945 Prophecy and the Church, Philadelphia.

Alonso-Schökel, L.
1961 Review of Vriezen 1954, Biblica 42: 231-

1963 'The Old Testament, a Christian Book', Biblica 44: 210-16 (review of Larcher 1962 and Grelot 1962a).

Alt, A.
1913-56 Kleine Schriften zur Geschichte des Volkes Israel, Munich I:1953, II:1953, III:1959 (originally 1913-56); ET of selection: Essays on Old Testament History and Religion, Oxford 1966 (originally 1925-51).

Althaus, P.
1933 Die deutsche Stunde der Kirche, Göttinge

1962 'Offenbarung als Geschichte und Glaube: Bemerkungen zu Wolfhart Pannenbergs Begriff der Offenbarung', TLZ 87: 321-30.

Amsler, S.
1952 'Où en est la typologie de l'Ancien Testament?', ETR 27: 75-81.

1953 'Prophétie et typologie', RThPh 3: 139-14

1960a L'Ancien Testament dans l'Église, Neuchâtel.

1960b 'Texte et événement' in Vischer Fs: 12-

1963 *David, Roi et Messie: La tradition davidique dans l'AT* Neuchâtel.

Anderson, A.A.
1963 'Old Testament Theology and Its Methods' in Hooke Fs: 7-19.

Anderson, B.W.
1955 'The Earth Is the Lord's: An Essay on the Biblical Doctrine of Creation', *Interpn* 9: 3-20.

1958 *The Living World of the Old Testament*, London.

1962 'Exodus Typology in Second Isaiah' in Muilenburg Fs: 177-195.

1964 'Introduction: The Old Testament as a Christian Problem' and 'The New Covenant and the Old' in *OTCF*: 1-7, 225-42.

1965a 'The Problem of Old Testament History', *LQHR* 190: 5-11.

1965b 'The New Heilsgeschichte', *Interpn* 19: 337-41 (review of von Rad 1957).

1969 'The Old and the New', *Interpn* 23: 88-93 (review of von Rad 1960).

1970 'Myth and the Biblical Tradition', *ThTo* 27: 44-62.

Anderson, G.W.
1962 'Th.C. Vriezen's "Outline of Old Testament Theology"', *ExpT* 73: 113-116.

1963 'Israel's Creed: Sung not Signed', *SJT* 16: 277-85.

Anderson, H.
1972 'The Old Testament in Mark's Gospel' in Stinespring Fs: 280-306.

Armstrong, G.T.
1962 *Die Genesis in der Alten Kirche: Die drei Kirchenväter*, Tübingen (BGBH 4).

Atkinson, B.F.C.
1947 'The Textual Background of the Use of the Old Testament by the New', *JTVI* 79: 39-69.

1952 *The Christian's Use of the Old Testament*, London.

Atkinson, J.
1968 *The Great Light: Luther and Reformation*, Exeter.

Aulén, G.
1930 *Christus Victor: An Historical Study of the Three Main Types of the Idea of the Atonement*, ET: London 1931 (Swedish 1930; abridged German translation in *ZST* 1930:501-38).

Aune, D.E.
1966 'Justin Martyr's Use of the Old Testament', *BETS* 9: 179-197.

1969 'Early Christian Biblical Interpretatio *EQ* 41: 89-96.

1972 *The Cultic Setting of Realized Eschatology in Early Christianity*, Leiden (SNovT 28).

Baalen, J.K.van
1956 *The Chaos of Cults: A Study in Present-Day Isms*, London 1956[2] (n.d.[1]).

Bainton, R.H.
1930 'The Immoralities of the Patriarchs according to the Exegesis of the Late Middle Ages and of the Reformation', *HTR* 23: 39-49 (repr. in *Early and Medieval Christianity*, London 1965: 122-

1963 'The Bible in the Reformation', *CHB* III: 1-37.

Balchin, J.A.
1961-2 'Biblical Hermeneutics', *TSFB* 31: 8-13; 33: 9-11; 34: 5-8.

Balthasar, H.U.von
1950 *A Theology of History*, ET: London/ New York 1964[2] (German 1959[2], 1950[1]).

1951 *Karl Barth: Darstellung und Deutung seiner Theologie*, Cologne.

Bampfylde, G.P.
1966 or 67 'Old Testament quotations and imagery in the Gospel according to St John', M.A. Dissn, Hull.*

Bandstra, A.J.
1971 'Interpretation in I Corinthians 10: 1-11', CTJ 6: 5-21.

Banks, R.J.
1969 'Jesus and the Law in the Synoptic Tradition', Dissn, Cambridge.

Bardy, G.
1949 'Interprétation (histoire de l'): II. Exégèse patristique', SDB 4: 569-91.

Barnard, L.W.
1964 'The Old Testament and Judaism in the Writings of Justin Martyr', VT 14: 395-406.

1966 Studies in the Apostolic Fathers and their Background, Oxford.

Baron, D.
1915 The History of the Ten "Lost" Tribes: Anglo-Israelism Examined, London.

Barr, J.
1957a 'The Problem of Old Testament Theology and the History of Religion', CJT 3: 141-9.

1957b 'Tradition and Expectation in Ancient Israel', SJT 10: 24-34.

1959 'The Meaning of "Mythology" in Relation to the Old Testament', VT 9: 1-10.

1960 Review of Jacob 1955a, JSS 5: 166-9.

1961 The Semantics of Biblical Language, Oxford.

1962a Biblical Words for Time, London 1962[1], 1969[2] (SBT 33).

1962b 'Gerhard von Rad's Theologie des Alten Testaments', ExpT 73: 142-6.

1962c 'Hypostatisation of Linguistic Phenomena in Modern Theological Interpretation', JSS 7: 85-94.

1963 'Revelation Through History in the Old Testament and in Modern Theology', *Interpn* 17: 193-205.

1965 'Taking the Cue from Bultmann', *Interpn* 19: 217-20 (review of *OTCF*).

1966 *Old and New in Interpretation: A Study of the Two Testaments*, London.

1967 'Den teologiska värderingen av den efterbibliska judendomen',*SEA* 32: 69-78.

1968a 'Common Sense and Biblical Language', *Biblica* 49: 377-87.

1968b *Judaism - Its Continuity with the Bible* Southampton (The Seventh Montefiore Memorial Lecture).

1968c 'Le Judaïsme postbiblique et la théologie de l'Ancien Testament', *RThPh* 18: 209-17.

1969 'The Authority of the Bible: A Study Outline',*ER* 21: 135-150.

1970 'Themes from the Old Testament for the Elucidation of the New Creation', *Encounter* 31: 25-30.

1971 'The Old Testament and the New Crisis of Biblical Authority',*Interpn* 25: 24-40.

1972a 'Semantics and Biblical Theology - a Contribution to the Discussion' in *Congress Volume: Uppsala 1971*,Leiden (SVT 22): 11-19.

1972b 'Man and Nature - The Ecological Controversy and the Old Testament', *BJRL* 55: 9-32.

1973 *The Bible in the Modern World*, London (Croall Lectures 1970).

1974 'Trends and Prospects in Biblical Theology',*JTS* 25: 265-82.

Barrett, C.K.

1947 'The Old Testament in the Fourth Gospel',*JTS* 48: 155-169.

1962 *From First Adam to Last: A Study in Pauline Theology*, London.

1970 'The Interpretation of the Old Testament in the New', CHB I: 377-411.

Barth, C.
1963 'Grundprobleme einer Theologie des Alten Testaments', EvTh 23: 342-72.

Barth, K.
n.d. Prayer and Preaching, ET: London 1964 (French 1953 and 1961; originally a course of lectures delivered when Barth was 'comparatively young', p.64).

1918/21 The Epistle to the Romans, ET: Oxford 1933 (German 1918[1], 1921[2], 1928[6]).

1935 'Gospel and Law', ET in God, Grace and Gospel, Edinburgh/London 1959 (SJT Occasional Papers 8):1-27 (German 1956[2], 1935[1]).

1938a The Knowledge of God and the Service of God According to the Teaching of the Reformation, London.

1938b Church Dogmatics I.2, ET: Edinburgh 1956 (German 1945[3], 1938[1]).

1940 Church Dogmatics II.1, ET: Edinburgh 1957 (German 1946[2], 1940[1]).

1942 Church Dogmatics II.2, ET: Edinburgh 1957 (German 1942).

1945a Church Dogmatics III.1, ET: Edinburgh 1958 (German 1945).

1945b Eine Schweizer Stimme: 1938-1945, Zollikon-Zürich.

1950 Church Dogmatics III.3, ET: Edinburgh 1961 (German 1950).

1952 Christ and Adam: Man and Humanity in Romans 5, ET: Edinburgh/London 1956 (SJT Occasional Papers 5; German ThSt 35, 1952).

1953 Church Dogmatics IV.1, ET: Edinburgh 1956 (German 1953).

1955 Church Dogmatics IV.2, ET: Edinburgh 1958 (German 1955).

1962 Evangelical Theology: An Introduction ET: London 1963/reset 1965 (German 1962)

Barth, M.

1954 'The Christ in Israel's History', *ThTo* 11: 342-53.

1962 'The Old Testament in Hebrews: An Essay in Biblical Hermeneutics' in Piper Fs: 53-78.

Bauer, W.

1934 *Orthodoxy and Heresy in Earliest Christianity*, ET: London 1972 (German 1964^2, 1934^1).

Baumann, E.

1929 'שוב שבות: Eine exegetische Untersuchung', *ZAW* 47: 17-44.

Baumann, R.

1969 *Mitte und Norm des Christlichen: Eine Auslegung von 1.Korinther 1,1-3,4*, Münster (Neutestamentliche Abhandlungen 5)

Baumgärtel, F.

1925 *Die Bedeutung des Alten Testaments für den Christen*, Schwerin.

1933 'Das Alte Testament' in Künneth and Schreiner (1933): 97-114.

1936 'Das Christuszeugnis des Alten Testaments', *WuT* 12: 309-16.*

1938 'Zur Frage der theologischen Deutung des Alten Testaments', *ZST* 15: 136-162.

1951 'Erwägungen zur Darstellung der Theologie des Alten Testaments', *TLZ* 76: 257-72.

1952 *Verheissung: Zur Frage des evangelischen Verständnisses des Alten Testaments*, Gütersloh.

1953a 'Das alttestamentliche Geschehen als "heilsgeschichtliches" Geschehen' in Alt Fs: 13-28.

1953b '"Ohne Schlüssel vor der Tür des Wortes Gottes"?', *EvTh* 13: 413-21.

1954a 'The Hermeneutical Problem of the Old Testament', ET in *EOTI*: 134-159 (German *TLZ* 79,1954).

1954b 'Der Dissensus im Verständnis des Alten Testaments', EvTh 14: 298-313.

1961 'Gerhard von Rad's "Theologie des Alten Testaments"', TLZ 86: 801-16, 895-908.

1963 'Der Tod des Religionsstifters', KuD 9: 223-33.

1967 'Das Offenbarungszeugnis des Alten Testaments im Lichte der religionsgeschichtlich-vergleichenden Forschung', ZTK 64: 393-422.

Baumgartner, W.
1941 'Die Auslegung des Alten Testaments im Streit der Gegenwart', repr. in Zum Alten Testament und seiner Umwelt: Ausgewählte Aufsätze von Walter Baumgartner, Leiden 1959: 179-207 (originally Schweizerische theologische Umschau 11,1941:2/3.17-38).

Bea, A.
1959 '"Religionswissenschaftliche" oder "theologische" Exegese? Zur Geschichte der neueren biblischen Hermeneutik', Biblica 40: 322-41.

Bear, J.E.
1956 'The Seventh-Day Adventists', Interpn 10: 45-71.

Beauchamp, P.
1971 'La figure dans l'un et l'autre Testament', RechSR 59: 209-24.

Beck, J.T.
1841 Die Christliche Lehr-Wissenschaft nach den biblischen Urkunden: Ein Versuch. Erster Theil. Die Logik der christlichen Lehre, Stuttgart.

Bell, R.D.
1970 'An examination of the presuppositions and methodology of Gerhard von Rad in his Old Testament Theology', Dissn, Baylor University.

Bennett, W.H.
1890 'The Old Testament and the New Reformation', Exp IV.2: 401-18.

1893 'Old Testament' in Congregationalists (1893): 1-47.

1914 The Value of the Old Testament for the Religion of Today, London.

Benoit, A.
1960 Saint Irénée: Introduction à l'étude de sa théologie, Paris (Études d'histoire et de philosophie religieuses 52

Benoit, P.
1960 'La plénitude de sens des Livres Saints', RB 67: 161-196.

Bentzen, A.
1948 King and Messiah, ET: London 1955 (German: Messias - Moses redivivus - Menschensohn: Skizzen zum Thema Weissagung und Erfüllung, 1948).

1950 'The Old Testament and the New Covenant', HervTS 7: 1-15.

Berge, W.
1958 Gesetz und Evangelium in der neueren Theologie: Interpretation einer theologischen Kontroverse, Berlin.

Berger, K.
1971 'Zum traditionsgeschichtlichen Hintergrund christologischer Hoheitstitel', NTS 17: 391-425.

1972 Die Gesetzesauslegung Jesu: Ihr historischer Hintergrund im Judentum und im Alten Testament. Teil I: Markus und Parallelen, Neukirchen (WMANT 40).

Bergmann, E.
1934 The 25 Theses of the German Religion: A Catechism, ET (with foreword by F.W. Norwood): London 1936 (German 193

Berkhof, H.
1965 'Over de methode der eschatologie', NedTT 19: 480-91.

1969 'Israel as a theological problem in the Christian church', JES 6: 329-47; with a 'Jewish response' by J.J. Petuchowski: 348-53.

Berkhof, L.
1950 Principles of Biblical Interpretation (Sacred Hermeneutics), Grand Rapids,Mi

Berkouwer, G.C.
1952 — _Studies in Dogmatics: The Person of Christ_, ET: Grand Rapids, Mich. 1954 (Dutch 1952).

Bernhardt, K.-H.
1968 — 'Gamla testamentets betydelse för Martin Luthers reformatoriska gärning', _SvTK_ 44: 69-83.

Berry, G.R.
1930 — 'The Old Testament: A Liability or an Asset', _CRDSB_ 1930: 8-22.

Berten, I.
1969 — _Geschichte. Offenbarung. Glaube: Eine Einführung in die Theologie Wolfhart Pannenbergs_, German translation: Munich 1970 (French 1969).

Betz, H.D.
1969 — 'The Concept of Apocalyptic in the Theology of the Pannenberg Group', _JTC_ 6: 192-207.

Betz, O.
1962 — 'Biblical Theology, History of', _IDB_ 1: 432-7.

1973 — '"Kann denn aus Nazareth etwas Gutes kommen?" (Zur Verwendung von Jesaja Kap.11 in Johannes Kap.1)' in Elliger Fs: 9-16.

Bewer, J.A.
1930 — 'The Christian Minister and the Old Testament', _JR_ 10: 16-21.

1936 — 'The Authority of the Old Testament', _JR_ 16: 1-9.

Beyerlin, W.
1961 — _Origins and History of the Oldest Sinaitic Traditions_, ET: Oxford 1966 (German 1961).

Bianchi, U.
1967 — 'Marcion: Theologien biblique ou docteur gnostique?', _VigChr_ 21:141-9.

Bič, M.
1970 — 'Das Alte Testament und das Wort Gottes' in Eichrodt Fs: 143-156.

Bierberg, R.
1948 'Does Sacred Scripture Have a Sensus Plenior?', CBQ 10: 182-195.

Black, M.
1971 'The Christological Use of the Old Testament in the New Testament', NTS 18: 1-14.

Blackman, E.C.
1948 Marcion and His Influence, London.

1957 Biblical Interpretation: The Old Difficulties and the New Opportunity, London.

Bläser, P.
1952 'Schriftverwertung und Schrifterklärung im Rabbinentum und bei Paulus', ThQ 132: 152-169.

1965 'Typos in der Schrift', LTK[2] 10:422-3.

Bligh, J.
1970 Christian Deuteronomy (Luke 9-18), Langley,Bucks.

Boer, P.A.H.de
1951 'De functie van de Bijbel', NedTT 6: 5

Boer, W. den
1947 'Hermeneutic problems in early Christian literature', VigChr 1: 150-167.

Bohren, R.
1962 'Die Krise der Predigt als Frage an die Exegese', EvTh 22: 66-92.

Boman, T.
1952/68 Hebrew Thought Compared with Greek, ET: London 1960 (German 1954[2], 1952[1]). German 5th edn (1968) includes a reply to Barr's criticisms.

Boney, M.L.
1956 'Paul's Use of the Old Testament', Dissn, Columbia University.*

Bonhoeffer, D.
1951 Letters and Papers from Prison, ET: London 1959 (reset, originally 1953; USA: Prisoner for God, 1958; German 1951).

Bonnard, P.
1950 'L'encyclique *Divino afflante Spiritu et l'orientation de l'herméneutique biblique*', *RThPh* 38: 51-6.

Bonnardière, A.M.La
1960- *Biblia Augustinia A.T.*, Paris: volumes have so far appeared on the historical books (1960), the minor prophets (1963), Deuteronomy (1967), Wisdom (1970) and Jeremiah (1972).

Bonner, G.
1970 'Augustine as Biblical Scholar', *CHB* I: 541-63.

Bonsirven, J.
1939 *Exégèse rabbinique et exégèse paulinienne*, Paris.

n.d. 'Le règne de Dieu suivant l'Ancien Testament' in Robert Fs: 295-302.

Borgen, P.
1965 *Bread From Heaven: An Exegetical Study of the Concept of Manna in the Gospel of John and the Writings of Philo*, Leiden (SNovT 10).

1972 'Logos was the True Light: Contributions to the Interpretation of the Prologue of John', *NovT* 14:115-130.

Bornkamm, G.
1962 'Geschichte und Glaube im Neuen Testament: Ein Beitrag zur Frage der "historischen" Begründung theologischer Aussagen', *EvTh* 22: 1-15.

Bornkamm, H.
1948 *Luther and the Old Testament*, ET: Philadelphia 1969 (German 1948).

Borsch, F.H.
1967 *The Son of Man in Myth and History*, London.

Boundy, R.
1972 'Augustine's Evangelical Use of the Old Testament In "De Spiritu et Littera"', unpublished paper.

Bourke, J.
1959 'Le jour de Yahwé dans Joël', *RB* 66: 5-31, 191-212.

Bowden, J.
1969 *What about the Old Testament?*, London.

Box, G.H.
1925 'The Value and Significance of the Old Testament in Relation to the New' in Peake (1925): 433-67.

Boyd, R.F.
1956 'Mormonism', *Interpn* 10: 430-46.

Boyd, R.H.
1955 'Revelation - In History and Experience', *Interpn* 9: 213-16 (review of Rowley 1953).

Boyer, P.J.
1905 'The Value of the Old Testament: A German Estimate', *The Interpreter* 1: 258-63.

Bozzo, E.G.
1974 'Jesus as a Paradigm for Personal Life', *JES* 11: 45-63.

Braaten, C.E.
1965 'The Current Controversy on Revelation: Pannenberg and His Critics', *JR* 45: 225-37.

1966 *History and Hermeneutics*, Philadelphia (New Directions in Theology Today 2).

Braun, D.
1967 'Heil als Geschichte', *EvTh* 27: 57-76.

Braun, F.-M.
1951 'Le sens plénier et les encycliques', *RThom* 51: 294-304.

1953 'La théologie biblique: Qu'entendre par là?', *RThom* 53: 221-53.

1964 *Jean le Théologien (Les grandes traditions d'Israël et l'accord des Écritures selon le Quatrième Évangile)* Volume II, Paris.

Braun, H.
1962 'Das Alte Testament im Neuen Testament', *ZTK* 59: 16-31.

Bright, J.

1951 'Faith and Destiny: The Meaning of History in Deutero-Isaiah', _Interpn_ 5: 3-26.

1953 _The Kingdom of God: The Biblical Concept and Its Meaning for the Church_, New York/Nashville.

1956 _Early Israel in Recent History Writing: A Study in Method_, London.

1960 _A History of Israel_, London 1960[1], 1972[2].

1962 'Edmond Jacob's "Theology of the Old Testament"', _ExpT_ 73: 304-7.

1963 'Eschatology', _DB_[2]: 265-7.

1965 _Jeremiah: Introduction, Translation and Notes_, Garden City, N.Y.

1967 _The Authority of the Old Testament_, London.

Bring, R.

1948 'Autorité et rôle actuels de la Bible', _ETR_ 23: 16-21.

1969 _Christus und das Gesetz: Die Bedeutung des Gesetzes des Alten Testaments nach Paulus und sein Glaube an Christus_, Leiden.

1971 'Paul and the Old Testament: A Study of the ideas of Election, Faith and Law in Paul, with special reference to Rom 9:30-10:30', _StTh_ 25: 21-60.

Brown, J.

1969 Review of Miskotte 1956a, _SJT_ 22: 356-62.

Brown, P.E.

1955 'The Basis for Hope: The Principle of the Covenant as a Biblical Basis for a Philosophy of History', _Interpn_ 9: 35-40.

Brown, R.E.

1953 'The History and Development of the Theory of a Sensus Plenior', _CBQ_ 15: 141-162.

1955 _The Sensus Plenior of Sacred Scripture_, Baltimore.*

1963 'The *Sensus Plenior* in the Last Ten Years', *CBQ* 25: 262-85.

1967 'The Problems of the *Sensus Plenior*', *ETL* 43: 460-69.

1968 'Hermeneutics', *JBC*: II.605-23.

Brown, W.A.
1911 'Covenant Theology', *ERE* 4: 216-24.

Bruce, F.F.
1950 *The Books and the Parchments*, London 1950, 1963[3].

1955 *The Christian Approach to the Old Testament*, London (IVF Presidential Address 1955).

1959 *Biblical Exegesis in the Qumran Texts*, Grand Rapids 1959 (London 1960).

1961 'The Book of Zechariah and the Passion Narrative', *BJRL* 43: 336-53.

1963 'Promise and Fulfilment in Paul's Presentation of Jesus' in Hooke Fs: 36-50.

1968a *This is That: The New Testament Development of Some Old Testament Themes*, Exeter.

1968b 'Scripture and Tradition in the New Testament' in *Holy Book and Holy Tradition* (ed.F.F.Bruce and E.G.Rupp), Manchester: 68-9

1969 *New Testament History*, London.

Brunner, E.
1930 'The Significance of the Old Testament for Our Faith', ET in *OTCF*: 243-64 (German: *ZZ* 8, 1930: 30-48).

1934 *Die Unentbehrlichkeit des Alten Testamentes für die missionierende Kirche: Vortrag am Basler Missionsfest 1934*, Stuttgart/Basel (Basler Missionsstudien 12).

1941 *Revelation and Reason: The Christian Doctrine of Faith and Knowledge*, ET: London 1947 (German 1941).

1950 *The Christian Doctrine of Creation and Redemption: Dogmatics Vol.II*, ET: London 1952 (German 1950).

Brunner, P.

1967 'Gesetz und Evangelium: Versuch einer dogmatischen Paraphrase' in Schmaus Fs: 1315-37.

Buber, M.

1932 *Kingship of God*, ET: London 1967 (German 1956[2], 1932[1]).

1951 *Two Types of Faith*, London.

Buchanan, G.W.

1970 *The Consequences of the Covenant*, Leiden (SNovT 20).

Bugge, C.A.

1924 'L'Ancien Testament, Bible de la primitive Eglise', *RHPR* 4: 449-55.

Buis, P.

1968 'La nouvelle Alliance', *VT* 18: 1-15.

Bultmann, R.

1917-60 *Glauben und Verstehen* (Bultmann's collected essays):
I: 1933, ET as *Faith and Understanding*, London 1969;
II: 1952, ET as *Essays: Philosophical and Theological*, London 1955;
III: 1960, ET of some essays in *Existence and Faith: Shorter Writings of Rudolf Bultmann*, London 1961.

1930 'The Historicity of Man and Faith', ET in *Existence and Faith*: 92-110 (German: *ZTK* 11, 1930: 339-64).

1933a 'The Significance of the Old Testament for the Christian Faith', ET in *OTCF*: 8-35 (German: *Glauben und Verstehen* I, 1933: 313-36).

1933b 'The Problem of "Natural Theology"', ET in *Faith and Understanding*: 313-31 (German: *Glauben und Verstehen* I, 1933: 294-312).

1933c 'The Task of Theology in the Present Situation', ET in *Existence and Faith*: 158-165 (German: *ThBl* 12, 1933: 161-6).

1940 'Christ the End of the Law', ET in *Essays*: 36-66 (German: BEvTh 1, 1940).

1941 'New Testament and Mythology: The Mythological Element in the New Testament and the Problem of its Re-interpretation', originally published in Offenbarung und Heilsgeschehen, Munich 1941 (BEvTh 7); now in Bartsch (1948, ET: 1953).

1948a Theology of the New Testament I, ET: London 1952 (German 1948

1948b 'History of Salvation and History', ET in Existence and Faith: 226-40 (German: TLZ 73, 1948: 659-66).

1949a 'Prophecy and Fulfillment', ET in EOTI: 50-75, and earlier in Essays (German: StTh 2, 1949: 21-44; also: ZTK 1950: 360-83; Glauben und Verstehen II: 162-186).

1949b Primitive Christianity in its Contemporary Setting, ET: London/New York 1956 (German 1954[2], 1949[1]).

1950a 'The Problem of Hermeneutics', ET in Essays: 234-61 (German: ZTK 47, 1950: 47-69).

1950b 'Ursprung und Sinn der Typologie als hermeneutischer Methode', TLZ 75: 205-12.

1950c 'The Significance of the Jewish Old Testament Tradition for the Christian West', ET in Essays: 262-72 (German: Welt ohne Hass: Aufsätze und Ansprachen zum 1. Kongress über bessere menschliche Beziehungen in München, Berlin 1950: 43-54).

1954 'History and Eschatology in the New Testament', NTS 1: 5-16.

1957a History and Eschatology: The Gifford Lectures 1955, Edinburgh.

1957b 'Is Exegesis without Presuppositions Possible?', ET in Existence and Faith: 289-96 (German: ThZ 13, 1957:409-17).

1959 'Adam and Christ According to Romans 5', ET in Piper Fs: 143-165 (German: ZNW 55, 1959: 145-165).

1961 'On the Problem of Demythologizing', ET in Batey (1970): 35-44; repr. from JR 1962: 96-102 (German: in Il Problema della Demitizzazione, Rome 1961).

Burdett, D.
1974 'Wisdom Literature and the Promise Doctrine', TrJ 3: 1-13.

Burghardt, W.J.
1950 'On Early Christian Exegesis', ThSt 11: 78-116.

Burkitt, F.C.
1927 'The Debt of Christianity to Judaism', in Bevan and Singer (1927): 69-96.

Burney, C.F.
1921 The Gospel in the Old Testament, Edinburgh.

Burrows, M.
1946 An Outline of Biblical Theology, Philadelphia.

Busch, E.
1967 'Der Beitrag und Ertrag der Föderaltheologie für ein geschichtliches Verständnis der Offenbarung' in Cullmann Fs: 171-190.

Butterfield, H.
1949 Christianity and History, London.

Caird, G.B.
1959 'The Exegetical Method of the Epistle to the Hebrews', CJT 5: 44-51.

1965 Jesus and the Jewish Nation, London.

1966 A Commentary on the Revelation of St. John the Divine, London.

Calmet, A.
1837 'Type' in Calmet's Dictionary of the Holy Bible, London 1837[6] (first edn in 18th century): II.768-9.

Calvin, J.
1536-59 Institutes of the Christian Religion, ET: London 1961 (originally published in 6 Latin or French editions, 1536-59).

Camelot, T.
1946 'Clément d'Alexandrie et l'Écriture', RB 53: 242-8.
1951 'L'exégèse de l'Ancien Testament par les Pères' in Auvray (1951): 149-167.

Campbell, R.
1954 Israel and the New Covenant, Philadelphia.

Campenhausen, H. von
1968 The Formation of the Christian Bible, ET: London 1972 (German 1968).

Carpenter, E.
1963 'The Bible in the Eighteenth Century' in Nineham (1963): 89-124.

Carpenter, H.J.
1944 'The Bible in the Early Church' in Dugmore (1944): 1-22.

Carpenter, J.E.
1903 The Bible in the Nineteenth Century, London.

Carr, A.
1905 'The Eclectic Use of the Old Testament in the New Testament', Exp 6.11: 340-5.

Carrez, M.
1971 'La méthode de G. von Rad appliqué à quelques textes pauliniens: Petit essai de vérification', RSPT 55: 81-95.

Carter, C.S.
1928 The Reformers and Holy Scripture: A Historical Investigation, London.

Casserley, J.V.L.
1965 Toward a Theology of History, London.

Causse, A.
1938 'Le mythe de la nouvelle Jérusalem du Deutéro-Esaie à la IIIe Sibylle', RHPR 18: 377-414.

Cave, A.
1890 'The Old Testament and the Critics', ConRev 57: 537-51.

Cazelles, H.
1956 Review of Jacob 1955a, VT 6: 326-30.

1966 'The Unity of the Bible and the People of God', Scripture 18: 1-10.

1969 Review of von Rad 1957-60, BO 26: 376-80.

Cerfaux, L.

1951 'L'exégèse de l'Ancien Testament par le Nouveau Testament' in Auvray (1951): 132-148.

1966 'Le royaume de Dieu', 'Le peuple de Dieu' and 'La survivance du peuple ancien à la lumière du Nouveau Testament' in Ottaviani Fs: 777-802, 803-64, 919-26.

Černý, L.

1948 The Day of Yahweh and some relevant problems, Prague.

Chadwick, H.

1963 'The Bible and the Greek Fathers' in Nineham (1963): 25-39.

Chamberlain, H.S.

1899 The Foundations of the Nineteenth Century, ET: London/New York 1911 (German 1899).

Chandler, A.R.

1945 Rosenberg's Nazi Myth, New York.

Childs, B.S.

1958 'Prophecy and Fulfillment: A Study in Contemporary Hermeneutics', Interpn 12: 259-71.

1959 Review of Vriezen 1954, JBL 78: 256-8.

1960a Myth and Reality in the Old Testament, London (SBT 27).

1960b Review of Knight 1959a, Interpn 14: 202-4.

1962 Memory and Tradition in Israel, London (SBT 37).

1964 'Interpretation in Faith: The Theological Responsibility of an Old Testament Commentary', Interpn 18: 432-49.

1970 Biblical Theology in Crisis, Philadelphia.

1972 'A Tale of Two Testaments', Interpn 26: 20-29.

1974 Exodus: A Commentary, London.

Clark, K.W.
1972 'The Israel of God' in Wikgren Fs: 161-9.

Clark, W.M.
1964 'The Origin and Development of the Land Promise Theme in the Old Testament', Dissn, Yale.*

Clarke, W.N.
1907 _The Use of the Scriptures in Theology_, Edinburgh 1907.

Clements, R.E.
1965a _Prophecy and Covenant_, London (SBT 43).

1965b 'The Problem of Old Testament Theology', _LQHR_ 190: 11-17.

1970 'Theodorus C. Vriezen, _An Outline of Old Testament Theology_' in Laurin (1970): 121-140.

1975 _Prophecy and Tradition_, Oxford.

Clines, D.J.A.
1968 Review of Miskotte 1956a, _EQ_ 40: 173-5.

1973 'God in Human Form: A Theme in Biblical Theology', _JCBRF_ 24: 24-40.

1974 'Expounding the Old Testament', unpublished paper, presented at the Tyndale Fellowship Conference, 1974.

Clowney, E.P.
1962 _Preaching and Biblical Theology_, London.

Cole, R.A.
1973 'Are You Bleached in the Belly of the Whale?', _Interchange_ 13: 41-51.

Collins, J.J.
1974 'Apocalyptic Eschatology as the Transcendence of Death', _CBQ_ 36: 21-43.

Colpe, C.
1969 'ὁ υἱὸς τοῦ ἀνθρώπου', _TDNT_ 8: 400-477.

Congar, Y.M.J.
1949 'The Old Testament as a Witness to Christ', repr. in _The Revelation of God_, ET: London/New York 1968: 8-15 (originally in _La Vie Intellectuelle_ 17: 335-43).

Connell, J.C.
1969 'Review Article: Theology of Hope by Jurgen Moltmann', VoxEv 6: 72-7.

Conzelmann, H.
1964 'Fragen an Gerhard von Rad', EvTh 24: 113-125.

1967 An Outline of the Theology of the New Testament, ET: London 1969 (German 1967).

Cook, S.A.
1936 The Old Testament: A Reinterpretation, Cambridge.

Coppens, J.
1948 Les harmonies des deux Testaments: Essais sur les divers sens des Ecritures et sur l'unité de la Révélation, Tournai/Paris 1949[2], 1948[1] (Cahiers de la NRT 6).

1950 'Le problème d'un Sens biblique plénier' in Problèmes et Méthode d'exégèse théologique (L. Cerfaux et al.), Louvain/Bruges-Paris (ALBO 2.16): 11-19.

1951 Un nouvel essai d'Herméneutique biblique, Louvain/Bruges-Paris (ALBO 2.25; also: ETL 27, 1952:500-507).

1952a Vom Christlichen Verständnis des Alten Testaments - Les Harmonies des deux Testaments: Supplément bibliographique - Bibliographie J. Coppens, Leuven (Folia Lovaniensa Fasc.3-4).

1952b 'Nouvelles réflexions sur les divers sens des Saintes Ecritures', NRT 74: 3-20.

1958 Le Problème du Sens Plénier des Saintes Ecritures, Louvain/Bruges-Paris (ALBO 3.9, taken from ETL 34: 5-20).

1963 'La Nouvelle Alliance en Jer 31,31-34', CBQ 25: 12-21.

1967 'Levels of meaning in the Bible', Concilium 3.10: 62-9.

1968 Le Messianisme Royal, Paris.

1971 'La relève du Messianisme royal: Le Règne de Dieu et l'Attente de sa venue' and 'Le messianisme israélite: La relève prophétique', ETL 47: 114-143, 321-39.

Courtade, G.
1949 'Le sens de l'histoire dans l'Écriture et la classification usuelle des sens scripturaires',RechSR 36: 136-141.

1950 'Les Écritures ont-elles un sens "plénier"?', RechSR 37: 481-97.

Cox, D.
1961 History and Myth: The World Around Us and the World Within, London.

Craig, C.T.
1943 'Biblical Theology and the Rise of Historicism', JBL 62: 281-94.

Cranfield, C.E.B.
1965 'The Christian's Social Responsibility according to the New Testament' in The Service of God, London: 49-66.

Crehan, F.J.
1963 'The Bible in the Roman Catholic Church from Trent to the Present Day', CHB III: 199-237.

Crenshaw, J.L.
1971 Prophetic Conflict: Its Effect Upon Israelite Religion, Berlin (BZAW 124).

Crespy, G.
1963 'Une théologie de l'histoire est-elle possible?', RThPh 13: 97-123.

Crockett, L.C.
1966 'The Old Testament in the Gospel of Luke: With Emphasis on the Interpretation of Isaiah 61.1-2', Dissn, Brown University.

Cullmann, O.
1946 Christ and Time: The Primitive Christian Conception of Time and History, ET: London 1962[2],1951[1] (German 1962[3],1946

1949 'La nécessité et la fonction de l'exégèse philologique et historique de la Bible', repr.in Boisset(1955): 131-147 (originally in VerbC 3,1949).

1957a The State in the New Testament, London.

1957b The Christology of the New Testament, ET: London 1959 (German 1957).

1964 'The Connection of Primal Events and End Events with the New Testament Redemptive History', _OTCF_: 115-123.

1965 _Salvation in History_, ET: London 1967 (German 1965).

Cunliffe-Jones, H.

1945 _The Authority of the Biblical Revelation_, London.

1973 _A Word for our Time? Zechariah 9-14, the New Testament and Today_, London.

Curr, H.S.

1951 'Progressive Revelation', _JTVI_ 83: 1-23.

Dahl, N.A.

1941 _Das Volk Gottes: Eine Untersuchung zum Kirchenbewusstsein des Urchristentums_, Oslo 1941 (Darmstadt 1963[2]).

1956 'The People of God', _ER_ 9: 154-161.

Dahlberg, B.T.

1975 'The Typological Use of Jeremiah 1: 4-19 in Matthew 16: 13-23', _JBL_ 94: 73-80.

Dalman, G.

1896 _Das Alte Testament ein Wort Gottes: Ein Vortrag_, Leipzig.

Daniélou, J.

1948a _Origen_, ET: New York 1955 (French 1948).

1948b 'Les divers sens de l'Écriture dans la tradition chrétienne primitive', _ETL_ 24: 119-126.

1948c 'L'unité des deux Testaments dans l'oeuvre d'Origène', _RevSR_ 22: 27-56.

1950a _From Shadows to Reality: Studies in the Biblical Typology of the Fathers_, ET: London 1960 (French: _Sacramentum Futuri_, 1950).

1950b Review of Coppens 1948, _DV_ 16: 149-153.

1950c Review of Vischer 1934, _DV_ 15: 139-141.

1951 'Qu'est-ce que la typologie?' in Auvray (1951): 199-205.

1953 *The Lord of History: Reflections on the Inner Meaning of History*, ET: London 1958 (French 1953).

1954 'The Fathers and the Scriptures', *Theology* 57: 83-9 (originally in *Eastern Churches' Quarterly* 10: 265-73)

1966 *Études d'exégèse judéo-chrétienne (Les Testimonia)*, Paris.

1969 'Patristic Literature' in *Historical Theology* (The Pelican Guide to Modern Theology, II, by J. Daniélou *et al.*), Harmondsworth, Middx: 23-127.

1958-73 *A History of Early Christian Doctrine: I. The Theology of Jewish Christianity II. Gospel Message and Hellenistic Culture*, ET: London I: 1964; II:1973 (French I: 1958; II: n.d.).

Darlapp, A.
1960 'Heilsgeschichte: II. Zur Theologie der H.', *LTK*[2] 5: 153-6.

Daube, D.
1963 *The Exodus Pattern in the Bible*, London.

Davidson, A.B.
1900 'The Uses of the Old Testament for Edification', *Exp* 6.1: 1-18.

1903a *Old Testament Prophecy*, Edinburgh.

1903b *Biblical and Literary Essays*, London.

1904 *The Theology of the Old Testament*, Edinburgh (ed. after the author's death by S.D.F. Salmond).

Davidson, Richard
1941 'The Old Testament Preparation for the New Testament Doctrine of the Church', *RExp* 38: 49-56.

Davidson, Robert
1964 *The Old Testament*, London.

1970 'The Old Testament' in *Biblical Criticism* (The Pelican Guide to Modern Theology, III, by R. Davidson and A.R.C.Leaney), Harmondsworth, Middx: 23-165.

Davies, G.H.
1953 *The Approach to the Old Testament*, London (Inaugural lecture, Durham).

1956 'An Approach to the Problem of Old Testament Mythology', *PEQ* 88: 83-91.

1970 'Gerhard von Rad, *Old Testament Theology*' in Laurin (1970): 63-89.

Davies, W.D.
1948 *Paul and Rabbinic Judaism: Some Rabbinic Elements in Pauline Theology*, London 1955[2], 1948[1].

1968a 'Torah and Dogma: A Comment', *HTR* 61: 87-105 (repr. in *The Gospel and the Land: Early Christianity and Jewish Territorial Doctrine*, Berkeley/Los Angeles/London 1974: 390-404).

1968b 'Reflections on Judaism and Christianity' in Leenhardt Fs: 39-54 (repr. in *The Gospel and the Land*: 377-89).

1969 'The Relevance of the Moral Teaching of the Early Church' in Black Fs: 30-49.

Davis, L.
1965 'Typology in Barth's Doctrine of Scripture', *ATR* 47: 33-49.

Deissler, A.
1972 *Die Grundbotschaft des Alten Testaments: Ein theologischer Durchblick*, Freiburg/Basel/Wien 1972.

Delitzsch, Franz
1881 *Old Testament History of Redemption*, Edinburgh.

1883 *Neueste Traumgesichte des antisemitischen Propheten: Sendschreiben an Prof. Böckler in Greifswald*, Erlangen.

1888 *Der tiefe Graben zwischen alter und moderner Theologie: Ein Bekenntnis*, Leipzig.

1890 *Messianic Prophecies in Historical Succession*, ET: Edinburgh 1891 (German 1890).

Delitzsch, Friedrich
1920-21 *Die grosse Täuschung*, Stuttgart/Berlin I: 1920; II: 1921 (volume I was completed in 1914, though not published until after the First World War).

Delling, G.

1959 'πλήρης, πληρόω...', *TDNT* 6: 283-311.

Denbeaux, F.J.

1951 'The Biblical Hope', *Interpn* 5:285-303.

Dentan, R.C.

1950 *Preface to Old Testament Theology*, New York 1950, revd edn 1963 (Yale Studies in Religion 14).

1951 'The Unity of the Old Testament', *Interpn* 5: 153-173.

Dequeker, L.

1969 'Pourquoi les chrétiens lisent-ils encore l'Ancien Testament?', *Collectanea mechliniensia* 54: 329-41 (French translation from Dutch: *Getuigenis* 13, 1968-9: 37-48).

Devreese, R.

1946 'La méthode exégétique de Théodore de Mopsueste', *RB* 53: 207-41.

1948 *Essai sur Théodore de Mopsueste*, Vatican (Studi e Testi 141).

Diehn, O.

1958 *Bibliographie zur Geschichte des Kirchenkampfes 1933-1945*, Göttingen (AGK 1).

Diem, H.

1951 *Theologie als kirchliche Wissenschaft: I. Exegese und Historie*, Munich.

1953 'Die Einheit der Schrift', *EvTh* 13: 385-405 (a shortened version forms ch.9 of *Dogmatics*).

1954 'Jesus, der Christus des Alten Testamentes', *EvTh* 14: 437-48 (repr. with only slight changes as *Dogmatics*, ch

1955 *Dogmatics*, ET: London/Edinburgh 1959 (German: *Theologie als kirchliche Wissenschaft: II. Dogmatik*, 1955).

Diepold, P.

1972 *Israels Land*, Stuttgart/Berlin/Cologne/Mainz (BWANT 95).

Diestel, L.
1869 *Geschichte des Alten Testamentes in der christlichen Kirche*, Jena.

Diétrich, S.de
1945 *Le dessein de Dieu: Itinéraire biblique*, Neuchâtel.

Dillenberger, J.
1964 'Revelational Discernment and the Problem of the Two Testaments', *OTCF*: 159-175.

Dillistone, F.W.
1948 *The Word of God and the People of God*, London.

Dinkler, E.
1950 'Bibelautorität und Bibelkritik', *ZTK* 47: 70-93.

Dodd, C.H.
1928 *The Authority of the Bible*, London 1928, 1960 (reset and corrections made).

1935 *The Parables of the Kingdom*, London 1935, revd edn 1961.

1936 *The Apostolic Preaching and its Developments: Three lectures with an appendix on Eschatology and History*, London 1936, reset 1944.

1938 *History and the Gospel*, London 1938, revd edn 1964.

1946a *The Bible To-day*, Cambridge.

1946b 'Natural Law in the New Testament', repr. in his *New Testament Studies*, Manchester 1953: 129-142 (originally published as 'Natural Law in the Bible', *Theology* 49, 1946: 130-134,161-7).

1948 'Autorité et rôle de la Bible', *ETR* 23: 11-15.

1951a *Gospel and Law: The Relation of Faith and Ethics in Early Christianity*, Cambridge.

1951b 'The Relevance of the Bible' in Richardson and Schweitzer (1951): 157-162.

1952a According to the Scriptures: The Substructure of New Testament Theology, London.

1952b The Old Testament in the New, London (lecture, University of London).

1953 The Interpretation of the Fourth Gospel, Cambridge.

1971 The Founder of Christianity, London.

Douglass, P.F.
1935 God Among the Germans, Philadelphia.

Dressler, H.H.P.
1972 'The Authority of the Holy Scriptures in Some of the Contemporary German Protestant Theologians', Dissn, Northwest Baptist Theological College, Vancouver.

Dreyfus, F.
1955 'La doctrine du reste d'Israël chez le prophète Isaïe', RSPT 39: 361-86.

1967 'The Existential Value of the Old Testament', Concilium 3.10: 18-23.

Driver, S.R.
1892 'The Moral and Devotional Value of the Old Testament', ExpT 4: 110-113.

1901 'The Old Testament in the Light of Today', Exp 6.3: 27-49 (repr. in The Higher Criticism, S.R.Driver and A.F.Kirkpatrick, London 1912, new edn: ch.3).

1905 'The Permanent Religious Value of the Old Testament', The Interpreter 1: 10-21 (also repr. in The Higher Criticism: ch.4).

Dubarle, A.
1947 'Le sens spirituel de l'Écriture', RSPT 31: 41-72.

1951 'La lecture chrétienne de l'Ancien Testament' in Auvray (1951):206-33.

Ducros, P.
1945 La Bible et La méthode historique, Libourne (?).

Duesberg, H.
1967 '"He opened their minds to understand the Scriptures"', Concilium 3.10: 56-61.

Duff, A.
1910 History of Old Testament Criticism, London.

Duling, D.C.
1974 'The Promises to David and their Entrance into Christianity - Nailing down a Likely Hypothesis', NTS 20: 55-77.

Dupont, J.
1953 'L'utilisation apologétique de l'Ancien Testament dans les discours des Actes', ETL 29: 289-327.

1962 'L'interprétation des psaumes dans les Actes des Apôtres' in de Langhe (1962): 357-88.

1968 'Nova et vetera (Matthieu 13: 52)' in Leenhardt Fs: 55-63.

Durham, J.I.
1970 'George A.F. Knight, A Christian Theology of the Old Testament' in Laurin (1970): 171-190.

Ebeling, G.
1942 Evangelische Evangelienauslegung: Eine Untersuchung zu Luthers Hermeneutik, repr. Darmstadt 1969 (originally Munich 1942).

1950 'Die Bedeutung der historisch-kritischen Methode für die protestantische Theologie und Kirche', ZTK 47: 1-46.

1951 'Die Anfänge von Luthers Hermeneutik', ZTK 48: 172-230.

1955 'The Meaning of "Biblical Theology"', JTS 6: 210-25 (repr. in Hodgson (1960): 49-67).

Edgar, S.L.
1962 'Respect for Context in Quotations from the Old Testament', NTS 9: 55-62.

Edsman, C.M.
1947 'Gammal och ny typologisk tolkning av G.T.', SEA 12: 69-93.

Ehrhardt, A.

1968 'A Biblical View of the People of God', <u>AER</u> 159: 126-138.

Eichrodt, W.

1920 <u>Die Hoffnung des ewigen Friedens im alten Israel: Ein Beitrag zu der Frage nach der israelitischen Eschatologie</u>, Gütersloh (BFChTh 25.3).

1929 'Hat die alttestamentliche Theologie noch selbständige Bedeutung innerhalb der alttestamentlichen Wissenschaft?', <u>ZAW</u> 47: 83-91.

1933 <u>Theology of the Old Testament</u> I, ET: London 1961 (German 1959[6], 1933[1]).

1935-9 <u>Theology of the Old Testament</u> II, ET: London 1967 (German 1964[5], 1935-9[1]

1936 <u>Das Alte Testament und der christliche Glaube</u>, Stuttgart/Basel.*

1938 'Zur Frage der theologischen Exegese des Alten Testamentes', <u>ThBl</u> 17: 73-87.

1948a 'Offenbarung und Geschichte im Alten Testament', <u>ThZ</u> 4: 321-31.

1948b 'Le message social et économique de l'Ancien Testament pour le monde présent', <u>ETR</u> 23: 96-102.

1950 'The Right Interpretation of the Old Testament: A Study of Jeremiah 7: 1-15', <u>ThTo</u> 7: 15-25.

1951 <u>Gottes Ruf im Alten Testament: Die alttestamentliche Botschaft im Lichte des Evangeliums</u>, Zürich (Zwingli Bücherei 64).

1954 Review of Wright 1952, <u>JBL</u> 73: 240-42.

1955 'Les rapports du Nouveau Testament et de l'Ancien Testament' in Boisset (1955): 105-130.

1956 'Heilserfahrung und Zeitverständnis im Alten Testament', <u>ThZ</u> 12: 103-125.

1957a 'Is Typological Exegesis an Appropriate Method?', ET in EOTI: 224-45 (originally SVT 4, 1957: 161-180).

1957b 'Vom Symbol zum Typos: Ein Beitrag zur Sacharja-Exegese', ThZ 13: 509-22.

1957c 'The Law and the Gospel: The Meaning of the Ten Commandments in Israel and for Us', Interpn 11: 23-40.

1961 'The Problem of Old Testament Theology', Excursus to Theology of the Old Testament I, ET: London 1961: 512-20.

1965 'Covenant and Law: Thoughts on Recent Discussion', Interpn 20: 302-21.

1974 'Darf man heute noch von einem Gottesbund mit Israel reden?', ThZ 30: 193-206.

Eissfeldt, O.

1919 'Das Alte und das Neue Testament in ihrer Stellung zur Kultur', repr. in Kleine Schriften I, Tübingen 1962:44-55 (originally Preussische Jahrbücher 178, 1919: 373-84).

1921 'Christentum und Alte Testament: Eine Bemerkung zu Harnacks Marcion', repr. in Kleine Schriften I: 72-5 (originally Kartellzeitung des Eisenacher Kartells 31, 1920-21: 82-3 and Adolf von Harnack zum 70. Geburtstag, Leipzig 1921: 29-33).

1926 'Israelitisch-jüdische Religionsgeschichte und alttestamentliche Theologie', ZAW 44: 1-12 (repr. in Kleine Schriften I).

1931 'Werden, Wesen und Wert geschichtlicher Betrachtung der israelitisch-jüdisch-christlichen Religion', repr. in Kleine Schriften I: 247-65 (originally Zeitschrift für Missionskunde und Religionswissenschaft 46, 1-24).

1934 Einleitung in das Alte Testament, unter Einschluss der Apokryphen und Pseudipigraphen: Entstehungsgeschichte des Alten Testaments, Tübingen 1934[1] (1964[3], ET: 1965).

1947 'Ist der Gott des Alten Testaments auch der des Neuen Testaments?' in Geschichtliches und Übergeschichtliches im Alten Testament, Berlin (ThStKr 109.2): 37-54.

Eliade, M.
1949 *The Myth of the Eternal Return*, ET: London 1955 (USA: *Cosmos and History*, 1954; French 1949).

Elliger, K.
1951 'Der Jakobskampf am Jabbok: Gen 32, 22ff. als hermeneutisches Problem', *ZTK* 48: 1-31.

\- *Jesaja II*, Neukirchen (BK 11), 5 fascicles have appeared so far.

Elliger, W.
1973 'Müntzer und das Alte Testament' in K.Elliger Fs: 57-64.

Ellis, D.J.
1969 'The New Testament Use of the Old Testament' in Howley (1969): 130-138.

Ellis, E.E.
1957 *Paul's Use of the Old Testament*, Edinburgh.

1969 'Midrash, Targum and New Testament Quotations' in Black Fs: 61-9.

1971 'Midraschartige Züge in den Reden Apostelgeschichte', *ZNW* 62: 94-104.

Ellison, H.L.
1953a *The Centrality of the Messianic Idea for the Old Testament*, London.

1953b 'Typology', *EQ* 25: 158-166.

1959 Review of Vriezen 1954, *EQ* 31: 113-115.

1969 *The Message of the Old Testament*, Exet

Elmslie, W.A.L.
1948 *How Came Our Faith: A Study of the Religion of Israel and its Significanc for the Modern World*, Cambridge.

Emerton, J.A.
1958 'The Origin of the Son of Man Imagery' *JTS* 9: 225-42.

Engelbrecht, B.
1971 'A.A. van Ruler, moderne teokraat', *NGTT* 12: 188-211.

Erickson, M.J.
1974 'Pannenberg's Use of History as a Solution to the Religious Language Problem', JETS 17: 99-105.

Ernst, J.
1972 'Schriftauslegung und Auferstehungsglaube bei Lukas' in Ernst (1972): 177-192.

Ewald, H.
1871 Revelation: Its Nature and Record, ET: Edinburgh 1884 (German: Die Lehre der Bibel von Gott oder Theologie des Alten und Neuen Bundes: I. Die Lehre vom Wort Gottes, 1871).

Fahey, M.A.
1971 Cyprian and the Bible: a Study in Third-Century Exegesis, Tübingen (BGBH 9).

Fairbairn, P.
1864 The Typology of Scripture, Viewed in Connection with the Whole Series of The Divine Dispensations, Edinburgh 1870[5], 1864[4].

Farmer, H.H.
1952 'The Bible: Its Significance and Authority', IB 1: 3-31.

Farrar, F.W.
1886 History of Interpretation, London (Bampton Lectures 1885).

Fawcett, T.
1973 Hebrew Myth and Christian Gospel, London.

Feldges, F.
1936 'Die Frage des alttestamentlichen Christuszeugnisses: Zum Angriff von Gerhard von Rad auf Wilhelm Vischer', ThBl 15: 25-30.

Fensham, F.C.
1967 'Covenant, Promise and Expectation in the Bible', ThZ 23: 305-22.

1971 'The Covenant as Giving Expression to the Relationship between the Old and New Testament', TynB 22: 82-94.

Fernández, A.
1927 'Hermeneutica' in *Institutiones Biblicae, scholis accommodatae* (ed. A. Vaccari) I: Rome 1927[2]: 293-430 (1951[6]: 363-509).*

Ferré, N.F.S.
1959 'Notes by a Theologian on Biblical Hermeneutics', *JBL* 78: 105-114.

Festorazzi, F.
1967 'The Faith of Both Testaments as Salvific Experience: "We are safe." (Jeremiah 7.10)', *Concilium* 3.10: 24-31

Filson, F.V.
1950 'Method in Studying Biblical History', *JBL* 69: 1-18.

1951 'The Unity of the Old and the New Testaments: A Bibliographical Survey' *Interpn* 5: 134-152.

1952 'The Interpreter at Work: VIII. Adolf von Harnack and his "What is Christianity"', *Interpn* 6: 51-62.

1972 'The Unity between the Testaments', *IOVCB*: 989-93.

Fischer, J.
1929 'Das Problem des neuen Exodus in Isaias c.40-55.', *ThQ* 110: 111-130.

Fisher, L.R.
1964 'Betrayed by Friends: An Expository Study of Psalm 22', *Interpn* 18: 20-38.

Fitzmyer, J.A.
1957 '"4 Q Testimonia" and the New Testament *ThSt* 18: 513-37 (repr. in 1971: 59-89).

1961 'The use of explicit Old Testament quotations in Qumran literature and in the New Testament', *NTS* 7: 297-333 (repr. in 1971: 3-58).

1963 '"Now This Melchizedek..." (Heb 7,1)', *CBQ* 25: 305-21.

1971 *Essays on the Semitic Background of the New Testament*, London.

Florovsky, G.
1951 'Revelation and Interpretation' in Richardson and Schweitzer (1951): 163-1

Flusser, D.
1960 'Blessed Are the Poor in Spirit', *IEJ* 10: 1-13.

Foakes-Jackson, F.J.
1908-9 'The Old Testament before Modern Criticism', *The Interpreter* 5: 46-55, 157-166.

Fohrer, G.
1950 'Die zeitliche und überzeitliche Bedeutung des Alten Testaments', repr. in *Studien zur alttestamentlichen Theologie und Geschichte (1949-1966)*, Berlin 1969: 23-38 (originally *EvTh* 9:447-60).

1957 *Messiasfrage und Bibelverständnis*, Tübingen (Sammlung gemeinverständlicher Vorträge und Schriften aus dem Gebiet der Theologie und Religionsgeschichte 213/214).

1960 'Die Struktur der alttestamentlichen Eschatologie', *TLZ* 85: 401-20 (repr. in *Studien zur alttestamentlichen Prophetie (1949-1965)*, Berlin 1967, BZAW 99: 32-58).

1961 'Tradition und Interpretation im Alten Testament', *ZAW* 73: 1-30 (repr. in *Studien zur atl. Theologie*).

1964 'Prophetie und Geschichte', *TLZ* 89: 481-500.

1966 'The Centre of a Theology of the Old Testament', *NGTT* 7, 1966: 198-206 (German translation: *ThZ* 24: 161-172; also substantially incorporated into 1972: ch.4).

1970 'Das Alte Testament und das Thema "Christologie"', *EvTh* 30: 281-98 (a revised version of this article forms ch.1 of 1972).

1972 *Theologische Grundstrukturen des Alten Testaments*, Berlin (Theologische Bibliothek Töpelmann 24).

Forstman, H.J.
1962 *Word and Spirit: Calvin's Doctrine of Biblical Authority*, Stanford, Ca.

Fosdick, H.E.
1938 *A Guide to Understanding the Bible: The Development of Ideas within the Old and New Testaments*, London.

Foulkes, F.
1958 *The Acts of God: A Study of the Basis of Typology in the Old Testament*, London.

France, R.T.
1970 'In all the Scriptures - a Study of Jesus' Typology', *TSFB* 56: 13-16.

1971 *Jesus and the Old Testament: His Application of Old Testament Passages to Himself and His Mission*, London.

Franks, R.S.
1933 'The Interpretation of Holy Scripture in the Theological System of Alexander of Hales' in Harris Fs: 83-95.

Freed, E.D.
1965 *Old Testament Quotations in the Gospel of John*, Leiden (SNovT 11).

Freedman, D.N.
1967 'The Biblical Idea of History', *Interpn* 21: 32-49.

Fretheim, T.E.
1972 Review of van Ruler 1955, *Interpn* 26: 478-80

Friederichsen, D.W.
1970 'The Hermeneutics of Typology', Dissn, Dallas Theological Seminary.*

Fries, H.
1967 'Spero ut intelligam: Bemerkungen zu einer Theologie der Hoffnung' in Schmaus Fs: 353-75.

Fries, P.
1973 'Van Ruler on the Holy Spirit and the salvation of the earth', *RefR* 26: 123-135.*

Frisque, J.
1960 *Oscar Cullmann: Une théologie de l'histoire du salut*, Tournai, Belgium (Cahiers de l'actualité religieuse 11).

Fritsch, C.T.
1946-7 'Biblical Typology', *BS* 103: 293-305, 418-30; 104: 87-100, 214-22.

1951 'The Interpreter at Work: V. Bengel, the Student of Scripture', *Interpn* 5: 203-15.

1966 'ΤΟ 'ΑΝΤΙΤΥΠΟΝ' in Vriezen Fs: 100-107.

Fröhlich, K.
1967 'Die Mitte des Neuen Testaments: Oscar Cullmanns Beitrag zur Theologie der Gegenwart' in Cullmann Fs: 203-19.

Frör, K.
1961 Biblische Hermeneutik: Zur Schriftauslegung in Predigt und Unterricht, Munich 1964², 1961¹.

Frost, S.B.
1952a Old Testament Apocalyptic: Its Origins and Growth, London.

1952b 'Eschatology and Myth', VT 2: 70-80.

1957 'History and the Bible', CJT 3: 87-96.

1966 'Apocalyptic and History' in Hyatt (1966): 98-113.

Fruchon, P.
1971 'Sur l'herméneutique de Gerhard von Rad', RSPT 55: 4-32.

Fuchs, E.
1954a Hermeneutik, Bad Cannstatt.

1954b 'Gesetz, Vernunft und Geschichte: Antwort an Erwin Reisner', ZTK 51: 251-70.

1963 'Theologie oder Ideologie? Bemerkungen zu einem heilsgeschichtlichen Programm', TLZ 88: 257-60.

Fuhrmann, P.T.
1952 'The Interpreter at Work: XI. Calvin, The Expositor of Scripture', Interpn 6: 188-209.

Fuller, D.P.
1965 Easter Faith and History, London 1968 (USA 1965).

1966 'A New German Theological Movement', SJT 19: 160-175.

1968 'The Fundamental Presupposition of the Historical Method', ThZ 24: 93-101.

Fullerton, K.
1919 Prophecy and Authority: A Study in the History of the Doctrine and Interpretation of Scripture, New York.

Funk, R.W.
1966 Language, Hermeneutic, and Word of God: The Problem of Language in the New Testament and Contemporary Theology, New York.

1973 'The Looking-Glass Tree Is for the Birds: Ezekiel 17: 22-24; Mark 4:30-32' Interpn 27: 3-9.

Gaebelein, F.E.
1959 'The Unity of the Bible' in Henry (1959): 387-401.

Galloway, A.D.
1973 Wolfhart Pannenberg, London.

Gamble, C.
1951 'The Nature of Biblical Theology: a Bibliographical Study', Interpn 5: 462-7.

1953 'The Literature of Biblical Theology: A Bibliographical Survey', Interpn 7: 466-8

1955 'The Method of Biblical Theology: A Bibliographical Study', Interpn 9: 91-9.

Geest, J.E.L. van der
1972 Le Christ et l'Ancien Testament chez Tertullian: Recherche terminologique, Nijmegen 1972 (LCP 22).

Gehman, H.S.
1950 'The Covenant - The Old Testament Foundation of the Church', ThTo 7:26-41.

1955 'An Insight and a Realization: A Study of the New Covenant', Interpn 9: 279-93.

1960 Review of Knight 1959a, ThTo 17: 390-91.

Gerdes, H.
1955 Luthers Streit mit den Schwärmern um das rechte Verständnis des Gesetzes Mose, Göttingen.

Gerhardsson, B.
1961 Memory and Manuscript: Oral Tradition and Written Transmission in Rabbinic Judaism and Early Christianity, Uppsala.

Gerleman, G.
1956 'Gamla testamentet i förkunnelsen', _SvTK_ 32: 81-94.

1965 _Ruth . Das Hohelied_, Neukirchen (BK 18).

1973 _Esther_, Neukirchen (BK 21).

Gese, H.
1958 'The Idea of History in the Ancient Near East and the Old Testament', ET in _JTC_ 1, 1965: 49-64 (German: _ZTK_ 55, 1958: 127-145).

1968 'Psalm 22 und das Neue Testament: Der älteste Bericht vom Tode Jesu und die Entstehung des Herrenmahles', _ZTK_ 65: 1-22.

1970 'Erwägungen zur Einheit der biblischen Theologie', _ZTK_ 67: 417-36.

1974 _Vom Sinai zum Zion: Alttestamentliche Beiträge zur biblischen Theologie_, Munich (BEvTh 64) - includes reprints of the three preceding articles.

Geyer, H.G.
1962 'Geschichte als theologisches Problem: Bemerkungen zu W. Pannenbergs Geschichtstheologie', _EvTh_ 22: 92-104.

1965 'Zur Frage der Notwendigkeit des Alten Testamentes', _EvTh_ 25: 207-37.

1967 'Ansichten zu Jürgen Moltmanns "Theologie der Hoffnung"', _TLZ_ 92: 481-92, 561-76.

Gilbert, G.H.
1908 _Interpretation of the Bible: A Short History_, New York.

Gilkey, L.B.
1961 'Cosmology, Ontology, and the Travail of Biblical Language', _JR_ 41: 194-205.

Glasson, T.F.
1963 _Moses in the Fourth Gospel_, London (SBT 40).

Glen, J.S.
1951 'Jesus Christ and the Unity of the Bible', _Interpn_ 5: 259-67.

Glover, W.B.
1954 Evangelical Nonconformists and Higher Criticism in the Nineteenth Century, London.

Gogarten, F.
1933 Einheit von Evangelium und Volkstum?, Hamburg.

1934 Ist Volksgesetz Gottesgesetz? Eine Auseinandersetzung mit meinen Kritiker[n], Hamburg.

1953 'Theology and History', ET in JTC 4, 1967: 35-81 (German ZTK 50, 1953: 339-94).

Goldingay, J.
1972 '"That you may know that Yahweh is God": A study in the relationship between theology and historical truth in the Old Testament', TynB 23: 58-93.

Gollwitzer, H.
1956 'Zur Einheit von Gesetz und Evangelium in Barth Fs: 287-309.

1963 The Existence of God as Confessed by Faith, ET: London 1965 (German 1964[3], 1963[1], BEvTh 34).

Good, E.M.
1966 'The Meaning of Demythologization' in Kegley (1966): 21-40.

Goodenough, E.R.
1923 The Theology of Justin Martyr, Jena.

Goppelt, L.
1939 Typos: die typologische Deutung des Alten Testaments im Neuen, Gütersloh 1939, reprinted Darmstadt 1969.

1964 'Apokalyptik und Typologie bei Paulus', TLZ 89: 321-44 (repr. as appendix to Typos).

1969 'τύπος', TDNT 8: 246-59.

Gottwald, N.K.
1970 'W.Eichrodt, Theology of the Old Testament' in Laurin (1970): 23-62.

Goulder, M.D.
1964 Type and History in Acts, London.

Grant, R.M.

1951 'The Place of the Old Testament in Early Christianity', Interpn 5: 186-202.

1952 'History of the Interpretation of the Bible: I. Ancient Period', IB 1: 106-114.

1957 The Letter and the Spirit, London.

1963 'Scripture and Tradition in St. Ignatius of Antioch', CBQ 25: 322-35.

1965 A Short History of the Interpretation of the Bible, London (revd edn of The Bible in the Church, 1948).

Gray, J.

1974 'The Day of Yahweh in Cultic Experience and Eschatological Prospect', SEA 39: 5-37.

Grech, P.

1973 'The "Testimonia" and Modern Hermeneutics', NTS 19: 318-24.

Green, W.H.

1895 The Higher Criticism of the Pentateuch, London.

1899 General Introduction to the Old Testament: The Canon, London.

Greer, R.A.

1961 Theodore of Mopsuestia: Exegete and Theologian, London.

Greidanus, S.

1970 Sola Scriptura: Problems and Principles in Preaching Historical Texts, Kampen.

Greig, A.J.

1974 'Geschichte and Heilsgeschichte in Old Testament Interpretation with Particular Reference to the Work of Gerhard von Rad', Dissn, Edinburgh.

Grelot, P.

1957 'L'interprétation catholique des livres saints' in Robert and Feuillet (1957): 169-212.

1962a Sens chrétien de l'Ancien Testament: Esquisse d'un traité dogmatique, Paris.

1962b 'Les figures bibliques', NRT 84: 561-78, 673-98.

1965 La Bible, Parole de Dieu: Introduction théologique à l'étude de l'Ecriture Sainte, Paris.

1966 'Tradition as Source and Environment of Scripture', Concilium 2.10: 5-15.

1968 'La lecture chrétienne de l'Ancien Testament' in Weber and Schmitt (1968): 29-50.

Gressmann, H.
1905 Der Ursprung der israelitisch-jüdischen Eschatologie, Göttingen.

1929 Der Messias, Göttingen (rewritten form of 1905).

Gribomont, J.
1946 'Le lien des deux Testaments, selon la théologie de saint Thomas: Notes sur le sens spirituel et implicite des Saintes Écritures', ETL 22: 70-89.

1950 'Sens plénier, sens typique et sens littéral' in Problèmes et Méthode d'exégèse théologique (L. Cerfaux et al.), Louvain/Bruges-Paris (ALBO 2.16): 21-31.

Grin, E.
1961 'L'unité des deux Testaments selon Calvin', ThZ 17: 175-186.

Grobel, K.
1962 'Interpretation, History and Principles of', IDB 2: 718-24.

Grogan, G.W.
1967a 'The Experience of Salvation in the Old and New Testaments', VoxEv 5: 4-26.

1967b 'The New Testament Interpretation of the Old Testament', TynB 18: 54-76.

Grönbaek, J.H.
1959 'Zur Frage der Eschatologie in der Verkündigung der Gerichtspropheten', SEA 24: 5-21.

Gross, H.
1956 <u>Die Idee des ewigen und allgemeinen Weltfriedens im alten Orient und im Alten Testament</u>, Trier (Trierer theologische Studien 7).

1959 'Zum Problem Verheissung und Erfüllung', <u>BZ</u> 3: 3-17.

Grunow, R.
1955 'Dietrich Bonhoeffers Schriftauslegung', <u>EvTh</u> 15: 200-214.

Guersen, M.W.J.
1968 Review of Miskotte 1956a, <u>RefTR</u> 27: 73-5.

Guilding, A.
1960 <u>The Fourth Gospel and Jewish Worship: A study of the relation of St. John's Gospel to the ancient Jewish lectionary system</u>, Oxford.

Guillet, J.
1949 'Thème de la marche au désert dans l'Ancien et le Nouveau Testament', <u>RechSR</u> 36: 161-181.

Gundry, R.H.
1967 <u>The Use of the Old Testament in St Matthew's Gospel, with special reference to the Messianic Hope</u>, Leiden (SNovT 18).

Gundry, S.N.
1969 'Typology as a Means of Interpretation: Past and Present', <u>BETS</u> 12: 233-40.

Gunkel, H.
1895 <u>Schöpfung und Chaos in Urzeit und Endzeit: Eine religionsgeschichtliche Untersuchung über Gen 1 und Ap Joh 12</u>, Göttingen.

1914 'What is Left of the Old Testament?', ET in <u>What Remains of the Old Testament and Other Essays</u>, London 1928 (originally in <u>Die Deutsche Rundschau</u> 41, 1914: 13-56).

Gunneweg, A.H.S.
1968 'Über die Prädikabilität alttestamentlicher Texte', <u>ZTK</u> 65: 389-413.

Guthrie, H.H.
1961 <u>God and History in the Old Testament</u>, London.

Guzie, T.W.
1971 'Patristic Hermeneutics and the Meaning of Tradition', ThSt 32: 647-58.

Haag, H.
1971 Vom alten zum neuen Pascha: Geschichte und Theologie des Osterfestes, Stuttgart (Stuttgarter Bibelstudien 49).

Haenchen, E.
1963 'Hamans Galgen und Christi Kreuz' in Hirsch Fs: 113-133.

Hagen, K.
1970 'The Problem of Testament in Luther's Lectures on Hebrews', HTR 63: 61-90.

Hagner, D.A.
1973 The Use of the Old and New Testaments in Clement of Rome, Leiden (SNovT 34).

Hahn, Ferdinand
1971 'Genesis 15_6 im Neuen Testament' in von Rad Fs: 90-107.

Hahn, Fritz
1951 'Die heilige Schrift als Problem der Auslegung bei Luther', EvTh 10: 407-24.

Hahn, H.F.
1954 The Old Testament in Modern Research, Philadelphia 1966 (original edn 1954), esp. ch.7.

Hahn, V.
1969 Das wahre Gesetz: Eine Untersuchung der Auffassung des Ambrosius von Mailand vom Verhältnis der beiden Testamente, Münster (Münsterische Beiträge zur Theologie 33).

Hall, B.
1965 'The Old Testament in the History of the Church', LQHR 190: 30-36.

Hamerton-Kelly, R.G.
1970 'The Temple and the Origins of Jewish Apocalyptic', VT 20: 1-15.

1973 Pre-existence, Wisdom and the Son of Man, Cambridge (SNTS Mon 21).

Hamilton, F.E.
1927 The Basis of Christian Faith: A Modern Defense of the Christian Religion, New York/London 1946[3],1927[1].

Hamp, V.
1958 'Biblische Theologie: I. B.Th. des Alten Testamentes', LTK² 2: 439-44.

Hänel, J.
1919 Der Schriftbegriff Jesu: Studie zur Kanongeschichte und religiösen Beurteilung des Alten Testamentes, Gütersloh (BFChTh 24.5/6).

1931 Die Religion der Heiligkeit, Gütersloh.

Hanson, A.T.
1965 Jesus Christ in the Old Testament, London.

1974 Studies in Paul's Technique and Theology, London.

Hanson, P.D.
1975 The Dawn of Apocalyptic, Philadelphia.

Hanson, R.P.C.
1945 'Moses in the Typology of St Paul', Theology 48: 174-7.

1959 Allegory and Event: A Study of the Sources and Significance of Origen's Interpretation of Scripture, London.

1961 'Notes on Tertullian's Interpretation of Scripture', JTS 12: 273-9.

1970 'Biblical Exegesis in the Early Church', CHB I: 412-53.

Harman, A.M.
1968 'Paul's Use of the Psalms', Dissn, Westminster Theological Seminary.

Harnack, A.von
1902 The Mission and Expansion of Christianity in the First Three Centuries, ET: London/New York 1908², 1904-5¹ (German 1906², 1902¹, 1924⁴).

1921 Marcion: Das Evangelium vom fremden Gott, Leipzig 1921 (1924², repr. Darmstadt 1960).

1923 Neue Studien zu Marcion, Leipzig (TU 44.4).

1928 'Das Alte Testament in den Paulinischen Briefen und in den Paulinischen Gemeinden', SAB 1928: Philosophisch-historische Klasse: 123-141.

Haroutinian, J.
1947 'The Bible and the Word of God: The Importance of Biblical Theology', Interpn 1: 291-308.

Harrington, W.J.
1973 The Path of Biblical Theology, Dublin.

Harris, J.R.
1916-20 Testimonies, Cambridge i: 1916; ii: 1920

Harrison, R.K.
1970 Introduction to the Old Testament, London.

Harvey, J.
1971 'The New Diachronic Biblical Theology of the Old Testament (1960-1970)', BThB 1: 5-29.

Hasel, G.F.
1970 'The Problem of History in Old Testament Theology', AUSS 8: 23-50.

1972a Old Testament Theology: Basic Issues in the Current Debate, Grand Rapids, Mich. An article published in the same year ('Methodology as a Major Problem in the Current Crisis of Old Testament Theology', BThB 2: 177-198) is incorporated into chs 1 and 5 of this book.

1972b The Remnant: The History and Theology of the Remnant Idea from Genesis to Isaiah, Berrien Springs, Mich.

1972/74 'The Center of the OT and OT Theology', Old Testament Theology: 49-63; revd version : 'The Problem of the Center in the OT Theology Debate', ZAW 86, 1974: 65-82.

Hashimoto, S.
1970 'The functions of the Old Testament quotations and allusions in the Marcan Passion narrative', Dissn, Princeton Theological Seminary.

Hay, D.M.
1973 Glory at the Right Hand: Psalm 110 in Early Christianity, Nashville/New York (SBL Monograph Series 18).

Hebert, A.G.
1941 The Throne of David: A Study of the Fulfilment of the Old Testament in Jesus Christ and His Church, London.

1947a The Authority of the Old Testament, London.

1947b Scripture and the Faith, London.

1948 'The Church in the Bible' in Jalland (1948): 1-10.

1950 'The Interpretation of the Bible', Interpn 4: 441-52.

Hedinger, U.
1967 'Glaube und Hoffnung bei Ernst Fuchs und Jürgen Moltmann',EvTh 27: 36-51.

Heimann, E.
1966 Theologie der Geschichte: Ein Versuch, Berlin

Heinisch, P.
1940 Theologie des Alten Testamentes, Bonn.

1949-50 History of the Old Testament, ET: Collegeville, Minn. 1952 (German 1949-50).

Heintze, G.
1958 Luthers Predigt von Gesetz und Evangelium, Munich (FGLP 10.11).

Héléwa, F.J.
1964 'L'origine du concept Prophétique du "Jour de Yahvé"', EphC 15: 3-36.

Hellbardt, H.
1935 Der verheissene König Israels: Das Christuszeugnis des Hosea, Munich (EvTh Beih.1).*

1936a Abrahams Lüge: Zum Verständnis von 1. Mose 12,10-20, Munich (ThEx 42).

1936b 'Christus, das Telos des Gesetzes', EvTh 3: 331-46.*

1937a 'Die Auslegung des Alten Testaments als theologische Disziplin', ThBl 16: 129-143.

1937b 'Neuerscheinungen zum Alten Testament', EvTh 4: 244ff.

1938 — *Das Alte Testament und das Evangelium: Melchisedek*, Munich.*

1939a — *Das Bild Gottes: Eine Auslegung von 2. Mose 32*, Munich (ThEx 64).

1939b — 'Auslegung der Schrift oder Deutung der Religionsgeschichte?', *DPfBl* :354ff.

Hempel, J.

1932 — 'Das reformatorische Evangelium und das Alte Testament', *LuJ* 14: 1-32.

1936 — 'Chronik', *ZAW* 54: 293-309.

1938 — *Politische Absicht und politische Wirkung im biblischen Schrifttum*, Leipzig (Der Alte Orient 38.1).

1953 — 'Glaube, Mythos und Geschichte im Alten Testament', *ZAW* 65: 109-167.

1957 — 'Biblische Theologie und biblische Religionsgeschichte: I. AT', *RGG*[3] 1: 1256-

1958 — 'Alttestamentliche Theologie in protestantischer Sicht heute', *BO* 15: 206-14

1962 — Review of von Rad 1960, *BO* 19: 267-73.

1964 — *Geschichten und Geschichte im Alten Testament bis zur persischen Zeit*, Gütersloh.

Hendry, G.S.

1948 — 'The Exposition of Holy Scripture', *SJT* 1: 29-47.

Hengstenberg, E.W.

1829-35 — *Christology of the Old Testament and a commentary on the Messianic predictions of the Prophets*, ET: Edinburgh 1854-8[2], 1836-9[1], 1847 abridged (German 1829-35, 1854-7[2]).

1871 — *History of the Kingdom of God under the Old Testament*, 1871, repr. Cherry Hill, N.J. 1972 as *The Kingdom of God in the Old Testament*.

Hentschke, R.

1960 — 'Gesetz und Eschatologie in der Verkündigung der Propheten', *ZEE* 4: 46-56.

Hermann, E.
1935 Review of Vischer 1934, RHPR 15: 382-4.

Hermann, R.
1937 'Deutung und Umdeutung der Schrift: Ein Beitrag zur Frage der Auslegung', repr. in 1971: 38-61 (originally in Theologia militans 12, Leipzig 1937).

1959 'Offenbarung, Worte und Texte', EvTh 19: 99-116 (repr. in 1971: 201-15).

1971 Bibel und Hermeneutik (Gesammelte und nachgelassene Werke III), Göttingen (ed. G. Krause).

Herntrich, V.
1934 Völkische Religiosität und Altes Testament: Zur Auseinandersetzung der nationalsozialistischen Weltanschauung mit dem Christentum, Gütersloh.

1936 Theologische Auslegung des Alten Testaments? Zum Gespräch mit Wilhelm Vischer, Göttingen (expanded form of article in Monatschrift für Pastoraltheologie 32: 119-131,177-189).

1938 'Luther und das Alte Testament', LuJ 20: 93-124.

1942 'The "Remnant in the Old Testament', TDNT 4: 196-209.

Herrmann, S.
1965 Die prophetischen Heilserwartungen im Alten Testament: Ursprung und Gestaltwandel, Stuttgart (BWANT 85).

1971 'Die Konstruktive Restauration: Das Deuteronomium als Mitte biblischer Theologie' in von Rad Fs: 155-170.

Hertzberg, H.W.
1936 Review of Vischer 1934, TLZ 61: 435-9.

1950 Werdende Kirche im Alten Testament, Münich (ThEx 20).

1952 'Ist Exegese theologisch möglich?', repr. in 1962: 101-117 (originally University lecture in Kiel, 1952; also Norddeutsche Beilage zu "Für Arbeit und Besinnung" 5,1952: 362-75).

1962 <u>Beiträge zur Traditionsgeschichte und Theologie des Alten Testaments</u>, Göttingen (collected essays, 1926-60; note in particular a lecture given in 1960 and not previously published: 'Das Christusproblem im Alten Testament', 148-161.

Heschel, A.J.
1951 <u>Man Is Not Alone: A Philosophy of Religion</u>, New York.

Hesse, F.
1958 'Die Erforschung der Geschichte Israels als theologische Aufgabe', <u>KuD</u> 4: 1-19.

1959 'The Evaluation and Authority of Old Testament Texts', ET in <u>EOTI</u>: 285-313 (originally Baumgärtel Fs: 1959

1960a 'Kerygma oder geschichtliche Wirklichkeit? Kritische Fragen zu Gerhard von Rads "Theologie des Alten Testaments, I.Teil"', <u>ZTK</u> 57: 17-26.

1960b 'Das Alte Testament in der gegenwärtigen Dogmatik', <u>NZST</u> 2: 1-44.

1965 'Wolfhart Pannenberg und das alte Testament', <u>NZST</u> 7: 174-199.

1966 <u>Das Alte Testament als Buch der Kirche</u> Gütersloh.

1969 'Bewährt sich eine "Theologie der Heilstatsachen" am Alten Testament? Zum Verhältnis von Faktum und Deutung' <u>ZAW</u> 81: 1-18.

1971 <u>Abschied von der Heilsgeschichte</u>, Züric

Hesselink, I.J.
1967 'Calvin and Heilsgeschichte' in Cullmann Fs: 163-170.

1969 'Recent Developments in Dutch Protestant Theology', <u>RefTR</u> 28: 41-54.

Hicks, R.L.
1970 'Form and Content: A Hermeneutical Application' in May Fs: 304-24.

Higgins, A.J.B.
1949 *The Christian Significance of the Old Testament*, London.

1960 'The Old Testament and Some Aspects of New Testament Christology', *CJT* 6, 1960: 200-210 (revised form in Hooke Fs: 128-141).

1967 'The Priestly Messiah', *NTS* 13: 211-39.

Hill, D.
1967 *Greek Words and Hebrew Meanings: Studies in the Semantics of Soteriological Terms*, Cambridge (SNTS Mon 5).

1973 '"Son of Man" in Psalm 80 v. 17', *NovT* 15: 261-9.

Hillers, D.R.
1969 *Covenant: The History of a Biblical Idea*, Baltimore.

Hirsch, E.
1935 'Gottes Offenbarung in Gesetz und Evangelium: 20 Thesen', repr. in *Die Bekenntnisse und grundsätzlichen Äusserungen zur Kirchenfrage, III. Das Jahr 1935* (ed. K.D.Schmidt), Göttingen: 37-40 (originally in Hirsch, *Christliche Freiheit und politische Bindung*, Hamburg 1935: 76-82).

1936a *Das Alte Testament und die Predigt des Evangeliums*, Tübingen.

1936b *Das vierte Evangelium, in seiner ursprünglichen Gestalt verdeutscht und erklärt*, Tübingen.

Hitchcock, F.R.M.
1914 *Irenaeus of Lugdunum: A Study of his Teaching*, Cambridge.

Hitler, A.
1925-6 *Mein Kampf*, ET: London 1969[3] (1939[2], 1933[1]; numerous German edns, originally 1925-6).

Hodgson, L.
1960 'God and the Bible' in Hodgson (1960): 1-24.

Hoekema, A.A.
1963 *The Four Major Cults* Exeter 1969 (USA 1963).

Hoffmann, M.
1965 'Kerygma and History', JBR 33: 24-33.

Hofmann, J.C.K.von
1841-4 Weissagung und Erfüllung im alten und im neuen Testamente: Ein theologischer Versuch, Nördlingen.

1852-3 Der Schriftbeweis: Ein theologischer Versuch, Nördlingen.

1880 Biblische Hermeneutik, Nördlingen (ET: Interpreting the Bible, Minneapolis 1959).

Holtz, T.
1968 Untersuchungen über die alttestamentlichen Zitate bei Lukas, Berlin (TU 10

1974 'Zur Interpretation des Alten Testaments im Neuen Testament', TLZ 99: 19-32.

Hommes, T.G.
1967 'Sovereignty and Saeculum: Arnold A. van Ruler's Theocratic Theology', Dissn, Harvard (not available to me, but summary in HTR 60, 1967: 489-90).

Honecker, M.
1963 'Zum Verständnis der Geschichte in Gerhard von Rads Theologie des Alten Testaments', EvTh 23: 143-168.

Hooke, S.H.
1961 Alpha and Omega: A Study in the Pattern of Revelation, Welwyn,Herts.

Horst, F.
1932 'Das Alte Testament als Heilige Schrift und als Kanon', ThBl 11: 161-17

1968 Hiob: I. Teilband (1-19), Neukirchen (BK 16/1).

Houlden, J.L.
1973 Ethics and the New Testament, Harmondsworth, Middx.

Howard, G.
1968 'Hebrews and the Old Testament Quotations', NovT 10: 208-16.

Hubbard, D.A.
1974 'Old Testament', NIDCC: 725-9.

Hübner, E.
1956 Schrift und Theologie: Eine Untersuchung zur Theologie Joh. Chr. K. von Hofmanns, Münich (FGLP 10.8).

Huffmon, H.B.
1965 'The Exodus, Sinai and the Credo', CBQ 27: 101-113.

1969 'The Israel of God', Interpn 23: 66-77.

Hughes, P.E.
1956 Scripture and Myth: An Examination of Rudolf Bultmann's Plea for Demythologization, London.

Hummel, H.D.
1964 'The Old Testament Basis of Typological Interpretation', BR 9: 38-50.

Hutten, K.
1958 'Deutsch-christliche Bewegungen', RGG[3] 2: 104-7.

Hyatt, J.P.
1970 'Were There an Ancient Historical Credo in Israel and an Independent Sinai Tradition?' in May Fs: 152-170.

Irwin, W.A.
1950 'The Interpretation of the Old Testament', ZAW 62: 1-10.

1951 'Trends in Old Testament Theology', JBR 19: 183-190.

1959 'A Still Small Voice...Said, What are You Doing Here?', JBL 78: 1-12.

Jacob, E.
1945 'A propos de l'interprétation de l'Ancien Testament: Méthode christologique ou méthod historique?', ETR 20: 76-82.

1946 'La tradition historique en Israël', ETR 21: 5-208.

1950 'L'Ancien Testament et la prédication chrétienne', VerbC 4: 151-164.

1955a Theology of the Old Testament, ET: London 1958 (French 1955[1]) - see also 1968a.

1955b 'Considérations sur l'autorité canonique de l'Ancien Testament' in Boisset (1955): 71-85.

1961 'Un récent essai d'herméneutique chrétienne de l'Ancien Testament', RThPh 11: 341-6.

1963 Review of van Ruler 1955; RHPR 43: 90-92.

1965 Grundfragen Alttestamentlicher Theologie: Franz Delitzsch Vorlesungen 1965, Stuttgart 1970.

1966a 'Possibilités et limites d'une Théologie biblique', RHPR 46: 116-130.

1966b Review of Miskotte 1956a, RHPR 46: 392-4.

1968a Théologie de l'Ancien Testament[2], Neuchâtel (in spite of the claim on it title page to be revised and augmented, the only difference from the earlier edn, 1955a, is a new preface; and so the new edn is only cited when that preface is involved).

1968b 'La Théologie de l'Ancien Testament: état présent et perspectives d'avenir', ETL 44: 420-32.

Janssen, E.

1971 Das Gottesvolk und seine Geschichte: Geschichtsbild und Selbstverständnis im palästinensischen Schrifttum von Jesus Sirach bis Jehuda ha-Nasi, Neukirchen.

Jasper, F.N.

1967 'The Relation of the Old Testament to the New', ExpT 78: 228-35, 267-70.

Jenni, E.

1962 'Eschatology of the Old Testament' and 'Jewish Messiah', IDB 1: 126-133; 3: 360-

1971 'יוֹם jōm Tag', THAT I: 707-26.

Jepsen, A.

1954 'Probleme der Auslegung des Alten Testaments', ZST 23: 373-86.

1958 'The Scientific Study of the Old Testament', ET in EOTI: 246-84 (originally published as a pamphlet, Berlin 1958).

Jeremias, Joachim
1941 'Eine neue Schau der Zukunftsaussagen Jesu', ThBl 20: 216-22.

1956 Jesus' Promise to the Nations, ET: London 1958 (German 1956).

1962 The Parables of Jesus, revd ET: London 1963 (German 1962[6], 1954[3], 1947[1]).

1971 New Testament Theology, I: The Proclamation of Jesus, ET: London 1971 (German 1971).

Jeremias, Jörg
1965 Theophanie: Die Geschichte einer alttestamentlichen Gattung, Neukirchen--Vluyn (WMANT 10).

Jervell, J.
1972 Luke and the People of God: A New Look at Luke-Acts, Minneapolis, Minn.

Jewett, P.K.
1954 'Concerning the Allegorical Interpretation of Scripture', WTJ 17: 1-20.

Jocz, J.
1958 A Theology of Election: Israel and the Church, London.

1961 The Spiritual History of Israel, London.

1965 'Law and Grace: With Special Reference to the Fourth Commandment', Judaica 21: 166-177.

Joest, W.
1951 Gesetz und Freiheit: Das Problem des Tertius usus legis bei Luther und die neutestamentliche Parainese, Göttingen.

Johnston, O.R.
1951 'The Puritan Use of the Old Testament', EQ 3 : 183-209.

Johnstone, W.
1971 'The Mythologising of History in the Old Testament', SJT 24: 201-17.

Jones, J.C.
1966 'The Exegetical Method of Gerhard von Rad', Dissn, Southern Baptist Theological Seminary.*

Jordan, W.G.
1909 Biblical Criticism and Modern Thought: Or, The Place of the Old Testament Documents in the Life of Today, Edinburgh.

Jowett, B.
1860 'On the Interpretation of Scripture' in Temple (1860): 330-433.

Kaiser, W.C.
1973 'The Promise Theme and the Theology of Rest', BS 130: 135-150.

1974 'The Centre of Old Testament Theology: The Promise', Themelios 10.1: 1-10.

Käsemann, E.
1960 'The Beginnings of Christian Theology', ET in New Testament Questions of Today, 1969: 82-107; and JTC 6, 1969: 17-46 (German: ZTK 57, 1960).

Katz, P.
1958 'The Quotations from Deuteronomy in Hebrews', ZNW 49: 213-23.

Katz, W.
1962 'Erfüllung des Gesetzes',EvTh 22: 494-50

Kaufman, G.D.
1971 'What Shall We Do With the Bible?', Interpn 25: 95-112.

Kautsch, E.
1902 Die bleibende Bedeutung des Alten Testaments: Ein Konferenzvortrag, Tübingen/Leipzig 1903^2, 1902^1 (French translation 1903).

Kayayan, A.R.
1971 'Théologie de l'espérance', EtEv 31: 77-88.

Kayser, A.
1886 Die Theologie des Alten Testamentes in ihrer geschichtlichen Entwicklung dargestellt, Strasbourg (ed. by E. Reuss after the death of the author).

Keane, A.H.
1905 'The Moral Argument against the Inspiration of the Old Testament', HibJ 4: 147-162.

Kee, H.C.
1975 'The Function of Scriptural Quotations and Allusions in Mark 11-16' in Kümmel Fs: 165-188.

Keller, C.A.
1956 '"Existentielle" und "heilsgeschichtliche" Deutung der Schöpfungsgeschichte (Gen.1,1-2,4)', ThZ 12: 10-27.

Kellermann, U.
1971 Messias und Gesetz: Grundlinien einer alttestamentlichen Heilserwartung: Eine traditionsgeschichtliche Einführung, Neukirchen (Biblische Studien 61).

Kelly, B.H.
1956 'Word of Promise: The Incarnation in the Old Testament', Interpn 10: 3-15.

Kelly, J.N.D.
1958 Early Christian Doctrines, London.

1963 'The Bible and the Latin Fathers' in Nineham (1963): 41-56.

Kennett, R.H.
1925 'The Contribution of the Old Testament to the Religious Development of Mankind' in Peake (1925): 383-402.

Kent, C.F
1906 The Origin and Permanent Value of the Old Testament, London.

Kent, H.A.
1964 'Matthew's Use of the Old Testament', BS 121: 34-43.

Kenyon, F.G.
1948 The Bible and Modern Scholarship, London.

Kerrigan, A.
1952 St. Cyril of Alexandria, Interpreter of the Old Testament, Rome (AnaB 2).

Kidd, B.J.
1933 The Counter-Reformation 1550-1600, London.

Kirkpatrick, A.F.
1891 'The Use of the Old Testament in the Christian Church' in The Divine Library of the Old Testament, London: 112-143.

1903 'How to read the Old Testament' in Kirkpatrick (1903): 3-25.

Kistemaker, S.
1961 The Psalm Citations in the Epistle to the Hebrews, Amsterdam.

Kittel, R.
1916 Das Alte Testament und unser Krieg, Leipzig.

Klausner, J.
1902-1950 The Messianic Idea in Israel: from Its Beginning to the Completion of the Mishnah, ET: London 1956 (German and Hebrew 1902-21, Hebrew 1927², 1950³).

Klein, G.
1964 Theologie des Wortes Gottes und die Hypothese der Universalgeschichte: Zur Auseinandersetzung mit Wolfhart Pannenberg, Munich (BEvTh 37).

1970 'The Biblical Understanding of "The Kingdom of God"', ET in Interpn 26, 1972: 387-418 (German: EvTh 30, 1970)

1971 'Bibel und Heilsgeschichte: Die Fragwürdigkeit einer Idee', ZNW 62: 1-47.

Kline, M.G.
1972 The Structure of Biblical Authority, Grand Rapids, Mich. Most of the material from his earlier articles on Canon and Covenant (WTJ 1970 and in Payne (1970)) is incorporated into this book.

Knierim, R.
1971 'Offenbarung im Alten Testament' in von Rad Fs: 206-35.

Knight, D.A.
1973 Rediscovering the Traditions of Israel: The Development of the Traditio-Historical Research of the Old Testament, with Special Consideration of Scandinavian Contributions, n.p. (SBL Dissertation Series 9).

Knight, G.A.F.
1949 From Moses to Paul: A Christological Study in the Light of Our Hebraic Heritage, London.

1950 Ruth and Jonah: The Gospel in the Old Testament, London 1950, revd edn 1966.

1953 A Biblical Approach to the Doctrine of the Trinity, Edinburgh/London (SJT Occasional Papers 1).

1955 Esther, Song of Songs, Lamentations: Introduction and Commentary, London.

1958 'Israel - A Theological Problem', RefTR 17: 33-43.

1959a A Christian Theology of the Old Testament, London 1964[2] (1959[1]).

1959b Review of Vriezen 1954, SJT 12: 423-5.

1960a 'New Perspectives in Old Testament Interpretation', BT 19(1968): 50-58 (from McCormick Quarterly 14,1960:3-14).

1960b Hosea: Introduction and Commentary, London.

1961 Prophets of Israel (1): Isaiah, London.

1962 Law and Grace: Must a Christian Keep the Law of Moses?, London.

1966 Exile and After: Studies in Isaiah 40-55, London.

Knight, H.T.

1911 'The Public Reading of the Old Testament', The Interpreter 7: 187-194.

Köberle, J.

1906 'Heilsgeschichtliche und religionsgeschichtliche Betrachtungsweise des Alten Testaments',NKZ 17: 200-222.

Koch, K.

1961 'Spätisraelitisches Geschichtsdenken am Beispiel des Buches Daniel', HZ 193: 1-32.

1962 'Der Tod des Religionsstifters: Erwägungen über das Verhältnis Israels zur Geschichte der altorientalischen Religionen',KuD 8: 100-123.

1970 The Rediscovery of Apocalyptic: A polemical work on a neglected area of biblical studies and its damaging effects on theology and philosophy, ET: London 1972 (SBT 2.22; German 1970).

Köhler, L.
1935-6 'Alttestamentliche Theologie', ThRu 7: 255-76; 8: 55-69,247-84.

1936 Old Testament Theology, ET: London 1957 (German 1953[3], 1936[1]).

1953 'Christus im Alten und im Neuen Testament', ThZ 9: 241-59.

Kolfhaus, W.
1935 'The Church of Christ in the Old Testament', EQ 7: 129-139.

König, E.
1920 Friedrich Delitzsch's "Die grosse Täuschung" kritisch beleuchtet, Gütersloh.

1921a Moderne Vergewaltigung des Alten Testaments, Bonn.

1921b Wie weit hat Delitzsch Recht? Beantwortet durch kritische Beleuchtung des zweiten Teils von Delitzschs "Die grosse Täuschung", Berlin.

Koole, J.L.
1938 De Overname van het Oude Testament door de christelijke Kerk, Hilversum.

Kosak, H.
1968 Wegweisung in das Alte Testament, Stuttgart.

Köster, H.
1961 'Die Auslegung der Abraham-Verheissung in Hebräer 6' in von Rad Fs: 95-109.

Kraeling, E.G.
1955 The Old Testament Since the Reformation, London.

Kraus, H.J.
1952 'Gespräch mit Martin Buber: Zur jüdischen und christlichen Auslegung des Alten Testaments', EvTh 12: 59-77.

1956a Geschichte der historisch-kritischen Erforschung des Alten Testaments, Neukirchen 1969[2] (1956[1]).

1956b 'Das Problem der Heilsgeschichte in der "kirchlichen Dogmatik"' in Barth Fs: 69-83.

1956c 'Zur Geschichte des Überlieferungsbegriffs in der alttestamentlichen Wissenschaft', EvTh 16: 371-87.

1956d Klagelieder (Threni), Neukirchen (BK 20).

1958 The People of God in the Old Testament, London.

1960 Psalmen, Neukirchen 1961[2] (1960[1]; BK 15).

1965 'Vom Sinn des Alten Testaments', VF 1960/62 (Lieferung 3, published 1965): 184-191.

1968 'Calvins exegetische Prinzipien', ZKG 79: 329-41.

1970 Die Biblische Theologie: Ihre Geschichte und Problematik, Neukirchen-Vluyn.

1971 'Geschichte als Erziehung' Biblisch--theologische Perspektiven' in von Rad Fs: 258-74.

Krause, G.
1962 Studien zu Luthers Auslegung der Kleinen Propheten, Tübingen (BHTh 33).

Kudasiewicz, J.
1971 'Jednośċ dwu Testamentów jako zasada wyjaśnienia misterium Chrystusa w Kościele pierwotnym', RBL 24: 95-109.

Kühl, C.
1953 The Old Testament: Its Origins and Composition, ET: Edinburgh/London 1961 (German 1953).

Kuitert, H.M.
1962 Gott in Menschengestalt: Eine dogmatisch-hermeneutische Studie über die Anthropomorphismen der Bibel, German translation: Münich 1967 (BEvTh 45; Dutch 1962).

Kümmel, W.G.
1945 Promise and Fulfilment: The Eschatological Message of Jesus, ET: London 1957 (SBT 23) German 1956[3], 1953[2], 1945[1]).

1968 '"Mitte des Neuen Testaments"' in Leenhardt Fs: 71-85.

Küng, H.
1967 The Church, ET: London 1968 (German 1967).

Künneth, W.
1935 *Antwort auf den Mythus: Die Entscheidung zwischen dem nordischen Mythus und dem biblischen Christus*, Berlin.

Kuptsch, J.
1937 *Nationalsozialismus und positives Christentum*, Weimar, Thür.

Kuske, M.
1967 *Das Alte Testament als Buch von Christus: Dietrich Bonhoeffers Wertung und Auslegung des Alten Testaments*, Göttingen n.d. (Dissn 1967)

Kuss, O.
1972 'Zur Hermeneutik Tertullians' in Ernst (1972): 55-87.

Kutsch, E.
1962 'Heuschreckenplage und Tag Jahwes in Joel 1 und 2', *ThZ* 18: 81-94.

1971 'בְּרִית b^erīt Verpflichtung', *THAT* I: 339-52.

1972 *Verheissung und Gesetz: Untersuchungen zum sogenannten 'Bund' im Alten Testament*, Berlin (BZAW 131).

Lacomara, A.
1974 'Deuteronomy and the Farewell Discourse (Jn 13:31-16:33)', *CBQ* 36: 65-84

Ladd, G.E.
1964 'Israel and the Church', *EQ* 36: 206-13.

1966a *Jesus and the Kingdom: The Eschatology of Biblical Realism*, London 1966 (the only difference in the 1974 revd edn is the title, *The Presence of the Future*, and four extra pages in the first chapter).

1966b 'History and Theology in Biblical Exegesis', *Interpn* 20: 54-64.

1968 *The Pattern of New Testament Truth*, Grand Rapids, Mich.

1971 'The Search for Perspective', *Interpn* 25: 41-62.

Lambert, J.C.
1918 'Type', *HDAC* II: 623-6.

Lampe, G.W.H.
1953 'Typological Exegesis', Theology 56: 201-8.

1957 'The Reasonableness of Typology' in Lampe and Woollcombe (1957): 9-38.

1963 'The Bible since the Rise of Critical Study' in Nineham (1963): 125-144.

1965 'Hermeneutics and Typology', LQHR 190: 17-25.

1969 'The Exposition and Exegesis of Scripture: 1. To Gregory the Great', CHB II: 155-183.

Langford, N.F.
1951 'Gospel and Duty: A Study of Biblical Ethics', Interpn 5: 268-84.

Larcher, C.
1962 L'actualité chrétienne de l'Ancien Testament, d'après le Nouveau Testament, Paris (Lectio Divina 34).

Laurin, R.B
1970 'Edmond Jacob, Theology of the Old Testament' in Laurin (1970): 141-169.

Lawson, J.
1948 The Biblical Theology of Saint Irenaeus.

Lawton, A.
1974 'Christ: The End of the Law. A Study of Romans 10: 4-8', TrJ 3: 14-30.

Leclercq, J.
1951 'L'exégèse médiévale de l'Ancien Testament' in Auvray (1951): 168-182.

1969 'The Exposition and Exegesis of Scripture: 2. From Gregory the Great to Saint Bernard', CHB II: 183-197.

Leenhardt, F.J.
1955 'La Bible et le message de l'Eglise au monde' in Boisset (1955): 149-168.

1973 'Abraham et la conversion de Saul de Tarse, suivi d'une note sur "Abraham dans Jean VIII"', RHPR 53: 331-51.

Leeuwen, C. van
1974 'The Prophecy of the Yōm YHWH in Amos v 18-20' in _Language and Meaning: Studies in Hebrew Language and Biblical Exegesis_, Leiden (OTS 19): 113-134.

Leffler, S.
1935 _Christus im Dritten Reich der Deutschen: Wesen, Weg und Ziel der Kirchenbewegung "Deutsche Christen"_, Weimar, Thür.

Leist, F.
1965 'Das "überholte" Alte Testament' in Leist (1965): 21-6.

Leivestad, R.
1968 'Der Apokalyptische Menschensohn ein theologisches Phantom', _ASTI_ 6: 49-105

Léon-Dufour, X.
1968 'Une lecture chrétienne de l'Ancien Testament: Galates 3: 6 à 4: 20' in Leenhardt Fs: 109-115.

Lerch, D.
1950 _Isaaks Opferung christlich gedeutet: Eine auslegungsgeschichtliche Untersuchung_, Tübingen (BHTh 12).

Lestringant, P.
1955 'L'unité de la Bible' in Boisset (1955): 45-69.

Levie, J.
1951a 'Exégèse critique et interprétation théologique', _RechSR_ 39: 237-52.

1951b 'A la lumière de l'encyclique "Divino afflante Spiritu"' in Auvray (1951): 89-111.

1956 'L'Ecriture Sainte, parole de Dieu, parole d'homme', _NRT_ 78: 561-92, 706-29.

Lewis, T.W.
1965 'The Theological Logic in Heb 10:19-12:29 and the appropriation of the Old Testament', Dissn, Drew University.

Lieb, F.
1955 '"Geschichte und Heilsgeschichte in der Theologie Rudolf Bultmanns"', _EvTh_ 15: 507-22 (response to Ott 1955).

Lightfoot, R.H.
1944 'The Critical Approach to the Bible in the Nineteenth Century' in Dugmore (1944): 75-91.

Lindars, B.
1961 New Testament Apologetic: The Doctrinal Significance of the Old Testament Quotations, London.

Lindblom, J.
1936 'Zur Frage der Eigenart der alttestamentlichen Religion' in Hempel (1936): 128-137.

1952 'Gibt es eine Eschatologie bei den alttestamentlichen Propheten?', StTh 6: 79-114.

1962 Prophecy in Ancient Israel, Oxford (although he had earlier written Profetismen i Israel, 1934, this is an entirely new work).

Lipiński, E.
1960 'Kościół a Stary Testament', RBL 13: 407-13.

1965 La royauté de Yahwé dans la poésie et le culte de l'ancien Israël, Brussels.

1970 Essais sur la Révélation et la Bible, Paris.

Lofthouse, W.F.
1938 'The Old Testament and Christianity' in Robinson (1938): 458-80.

Lohfink, N.
1965 The Christian Meaning of the Old Testament, ET: London 1969 (German: Das Siegeslied am Schilfmeer, 1965).

1967 'Die historische und die christliche Auslegung des Alten Testamentes' in Bibelauslegung im Wandel: Ein Exeget ortet seine Wissenschaft, Frankfurt: 185-213.

Lohse, E.
1963 'Hosianna', NovT 6: 113-119.

1975 'Die Einheit des Neuen Testaments als theologisches Problem: Überlegungen zur Aufgabe einer Theologie des Neuen Testaments', EvTh 35: 139-154.

Longenecker, R.N.
1970 'Can we reproduce the Exegesis of the New Testament?', TynB 21: 3-38.

1975 Biblical Exegesis in the Apostolic Period, Grand Rapids, Mich.

Loretz, O.
1964 The Truth of the Bible, ET: London/New York 1968 (German 1964).

Lother, H.
1934 Neugermanische Religion und Christentum: Eine kirchengeschichtliche Vorlesung, Gütersloh.

Löwith, K.
1949 Meaning in History: The Theological Implications of the Philosophy of History, Chicago.

Lubac, H. de
1947 '"Typologie" et "Allégorisme"', RechSR 34: 180-226.

1949 '"Sens spirituel"', RechSR 36: 542-76.

1950 Histoire et Esprit: L'intelligence de l'Écriture d'après Origène, Paris (Théologie 16).

1959-64 Exégèse médiévale: Les quatres sens de l'Écriture, Paris (Théologie 41,42,59)

1966 L'Écriture dans la tradition, Paris.

Lubsczyk, H.
1970 Die Einheit der Schrift: Viele Theologien - ein Bekenntnis, Stuttgart.

Luther, M.
1523-34 'Prefaces to the Old Testament', ET: Luther's Works (American Edition) Vol.35, Philadelphia 1960: 233-333 (originally 1523-34).

Luz, U.
1974 'Theologia crucis als Mitte der Theologie im Neuen Testament', EvTh 34: 116-141.

Lys, D.
1967 The Meaning of the Old Testament: An Essay on Hermeneutics, Nashville/New York (rewriting and translation of 'A la recherche d'une méthode pour l'exégèse de l'Ancien Testament', ETR 30, 1955; and 'L'Appropriation de l'Ancien Testament', ETR 41, 1966: 1-12).

McAlear, R.
1970 'The Presence of Christ in the Old Testament', _Angelicum_ 47: 77-82.

McCarthy, D.J.
1972a _Old Testament Covenant: A Survey of Current Opinions_, Oxford.

1972b 'b^e^rîth in Old Testament History and Theology', _Biblica_ 53: 110-121 (review article on Perlitt 1969).

McCasland, S.V.
1954 'The Unity of the Scriptures', _JBL_ 73: 1-10.

1961 'Matthew Twists the Scriptures', _JBL_ 80: 143-8.

McConnell, R.S.
1969 _Law and Prophecy in Matthew's Gospel: The Authority and Use of the Old Testament in the Gospel of St Matthew_, Basel.

McCormick, S.
1958 'The Bible as Record and Medium: Contemporary Scholarship and the Word of God', _Interpn_ 12: 292-308.

McCullough, J.C.
1972 'Jesus Christ in the Old Testament', _Biblical Theology_ 22: 36-47.

McCurdy, J.F.
1897 'The Moral Evolution of the Old Testament', _AJT_ 1: 658-91.

McCurley, F.R.
1970 'The Christian and the Old Testament Promise', _LQ_ 22: 401-10.

McFadyen, J.E.
1903 _Old Testament Criticism and the Christian Church_, London.

MacFarland, C.S.
1934 _The New Church and the New Germany: A Study of Church and State_, New York.

McGaughey, D.H.
1963 'The Hermeneutic Method of the Epistle to the Hebrews', Dissn, Boston.

McKane, W.
1965 *Prophets and Wise Men*, London (SBT 44)

McKenzie, J.L.
1951 'A Chapter in the History of Spiritual Exegesis: De Lubac's *Histoire et esprit*', *ThSt* 12: 365-81.

1956 *The Two-Edged Sword: An Interpretation of the Old Testament*, London 1959 (USA 1956).

1958 'Problems of Hermeneutics in Roman Catholic Exegesis', *JBL* 77: 197-204.

1959 'Myth and the Old Testament', *CBQ* 21: 265-82 (repr. in *Myths and Realities*, Milwaukee 1963: 182-200).

1964 'The Significance of the Old Testament for Christian Faith in Roman Catholici[sm]' in *OTCF*: 102-114.

1967 'The Values of the Old Testament', *Concilium* 3.10: 4-17.

1968 'Aspects of Old Testament Thought', *JBC* II: 736-67.

1972 'Biblical Anthropomorphisms and the Humaneness of God' in Robinson (1972): 172-186.

1974 *A Theology of the Old Testament*, Londo[n]

MacKenzie, R.A.F.
1963 *Faith and History in the Old Testament*, Minneapolis, Minn.

Mackintosh, H.R.
1937 *Types of Modern Theology: Schleiermacher to Barth*, London.

McNally, R.E.
1959 *The Bible in the Early Middle Ages*, Westminster, Md (Woodstock Papers 4).

McNeile, A.H.
1913 *The Old Testament in the Christian Church*, London.

McNeill, J.T.
1952 'History of the Interpretation of the Bible: II. Medieval and Reformation Period', *IB* 1: 115-126.

Macquarrie, J.
1955 An Existentialist Theology: A Comparison of Heidegger and Bultmann, London 1955 (again, Harmondsworth 1973).

1971 'Theologies of Hope: A Critical Examination', ExpT 82: 100-105.

Malden, R.H.
1919 The Old Testament: Its Meaning and Value for the Church Today, London.

Malet, A.
1962 Mythos et Logos: La pensée de Rudolf Bultmann, Geneva.

Malevez, L.
1958 The Christian Message and Myth: The Theology of Rudolf Bultmann, London.

1964 'Les dimensions de l'histoire du salut', NRT 86: 561-78.

Manson, T.W.
1944 'The Failure of Liberalism to Interpret the Bible as the Word of God' in Dugmore (1944): 92-107.

1952 'The Old Testament in the Teaching of Jesus', BJRL 34: 312-32.

Marbury, C.H.
1968 'Old Testament Textual Traditions in the New Testament: Studies in Text-Types', Dissn, Harvard (not available to me, but summary in HTR 61, 1968: 643-4).

Marcel, P.C.
1959 'Our Lord's Use of Scripture' in Henry (1959): 119-134.

Marcus, R.A.
1957 'Presuppositions of the Typological Approach to Scripture', CQR 158: 442-51.

Margoliouth, D.S.
1906 'Dr. Orr on the Problem of the Old Testament', Exp 7.2: 19-28.

Markus, R.A.
1954 'Pleroma and Fulfilment: The Significance of History in St. Irenaeus' Opposition to Gnosticism', VigChr 8: 193-224.

Marquardt, F.-W.
1968 'Christentum und Zionismus', EvTh 28: 629-60.

Marlé, R.
1956 'Bultmann et l'Ancien Testament', NRT 78: 473-86 (ET in Rudolf Bultmann in Catholic Thought, ed. T.O'Meara and D.Weisser, New York/London 1968: 110-124).

Marsh, J.
1951 'History and Interpretation' in Richardson and Schweitzer (1951):181-19

Marti, K.
1906 The Religion of the Old Testament: Its Place Among the Religions of the Nearer East, ET: London 1907 (German 1906).

1912 Stand und Aufgabe der alttestamentlichen Wissenschaft in der Gegenwart, Bern.

Martin-Achard, R.
1956 From Death to Life: A Study of the Development of the Doctrine of the Resurrection in the Old Testament, ET: Edinburgh/London 1960 (French 1956)

1959a A Light to the Nations: A Study of the Old Testament Conception of Israel's Mission to the World, ET: Edinburgh/London 1962 (French 1959).

1959b 'Les voies de la théologie de l'Ancien Testament', RThPh 9: 217-26.

1962 'La nouvelle alliance, selon Jérémie', RThPh 12: 81-92.

Matthews, I.G.
1947 The Religious Pilgrimage of Israel, New York/London.

Matthias, W.
1962 'Der anthropologische Sinn der Formel Gesetz und Evangelium', EvTh 22: 410-25.

Mauchline, J.
1959 Review of Vriezen 1954, JSS 4: 393-5.

Mauser, U.
1963 Christ in the Wilderness: The Wilderness Theme in the Second Gospel and its Basis in the Biblical Tradition, London (SBT 39).

1970 'Image of God and Incarnation', Interpn 24: 336-56.

1971 Gottesbild und Menschwerdung: Eine Untersuchung zur Einheit des Alten und Neuen Testaments, Tübingen (BHTh 43).

Mead, R.T.
1964 'A Dissenting Opinion about Respect for Context in Old Testament Quotations', NTS 10: 279-89 (a reply to Edgar 1962).

Means, P.B.
1935 Things That are Caesar's: The Genesis of the German Church Conflict, New York.

Meeks, W.A.
1967 The Prophet-King: Moses Traditions and the Johannine Christology, Leiden (SNovT 14).

Meinhold, J.
1903 Studien zur israelitischen Religionsgeschichte. Band I: Der heilige Rest. Teil I: Elias Amos Hosea Jesaja, Bonn (no more of the work was published).

Mellor, E.B.
1972 'The Old Testament for Jews and Christians Today' in The Making of the Old Testament, Cambridge: 167-201.

Mercer, J.E.
1909 'Is the Old Testament a Suitable Basis for Moral Instruction?', HibJ 7: 333-45.

Meyer zu Uptrup, K.
1966 Die Bedeutung des Alten Testaments für eine Transformation der Kirche heute: Versuch zu einer kirchlichen "Kybernetik", München (ThEx 135).

Michaeli, F.
1957 How to understand the Old Testament, London 1961, simplified and abridged ET of L'Ancien Testament et l'Église chrétienne d'aujourd'hui (1957).

Michalson, C.
1964 'Bultmann against Marcion' in _OTCF_: 49-63.

Michel, O.
1929 _Paulus und seine Bibel_, Gütersloh (BFChTh 2.18).

Mickelsen, A.B.
1963 _Interpreting the Bible_, Grand Rapids, Mich.

Micklem, N.
1953 'Leviticus', _IB_ 2: 1-134.

Miegge, G.
1958 'La valutazione teologica dell' Antico Testamento nell'esegesi protestante recente', _Protestantesimo_ 13: 129-142.

Mildenberger, F.
1964 _Gottes Tat im Wort: Erwägungen zur alttestamentlichen Hermeneutik als Frage nach der Einheit der Testamente_, Gütersloh.

Miller, A.
1951 'Zur Typologie des Alten Testamentes', _BenM_ 27: 12-19.

Miller, A.A.
1970 'The Theologies of Luther and Boehme in the Light of their _Genesis_ Commentaries',_HTR_ 63: 261-303.

Miller, D.G.
1956 Review of Boisset 1955, _Interpn_ 10: 85-

Miller, M.P.
1971 'Targum, Midrash and the Use of the Old Testament in the New Testament', _JSJ_ 2: 29-82.

Minear, P.S.
1948 _Eyes of Faith: A Study in the Biblical Point of View_, London/Redhill.

Mirtow, P.
1957 _Jesus and the Religion of the Old Testament_, London.

Miskotte, H.H.
1966 _Sensus spiritualis: De verhouding tussen het Oude Testament en het Nieuwe Testament in de rooms-katholiek hermeneutiek sinds het verschijnen van de encycliek 'Divino afflante Spiritu' in 1943_, Nijkerk.

Miskotte, K.H.

1932 — _Het Wezen der Joodsche Religie: Vergelijkende Studie over de voornaamste Strukturen der joodsche Godsdienstphilosophie van dezen Tijd_, Amsterdam.

1936 — 'Das Problem der theologischen Exegese' in Barth Fs: 51-77.

1939 — _Edda en Thora: Een vergelijking van germaansche en israëlitische religie_, Nijkerk 1939, 1970[2].

1948a — _Om het levende Woord: Opstellen over de praktijk der exegese_, The Hague.

1948b — 'De prediking van het Oude Testament' in Berkelbach and Abbing(1948): I. 353ff.*

1952 — 'Naturrecht und Theokratie' in _Die Freiheit des Evangeliums und die Ordnung der Gesellschaft_, Münich (BEvTh 15): 29-72.

1956a — _When the Gods are Silent_, ET: London 1967 (Dutch 1956, revd German edn 1963). The subtitle, 'On the Significance of the Old Testament', is omitted in the English edition, though it is mentioned on the dust-cover.

1956b — 'Die Erlaubnis zu schriftgemässem Denken' in Barth Fs: 29-51.

1959 — _Zur biblischen Hermeneutik_, Zollikon (ThSt 55; repr. in 1966: 200-229).

1965 — 'Fragende Existenz' in Leist (1965): 27-33.

1966 — _Geloof en Kennis: theologische voordrachten_, Haarlem.

1969 — _Miskende majesteit_, Nijkerk.

Moltmann, J.

1962 — 'Exegesis and the Eschatology of History', ET in _Hope and Planning_, London 1971: 56-98 (originally in _EvTh_ 22, 1962: 31-66).

1964 — _Theology of Hope: On the Ground and Implications of a Christian Eschatology_, ET: London 1967 (German 1964, BEvTh 38).

Mondin, B.
1972 'Theology of Hope and the Christian Message', *BThB* 2: 43-63.

Moorehead, W.G.
1939 'Type', *ISBE*: 3029-30.

Morgan, R.
1957 'Fulfillment in the Fourth Gospel: The Old Testament Foundations', *Interpn* 11: 155-165.

Morris, L.
1964 *The New Testament and the Jewish Lectionaries*, London.

1969 *The Revelation of St John: An Introduction and Commentary*, London.

1973 *Apocalyptic*, London.

Motyer, A.
1972 'Bible study and the unity of the Bible' in Job (1972): 11-23.

Moule, A.W.H.
1971 'Pattern of the Synoptists', *EQ* 43: 162-171.

Moule, C.F.D.
1962 *The Birth of the New Testament*, London

1968 'Fulfilment-Words in the New Testament Use and Abuse', *NTS* 14: 293-320.

Mowinckel, S.
1922 *Psalmenstudien II. Das Thronbesteigungsfest Jahwäs und der Ursprung der Eschatologie*, Christiana.

1938 *The Old Testament as Word of God*, ET: Oxford 1960 (Norwegian 1938).

1951 *He That Cometh*, ET: Oxford 1956 (Norwegian 1951).

1958 'Jahves dag', *NorTT* 59: 1-56,209-29.*

Mozley, J.B.
1874-5 *Ruling Ideas in Early Ages, and their Relation to Old Testament Faith* (on spine: *Lectures on the Old Testament*), London 1889[4] (n.d.[1], lectures originally given 1874-5).

Muilenburg, J.
1951 'The Interpretation of the Bible' in Richardson and Schweitzer (1951): 198-218.

1958 'Preface to Hermeneutics', JBL 77: 18-26.

Müller, H.-P.
1964 'Zur Frage nach dem Ursprung der biblischen Eschatologie', VT 14: 276-93.

1969 Ursprünge und Strukturen alttestamentlicher Eschatologie, Berlin (BZAW 109).

Müller, W.E.
1939 Die Vorstellung vom Rest im Alten Testament, Borsdorf-Leipzig (new edn by H.D.Preuss, Neukirchen-Vluyn 1973).*

Mulrooney, J.
1971 'Covenant and Conscience', The Way 11: 283-90.

Munck, J.
1954 Paul and the Salvation of Mankind, ET: London 1959 (German 1954).

Murdock, W.R.
1967 'History and Revelation in Jewish Apocalypticism', Interpn 21: 167-187.

Murphy, R.E.
1961 'A New Theology of the Old Testament', CBQ 23: 217-23 (re von Rad).

1964 'The Relationship between the Testaments', CBQ 26: 349-59.

Myers, J.M.
1959 Review of Vriezen 1954, Interpn 13: 333-6.

Neil, W.
1963 'The Criticism and Theological Use of the Bible, 1700-1950', CHB III: 238-93.

Nesbit, W.G.
1969 'A Study of Methodologies in Contemporary Old Testament Theologies', Dissn.

Nicholson, E.W.
1973 Exodus and Sinai in History and Tradition, Oxford.

Nicolaisen, C.
1966 Die Auseinandersetzung um das Alte Testament im Kirchenkampf 1933-1945, Hamburg.

1971 'Die Stellung der "Deutschen Christen" zum Alten Testament' in Zur Geschichte des Kirchenkampfes: Gesammelte Aufsätze II (ed. H. Brunotte, AGK 26), Göttingen: 197-220.

Nicole, R.
1959 'New Testament Use of the Old Testament' in Henry (1959): 135-151.

Niebuhr, R.
1949 Faith and History: A Comparison of Christian and Modern Views of History, London.

Nielen, J.M.
1965 'Jesus und das Alte Testament' in Leist (1965): 481-97.

Niemöller, M.
1934 Das Bekenntnis der Väter und die bekennende Gemeinde, Munich.

Niemöller, W.
1956 Die Evangelische Kirche im Dritten Reich: Handbuch des Kirchenkampfes, Bielefeld.

Niesel, W.
1938 The Theology of Calvin, ET: London 1956 (German 1938).

Nineham, D.E.
1969 'The Use of the Bible in Modern Theology', BJRL 52: 178-199.

Nixon, R.E.
1963 The Exodus in the New Testament, London.

North, C.R.
1948 The Suffering Servant in Deutero-Isaiah: An Historical and Critical Study, Oxford.

North, R.
1971 'Pannenberg's Historicizing Exegesis', HeyJ 12: 377-400.

1973 'Bibliography of Works in Theology and History', HT 12: 55-140.

Noth, G.
1966 'Das Evangelium im Alten Testament: Eine Besinnung auf die Väter unseres Glaubens', ZdZ 20: 414-20.

Noth, M.
1937 'Zur Auslegung des Alten Testamentes', repr. in Gesammelte Studien zum Alten Testament II, Münich 1969 (ThB 39): 48-61 (originally DPfBl 41, 1937: 341-2, 359-60, 373-4).

1948 A History of Pentateuchal Traditions, ET: Englewood Cliffs, N.J. 1972 (German 1948).

1949 'History and Word of God in the Old Testament', (slightly shortened) ET: BJRL 32(1950): 194-206 (repr. as booklet, and also in The Laws in the Pentateuch and other studies, Edinburgh/London 1966: 179-193; German: Bonner Akademischen Reden 3, 1949).

1950 The History of Israel, ET: London 1960[2] (1958[1]; German 1954[2], 1950[1]).

1952 'The "Re-presentation" of the Old Testament in Proclamation', ET in EOTI: 76-88 (and Interpn 15, 1961: 50-60; German: EvTh 12, 1952: 6-17).

1953 'The Understanding of History in Old Testament Apocalyptic', ET in The Laws in the Pentateuch: 194-214.

1968 Könige: I. Teilband (I.1-16), Neukirchen (BK 9/1).

Nötscher, F.
1958 Gotteswege und Menschenwege in der Bibel und in Qumran, Bonn (Bonner Biblischer Beiträge 15).

Nygren, A.
1930-36 Agape and Eros: I A Study of the Christian Idea of Love; II The History of the Christian Idea of Love, ET: London 1932-9 (Swedish 1930-36).

Obayashi, H.
1970 'Pannenberg and Troeltsch: History and Religion', JAAR 38: 401-19.

O'Collins, G.G.
1966 'Revelation as History', HeyJ 7: 394-406.

1968a 'Spes Quaerens Intellectum', Interpn 22: 36-52.

1968b 'The Theology of Hope', The Way 8: 260-69.

Oehler, G.F.
1973 Theology of the Old Testament, ET: Edinburgh I: 1874; II: 1875 (German 1873, ed. after the author's death by his son).

Oesterreicher, J.M.
1963 The Israel of God: On the Old Testament Roots of the Church's Faith, Englewood Cliffs, N.J.

Oettli, S.
1896 Der gegenwärtige Kampf um das Alte Testament, Gütersloh,

O'Grady, C.
1972 'The Theology of Hope', DL 22: 419-30, 451-60, 589-94.

Ohler, A.
1973 Gattungen im Alten Testament: Ein biblisches Arbeitsbuch, Düsseldorf: II: 153-218.

O'Malley, T.P.
1967 Tertullian and the Bible: Language - Imagery - Exegesis, Nijmegen.

O'Rourke, J.J.
1962 'The Fulfillment Texts in Matthew', CBQ 24: 394-403.

Orr, J.
1895 'The Old Testament Question in the Early Church', Exp 5.1: 346-61.

1906 The Problem of the Old Testament, Considered with Reference to Recent Criticism, London.

n.d. The Bible under Trial: Apologetic Papers in view of present-day assaults of Holy Scripture, London.

1910 Revelation and Inspiration, London.

Osborn, R.T.
1967 'Pannenberg's Programme', CJT 13: 109-122.

Osswald, E.
1974 'Theologie des Alten Testaments - eine bleibende Aufgabe alttestamentlicher Wissenschaft', TLZ 99: 641-58.

Ott, H.
1955 Geschichte und Heilsgeschichte in der Theologie Rudolf Bultmanns, Tübingen (BHTh 19).

1959 'Heilsgeschichte', RGG[3] 3: 187-9.

1966 'Rudolf Bultmann's Philosophy of History' in Kegley (1966): 51-64.

Ottley, R.L.
1897 Aspects of the Old Testament, London (Bampton Lectures 1897).

Pache, R.
1969 The Inspiration and Authority of Scripture, ET: Chicago 1969 (no mention of original).

Pancaro, S.
1975 'The Relationship of the Church to Israel in the Gospel of St John', NTS 21: 396-405.

Pannenberg, W.
1953 'Zur Bedeutung des Analogiegedankens bei Karl Barth: Eine Auseinandersetzung mit Urs von Balthasar', TLZ 78: 17-24.

1959 'Redemptive Event and History', ET in 1967a: I.15-80 (first part is also translated in EOTI: 314-335; German: KuD 5, 1959: 218-37,259-88).

1961a 'Dogmatic Theses on the Doctrine of Revelation' in Pannenberg (1961):123-158.

1961b 'Kerygma and History', ET in 1967a: I.81-95 (German: von Rad Fs (1961): 129-140).

1964 Jesus - God and Man, ET: London 1968 (German 1964).

1965 'The God of Hope', ET in 1967a: II. 234-49 (originally in <u>Ernst Bloch zu Ehren</u> (ed. S. Unseld), Frankfurt 1965: 209-25).

1967a <u>Basic Questions in Theology</u>, ET: London I: 1970; II: 1971 (German 1967; a collection of his essays).

1967b 'On Historical and Theological Hermeneutic', a previously unpublised lecture in 1967a: I.137-181.

1967c 'Appearance as the Arrival of the Future', <u>JAAR</u> 35: 107-118.

1971 'Weltgeschichte und Heilsgeschichte' in von Rad Fs: 349-66.

1973 'Glaube und Wirklichkeit im Denken Gerhard von Rads' in Wolff(1973): 37-5

Park, A.P.
1971 'The Christian Hope According to Bultmann, Pannenberg, and Moltmann', <u>WTJ</u> 33: 153-174.

Patience, D.G.
1970 'The Contribution to Christology of the Quotations of the Psalms in the Gospels and Acts', Dissn, Southwestern Baptist Theological Seminary.

Patton, F.L.
1926 <u>Rundamental Christianity</u>, New York.

Payne, J.B..
1962 <u>The Theology of the Older Testament</u>, Grand Rapids, Mich.

1970 'The B'rith of Yahweh' in Payne (1970): 240-64.

1973 <u>Encyclopedia of Biblical Prophecy: The Complete Guide to Scriptural Predictions and their Fulfillment</u>, London.

Payot, C.
1968 'Les infortunes de la théologie biblique et de l'herméneutique: A propos de quelques ouvrages récents de James Barr et Robert W. Funk', <u>RThPh</u> 18: 218-35.

Peake, A.S.
1897 A Guide to Biblical Study, London 1897[2] (n.d.[1]).

1907,1912 'The Permanent Value of the Old Testament', two lectures with the same title, reprinted in The Nature of Scripture, London 1922: 137-198 (the later essay is printed first).

1913 The Bible: Its Origin, its Significance, and its Abiding Worth, London.

1914 'The History of Theology' in Germany in the Nineteenth Century (A.S.Peake et al.), Manchester 1912-14: 129-184.

Peel, A.
1944 'The Bible and the People: Protestant Views of the Authority of the Bible' in Dugmore (1944): 49-74.

Pelikan, J.
1959 Luther the Expositor: Introduction to the Reformer's Exegetical Writings, St Louis.

Pepler, C.
1944 'The Faith of the Middle Ages' in Dugmore (1944): 23-48.

Perlitt, L.
1969 Bundestheologie im Alten Testament, Neukirchen-Vluyn (WMANT 36).

Perrin, N.
1966 'The Son of Man in Ancient Judaism and Primitive Christianity: A Suggestion', BR 9: 17-28.

Peter, J.
1970 'Salvation History as a Model for Theological Thought', SJT 23: 1-12.

Peter, M.
1969 'Jedność całej Biblii jako zasada hermeneutyczna', AK 72: 398-407.

Phillips, G.E.
1942 The Old Testament in the World Church: With Special Reference to the Younger Churches, London/Redhill (Lutterworth Library 13).

Phythian-Adams, W.J.

1934 *The Call of Israel: An Introduction to the Study of Divine Election*, Oxford

1938 *The Fulness of Israel: A Study of the Meaning of Sacred History*, Oxford (Warburton Lectures 1935-7).

1942 *The People and the Presence: A Study of the At-one-ment*, Oxford.

1944 *The Way of At-one-ment: Studies in Biblical Theology*, London.

1947 'Shadow and Substance: The Meaning of Sacred History', *Interpn* 1: 419-35.

Piccard, D.

1960 'Réflexions sur l'interprétation chrétienne de trois récits de la Genèse' in Vischer Fs: 181-190.

Pieper, K.

n.d. *Ludendorff und die Heilige Schrift: Antwort auf die Schrift: "Das grosse Entsetzen - Die Bibel nicht Gottes Wort"*, Munich n.d. (received in the Bodleian Library, 1946).

Pierson, A.T.

1906 *The Bible and Spiritual Criticism*, London (lectures delivered in 1904).

Pinnock, C.H.

1971 'Theology and Myth: An Evangelical Response to Demythologizing', *BS* 128: 215-26.

Piper, O.A.

1957 'Unchanging Promises: Exodus in the New Testament', *Interpn* 11: 3-22.

Pirot, L.

1913 *L'oeuvre exégétique de Théodore de Mopsueste: 350-428 après J.-C.*, Rome.

Pius XII

1943 'Divino afflante Spiritu', *Acta Apostolicae Sedis* 35: 297-326 (ET: London 1944).

Ploeg, J. van der
1947 'L'Exégèse de l'Ancien Testament dans l'Épître aux Hébreux', RB 54: 187-228.

1954 'L'espérance dans l'Ancien Testament', RB 61: 481-507.

1962 'Une "Théologie de l'Ancien Testament" est-elle possible?', ETL 38: 417-34.

1972 'Eschatology in the Old Testament' in The Witness of Tradition, Leiden (OTS 17): 89-99.

Plöger, O.
1959 Theocracy and Eschatology, ET: Oxford 1968 (German 1959, WMANT 2).

Pöhlmann, H.G.
1965 Analogia entis oder Analogia fidei? Die Frage der Analogie bei Karl Barth, Göttingen.

Polley, M.E.
1972 'H. Wheeler Robinson and the Problem of Organizing an Old Testament Theology' in Stinespring Fs: 149-169.

Polman, A.D.R.
1955 The Word of God According to St. Augustine, ET: London 1961 (Dutch 1955).

Porteous, N.W
1948 'Towards a Theology of the Old Testament', SJT 1: 136-149 (repr. in 1967: 7-19).

1950 'Semantics and Old Testament Theology', OTS 8: 1-14 (repr. in 1967: 21-30).

1951 'Old Testament Theology' in Rowley (1951): 311-45.

1954 'The Old Testament and Some Theological Thought-Forms', SJT 7: 153-169 (repr. in 1967: 31-46).

1961 'Jerusalem - Zion: the Growth of a Symbol', repr. in 1967: 93-111 (originally in Verbannung und Heimkehr: Wilhelm Rudolph zum 70. Geburtstage, Tübingen 1961).

1962 'The Theology of the Old Testament', PCB: 151-9.

1963a 'Actualization and the Prophetic Criticism of the Cult' in Weiser Fs: 93-105 (repr. in 1967: 127-141).

1963b 'Second Thoughts: II. The Present State of Old Testament Theology', _ExpT_ 75: 70-74.

1963c Review of Vriezen 1954, _JTS_ 14: 116-118.

1966 'The Relevance of the Old Testament as the Rule of Life' in Vriezen Fs: 278-89 (repr. in 1967: 157-168).

1967 _Living the Mystery: Collected Essays_, Oxford.

1970a 'A Question of Perspectives' in Eichrodt Fs: 117-131

1970b 'The Limits of Old Testament Interpretation' in Davies Fs: 3-17.

1971 'Magnalia Dei' in von Rad Fs: 417-27.

1972 'Old Testament and History', _ASTI_ 8: 21-77.

Porter, J.R.
1950 Review of Vischer 1934, _Theology_ 53: 192-3.

Premsagar, P.V.
1974 'Theology of Promise in the Patriarchal Narratives', _IJT_ 23: 112-122.

Prenter, R.
1956 'Die systematische Theologie und das Problem der Bibelauslegung', _TLZ_ 81: 577-86.

Press, R.
1934 'Das Alte Testament als Wort Gottes', _ThBl_ 13: 225-9.

Preus, J.S.
1967 'Old Testament _Promissio_ and Luther's New Hermeneutic', _HTR_ 60: 145-161.

1969 _From Shadow to Promise: Old Testament Interpretation from Augustine to the Young Luther_, Cambridge,Mass.

Preuss, C.
1950 'The Contemporary Relevance of Von Hofmann's Hermeneutical Principles', _Interpn_ 4: 311-21.

Preuss, H.D.
1968 Jahweglaube und Zukunftserwartung, Stuttgart (BWANT 87).

Prigent, P.
1964 Justin et l'Ancien Testament: L'argumentation scripturaire du Traité de Justin contre toutes les hérésies comme source principale du Dialogue avec Tryphon et de la Première Apologie, Paris.

Prins, R.
1972 'The Image of God in Adam and the Restoration of Man in Jesus Christ: A Study in Calvin', SJT 25: 32-44.

Procksch, O.
1925a 'Die Geschichte als Glaubensinhalt', NKZ 36: 485-99.

1925b 'Ziele und Grenzen der Exegese', NKZ 36: 715-30.

1931 'Die kirchliche Bedeutung des Alten Testaments: Nach einem Vortrag', NKZ 42: 295-306.

1933 'Christus im Alten Testament', NKZ 44: 57-83.

1935 Review of Vischer 1934, ThLBl 56: 326-8.

1950 Theologie des Alten Testaments, Gütersloh.

Prussner, F.C.
1968 'The Covenant of David and the Problem of Unity in Old Testament Theology' in Rylaarsdam (1968): 17-41.

Quervain, A. de
1935-6 Das Gesetz Gottes: Die erste Tafel, Predigten; Die zweite Tafel, Munich (ThEx 34, 39).

Rad, G. von
1933 'There still remains a rest for the people of God: An Investigation of a Biblical Conception', ET in 1958: 94-102 (German: ZZ 11, 1933: 104-111).

1935 'Das Christuszeugnis des Alten Testaments: Eine Auseinandersetzung mit Wilhelm Vischers gleichnamigen Buch', ThBl 14: 249-54.

1936a 'The Theological Problem of the Old Testament Doctrine of Creation', ET in 1958: 131-143 (originally in Hempel (1936)).

1936b 'Sensus Scripturae Sacrae duplex? Eine Erwiderung', ThBl 15: 30-34.

1937 'Gesetz und Evangelium im Alten Testament. Gedanken zu dem Buch von E. Hirsch: Das Alte Testament und die Predigt des Evangeliums', ThBl 16: 41-7.

1938 'The Form-Critical Problem of the Hexateuch', ET in 1958: 1-78 (originally published as a monograph in BWANT, 1938).

1943 'Grundprobleme einer biblischen Theologie des Alten Testaments', TLZ 68: 225-34.

1947 Studies in Deuteronomy, ET: London 1953 (SBT 9; German 1948,revd; 1947[1]).

1948 'Theologische Geschichtsschreibung im Alten Testament', ThZ 4: 161-174.

1952a 'Typological Interpretation of the Old Testament', ET in EOTI: 17-39 (also: Interpn 15, 1961: 174-192; German: EvTh 12, 1952: 17-33).

1952b 'Predigt über Ruth 1', EvTh 12: 1-6.

1952c 'Kritische Vorarbeiten zu einer Theologie des Alten Testaments (Ein Bericht)' in Hennig (1952): 9-34.

1953a Genesis, ET: London 1961 (German 1958[2], 1953[1]).

1953b 'Verheissung: Zum gleichnamigen Buch Fr. Baumgärtels', EvTh 13: 406-13.

1957 Old Testament Theology: I. The Theology of Israel's Historical Traditions, ET: Edinburgh 1962 (German 1957).

1958 The Problem of the Hexateuch and other essays, ET: Edinburgh/London 1966 (German 1958). A collection of essays originally published 1931-1964.

1959 'The Origin of the Concept of the Day of Yahweh', JSS 4: 97-108 (much of it is incorporated into 1960: 119-125).

1960 *Old Testament Theology: II. The Theology of Israel's Prophetic Traditions*, ET: Edinburgh 1965 (German 1960). An abridged French translation of pp. 99-125 was published as 'Les idées sur le temps et l'histoire en Israël et l'eschatologie des prophètes' in Vischer Fs: 198-209.

1961a 'Ancient Word and Living Word: The Preaching of Deuteronomy and Our Preaching', *Interpn* 15: 3-13.

1961b 'History and the Patriarchs', *ExpT* 72: 213-16.

1963 'Offene Fragen im Umkreis einer Theologie des Alten Testaments', *TLZ* 88: 401-16. A slightly abridged ET is printed as a postscript to the ET of 1960: 410-29.

1964 'Antwort auf Conzelmanns Fragen', *EvTh* 24: 388-94.

1971 'Christliche Weisheit?', *EvTh* 31: 150-155.

Rahner, K.
1968 'Bible: I. Introduction: B. Theology' in *Sacramentum Mundi: An Encyclopedia of Theology* (ed. K. Rahner *et al.*), English edn: New York/London, I: 1968: 171-8.

Ramlot, L.
1964-5 'Une décade de théologie biblique', *RThom* 64: 65-96; 65: 95-135.

Ramm, B.
1953 *Protestant Biblical Interpretation: A Textbook of Hermeneutics*, Grand Rapids, Mich. 1970[3] (Chicago 1953[1]).

Ratschow, C.H..
1957 *Der angefochtene Glaube: Anfangs- und Grundprobleme der Dogmatik*, Gütersloh 1960[2], 1957[1].

Redpath, H.A.
1907 'Christ, the Fulfilment of Prophecy', *Exp* 7.3: 1-20.

Rehm, M.
1968 *Der königliche Messias: im Licht der Immanuel-Weissagungen des Buches Jesaja*, Kevelaer, Rheinland.

Reid, J.K.S.
1957 The Authority of Scripture, London.

Reid, R.
1964 'The Use of the Old Testament in the Epistle to the Hebrews', Dissn, Union Theological Seminary, New York.*

Reid, W.S.
1952 'The New Testament Belief in an Old Testament Church', EQ 24: 194-205.

Reim, G.
1973 Studien zum alttestamentlichen Hintergrund des Johannesevangeliums, Cambridge (SNTS Mon 22).

Reisner, E.
1952 'Hermeneutik und historische Vernunft', ZTK 49: 223-38 (a response to Ebeling 1950).

Reist, I.
1971 'The Old Testament Basis for the Resurrection Faith', EQ 83: 6-24.

Rendtorff, R.
1960 'Hermeneutik des Alten Testaments als Frage nach der Geschichte', ZTK 57: 27-40.

1961a 'The Concept of Revelation in Ancient Israel' in Pannenberg (1961): 23-53. A shorter form of the same article appeared in TLZ 85: 833-8.

1961b 'Geschichte und Überlieferung' in von Rad Fs: 81-94.

1962 'Geschichte und Wort im Alten Testament', EvTh 22: 621-49.

1963 'Alttestamentliche Theologie und israelitisch-jüdische Religionsgeschichte' in Kupisch Fs: 208-22.

1971 'Beobachtungen zur altisraelitischen Geschichtsschreibung' in von Rad Fs: 428-39.

1973 'Die alttestamentlichen Überlieferungen als Grundthemen der Lebensarbeit Gerhard von Rads' in Wolff (1973): 21-35

Rese, M.
1967 'Die Rolle des Alten Testaments im Neuen Testament', VF 12.2: 87-97.

1969 Alttestamentliche Motive in der Christologie des Lukas, Gütersloh 1969 (Studien zum Neuen Testament 1).

Reventlow, H.G.
1961 'Grundfragen der alttestamentlichen Theologie im Lichte der neueren deutschen Forschung', ThZ 17: 81-98.

1965 'Die Auffassung vom Alten Testament bei Hermann Samuel Reimarus und Gotthold Ephraim Lessing', EvTh 25: 429-48.

1971 Rechtfertigung im Horizont des Alten Testaments, Munich (BEvTh 58).

Rhodes, A.B.
1959 Review of Jacob 1955, Interpn 13: 468-70.

Richardson, A.
1947 Christian Apologetics, London.

1948 'Autorité et rôle actuels de l'éthique de l'Ancien Testament', ETR 23: 37-40.

1960 Review of Knight 1959a, JTS 11: 376-7.

1963 'The Rise of Modern Biblical Scholarship and Recent Discussion of the Authority of the Bible', CHB III: 294-338.

1964a 'Is the Old Testament the Propaedeutic to Christian Faith?', OTCF: 36-48.

1964b History Sacred and Profane, London (Bampton Lectures 1962).

Richardson, P.
1969 Israel in the Apostolic Church, Cambridge (SNTS Mon 10).

1970 'The Israel-Idea in the Passion Narratives' in Moule Fs: 1-10.

Richter, G.
1972 'Die alttestamentlichen Zitate in der Rede vom Joh 6,26-51a' in Ernst (1972): 193-279.

Richter, W.
1967 'Beobachtungen zur theologischen Systembildung in der alttestamentlichen Literatur anhand des "kleinen geschichtlichen Credo"' in Schmaus Fs: 175-212.

Ridderbos, H.
1966 *Paulus: Ontwerp van zijn Theologie*, Kampen. ET: Grand Rapids, Mich. 1975.

Ridderbos, J.
1954 'Oud en Nieuw Verbond' in Kampen (1954): 7-38.

Ridderbos, N.H.
1961 'Typologie (Speciaal de typologie naar Von Rads conceptie)', *VoxTh* 31: 149-159.

Riedinger, R.
1975 'Zur antimarkionitischen Polemik des Klemens von Alexandreia', *VigChr* 29: 15-32.

Ringgren, H.
1956 *The Messiah in the Old Testament*, London (SBT 18).

1964 Review of Amsler 1960a, *Interpn* 18: 79-8

Robinson, H.W.
1913 *The Religious Ideas of the Old Testament*, London 1956[2] (revd by L.H.Brockington, it has only minor changes from the first edn, 1913).

1916-26 *The Cross in the Old Testament*, London 1955 (originally 3 monographs: 1916, 1938[2]; 1926; 1925).

1938 'The Theology of the Old Testament' in Robinson (1938): 303-48.

1943 'The Higher Exegesis', *JTS* 44: 143-7.

1946 *Inspiration and Revelation in the Old Testament*, Oxford.

Robinson, J.A.
1904 *Some Thoughts on Inspiration*, London 1908 (new impression, 3 lectures given 1904).

Robinson, J.M.
1964 'The Historicality of Biblical Language' *OTCF*: 124-158. It is essentially the same article as 'Heilsgeschichte und Lichtungsgeschichte: Friedrich Gogarten zum 75. Geburtstag', *EvTh* 22: 113-141.

1965 'Scripture and Theological Method: A Protestant Study in *Sensus Plenior*', *CBQ* 27: 6-27.

Robinson, T.H.

1951 'The Old Testament and the Modern World' in Rowley (1951): 346-70.

Rohland, E.

1956 *Die Bedeutung der Erwählungstraditionen Israels für die Eschatologie der alttestamentlichen Propheten*, Munich (photocopy of Heidelberg dissn).

Röhr, H.

1973 'Buddhismus und Christentum: Untersuchung zur Typologie zweier Weltreligionen', *ZRG* 25: 289-303.

Rordorf, W.

1967 'The Theology of Rudolf Bultmann and Second-Century Gnosis', *NTS* 13: 351-62.

Rose, A.

1962 'L'influence des psaumes sur les annonces et les récits de la Passion et de la Résurrection dans les Évangiles' in de Langhe (1962): 297-356.

Rosenberg, A.

1930 *Der Mythus des 20. Jahrhunderts: Eine Wertung der seelisch-geistigen Gestaltkämpfe unserer Zeit*, Munich 1934[29-30] (1930[1]).

1938 *Protestantische Rompilger: Der Verrat an Luther und der "Mythus des 20. Jahrhunderts"*, Munich.

Rössler, D.

1960 *Gesetz und Geschichte: Untersuchungen zur Theologie der jüdischen Apokalyptik und der pharisäischen Orthodoxie*, Neukirchen (WMANT 3).

1961 'Die Predigt über alttestamentliche Texte' in von Rad Fs: 153-162.

Rost, H.

1939 *Die Bibel im Mittelalter: Beiträge zur Geschichte und Bibliographie der Bibel*, Augsburg.

Rost, L.

1947 'Sinaibund und Davidsbund', *TLZ* 72: 129-134.

1965 *Das kleine Credo und andere Studien zum Alten Testament*, Heidelberg (all but the title essay are reprints from earlier publications).

Rothfuchs, W.
1969 *Die Erfüllungszitate des Matthäus-Evangeliums: Eine biblisch-theologisch Untersuchung*, Stuttgart (BWANT 88).

Rottenberg, I.C.
1964 *Redemption and Historical Reality*, Philadelphia.

Rowley, H.H.
1939 *Israel's Mission to the World*, London.

1941 *The Relevance of the Bible*, London n.d. (preface 1941).

1944a *The Relevance of Apocalyptic: A Study of Jewish and Christian Apocalypses from Daniel to the Revelation*, London 1947[2] (1944[1], 1963[3]).

1944b *The Missionary Message of the Old Testament*, London.

1946a *The Re-Discovery of the Old Testament*, London n.d. (preface 1945, this date from Rowley Fs: xiv).

1946b 'The Unity of the Old Testament', *BJRL* 29: 326-58.

1947 'The Relevance of Biblical Interpretation', *Interpn* 1: 3-19.

1949 'The Authority of the Bible', repr. in *From Moses to Qumran*, London 1963: 3-31 (reprinted from the Joseph Smith Memorial Lecture, Birmingham 1949).

1950a *The Biblical Doctrine of Election*, London 1950[1], 1964[2].

1950b 'The Suffering Servant and the Davidic Messiah', *OTS* 8: 100-136, revised edn in *The Servant of the Lord, and other essays on the Old Testament*, London 1952[1]: 59-88; 1965[2]: 61-93.

1950c 'The Gospel in the Old Testament' in Smith (1950): 19-35.

1952 'The Servant of the Lord in the Light of Three Decades of Criticism' in *The Servant of the Lord*, 1952[1]: 1-57; 1965[2]: 1-60.

1953 *The Unity of the Bible*, London.

1956 *The Faith of Israel*, London.

1959 Review of Knight 1959a, *ExpT* 71: 73.

Ruler, A.A.van

1942 'De waarde van het Oude Testament', *VoxTh* 13: 113-117.

1945 *Religie en Politiek*, Nijkerk.

1947 *De vervulling van de wet: Een dogmatische studie over de verhouding van openbaring en existentie*, Nijkerk.

1955 *The Christian Church and the Old Testament*, ET: Grand Rapids, Mich. 1966 (reissued 1971 without change; German BEvTh 23, 1955).

1960 *God's Son and God's World: Sixteen Meditations on the Person of Christ and the Psalm of Nature*, ET: Grand Rapids, Mich. 1960 (Dutch n.d.)

1962 *Zechariah Speaks Today*, ET: London 1962 (abridged from *Heb Moed voor de Wereld*, n.d.).

1965 *Reformatorische opmerkingen in de ontmoeting met Rome*, Antwerp.

Runia, K.

1967 'The Interpretation of the Old Testament by the New Testament', *TSFB* 49: 9-18.

Rupp, E.G.

1945 *Martin Luther: Hitler's Cause - or Cure?*, London/Redhill. A response to Wiener 1945.

1963 'The Bible in the Age of the Reformation' in Nineham (1963): 73-87.

Russell, D.S.

1964 *The Method and Message of Jewish Apocalyptic: 200 BC - AD 100*, London.

Russell, S.H.

1968 'Calvin and the Messianic Interpretation of the Psalms', *SJT* 21: 37-47.

Rust, E.C.

1963 *Towards a Theological Understanding of History*, New York.

Rylaarsdam, J.C.
1958 'The Problem of Faith and History in Biblical Interpretation', JBL 77: 26-32.

1972 'Jewish-Christian relationship: The Two Covenants and the Dilemmas of Christology', JES 9: 249-70.

Sagnard, F.M.M.
1959 'Holy Scripture in the Early Fathers of the Church', StEv I (TU 73): 706-13.

Sahlin, H.
1950 Zur Typologie des Johannesevangeliums, Uppsala (Uppsala Universitets Årsskrift 1950: 4).

Sailer, J.
1947 Über Typen im Neuen Testament', ZKT 69: 490-96.

Sand, A.
1972a 'Zur Frage nach dem "Sitz im Leben" der Apokalyptischen Texte des Neuen Testaments', NTS 18: 167-177.

1972b '"Wie geschrieben steht...": Zur Auslegung der jüdischen Schriften in den urchristlichen Gemeinden' in Ernst (1972): 331-57.

Sanday, W.
1891 The Oracles of God: Nine Lectures, London.

Sanders, J.A.
1972 Torah and Canon, Philadelphia.

1974 'Reopening Old Questions About Scripture', Interpn 28: 321-30 (a review of Barr 1973).

Saphir, A.
1867 Christ and the Scriptures, London n.d. (this date from British Museum catalogue).

1894 The Divine Unity of Scripture, London.

Sauer, E.
1937a The Dawn of World Redemption: A Survey of Historical Revelation in the Old Testament, ET: London 1951 (German 1937).

1937b The Triumph of the Crucified: A Survey of Historical Revelation in the New Testament, ET: London 1951 (German 1937).

Sauter, G.
1965 Zukunft und Verheissung: Das Problem der Zukunft in der gegenwärtigen theologischen und philosophischen Diskussion, Zürich.

Schaff, P.
1877 The Creeds of Christendom: Volume II. The Greek and Latin Creeds, with translations, New York.

Schairer, J.B.
1933 Volk - Blut - Gott: Ein Gruss des Evangeliums an die deutsche Freiheitsbewegung, Berlin.

Scharleman, M.H.
1972 'Roman Catholic Biblical Interpretation' in Gingrich Fs: 209-22.

Schedl, C.
1965 'Die messianische Hoffnung' in Leist (1965): 434-47.

Schelkle, K.H.
1968- Theologie des Neuen Testaments, Düsseldorf, 1: 1968; 2: 1973; 3: 1970; 4.1: 1974; 4.2: not yet available.

Schierse, F.J.
1957 'Die interpretatio christiana des Alten Bundes', LTK[2] 1: 393-6.

Schildenberger, J.
1943 'Weissagung und Erfüllung', Biblica 24: 107-124, 205-30.

1965 'Die Opfer des Alten Testamentes und das Opfer Jesu Christi' in Leist (1965): 488-509.

Schlatter, A.
1904 'J.T. Beck's theologische Arbeit', BFChTh I.8.3: 25-46, Gütersloh.

1933 Die neue deutsche Art in der Kirche, Bethel bei Bielefeld (repr. from the journal Beth-El).

Schleiermacher, F.
1821 The Christian Faith, ET: Edinburgh 1928 (German 1830[2], 1821[1]).

Schlink, E.
1937 *Gesetz und Evangelium: Ein Beitrag zum lutherischen Verständnis der 2. Barmer These*, Munich (ThEx 53).

1956 'Gesetz und Paraklese' in Barth Fs: 323-35.

1961 'Law and Gospel as a Controversial Theological Problem' in The Coming Christ and the Coming Christ and the Coming Church, ET: Edinburgh/London 1967 (German 1961): 144-185.

Schmid, H.
1965 'Die Einheit der Testamente', *Judaica* 21: 150-166.

Schmid, J.von
1959 'Die alttestamentlichen Zitate bei Paulus und die Theorie vom sensus plenior', *BZ* 3: 161-173.

Schmidt, H.
1933 *Luther und das Buch der Psalmen: Ein Beitrag zur Frage der Wertung des Alten Testaments*, Tübingen (Sammlung Gemeinverständlicher Vorträge 167).

Schmidt, J.M.
1969 *Die jüdische Apokalyptik: Die Geschichte ihrer Erforschung von den Anfängen bis zu den Textfunden von Qumran*, Neukirchen-Vluyn.

1970 'Erwägungen zum Verhältnis von Auszugs- und Sinaitraditionen', *ZAW* 82: 1-31.

Schmidt, K.L.
1950 'Jerusalem als Urbild und Abbild', *ErJb* 18: 207-48.

Schmidt, L.
1975 'Die Einheit zwischen Altem und Neuem Testament im Streit zwischen Friedrich Baumgärtel und Gerhard von Rad', *EvTh* 35: 119-139.

Schmidt, M.A.
1967 'Zum Problem der Heilsgeschichte in der Hochscholastik' in Cullmann Fs: 155-162.

Schmidt, W.H.

1969 — Das erste Gebot: Seine Bedeutung für das Alte Testament, Munich (ThEx 165).

1972 — '"Theologie des Alten Testaments" vor und nach Gerhard von Rad', VF 17: 1-25.

\- — Exodus, Neukirchen (BK 2/1; one fascicle appeared so far).

Schmithals, W.

1966 — An Introduction to the Theology of Rudolf Bultmann, ET: London 1968 (German 1967[2], 1966[1]).

Schmitz, O.

1934 — 'Das Alte Testament im Neuen Testament' in Heim Fs: 49-74.

Schnackenburg, R.

1960 — 'Heilsgeschichte: I. Die biblische H.', LTK[2] 5: 148-153.

1963 — 'Zum Offenbarungsgedanken in der Bibel', BZ 7: 2-22.

1972 — 'Joh 12, 39-41: Zur christologischen Schriftauslegung des vierten Evangelisten' in Cullmann Fs: 167-177.

Schneider-Hume, G.

1971 — Die politische Theologie Emanuel Hirschs 1918-1933, Bern/Frankfurt-on--Main (Europäische Hochschulschriften 23.5).

Schniewind, J.

1936 — 'Die Eine Botschaft des Alten und des Neuen Testaments' in Julius Schniewind: Nachgelassene Reden und Aufsätze (ed. E. Kähler), Berlin 1952: 58-71 (from typescript of previously unpublished 1936 lecture).

1966 — 'Die Beziehung des Neuen Testaments zum Alten Testament', ZdZ 20: 3-10.

Schofield, J.N.

1964 — Introducing Old Testament Theology, London.

1970 — 'Otto Procksch, Theology of the Old Testament' in Laurin (1970): 91-120.

Schreiner, H.
1936 *Die Verkündigung des Wortes Gottes: Homiletik*, Schwerin.

Schreiner, J.
1966 'The Development of the Israelite "Credo"', *Concilium* 2.10: 16-21.

1969 'Die Hoffnung der Zukunftsschau Israels' in Kleinedam Fs: 29-48.

Schrenk, G.
1923 *Gottesreich und Bund im älteren Protestantismus, vornehmlich bei Johannes Cocceius*, Gütersloh (BFChTh 2.5).

1933 'γράφω, γραφή, γράμμα, ἐγγράφω, προγράφω, ὑπογραμμός', *TDNT* 1: 742-73.

Schröger, F.
1968 *Der Verfasser des Hebräerbriefes als Schriftausleger*, Regensburg.

Schubert, K.
1965 'Das Zeitalter der Apokalyptik' in Leist (1965): 461-80.

Schulte, H.
1962 'In den Tatsachen selbst ist Gott: Die Bedeutung des Alten Testaments für die christliche Verkündigung nach D. Bonhoeffers letzten Briefen', *EvTh* 22: 441-8.

1966 'The Old Testament and its Significance for Religious Instruction' in Kegley (1966): 221-35.

Schultz, H.
1860 *Old Testament Theology*, ET: Edinburgh 1892 (German n.d.^{4}, 1860^{1}).

Schultz, S.
1961 'Markus und das Alte Testament', *ZTK* 58: 184-197.

Schulz, S.
1962 'Die römisch-katholische Exegese zwischen historisch-kritischer Methode und lehramtlichem Machtspruch', *EvTh* 22: 141-156.

Schunk, K.-D.
1964 'Strukturlinie in der Entwicklung der Vorstellung vom "Tag Jahwes"', *VT* 14: 319-30.

1974 'Die Eschatologie der Propheten des Alten Testaments und ihre Wandlung in exilisch-nachexilischer Zeit' in Studies on Prophecy: A Collection of Twelve Papers, Leiden (SVT 26): 116-132.

Schütte, H.-W.
1970 'Christlicher Glaube und Altes Testament bei Friedrich Schleiermacher' in Doerne Fs: 291-310.

Schwarzwäller, K.
1966a Das Alte Testament in Christus, Zürich (ThSt 84).

1966b Theologie oder Phänomenologie: Erwägungen zur Methodik theologischen Verstehens, Münich (BEvTh 42).

1966c 'Geschichte oder AltesTestament?', VF 11: 57-62. A discussion of Hempel 1964.

1969 'Das Verhältnis AltesTestament - NeuesTestament im Lichte der gegenwärtigen Bestimmungen', EvTh 29: 281-307.

1971 'Probleme gegenwärtiger Theologie und das Alte Testament' in von Rad Fs: 479-93.

Schweitzer, W.
1950 'Das Problem der biblischen Hermeneutik in der gegenwärtigen Theologie', TLZ 8: 467-78.

Seebass, H.
1965 'Der Beitrag des Alten Testaments zum Entwurf einer biblischen Theologie', WuD 8: 20-49.

Seeligmann, I.L.
1963 'Menschliches Heldentum und göttliche Hilfe: Die doppelte Kausalität im alttestamentlichen Geschichtsdenken', ThZ 19: 385-411.

Sekine, M.
1963 'Vom Verstehen der Heilsgeschichte: Das Grundproblem der alttestamentlichen Theologie', ZAW 75: 145-154.

Selbie, W.B.
1927 'The Influence of the Old Testament on Puritanism' in Bevan and Singer (1927): 407-31.

Sellin, E.
1921 Das Alte Testament und die evangelische Kirche der Gegenwart, Leipzig-Erlangen.

1933 Alttestamentliche Theologie II: Theologie des Alten Testaments, Leipzig 1936[2] (1933[1])

Senior, D.
1972 'The Fate of the Betrayer: A Redactional Study of Matthew XXVII, 3-10', ETL 48: 372-426.

Sheppard, G.T.
1974 'Canon Criticism: The Proposal of Brevard Childs and an Assessment for Evangelical Hermeneutics', Studia Biblica et Theologica 4.2: 3-17.

Shih, D.P.
1971 'The Unity of the Testaments as a Hermeneutical Problem', Dissn, Boston.

Shotwell, W.A.
1965 The Biblical Exegesis of Justin Martyr, London.

Shuster, G.N.
1935 Like a Mighty Army: Hitler versus Established Religion, New York/London.

Sick, H.
1959 Melanchthon als Ausleger des Alten Testaments, Tübingen (BGBH 2).

Siegwalt, G.
1971 La Loi, chemin du Salut: Étude sur la signification de la loi de l'Ancien Testament, Neuchâtel.

Siertsema, B.
1969 'Language and World View (Semantics for Theologians)', BT 20: 3-21.

Simon, M.
1932 'Die Beziehung zwischen Altem und Neuem Testament in der Schriftauslegung Calvins', RKZ 82: 19-20.*

Simon, U.
1970 Review of Miskotte 1956a, RelSt 6(1970): 190-191, and again in 7(1971): 191-2.

Simpson, C.A.
1961 'An Inquiry into the Biblical Theology of History', JTS 12: 1-13.

Smalley, B.
1952 The Study of the Bible in the Middle Ages, Oxford.

1963 'The Bible in the Middle Ages' in Nineham (1963): 57-71.

1969 'The Exposition and Exegesis of Scripture: 3. The Bible in the Medieval Schools', CHB II: 197-220.

Smart, J.D.
1960 Review of Knight 1959a, JBL 79: 290-91.

1961 The Interpretation of Scripture, London.

1965 The Old Testament in Dialogue with Modern Man, London.

1970 The Strange Silence of the Bible in the Church: A Study in Hermeneutics, London.

Smend, R. (1)
1893 Lehrbuch der alttestamentlichen Religionsgeschichte, Freiburg/Leipzig 1899[2] (1893[1]).

Smend, R. (2)
1970 Die Mitte des Alten Testaments, Zürich (ThSt 101).

Smith, D.M.
1972 'The Use of the Old Testament in the New' in Stinespring Fs: 3-65.

Smith, G.A.
1899 Modern Criticism and the Preaching of the Old Testament, London n.d. (lectures given at Yale, 1899).

1927 'The Hebrew Genius as Exhibited in the Old Testament' in Bevan and Singer (1927): 1-28.

Smith, H.P.
1921 Essays in Biblical Interpretation, London.

Smith, J.M.P.
1901 'The Day of Yahweh', AJT 5: 505-33.

Smith, R.
1952 'The Relevance of the Old Testament for the Doctrine of the Church', SJT 5: 14-23.

Smith, R.H.
1962 'Exodus Typology in the Fourth Gospel', JBL 81: 329-42.

Smith, R.P.
1862 The Authenticity and Messianic Interpretation of the Prophecies of Isaiah Vindicated in a Course of Sermons Preached Before the University of Oxford, Oxford/London.

1869 Prophecy a Preparation for Christ, London (Bampton Lectures 1869).

Smith, W.R.
1881 The Old Testament in the Jewish Church: A Course of Lectures on Biblical Criticism, London 1892[2] (1881[1]).

1884 'The Attitude of Christians to the Old Testament', Exp 2.7: 241-51.

Smits, C.
1952-63 Oud-testamentische citaten in het Nieuwe Testament, 4 volumes, 's-Hertogenbosch (Collectanea Franciscana Nederlandica 8).

Snaith, N.H.
1944 The Distinctive Ideas of the Old Testament, London.

1956 The Inspiration and Authority of the Bible, London (A.S.Peake Memorial Lecture 1).

1960 Review of Knight 1959a, SJT 13: 90-91.

Sneen, D.J.
1972 'The Hermeneutics of N.F.S.Grundtvig', Interpn 26: 42-61.

Soggin, J.A.
1961a 'Altestamentliche Glaubenszeugnisse und geschichtliche Wirklichkeit', ThZ 17: 385-98.

1961b 'L'Antico Testamento nella Chiesa', Protestantesimo 16: 211-17. Discussion of Amsler 1960a.

1964 'Geschichte, Historie und Heilsgeschichte im Alten Testament: Ein Beitrag zur heutigen theologisch-hermeneutische Diskussion', TLZ 89: 721-36.

Sowers, S.G.
1965 *The Hermeneutics of Philo and Hebrews: A Comparison of the Interpretation of the Old Testament in Philo Judaeus and the Epistle to the Hebrews*, Zürich.

Sparks, H.F.D.
1944 *The Old Testament in the Christian Church*, London.

Sperber, A.
1940 'New Testament and Septuagint', *JBL* 59: 193-293.

Spicq, C.
1944 *Esquisse d'une histoire de l'exégèse latine au Moyen Age*, Paris (BThom 26).

1951 'L'avènement de la théologie biblique', *RSPT* 35: 561-74.

Spriggs, D.G.
1971/74 'Towards an Understanding of Old Testament Theology', Dissn, Oxford 1971; abridged version published as *Two Old Testament Theologies: A Comparative Evaluation of the Contributions of Eichrodt and von Rad to our Understanding of the Nature of Old Testament Theology*, London 1974 (SBT 2.30).

Stachowiak, L.
1969 'W poszukiwaniu chrześcijańskiego sensu Starego Testamentu', *AK* 72: 418-26.

Stadtke, J.
1972 'Die Hoffnung des Glaubens und die Veränderung der Welt', *KuD* 18: 71-81.

Stamm, J.J.
1940 *Erlösen und Vergeben im Alten Testament: Eine begriffsgeschichtliche Untersuchung*, Bern.

1956 'Jesus Christ and the Old Testament: A Review of A.A. van Ruler's book: *Die christliche Kirche und das Alte Testament*', ET in *EOTI*: 200-210 (originally in *EvTh* 16,1956: 387-95).

Stauffer, E.
1941 *New Testament Theology*, ET: London 1955 (German 1948[5], 1941[1]).

Steck, K.G.

1959 Die Idee der Heilsgeschichte: Hofmann - Schlatter - Cullmann, Zollikon (ThSt 56).

1960 'Heilsgeschichte: III. Das ev. Verständnis der H.', LTK[2] 5: 156-7.

Steck, O.H.

1967 Israel und das gewaltsame Geschick der Propheten: Untersuchungen zur Überlieferung des deuteronomistischen Geschichtsbildes im Alten Testament, Spätjudentum und Urchristentum, Neukirchen-Vluyn (WMANT 23).

1971 'Genesis 12: 1-3 und die Urgeschichte des Jahwisten' in von Rad Fs: 525-54.

Stegeman, U.

1969 'Der Restgedanke bei Isaias', BZ 13: 161-186.

Steiger, L.

1962 'Revelation-History and Theological Reason: A Critique of the Theology of Wolfhart Pannenberg', ET in JTC 4(1967): 82-106 (German: ZTK 59, 1962: 88-113).

Steinlein, H.

1937 'Luther und das Alte Testament', Luthertum 48: 172-184, 193-200.

Stek, J.H.

1970 'Biblical Typology Yesterday and Today', CTJ 5: 133-162.

Stendahl, K.

1954 The School of St. Matthew, and its Use of the Old Testament, Philadelphia 1968[2] (1954[1]).

1962 'Biblical Theology, Contemporary', IDB 1: 418-32.

Steuernagel, C.

1925 'Alttestamentliche Theologie und alttestamentliche Religionsgeschichte' in Vom Alten Testament: Karl Marti zum siebzigsten Geburtstage (ed. K. Budde), Giessen (BZAW 41).

Stierle, B.

1971 'Schriftauslegung der Reformationszeit' VF 16.1: 55-88.

Stoebe, H.J.
1954 'Der heilsgeschichtliche Bezug der Jabbok-Perikope', EvTh 14: 466-74.

Stol, M.
1971 Review of Miskotte 1956a, BO 28: 372-4.

Stott, W.
n.d. 'The Jewish Background to the Epistle to the Hebrews, with special reference to the Writings of the Qumran Sect and the use of the Old Testament', Dissn, B.Litt.Oxford n.d. (the most recent reference is 1962).

Stoughton, J.
n.d. The Progress of Divine Revelation, or The Unfolding Purpose of Scripture, London.

Strathmann, H.
1936 'Zum Ringen um das christliche Verständnis des Alten Testaments', ThBl 15: 257-60.

Strauss, G.
1959 Schriftgebrauch, Schriftauslegung und Schriftbeweis bei Augustin, Tübingen (BGBH 1).

Strohl, H.
1955 'La méthode exégétique des Réformateurs' in Boisset (1955): 87-104.

Stuermann, W.E.
1956 'Jehovah's Witnesses', Interpn 10: 323-46.

Stylianopoulos, T.G.
1972 'Shadow and Reality: Reflections on Hebrews 10: 1-18', GOTR 17: 215-30.

Suhl, A.
1965 Die Funktion der alttestamentlichen Zitate und Anspielungen in Markusevangelium, Gütersloh.

Sundberg, A.C.
1964 The Old Testament of the Early Church, Cambridge, Mass./London (Harvard Theological Studies 20).

Surburg, R.F.
1974 'The New Hermeneutic Versus the Old Hermeneutics in New Testament Interpretation', The Springfielder 38: 13-21 (not available to me, but summary in New Testament Abstracts 19.27).

Sutcliffe, E.F.
1953 'The Plenary Sense as a Principle of Interpretation', Biblica 34: 333-43.

Swetnam, J.
1974 'Why was Jeremiah's new covenant new?' in Studies on Prophecy: A Collection of Twelve Papers, Leiden (SVT 26): 111-115.

Sykes, N.
1963 'The Religion of Protestants', CHB III: 175-198.

Synge, F.C.
1959 Hebrews and the Scriptures, London.

Talmon, S.
1971 'Typen der Messiaserwartung um die Zeitenwende' in von Rad Fs: 571-88.

Tångberg, K.A.
1973 'Linguistics and Theology', BT 24: 301-10.

Tanner, E.S.
1942 The Nazi Christ, Tulsa, Okla.

Tasker, R.V.G.
1946 The Old Testament in the New Testament, London 1946[1], 1954[2].

Temiño Saiz, A.
1955 'En torno al problema del "sensus plenior"', EstB 14: 5-47.

Terrien, S.
1952 'History of the Inteprretation of the Bible: III. Modern Period', IB 1: 127-141.

Terry, M.S.
1883 Biblical Hermeneutics, repr. Grand Rapids, Mich. 1961 (originally 1890[2], 1883[1]).

Theis, J.
1921 Friedrich Delitzsch und seine "Grosse Täuschung" oder Jaho und Jahwe, Trier.

Thielicke, H.
1948 'Law and Gospel as Constant Partners', incorporated into Theological Ethics, I: Foundations, abridged ET: London 1968 (German 1958-9[2]): 100-125 (originally in Auf dem Grunde der Apostel und Propheten: Festgabe für Landesbischof D. Theophil Wurm zum 80. Geburtstag (ed. M.Loeser), Stuttgart 1948: 173-197).

Thils, G.
1971 '"Soyez riches d'espérance par la vertu du Saint-Esprit" (Rom.15,13): La théologie de l'espérance de J. Moltmann', _ETL_ 47: 495-503.

Thomas, K.J.
1965 'The Old Testament Citations in Hebrews', _NTS_ 11: 303-25.

Thomas, T.G.
1966 'The Unity of the Bible and the Uniqueness of Christ', _LQHR_ 191: 219-27.

Thornton, L.S.
1950 _Revelation and the Modern World: being the first part of a treatise on The Form of the Servant_, London.

Throckmorton, B.H.
1959 _The New Testament and Mythology_, London.

Thurneysen, E.
1965 'Die Bedeutung der theologischen Arbeit Wilhelm Vischers', _KBRS_ 121: 130-134.*

Tilden, E.E.
1953 'The Study of Jesus' Interpretive Methods', _Interpn_ 7: 45-61.

Tinsley, E.J.
1963 Review of Amsler 1960a, _JTS_ 14: 485-7.

Tollinton, R.B.
1916 'The Two Elements in Marcion's Dualism', _JTS_ 17: 263-70.

Tomes, R.
1969 'Exodus 14: The Mighty Acts of God: An Essay in theological criticism', _SJT_ 22: 454-78.

Toombs, L.E.
1969 'The Problematic of Preaching from the Old Testament', _Interpn_ 23: 302-14.

Torrance, T.F.
1950 'Salvation is of the Jews', _EQ_ 22: 164-173.

1956 'The Israel of God: Israel and the Incarnation', _Interpn_ 10: 305-20.

1962 'Scientific Hermeneutics According to St. Thomas Aquinas', _JTS_ 13: 259-89.

Traub, F.
1935 'Die Kirche und das Alte Testament', ZTK 43: 175-189.

Trench, R.C.
1845-6 The Hulsean Lectures for M.DCCC.XLV (The Fitness of Holy Scripture for Unfolding the Spiritual Life of Men) and M.DCCC.XLVI (Christ the Desire of All Nations, or, the Unconscious Prophecies of Heathendom), Cambridge 1859[4] (revised).

1870 Notes on the Parables of our Lord, London 1870[11] (n.d.[1], about 1850?).

Tresmontant, C.
1965 'Biblisches und griechisches Denken' in Leist (1965): 34-46.

Trilling, W.
1959 Das Wahre Israel: Studien zur Theologie des Matthäus-Evangeliums, Munich 1964[3] (1959[1]).

Tupper, E.F.
1974 The Theology of Wolfhart Pannenberg, London.

Tyng, D.
1931 'Theodore of Mopsuestia as an Interpreter of the Old Testament', JBL 50: 298-303.

Uhlig, S.
1974 'Die typologische Bedeutung des Begriffs Babylon', AUSS 12: 112-125.

Ulonska, H.
1963 'Die Funktion der alttestamentlichen Zitate und Anspielungen in den Paulinischen Briefen', Dissn, Münster.*

Unnik, W.C. van
1960 'La conception paulinienne de la Nouvelle Alliance', repr. in Sparsa Collecta: The Collected Essays of W.C.van Unnik I, Leiden 1973 (SNovT 29): 174-193 (originally in Littérature et théologie pauliniennes, ed. J.Copper Bruges 1960: 109-126).

1966 'Der Ausdruck ἙΩΣ ἘΣΧΑΤΟΥ ΤΗΣ ΓΗΣ (Apostelgeschichte 1:8) und sein alttestamentlicher Hintergrund' in Vriezen Fs: 335-49 (repr. in Sparsa Collecta I: 386-401).

Vatke, W.
1835 <u>Die biblische Theologie wissenschaftlich dargestellt</u>, Berlin.

Vaux, R.de
1933 'The "Remnant of Israel" According to the Prophets', ET in <u>The Bible and the Ancient Near East</u>, London 1972: 15-30 (French: <u>RB</u> 42: 526-39).

1950,1952 Reviews of Vischer 1934, <u>RB</u> 57: 284-5 and 59: 282-3.

1963 Review of von Rad 1957-60, <u>RB</u> 70: 291-3.

1967 'Is It Possible to Write a "Theology of the Old Testament"?', ET in <u>The Bible and the Ancient Near East</u>: 49-62 (French: <u>Mélanges Chenu</u>, Paris 1967, BThom: 439-49).

1969 'God's Presence and Absence in History: the Old Testament View', <u>Concilium</u> 5.10: 5-11.

Vawter, B.
1960 'Apocalyptic: Its Relation to Prophecy', <u>CBQ</u> 22: 33-46.

1964 'The Fuller Sense: Some Considerations', <u>CBQ</u> 26: 85-96.

1967 'History and the Word', <u>CBQ</u> 29: 512-23.

1971 Review of Childs 1970, <u>Biblica</u> 52: 567-70.

Veenen, S.F.van
1948 'La signification de l'Ancien Testament pour les questions sociales et politiques', <u>ETR</u> 23: 32-6.

Velema, W.H.
1962 <u>Confrotatie met Van Ruler: Denken vanuit het einde</u>, Kampen.

Venard, L.
1934 'Citations de l'Ancien Testament dans le Nouveau Testament', <u>SDB</u> 2: 23-51.

Verhoef, P.A.
1962 'Some Notes on Typological Exegesis' in <u>New Light on Some Old Testament Problems: Papers read at 5th Meeting of OTWSA</u>, Pretoria: 58-63.

1970a 'The Relationship between the Old and the New Testaments' in Payne (1970): 280-303.

1970b 'Some Thoughts on the Present-Day Situation in Biblical Theology', WTJ 33: 1-19.

Vernon, A.W.
1908 The Religious Value of the Old Testament, London.

Vesco, J.-L.
1971 'Abraham: actualisation et relectures: Les traditions vétérotestamentaires', RSPT 55: 33-80.

Via, D.O.
1974 'A Structuralist Approach to Paul's Old Testament Hermeneutic', Interpn 28: 201-220.

Vidler, A.
1934 The Modernist Movement in the Roman Church: Its Origins and Outcome, Cambridge.

Vink, J.
1967 '"In Yahweh alone is the salvation of Israel" (Jer.3.23)', Concilium 3.10: 32-7.

Vis, A.
1936 An Inquiry into the Rise of Christianit out of Judaism, Amsterdam.

Vischer, W.
1927 'Das Alte Testament als Wort Gottes', ZZ 5: 379ff.*

1929 Jahweh der Gott Kains, Munich.*

1930a 'Le Serviteur du Seigneur: Une contribution à l'exégèse d'Esaïe 40 à 55', French translation in 1958: 125-188 (German: a lecture given in 1929 and published in Jahrbuch der Theologischen Schule Bethel bei Bielefeld 1930).

1930b 'Der Gott Abrahams, Isaaks u. Jakobs', in ZZ 8.*

1931 'Das Alte Testament und die Verkündigun ThBl 10: 1-12.

1932a 'Das Alte Testament und die Geschichte' ZZ 10: 22ff.*

1932b 'Gehört das Alte Testament heute noch in die Bibel des deutschen Christen?', Beth-El 24: 91-101.*

1933 'Job, un témoin de Jésus-Christ', French translation in 1958: 35-70 (German *ZZ* 11, 1933: 386-413).

1934 *The Witness of the Old Testament to Christ I: The Pentateuch*, ET: London 1949 (German 1936[3], 1934[1]).

1937 'The Book of Esther', ET in *EQ* 11(1939): 3-21 (German: ThEx 48, 1937; revd French edn in 1958: 73-98).

1938 'The Significance of the Old Testament for the Christian Life' in Edinburgh (1938): 237-60 (also published in French - *Études sur l'Ancien Testament* 1938, repr. in 1958: 9-32 - and in German - ThSt 3, 1938,1947[2]).

1942 *Das Christuszeugnis des Alten Testaments II: Die Propheten 1.Die früheren Propheten*, Zollikon-Zürich 1946[2](1942[1]).

1949 'Words and the Word: The Anthropomorphisms of the Biblical Revelation', *Interpn* 3: 3-18.

1954a *Die Immanuel-Botschaft im Rahmen des königlichen Zionsfestes*, German translation: Zollikon-Zürich 1955 (ThSt 45; French: *ETR* 29, 1954: 55-97).

1954b 'L'Ecclésiaste, témoin du Christ Jésus', first published in French in 1958: 101-121 (originally published in Italian translation in *Protestantesimo* 1954).

1954c 'Return, Rebel Sons! A Sermon on Jeremiah 3: 1,19 - 4:4', *Interpn* 8: 43-7.

1955a 'The Vocation of the Prophet to the Nations: An Exegesis of Jeremiah 1: 4-10', *Interpn* 9: 310-17.

1955b 'Le "kerygme" de l'Ancien Testament', *ETR* 30, 1955: 24-48 (German: *Das Kerygma des Alten Testaments*, Zürich 1955, Kirchliche Zeitfragen 8).*

1956 'Du sollst dir kein Bildnis machen' in Barth Fs: 764-72.

1957 *Versöhnung zwischen Ost und West: Zwei Bibelstudien*, Munich (ThEx 56; French translation in *VerbC* 1957).

1958 *Valeur de l'Ancien Testament: Commentaires des livres Job, Esther, l'Ecclésiaste, le second Esaïe, précédés d'une introduction*, Geneva (see 1938, 1933, 1937, 1954b, 1930a).

1959 'Perhaps the Lord will be Gracious: A Sermon', *Interpn* 13: 286-95.

1960 'La méthode de l'exégèse biblique', *RThPh* 10: 109-123.

1961a 'God's Truth and Man's Lie: A Study of the Message of the Book of Job', *Interpn* 15: 131-146.

1961b 'The Love Story of God: A Sermon', *Interpn* 15: 304-9.

1961c 'Zum Problem der Hermeneutik', German translation: *EvTh* 24: 98-112 (French: 'Eglise et Théologie', Paris 1961).

1962 'Der Hymnus der Weisheit in den Sprüchen Salomos 8,22-31', *EvTh* 22: 309-26.

1964a 'Everywhere the Scripture Is about Christ Alone', *OTCF*: 90-101.

1964b 'Foi et Technique (Méditation sur Deutéronome 11_{10-15})', *RHPR* 44: 102-109.

1965 'Calvin, exégète de l'Ancien Testament', *ETR* 40: 213-31 (repr. in *La Revue Réformée* 18.1, 1967: 1-20).

1966 '"Der im Himmel Thronende lacht"' in de Quervain Fs: 129-135.

1969 *Ils annoncent Jésus-Christ: Les patriarches*, Paris (Foi Vivante 103).*

1971 'Nehemia, der Sonderbeauftragte und Statthalter des Königs: Die Bedeutung der Befestigung Jerusalems für die biblische Geschichte und Theologie' in von Rad Fs: 603-10.

Voegelin, E.
1964 'History and Gnosis', *OTCF*: 64-89.

Voeltzel, R.
1953 'Le Rôle de l'Ancien Testament dans l'instruction des catéchumènes', *RHPR* 33: 308-21.

Volz, P.

1897 *Die vorexilische Jahweprophetie und der Messias: In ihrem Verhältnis dargestellt*, Göttingen.

1937 'Das Alte Testament und unsere Verkündigung', *Luthertum* 48: 326-40.

Vos, G.

1948 *Biblical Theology: Old and New Testaments*, Grand Rapids, Mich.

Vriezen, T.C.

1953a 'Die Hoffnung im Alten Testament: Ihre inneren Voraussetzungen und äusseren Formen', *TLZ* 78: 577-86 (ET in *HervTS* 10: 121-130).

1953b 'Prophecy and Eschatology' in *Congress Volume: Copenhagen 1953*, Leiden (SVT 1): 199-229 (partly incorporated into 1966).

1954 *An outline of Old Testament theology*, ET: Oxford 1958 (Dutch 1954[2], 1949[1]) - see also: 1966.

1956 'Theocracy and Soteriology: Comments on A.A.van Ruler's book: *Die christliche Kirche und das Alte Testament*', ET in *EOTI*: 211-23 (German: *EvTh* 16: 395-404).

1963a *The Religion of Ancient Israel*, ET: London 1967 (Dutch 1963).

1963b 'The Credo in the Old Testament' in *Studies on the Psalms: Papers read at 6th Meeting of OTWSA*, Potschefstroom: 5-17.

1965 'Geloof, openbaring en geschiedenis in de nieuwste Oud-Testamentische Theologie', *KT* 16: 97-113, 210-18.

1966 *An outline of Old Testament theology*, revd ET: Oxford 1970 (Dutch 1966[3]) - cf. 1954.

1967 'Exodusstudien Exodus I', *VT* 17: 334-53.

1970 'Erwägungen zu Amos 3,2' in Galling Fs: 255-8.

1972 'The Exegesis of Exodus xxiv 9-11' in *The Witness of Tradition* (M.A.Beek *et al.*), Leiden (OTS 17): 100-133.

Wagner, S.
1970 'Zur Frage nach dem Gegenstand einer Theologie des Alten Testaments' in Doerne Fs: 391-411.

Wallace, D.H.
1963 'Biblical Theology: Past and Future', ThZ 19: 88-105.

Wallace, R.S.
1953a Calvin's Doctrine of the Word and Sacrament, Edinburgh/London.

1953b 'The Preaching of the Old Testament - A Preliminary Discussion', TSFB 6: 2-4.

1957 Elijah and Elisha: Expositions from the Book of Kings, Edinburgh/London.

1965 The Ten Commandments: A Study of Ethical Freedom, Edinburgh/London.

Walvoord, J.F.
1948-9 'The Incarnation of the Son of God: II. Christological Typology', BS 105: 286-96, 404-17; 106: 27-33.

Wapler, P.
1914 Johannes v. Hofmann: Ein Beitrag zur Geschichte der theologischen Grundprobleme, der kirchlichen und der politischen Bewegungen im 19. Jahrhundert, Leipzig.

Warfield, B.B.
1886-1917 Biblical and Theological Studies, Philadelphia 1952 (a collection of articles originally published 1886-1917).

1892-1915 The Inspiration and Authority of the Bible, Philadelphia 1948 (an earlier edn was entitled Revelation and Inspiration, 1927; articles originally published 1892-1915).

Watson, P.S.
1962 'The Nature and Function of Biblical Theology', ExpT 73: 195-200.

Watts, J.D.W.
1956 'The People of God: A Study of the Doctrine in the Pentateuch', ExpT 67: 232-7.

Weippert, M.
1973 'Fragen des israelitischen Geschichtsbewusstseins', VT 23: 415-42.

Weiser, A.
1931 Glaube und Geschichte im Alten Testament, Stuttgart (BWANT 4.4) 1931 (repr. in a volume of essays with the same title, 1961: 99-182).

1945 'Vom Verstehen des Alten Testaments', ZAW 61: 17-30 (repr. in Glaube und Geschichte, 1961: 290-302).

Weiss, M.
1966 'The Origin of the "Day of the Lord" - Reconsidered', HUCA 37: 29-72.

Welch, A.C.
1933 The Preparation for Christ in the Old Testament, Edinburgh.

Wellhausen, J.
1878 Prolegomena to the History of Israel, ET: Edinburgh 1885 (German 1883, originally 1878, under the title 'History of Israel, Vol.1').

Wenham, J.W.
1972 Christ and the Bible, London.

Wernberg-Möller, P.
1960 'Is There an Old Testament Theology?', HibJ 59: 21-9.

Westcott, B.F.
1864 The Bible in the Church: A Popular Account of the Collection and Reception of the Holy Scriptures in the Christian Churches, London/Cambridge.

1889 The Epistle to the Hebrews: The Greek Text with Notes and Essays, London 1892[2] (1889[1], 1903[3]).

Westermann, C.
1952 'Das Hoffen im Alten Testament: Eine Begriffsuntersuchung', repr. in Forschung am Alten Testament: Gesammelte Studien, Munich 1964 (ThB 24): 219-65 (originally Theologia Viatorum 4, 1952-3: 19-70).

1955 'Zur Auslegung des Alten Testaments', Vergegenwärtigung, Berlin 1955: 88-116. This was not available to me, but an abridged ET appears in EOTI as 'The Interpretation of the Old Testament - A Historical Introduction', 40-49; and 'Remarks on the Theses of Bultmann and Baumgärtel', 123-133.

1962 Review of Amsler 1960a, *TLZ* 87: 507-10.

1963 'Vergegenwärtigung der Geschichte in den Psalmen' in Kupisch Fs: 253-80, repr. in *Forschung am Alten Testament*: 306-35.

1964 'The Way of the Promise through the Old Testament', *OTCF*: 200-224.

1966 *Isaiah 40-66: A Commentary*, ET: London 1969 (German 1966).

1967 'Prophetenzitate im Neuen Testament', *EvTh* 27: 307-17.

1968a *The Old Testament and Jesus Christ*, ET: Minneapolis, Minn. 1970 (German 1968).

1968b 'Zur Auslegung des Alten Testaments' in Loretz and Strolz (1968): 181-239.

1971 'Zum Geschichtsverständnis des Alten Testaments' in von Rad Fs: 611-19.

1974a *Genesis: I. Teilband, Genesis 1-11*, Neukirchen (BK 1/1).

1974b 'Zu zwei Theologien des Alten Testaments', *EvTh* 34: 96-112.

Westphal, A.
1903-7 *The Law and the Prophets, or, The Revelation of Jehovah in Hebrew History from the Earliest Times to the Capture of Jerusalem by Titus*, ET: London 1910 (French: *Jéhovah*, 1923[4], 1903-7[1]).

Wette, W.M.L.De
1813 *Lehrbuch der christlichen Dogmatik, in ihrer historischen Entwicklung dargestellt I. Biblische Dogmatik Alten und Neuen Testaments*, Berlin 1831[3] (1813[1]).

1846 *Das Wesen des christlichen Glaubens vom Standpunkt des Glaubens*, Basel,

Whitley, C.F.
1963 *The Prophetic Achievement*, London.

Wieneke, F.
1933 *Deutsche Theologie im Umriss*, Soldin (Schriftenreihe der "Deutschen Christen" 5).

Wiener, P.F.
1945 *Martin Luther: Hitler's Spiritual Ancestor*, London n.d. (British Museum catalogue: 1945).

Wiesemann, H.
1965 Das Heil für Israel, Stuttgart.

Wiesner, W.
1957 'Bund: V.Alter und neuer Bund, dogmatisch', RGG[3] 1: 1521-3.

Wifall, W.
1974 'David - Prototype of Israel's Future?', BThB 4: 94-107.

Wilckens, U.
1961 'Die Rechtfertigung Abrahams nach Römer 4' in von Rad Fs: 111-127.

Wildberger, H.
1956 'Israel und sein Land', EvTh 16: 404-22.

1959 'Auf dem Wege zu einer biblischen Theologie: Erwägungen zur Hermeneutik des Alten Testamentes', EvTh 19: 70-90.

1972 Jesaja: I.Teilband (1-12), Neukirchen (BK 10/1). The first fascicle of vol. II appeared in 1974.

Wilde, W.J.de
1938 Het probleem van het Oude Testament in verband met de verkondigung van den Christus Jezus, Nijkerk.*

Wilder, A.N.
1947 'New Testament Theology in Transition' in Willoughby (1947): 419-36.

1955 Otherworldliness and the New Testament, London.

1956 'Kerygma, Eschatology and Social Ethics' in Dodd Fs: 509-36.

Wiles, M.F.
1955 'The Old Testament in Controversy with the Jews', SJT 8: 113-126.

1970 'Origen as Biblical Scholar' and 'Theodore of Mopsuestia as Representative of the Antiochene School' in CHB I: 454-89, 489-510.

Willi, T.
1971 Herders Beitrag zum Verstehen des Alten Testaments, Tübingen (BGBH 8).

Williamson, R.
1970 Philo and the Epistle to the Hebrews, Leiden.

Wingren, G.

1956 'Evangelium und Gesetz' in Barth Fs: 310-22.

1958 *Creation and Law*, ET: Edinburgh/London 1961 (Swedish 1958).

Winkler, E.

1965 *Exegetische Methode bei Meister Eckhart*, Tübingen (BGBH 6).

Wintermute, O.

1972 'A Study of Gnostic Exegesis of the Old Testament' in Stinespring Fs: 241-70.

Wolf, E.

1957 'Bekennende Kirche', *RGG*^{3} 1: 984-8.

1959 'Kirchenkampf', *RGG*^{3} 3: 1443-53.

Wolf, H.H.

1958 *Die Einheit des Bundes: Das Verhältnis von Altem und Neuem Testament bei Calvin*, Neukirchen (Beiträge zur Geschichte und Lehre der Reformierten Kirche 10).

Wolff, H.W.

1942 *Jesaja 53 im Urchristentum*, Berlin n.d. (1952^3,1949^1; Dissn 1942).

1952 'Der grosse Jesreeltag (Hosea 2,1-3): Methodologische Erwägungen zur Auslegung einer alttestamentlichen Perikope', *EvTh* 12: 78-104.

1956a 'The Hermeneutics of the Old Testament', ET in *EOTI*: 160-199 (also in *Interpn* 15, 1961: 439-72; originally in *EvTh* 16, 1956: 337-70).

1956b 'The Old Testament in Controversy: Interpretive Principles and Illustration', ET in *Interpn* 12: 281-91 (German: *Alttestamentliche Predigten*, Neukirchen 1956: 7ff.; also part of the article appeared in *ZdZ* 10, 1956: 446-8, as 'Erwägungen zur typologischen Auslegung des Alten Testaments').

1960 'The Understanding of History in the Old Testament Prophets', ET in *EOTI*: 336-55 (originally in *EvTh* 20: 218-35).

1961 *Dodekapropheton 1: Hosea*, Neukirchen (BK 14/1). ET: Philadelphia (Hermeneia) 1974.

1963 'Das Alte Testament und das Problem der existentialen Interpretation', *EvTh* 23: 1-17.

1964 'Das Kerygma des Jahwisten', *EvTh* 24: 73-98.

1969 *Dodekapropheton 2: Joel und Amos*, Neukirchen (BK 14/2).

1973 'Gerhard von Rad als Exeget' in Wolff (1973): 9-20.

Wolfzorn, E.E.
1962 'Realized Eschatology: An Exposition of Charles H. Dodd's Thesis', *ETL* 38: 44-70.

Wood, A.S.
1960 *Luther's Principles of Biblical Interpretation*, London.

Wood, J.D.
1958 *The Interpretation of the Bible: A Historical Introduction*, London.

Wood, J.E.
1968 'Isaac Typology in the New Testament', *NTS* 14: 583-9.

Woods, J.
1949 *The Old Testament in the Church*, London.

Woollcombe, K.J.
1957 'The Biblical Origins and Patristic Development of Typology' in Lampe and Woollcombe (1957): 39-75.

Wright, G.E.
1944 *The Challenge of Israel's Faith*, London 1946 (USA 1944).

1946 'Interpreting the Old Testament', *ThTo* 3: 176-191.

1947 'The Christian Interpreter as Biblical Critic: The Relevance of Valid Criticism', *Interpn* 1: 131-8.

1950a *The Old Testament Against Its Environment*, London (SBT 2).

1950b 'Recent European Study in the Pentateuch', *JBR* 18: 216-25.

1951a Introduction and conclusion to a symposium on 'The Unity of the Bible', *Interpn* 5: 131-3, 304-17.

1951b 'From the Bible to the Modern World' in Richardson and Schweitzer (1951): 219-39.

1952 God Who Acts: Biblical Theology as Recital, London (SBT 8).

1955 'The Unity of the Bible', SJT 8: 337-52.

1960 'Modern Issues in Biblical Studies: History and the Patriarchs', ExpT 71: 292-6.

1964 'History and Reality: The Importance of Israel's "Historical" Symbols for the Christian Faith', OTCF: 176-199.

1966 'Reflections concerning Old Testament Theology' in Vriezen Fs: 376-88.

1969 The Old Testament and Theology, New York.

1970 'Historical Knowledge and Revelation' in May Fs: 279-303 (a new, considerably expanded version of 1947).

1972 'The Theological Study of the Bible', IOVCB: 983-8.

Wright, J.S.
1956 'The Place of Myth in the Interpretation of the Bible', JTVI 88: 17-30.

Würthwein, E.
1971 'Zur Theologie des Alten Testaments', ThRu 36: 185-208.

Young, E.J.
1958 Daniel's Vision of the Son of Man, London.

Young, N.J.
1966 'Bultmann's View of the Old Testament', SJT 19: 269-79.

1969 History and Existential Theology: The Role of History in the Thought of Rudolf Bultmann, London.

Zerafa, P.
1964 'Christological interpretation of the Old Testament', Angelicum 41: 51-62.

Zimmerli, W.

1940 'Auslegung des Alten Testamentes', *ThBl* 19: 145-157.

1952 'Promise and Fulfillment', ET in *EOTI*: 89-122 (also in *Interpn* 15, 1961: 310-38; German: *EvTh* 12: 34-59).

1956 'Das Alte Testament in der Verkündigung der christlichen Kirche' in *Das Alte Testament als Anrede*, Munich (BEvTh 24): 62-88.

1960a 'Le nouvel "exode" dans le message des deux grands prophètes de l'exil' in Vischer Fs: 216-27 (German translation in 1963a: 192-204.

1960b 'Das Gesetz im Alten Testament',repr. in 1963a: 249-76 (originally in *TLZ* 85, 1960: 481-98).

1962 '"Offenbarung" im Alten Testament: Ein Gespräch mit R.Rendtorff', *EvTh* 22: 15-31.

1963a *Gottes Offenbarung: Gesammelte Aufsätze zum Alten Testament*, Munich (ThB 19).

1963b Review of von Rad 1957-60, *VT* 13: 100-111.

1965 *The Law and the Prophets: A Study of the Meaning of the Old Testament*, Oxford 1965 (abridged from 'Das Gesetz und die Propheten',1963).

1968 *Man and His Hope in the Old Testament*, ET: London 1971 (German 1968).

1969 *Ezechiel*, Neukirchen (BK 13).

1971a *Die Weltlichkeit des Alten Testamentes*, Göttingen (Kleine Vandenhoeck-Reihe 327).

1971b 'Alttestamentliche Traditionsgeschichte und Theologie' in von Rad Fs: 632-47.

1972 *Grundriss der alttestamentlichen Theologie*, Stuttgart.

1973 'Erwägungen zur Gestalt einer alttestamentlichen Theologie', *TLZ* 98: 81-98.

1975 'Zum Problem der "Mitte des Alten Testamentes"',*EvTh* 35: 97-118.

11.4 SUPPLEMENTARY BIBLIOGRAPHY

Accra (1974) — 'La relation entre l'Ancien et le Nouveau Testament', Istina 20 (1975): 253-61.

Achtemeier, E.
1973 — The Old Testament and the Proclamation of the Gospel, Philadelphia.

1974 — 'The Relevance of the Old Testament for Christian Preaching' in Myers Fs: 3-24.

Andersen, F.I.
1975 — 'Dietrich Bonhoeffer and the Old Testament', RefTR 34: 33-44.

Berkouwer, G.C.
1966-7 — Studies in Dogmatics: Holy Scripture, ET: Grand Rapids, Mich. 1975 (Dutch I: 1966; II: 1967).

Bijlsma, R.
1975 — 'Openbaring en Schrift', VoxTh 45: 48-59.

Boman, T.
1973 — 'Historieforskningen og virkelighetsbildet: Til Harnacks og Bultmanns historiesyn', NorTT 74: 243-53.

Bruce, F.F.
1975 — 'Paul and the Law of Moses', BJRL 57: 259-79.

Childs, B.S.
1972 — 'The Old Testament as Scripture of the Church', Concordia Theological Monthly 43: 709-22.*

Delgado, A.
1972 — 'La unidad de las Escrituras', Scripta Theologica 4: 7-82, 279-354.*

Derrett, J.D.M.
1974 'Allegory and the Wicked Vinedressers', JTS 25: 426-32.

DeVries, S.J.
1975 Yesterday, Today and Tomorrow: Time and History in the Old Testament, Grand Rapids, Mich.

Documents (1975) 'Documents: Le dialogue avec le Judaïsme', Istina 20: 338-66.

Freed, E.D.
1974 'Some Old Testament Influences on the Prologue of John' in Myers Fs: 145-161.

Gordon, R.P.
1975 'Preaching from the Patriarchs: Background to the Exposition of Genesis 15', Themelios 1: 19-23.

Grech, P.
1975 'The Old Testament as a Christological Source in the Apostolic Age', BThB 5: 127-145.

Gross and Mussner (1974) 'Die Einheit von Altem und Neuem Testament', Internationale Katholische Zeitschrift / Communio 3: 544-55 (H.Gross and F.Mussner).*

Jenson, R.W.
1970 'Die Kontinuität von Altem und Neuem Testament als Problem für Kirche und Theologie heute' in Zeddies (1970): 88-103.

Kaiser, W.C.
1975 'The Present State of Old Testament Studies', JETS 18: 69-79.

Kasper, W.
1975 'Tradition als Erkenntnisprinzip: Systematische Überlegungen zur theologischen Relevanz der Geschichte', ThQ 155: 198-215.

Kelsey, D.H.
1975 The Uses of Scripture in Contemporary Theology, Philadelphia.

Kline, M.G.
1975 'The Old Testament Origins of the Gospel Genre', WTJ 38: 1-27.

Küng and Kasper (1974) 'Christians and Jews', Concilium 10.7/8: 101-186 (ed. H.Küng and W.Kasper).

Labuschagne, C.J.
1973 'De verhouding tussen het Oude en het Nieuwe Testament', Rondom het Woord 15: 118-132.*

Limbeck, M.
1975 'Bedarf der Christ des Alten Testaments? Der Ausfall des Alten Testaments im gegenwärtigen Bewusstsein', Herder Korrespondenz 29: 77-84.

Merrill, E.H.
1975 'Rashi, Nicholas de Lyra, and Christian Exegesis', WTJ 38: 66-79.

Mildenberger, F.
1975 'The Unity, Truth, and Validity of the Bible: Theological Problems in the Doctrine of Holy Scripture', Interpn 29: 391-405.

Miskotte, K.H.
1975 Der Gott Israels und die Theologie: Ausgewählte Aufsätze (ed. H.Stoevesandt and H.J.Weber), Neukirchen.

Myers Fs (1974) A Light unto My Path: Old Testament Studies in Honor of Jacob M. Myers (ed. H.N.Bream et al.), Philadelphia (Gettysburg Theological Studies 4).

Myers, J.M.
1975 Grace and Torah, Philadelphia.

Nicol, I.G.
1974 'Event and Interpretation: Oscar Cullmann's conception of Salvation History', Theology 77: 14-21.

Noack, B.
1970 'Die Relevanz der alttestamentlichen Verheissung für Glauben und Verkündigung des Urchristentums' in Zeddies (1970): 75-87.

Pancaro, S.
1975 The Law in the Fourth Gospel: The Torah and the Gospel Moses and Jesus, Judaism and Christianity according to John, Leiden (SNovT 42).

Rendtorff, R.
1970 'Die alttestamentliche Verheissung in Theologie und Verkündigung der Kirche' in Zeddies (1970): 62-74.

Sanders, J.A.
1975 'Torah and Christ', Interpn 29: 372-90.

Schmid, H.
1974 'Das Alte Testament im evangelischen Religionsunterricht', VF 19: 66-86.

Schnackenburg, R.
1972 'Das Schriftzitat in Joh 19,37' in Wort, Lied und Gottesspruch: Beiträge zu Psalmen und Propheten: Festschrift für Joseph Ziegler (ed. J.Schreiner, Forschung zur Bibel 2), Würzburg: 239-47.

Shires, H.M.
1974 Finding the Old Testament in the New, Philadelphia.

Smith, G.V.
1975 'Paul's Use of Psalm 68:18 in Ephesians 4:8', JETS 18: 181-9.

Stolz, F.
1974 Interpreting the Old Testament, ET: London 1975 (German 1974, Das Alte Testament).

Stramare, T.
1974 'Quod in novo patet in vetere latet', Bibbia e Oriente 16: 199-210.*

Vischer (1974) 'Biblical Interpretation and the Middle East: I.The Relationship between Old and New Testament', Immanuel 4: 68-73 (L.Vischer et al.).

Waal, C.van der
1974 'Enkele opmerkinges oor Tipologie', NGTT 15: 225-35.*

Weinfeld, M.
1975 'Bᵉrit - Covenant vs. Obligation', Biblica 56: 120-128 (review article on Kutsch 1972).

Wifall, W.
1974 'Gen 3:15 - A Protevangelium?', CBQ 36: 361-5.

Zeddies (1970) Hoffnung ohne Illusion: Referate und Bibelarbeiten (ed. H.Zeddies), Berlin.

INDEXES

12.1 AUTHORS

12.2 SUBJECTS

12.3 BIBLICAL REFERENCES